FOREST LIFE
IN
CEYLON

FOREST LIFE IN CEYLON

W. KNIGHTON

IN TWO VOLUMES

VOLUME 1

Published by

Facsimile Publisher
12 Pragati Market
Ashok Vihar, Ph-2
Delhi-110052
facsimilepublisher.com

Distribution Network
gyanbooks.com
India, USA, Canada, UK, Australia, France

ISBN : 978-93-5324-489-7 (Set)
ISBN : 978-93-5324-490-3 Vol. 1 (HB)
First Published, London, 1854

2nd Impression 2020

Printed at: Gyan Press, Delhi.

Forest Life in Ceylon
Author: W. Knighton

FOREST LIFE

IN

CEYLON.

BY W. KNIGHTON, M.A.

FORMERLY SECRETARY TO THE CEYLON BRANCH ROYAL ASIATIC SOCIETY.

Second Edition.

IN TWO VOLUMES.

VOL. I.

LONDON:

HURST AND BLACKETT, PUBLISHERS,

SUCCESSORS TO HENRY COLBURN,

13, GREAT MARLBOROUGH STREET.

1854.

CONTENTS OF VOLUME I.

PREFACE.

In journeying through a desert the eye of the traveller lingers with interest and pleasure upon the oasis he has left, and which he is not again likely to revisit; and so, in the life of every man, there is probably some period of shorter or longer duration on which the memory, in subsequent years, delights to dwell. Of such a character to the author was his residence in Ceylon.

During four years he lived in that interesting island as a Coffee-planter and the Editor of a newspaper, and those four years were so filled with incident, with employment, with variety and adventure, that, despite the pecuniary losses sustained in a ruinous speculation, they have ever since afforded him ample and pleasing themes for reflection.

In the following pages it has been his aim to give an interesting, and, at the same time, a truthful picture of jungle life—such a picture as may bring it before the mind of the European reader without exaggeration or false glitter. The scenes described and the incidents recorded are such as every resident in the East will acknowledge to be common and usual to a life spent in the recesses of an Oriental forest. In such a life, scenery, inhabitants, costume, and characteristics are so different from those to which the novice has been accustomed in his European home, that they have for him at first all the effect of enchantment. It was the author's lot to return from the East before this fresh feeling of pleased surprise had been quite removed—before the novel charm of Oriental life had worn off, to give place to satiety and monotony.

The lives of a Parsee and of a Kandian chief—which will be found, the one at the conclusion of the first, the other near the end of the second, volume—are intended to show how strangely the old life of the East, with its antiquated habits and forms of thought, is influenced by the new life of the progressive West—busy, bustling, and innovating. These accounts are founded upon facts related to the author by Parsees and Budhists. Hormanjee and Marandhan, indeed, are fictitious names, but such men *have* lived, and *are* living, in India and Ceylon; nor are the events recorded of them more extraordinary than those which, for the last fifty years, have been constantly occurring, wherever Eastern and Western races have been brought into collision—a collision as much of souls as of bodies.

There is something inexpressibly pleasing in thus minutely recalling some of the happiest passages of one's early life, particularly when the strong light of reality has been mellowed into a twilight glow by the lapse of a few intervening years; so that if the reader receive but a tithe of the pleasure in its perusal which the author has obtained from the compilation of this work, the labour of both will have been amply remunerative.

London, November, 1853.

FOREST LIFE

IN

CEYLON.

CHAPTER I.

ARRIVAL IN CEYLON—GALLE TO COLOMBO.

"I would entreat thy company
To see the wonders of the world abroad."
Two Gentlemen of Verona, act i., sc. 1.

I WAS leaning over the side of the good ship, *Parsee*, watching a nautilus hoisting sail, and steering its tiny shell over the ocean, when the Captain, who had been as usual peering through a telescope, muttered to the chief officer, "O yes, it's very plain. I see it distinctly."

"See what?" I asked.

"Ceylon," said he; "I told you we should see it to-day."

He handed me the telescope—a group of passengers, attracted by the interesting information, surrounded us, some armed with glasses of their own, others eagerly awaiting a loan of one. I strained my eyes; I looked intently in the direction indicated; I readjusted the glass, and wiped the lenses; I looked again as earnestly as if some important result depended on the issue, but, in vain; I saw no Ceylon: other passengers were equally unsuccessful. One tall yellow-haired man, that prided himself on his nautical dress and knowledge, declared he did, but no one ever minded what he said.

"You don't see it," said the Captain, "that's strange—it's very distinct—just on the horizon, by the end of the jib-boom—look again." "Keep her three points off," said he to the steersman, as he walked away.

I looked again, but there was the same impenetrable haze on the horizon—everything misty and obscure.

"Very distinct indeed," said the chief officer, as he too walked away.

The sun was shining as fiercely as the sun only can shine towards the end of May at the Equator. We were all grilling—the boards of the ship hot—the pitch and tar clammy on the ropes, and in the oakum between the planks of the deck

—the awning scorching—the air agitated into the faintest possible wind, dry and stifling—whilst an incessant drop, drop, drop, coursing each other from the forehead to the neck, plainly proved that there was still moisture left in us.

"We must see it," resolved the passengers, and away we went in a body, into the broiling sunshine, to the fore-part of the ship. The tall man with the yellow hair, smiled at our want of nautical vision, and followed us—the ladies, one by one, threw handkerchiefs and veils over their necks, and came too.

"This is much better," we all exclaimed, as we poised our glasses, like rifles, some on the bulwarks, some on the ropes, and looked intently. Still it was no use! not a hill the size of a grain of sand could we discern on the horizon, close by the jib-boom or elsewhere—all was haziness and impenetrable gloom ahead, watery-looking decidedly, but, to our unpractised eyes, far from land-looking. The ladies tried. One lady thought she discerned something.

"Bravo," said the tall yellow-haired man, in ecstacy, "you see it. I thought you would, as I placed the glass."

She looked again. "Why, bless me," said she, "that's the end of a stick, of that stick there with the sail tied to it—the jib—jib, what do you call it?"

It was tantalizing to know that the glorious island was right ahead, visible to the eye of the Captain, the chief officer, and our tall yellow-haired friend, and that we could not even faintly discern it. Yet so it was, and so it continued to be all that day. With heroic perseverance we combated the sun and the heat, again and again, but all to no purpose—at last coming to the conclusion that imagination had a great deal to do with the matter, and that the Captain, the chief officer, and the yellow-haired man, knew the land ought to be there, and therefore they saw it.

Even during the night, before we went to bed—a clear star-light night, without a moon—we gazed intently in the direction indicated, as if then, without glass or sun, we might perchance succeed in catching a glimpse of the wished-for island. Those only who have spent four monotonous months on the ocean, without touching at a single port, as was our case, can realize to themselves the eagerness with which the weary passengers look out for land. And Ceylon too! such an island of mysterious interest and beauty—" its breezes, perfumes; its forests, the rarest and choicest trees; its pebbles, gems," as a flowery writer describes it. Only two of us had ever been there before—the only two that seemed to know nothing of the island indeed, for all the others had read of it, had talked of it, had studied it; they, on the other hand, thought they should have enough of it when they got there, as had been the case before, and were therefore but too anxious to banish it from their thoughts.

The next morning the line of hills on the horizon, although still distant, was near enough to be distinctly seen by the naked eye—the sea had lost much of its deep blue shade, and was more greenish and dull, even the sun did not appear to shine so brightly to those whose thoughts were drawn off from a contemplation of him, and fixed on the island, on which we soon hoped to enjoy liberty and the delights of shore, after we had escaped from the imprisonment of our floating castle.

The *Parsee* was bound for Point de Galle, on the south-western coast of Ceylon, and it was not until the following morning, that we neared the harbour sufficiently to fire off a gun as a signal for a pilot; for, open and safe as the bay looks, it is filled with sunken rocks and hidden dangers of all kinds. The long line of green vegetation which fringed the shore, consisting entirely of cocoa-nut trees, contrasted beautifully with the white foam of the sea as it broke impetuously on the rocks, whilst, far away in the harbour, masses of white and red, without apparent order or regularity, indicated the town. Above all rose the eternal hills, stretching away higher and higher into the distance, and ending in irregular, hazy lines of considerable elevation, particularly to the north, where Adam's Peak was pointed out to us—by far the most celebrated of Ceylonese mountains.

We fired another gun—the loud booming report coming back to us from the shore, as if the genius of the place resented our intrusion and the noise—and, as the Captain swept the harbour with his glass, he descried a boat pulling towards us, and was satisfied. I shall never forget the impression made upon me by that boat and its occupants, as it slowly came nearer and nearer to the huge vessel. About the boat itself there was, perhaps, nothing that, in any other place, would have much attracted my attention; but when I compared it with the unclad, attenuated individuals that occupied it, it seemed to me the widest and deepest boat, of its length, I had ever seen. In England, one associates the idea of stout frames, well wrapped up, glazed hats, and groggy-looking faces, with a pilot-boat, or any other, in fact, that makes its way at all into the sea. To my unsophisticated eyes, the crew of this boat appeared to be tame monkeys. So completely was my conception of humanity mixed up with clothes and white or black skins, that it was, for a time, impossible for me to realise to myself the idea that these gibbering, long-armed, brown, naked animals were fellow-creatures. Even now, after having had many years' experience of the East, I still believe that more unfavourable specimens of the natives of Ceylon could scarcely have been met with than those in that boat. Three of them were old men, their ribs too distinguishable through their leather-like skin, their arms dry and shrivelled; yet their advanced age was not to be seen at once — their long, bony, and muscular arms, deprived of every particle of fat; their fingers rendered remarkable by the white nails at the tips; the palms of their hands white from constant labour; and the contrast between their brown, shrivelled-up, wrinkled skins, and the scanty white or blue cloth which they wore round their loins, all formed a picture so like that which a party of tamed monkeys would present, that it was not without disgust I gazed at them — disgust, mingled with something of indignation, that these animals should be of the same species as myself. Nor did the grizzled beards, and the bare, shaggy heads, from which they had removed their straw fishermen's hats, tend to improve the picture, or make them more human-like. My feelings were shared by my companions, and, as we muttered to each other, "These are the natives," we could not help wondering how humanity could degenerate into such figures; forgetting that the want of dress and difference of colour were the only real points of contrast between them and similar specimens of our own countrymen.

Our Portuguese pilot interested us much; he was dressed in a neat nautical uniform; a blue jacket, tightly buttoned up, white unmentionables, and an enormous straw hat that contrasted oddly with the slight form which it crowned—a form which, although far from tall, appeared to be so, in consequence of its extreme spareness; his face and hands were much darker than those of the natives; but, strange to say, whilst we were astounded by the dusky brown skins of his crew, we saw nothing wonderful in the black one of the pilot; so apt are we to take the accustomed for the natural, the unaccustomed and strange for the unnatural.

The anchor had scarcely been dropped ere we were surrounded by a little fleet of boats of the most heterogeneous characters. The majority of them had the curious "outrigger," peculiar to Ceylon and some of the Pacific Islands. A hollowed trunk forms the canoe-proper, and, from one side of it, project two or three beams, to the end of which is attached a solid block of the shape of the canoe itself, but considerably smaller. This contrivance prevents the boat from upsetting, and as the outrigger, as it is called, is always of a light, buoyant wood, even should the canoe fill with water, the consequences are not likely to be serious. The occupants were not less strange and new to us than were the spider-like machines which they guided so skilfully. The long hair tied up on the back of the head, with a high tortoise-shell comb stuck into it, the petticoats—scanty though they were—and the small feet and hands, were all things we were so much accustomed to associate with the idea of the fairer sex, that there was something repulsive in seeing them belong to fellows with huge black beards and moustaches; whilst, to our wondering eyes, there seemed no other difference between the men and women than the presence or absence of the beard. True, one becomes familiarised to these things after a time; but I do not think any one can first witness them without a sentiment of disgust—so utterly incongruous do the long twisted hair, with the crowning comb, appear to be with the hirsute and unshaven faces. But these were the Singhalese-proper alone. There were, besides, several Moors, more man-like in their habiliments and character, and infinitely more dangerous to the purse of the newly-arrived European, or "Griffin," as he is elegantly styled. The small white cap stuck on the very top of his shaven crown, gives the Moorman of Ceylon and the Southern Indian coast quite a distinctive character, which is rendered more marked by the ample volume of the cloth girdle, worn round his waist, and in which he keeps his money, his accounts, his writing materials, and, very often, his stock in trade too.

Our decks soon presented a strange appearance. Singhalese and Moormen having obtained the Captain's permission to come on board, were wandering about to effect sales of their various wares, oddly contrasting with the sun-burnt countenances and square forms of the sailors, forms with which our long voyage had made us so intimately acquainted. The scraps of English the Asiatics had picked up, and of which they now made their utmost use, rose shrilly above the din of ropes being coiled up, sails furled, hatches opening, chains rattling, and all the other usual concomitants of a ship's arrival in port. The Moormen, for the most part, had "jewels," toys, ornaments, and knick-knacks of various kinds for sale. People naturally expect to find jewels in an island so celebrated for them, from the time of Pliny* to the present day. As the wily Asiatic produces a little bundle from his ample girdle, carefully wrapped up in many folds, and, after a time, exhibits, imbedded in the downiest cotton, some sparkling particles, whispering the imposing name "diamonds," the European feels as if it would be folly to lose the chance—he is a young officer going home from Calcutta or Madras, or an enterprising traveller from China or Singapore—there are sisters, cousins, and fair flames afar off, awaiting presents, and he thinks if he can get the whole quantity for a trifle, it will be very hard indeed if there be

* Vid. Hist. Nat. vi. 22.

no real ones, however small, amongst them; and so he makes an offer—he is almost ashamed to make it, so small an offer for so valuable a collection. The crafty Asiatic grins, laughs outright, but submissively, at the sum named, and commences to refold his store, glancing sideways at the victim to see if the laugh has not moved him, and then offers the collection for double his bid. John Bull often bites at this—he has been but nibbling before—and exclaiming, "Well, it is but a trifle after all," pulls out his purse. Should he still continue immovable, however, he will have them at his own price, for Moorman protests he must sell them to get a little bread for himself and his starving children, although they cost him so much more. But what does John find them to be when he gets home? The following incident will show—a true incident, well known to most of the residents at Point de Galle:—

Mr. R., an English merchant there, had imported some coloured glass. Several panes were smashed in the landing, and all the broken pieces were thrown into an empty barrel in his warehouse. There they lay unheeded for a time, until Zambo, a well-known Moorman, made his salaam to Mr. R. one morning, just as he had arrived at home after his matutinal ride.

"Well, Zambo," said the Englishman, "how do you do? What brings you so early?"

"You-have-got-the-broke-up-glass-in-your-godowns,-Saar," said Zambo.

"Broken glass," said the merchant, musing. "Yes, yes, there were several panes of that coloured glass broken. I suppose they're there still."

"Your - coolies - do - steal - it - every - day - I know," said Zambo mysteriously. "I-will-buy-it-all-at-once-now."

Glad to get so worthless an article off his hands, Mr. R. readily consented to Zambo's proposal, and agreed to let him have the glass at his own price.

"And now, Zambo," said the Englishman, "may I ask what you want with the glass?"

Zambo looked round to see that there was no one within hearing-distance, and then, stretching his hairy chin forwards, said "You-no-tell-though?"

"Tell," said the merchant, "no, I don't want to tell anything. What do you want this glass for?"

"To-make-diamonds-for-steamer-passengers,"

said Zambo, his small grey eyes twinkling with cunning.

No one need ask, after having heard that, what our friend John will find his diamonds, emeralds, and garnets to be, when he reaches the paternal roof.

This sort of trade is almost entirely confined to the Moormen, by far the most expert retail dealers in the island. I was not disposed on landing to encumber myself with jewellery, wisely considering that if precious stones were so common in Ceylon, I should have innumerable opportunities of collecting them whilst living in the jungle.

The scene which presented itself on landing had all the interest and freshness of unwonted novelty for us. Accustomed, as I had been, previously to an English life, diversified by two hurried trips to the Continent alone, there was nothing in the reminiscences with which my memory was stored to detract from the novelty of the picture that now spread widely around us on every side. The small huts of mud, with their cocoa-nut leaf thatch; the wicker-work trays exhibiting heaps of chillies or other equally piquant stimulants; the amazing variety of fruit common to all tropical countries; the strange costume of the women and still stranger of the men; their shrill voices as they called upon the passers-by to purchase, or loudly conversed with each other across the street, all—men, women, and children—squatted on their heels; the fish-women, as in all countries, most voluble of tongue, light-hearted, and merry, exchanging badinage with the male passers-by, or making their own remarks on the pale faces—all was new and striking, and told us, with all the eloquence of vision, that we had left the cold north behind, with its frosts and snows, and wintry churlishness, and brave battling with a thousand evils that more favoured climes know nothing of, and that we had reached a land of the sun where there was food upon every tree, and clothing was little more than an encumbrance, where the battle of life was not for existence, but for luxury and enjoyment.

The soldiers seemed the only melancholy objects in the bright, ever-moving panorama. Malays, with horsehair-like whiskers and moustaches, dressed up in the darkest and most sombre green, the "Ceylon Rifles" as they are called, stood at their posts, or marched or loitered about the verandah of their guard-house, as if they were only gloomy visitants upon the glorious island, but not of it—as if they felt that their execrable trade was a thing in which man should not rejoice, which should stifle all mirth—a necessary evil. It may not be so in other parts of the island, and I do not remember that the idea was impressed afterwards upon my mind, but certainly the first few specimens of the Ceylon Rifles that we saw loitering about the great archway that leads from the harbour into the old Dutch fort suggested the idea of gloom, moroseness, taciturnity, and cruelty to our entire party.

The fort itself was by no means so interesting an object to us as the bazaar that stretches along the shore without it. The kaleidoscopic aspect of that strange scene was gone, and the lines of glistening white houses, with their green or black Venetians, diligently barricading them from the sun and the intense glare without, were but poor substitutes for it. Arrived at the hotel, which, with very questionable taste, like almost all the other European buildings, is situated within the fort, our party separated. Some, fatigued with their walk, spoke energetically of beefsteaks and pine-apples, as they threw themselves upon the various couches, whilst others, of whom I was one, ordered vehicles to call upon those to whom they had letters of introduction. I had but one visit to pay, to a merchant of whom I had no personal knowledge, but whom my uncle, the head of a mercantile house in Colombo, wished me particularly to become acquainted with; so, having first enjoyed the luxury of a glass of Allsopp or Bass, I made my way into the palanquin-carriage,—a conveyance not very dissimilar from a London cab, denuded of its coach-box, save that Venetian blinds take the place of the panelled sides and glass front—and was soon rapidly whirled along through a few narrow and uneven streets to my destination. Yet although the vehicle was one that not even an idle crossing-sweeper would turn to gaze after in London, and although the horse was only a respectable grey hack, without either points or sores, what a sensation we should have created in the Strand or Regent Street, had our course lain there instead of through Point de Galle! At the head of the horse, and firmly grasping the rein in one hand, whilst in the other he held a short whip, ran a wild savage-looking fellow, with a red handkerchief wrapped round his head, and a scanty red cloth round his loins. Fast as the horse could trot did this Jehu scamper along by his side, bounding over the road with bare feet, his well-oiled skin glistening in the fierce rays of the sun as the moving muscles of the back caught and reflected the light. I thought it was very barbarous, but what could I do? it was "the custom of the country" evidently, for there was no coach-box on the carriage, and no one seemed to consider it strange. At length, as I saw a stream of perspiration making its way down his back between his shoulder-blades, I shouted out in English, a language of which he apparently did not understand a single word. He looked round, still running on as before. I cried out "stop" with an energy that I hoped would force him to arrest his wild race. He pointed with his whip as he turned round, and went on more rapidly than ever. Poor fellow! he evidently thought that I was chiding him for not going fast enough instead of being full of benevolence for him, so he cut the horse with a skilful back-hand stroke of the short whip, and coursed on still faster. I saw it was no use to attempt anything further, so

I threw myself back, tired and hot, into the carriage, and allowed him to do as he pleased. I mentioned the matter to my newly-acquired friend on reaching his house, and he smiled, assuring me that every one went about so, that the natives were used to it, and that if I had spoken the language and told the *syce* or horse-keeper, to get up on the top whilst I drove, he would not have done so. Under these circumstances, heartily as I pitied the poor fellow, I interfered no further, and, in the same wild style, we made our way back to the hotel—horse and man rushing madly along, up one street and down another, over shingle and gravel and a little piece of good macadamised road, with the same indifference. We passed another vehicle too, of the same kind, similarly led, and, as I felt assured from this, that other people were equally barbarous, my mind was quite relieved—a circumstance that might be well moralised, were one "i' th' vein," or did one feel one's self equal to it.

We had a very comfortable dinner at the hotel—our party having diminished to four, of whom I was the only one intending to proceed the following morning, by the mail coach, to Colombo. The native servants, in spotless white, petticoats and all—proud that they understood how to wait at table—their black beards, and large tortoise-shell combs stuck in the back of their heads, appearing to me so incongruous, that I felt disposed to laugh every time I looked at them. Nor was it without a feeling of unpleasantness that I saw my plate handed about by the dark fingers—a transient feeling, which I distinctly remember having once felt, but which must very soon have passed away with use. After a long voyage, people are not disposed for some time to be very critical respecting their meals. We found everything excellent at our dinner, including the beef—the fact is, people get so much mutton on board, that, I believe, they would willingly declare the roast ribs of a sexagenarian cart-horse exquisite after a four months' voyage—my subsequent experience of Point de Galle did not lead me to believe that anything like good beef was ever to be got there in those days (1843), and therefore I attribute our satisfaction to our position and condition. There was something so completely novel in being waited upon by the brown natives in white garments; in the open room leading into an equally open verandah; in the large fan, called a punkah, pulled backwards and forwards by a servant, to create a current of air in the room—there was something so novel in all this, that one could not be critical; and soup, beef, curry, tarts, and fruit, were all found to be equally excellent and palatable, although I have no doubt, had the same dinner been presented to any one of us a month after, we should have found the soup bad, the tarts worse, and the beef worst of all; that, in fact, the curry and the fruits would be pronounced to be the only eatable things on the table. Indeed I must say, that notwithstanding the variety of Indian cookery—the pillaws, and coftahs, and cabobs, and kitchery of the presidencies—there is no place where better curries are made than in Ceylon, and this I say, not as a griffin just arrived from England, but as an experienced *quyhy*—one who knows Ceylon, and who has lived both in Madras and Calcutta.

That evening I first made acquaintance with the fire-flies, and was surprised and delighted with the appearance produced by numbers of them, shining like so many tiny stars upon a tree. The effect was altogether so strange and pretty, rather than grand or beautiful, that it looked far more like an artificial one, produced by the handiwork of man, than the simple operation of nature.

Having heard that the coach to Colombo started at gun-fire, or the first faint dawn of day, I retired early, requesting to be called at four o'clock. The bed-room differed as much from what a bed-room would have been in England, as everything else in the house from their European prototypes. The object in it was to obtain air and some slight degree of coolness, not to be snug and comfortable as one expects a bed-room to be in colder climes. A mat that crackled under the feet covered the floor. The bed itself was near the middle of the room, detached from the wall, completely isolated. Thin net curtains hung round it, tucked under the mattrass, which bore no similarity at all to a feather bed. The feet were elevated upon curious little blocks, that reminded one of extremely-small flower-pots, with an elevation in the centre to support them, a deep groove all round which, was full of water or some other fluid. I had no idea of the use of these stands at the time, but subsequently found that they prevented the ants from making their way into the bed, and that many other articles of furniture, such as sideboards, were similarly protected. Altogether, as I advanced lamp in hand into the apartment, it struck me that there was a cold, cheerless, uncomfortable look about it, even after having spent months in the cabin of a ship—a reflection that the oppressive heat of the atmosphere might have convinced me was a foolish one, for the cooler such an apartment could be made the better. The true model, indeed, of an Indian bed-room, is a large empty apartment, with a bed in the middle, surmounted by a fan or punkah, to be pulled backwards and forwards all night by servants employed for the purpose. In the Presidencies this arrangement is common—the rope from the punkah going through the wall into the verandah, where the *punkah-wallah*, as he is called, sits and nods—pulling, however, as he nods—easy, though monotonous work. To prevent his going to sleep over the operation—an accident that but too frequently happens, and which causes the sleeper within to start up bathed in perspiration, and infuriated with musquitoes—some benevolent individual has invented the plan of perching punkah-wallah upon a high stool, made for the purpose, when, if he goes to sleep, his balance must be lost, and he comes to the ground with sufficient violence to wake him were he never so drowsy.

I jumped into my novel bed at Point de Galle as yet innocent of the greatest plagues of Indian existence. The window, which looked into the verandah, with a garden beyond, had the glass compartments open and the Venetian shutters closed, whilst the laths of the Venetians themselves were laid perfectly horizontal, to admit, through the interstices, as much air as possible. As I lay, covered with one flimsy sheet, I could see the stars through the window, peering brightly above the trees without, and the fire-flies flitting ceaselessly from leaf to leaf, and lighting up the dark shadows of a dark moonless night with ever-changing variety. I should have enjoyed the scene with infinitely more gusto, had it not been for the excessive heat. Throwing off the sheet, with which alone I was covered, was but a temporary relief. I tossed about from side to side to find some cooler corner, but as fatigue threw me into a short-lived doze, the stifling heat laid its hand heavily upon me, and I awoke with a sense of oppression and liquefaction that was anything but comfortable. At length, as I looked through the open jalousies of the window, it struck me that the net-curtains by which I was surrounded, thin as they were, must tend to increase the heat considerably, and to prevent that circulation of the cool night air about my person, which I so much desired. I wonder they don't think of that, I thought, as I threw the curtains up over the roof of the bed,—they have much to learn yet in order to accommodate this Indian climate to British constitutions. The change was delightful; the cool air of the night without was wafted insensibly around me, and I dozed off into what promised to be a delightful sleep.

I was awoke by a sharp stinging pain upon my forehead, accompanied by a similar sensation on both my feet. I put my hand to all three places successively, but could discover nothing, at the same time that a little rubbing on each was agreeable. Never mind, thought I, I have got rid of the excessive heat at all events, I shall soon be asleep. The quiet that now reigned in the house, assured me that the others had similarly sought their couches, but, like myself, as I afterwards learned, not to sleep. I had scarcely settled myself into a new and more comfortable position than any I had yet found—I had scarcely had time to close my eyes, and fancy myself on the high road to a sound slumber—four o'clock always looming in the distance, as the hour of rising—when I felt a number of similar sharp pains over various parts of my exposed person, whilst a ringing "hum-m" in my ears told me of formidable enemies I had forgotten—the musquitoes. In getting rid of one evil by raising the curtains, I had induced another and a more formidable one. True, I was as yet, or rather I had been, up to this moment, ignorant of the appearance and character of those blood-thirsty insects, save what I had heard from others, but their descriptions had made me too well acquainted with the peculiar "hum-m-m," in which the little wretches delight, to feel a doubt as to the nature of my assailants. The more I rubbed the places they had bitten, the more they swelled, until I was literally covered with small excrescences, red and purple, such as a devoted attachment to the brandy bottle often produces upon the nose of the toper; and, what was worse, each pimple itching most acutely. At length I could stand it no longer. I sprung from the bed, and determined to seek a light. I had, fortunately for my convenience, a small box of lucifers in my dressing-case, and soon lit the lamp. My first visit, lamp in hand, was to the looking-glass, in which I discovered my forehead all blotched over in the most frightful way. I then went to the bed, and as I held the light over the pillow, I saw two of the ugliest-looking little monsters I had ever set my eyes upon. "These are musquitoes," I muttered, as I surveyed them—gnat-like insects, with swollen bodies, curved up at the tail. I brought my hand down heavily upon one of them, I fancy indeed he was too full to fly, and a blot of blood upon the pillow marked where he had been. I felt glad, although I knew but too well whose blood it was, that I had thus scattered; at the same time that sundry smarts upon my legs assured me that many of them had not yet had enough.

I put down the lamp on a chair, and then jumped into bed, carefully tucking the curtains below the mattrass as I had seen them at first, preparatory to engaging in a general *battue* against all the musquitoes that they imprisoned. I commenced by arming myself with the pillow, and having swept it round the sides of the enclosure to collect them all as much as possible into the middle, I brought it down three or four times with terrible energy upon the bed. A solitary delinquent, however, was the sole result, and as I surveyed him with interest, others attacked me in the rear, and I was obliged to renew operations. I found, after a time, that the pillow would not do—my exertions had thrown me into a perfect bath of perspiration, and only two victims the result! so depositing the pillow in its place, I proceeded to close quarters, first wrapping myself well up in the sheet, and then endeavouring to squash my adversaries between my open palms. What other people without must have thought of the various noises I was making, if any were listening, I did not stop to inquire, for I was delighted to find that my new mode of procedure was more successful than the former. Clap, clap, clap, went my hands, and one after another of the assailants lost his life, until I could find no more of them. I then lay down, hot, weary, and exhausted with my recent energetic proceedings, and, notwithstanding the heat, fell asleep.

I had not slept long, however, when I was again awoke by heat and musquitoes combined—some of the latter, I suppose, having made their way in subsequently, or escaped my sanguinary onslaught. Again forsaking my bed, I partially dressed, and spent the remainder of that dreadfully long night in the verandah. Most heartily did I wish that the coach left at three instead of five, but wishes were unavailing, and, for more than three hours, I walked up and down, smoking the while, and listening to the strange hum of insect and reptile life, that makes the night of the tropics far noisier than the day.

When it was four o'clock, I returned into my room to dress. I had more than half got through my toilet, when a knock at my door informed me that the servant who had promised faithfully to wake me at four, had just awoke himself. It was then twenty minutes past, and as my kind Mentor informed me it was "plenty time for master to get up." I quite agreed with him, informing him at the same time that I had been up since two o'clock, and was then in expectation of coffee, not of being called. In ten minutes the coffee made its appearance, and as the old, grey-bearded "boy," (for, strange to say, they call all servants of all ages, *boys* in Ceylon,) informed me that the coach office was not five minutes' walk distant, I had another long wait in the verandah, feeling considerably refreshed, however, by the ablution and the coffee. At length it was ten minutes to five, and, with a coolie or porter carrying my portmanteau, I bid adieu to the "hotel," and commenced my journey to Colombo—my heavier luggage having been left in the *Parsee*, which was to proceed to Colombo in a few days.

The moon had risen an hour before, and its light, with that of the stars, was sufficient to enable us to distinguish objects faintly as we went along. At length we arrived opposite a large door, with two stunted trees on each side. "Here, Saar," said the coolie, as he put my portmanteau down against one of the trees, exhausting in those two words nearly his whole available stock of English. I looked around, but saw no signs of coach or horses, of people or bustle. All was still. The coolie has made some mistake, thought I, and can't speak English. Perhaps the coach starts from some other place.

"Where's the coach that goes to Colombo?" shouted I in his ear, hoping, by the loudness with which I spoke, to make him comprehend me.

"Here, Saar," said he again, as he coolly proceeded, having found a large stone, to ham mer it on the iron hinges of the door, shouting out some words all the time, that seemed invariably to end with " man gee," in a singing tone. At length the violent knocking, and no less violent shouting, elicited a reply from within. The coolie turned to me with a grin, as if he would have said, " You see." I so understood his look at all events, and replied, " I see nothing extraordinary in your waking somebody with all that. But where's the mail-coach ?"

" Here, Saar," shouted he again, grinning; and again commencing the vociferation of the Singhalese sentence invariably ending in " man gee." At length the door opened, and a huge, half-dressed, negro-like Portuguese stood before us. His black hair stood up straight from his head like the bristles of a hedgehog, and added some inches to his height, which was in itself great.

" Does the coach start from here ?" I asked, delighted to see a pair of pantaloons under such circumstances.

" Yes, Sir," he replied, squeakingly; " in five minutes it will be off."

" O, then it only calls here," I observed.

" No, Sir," said he, in a half-feminine, half-boyish voice, that contrasted strangely with his uncouth figure—"No, Sir, it starts from here;" and, as he said so, I saw a strange waggon-like vehicle lumbering up to us, drawn by four coolies. This was the mail-coach—a miserable cart, with canvas curtains hanging down on either side, and room inside for six at the utmost, whilst the driver might possibly accommodate one or two on his box! A flat roof covered it, whence depended the aforesaid canvas curtains, and on which I suppose luggage is sometimes packed. Two horses, that did not look as if they were particularly disposed to go on, were speedily harnessed, and after another delay of five minutes for the coachman, also a Portuguese, preparations were made for starting. It took the united force of the establishment—coachman, grooms, coolies, and all—to set the machine in motion. Some turned round the wheels, others belaboured the horses, others pushed from behind, whilst two pulled vigorously at the horses' heads and ears. At length we were fairly off—I the only passenger, my leathern portmanteau constituting all the luggage! It was then a quarter past five; when they would have started, had I not been going, I cannot conjecture. We rattled through the streets at a capital pace; but to my surprise, as I looked round I found our vehicle literally covered with natives holding on, on all sides, like shell-fish stuck to a ship's bottom. Even my friend the negro-like Portuguese, in the same elegant *déshabille,* was sitting composedly on the step by which I had mounted. I thought it very odd, but for a time said nothing. At length I asked my mop-headed companion whether they were all coming to Colombo. "No, Sir," he squeaked out; "but there's another start at the post-office." That explained it, and I was satisfied.

Arrived at the post-office, we stopped. There was a man in the verandah to be woke first, which took some time. He then proceeded to wake those within, by a repetition of the same process my coolie had employed to wake the "mail-coach office." There was the same hammering of a stone on the iron-work of the door—the same vociferation of sentences ending in "man gee"—the same intervals of repose and renewals of the assault, and with the same result. A voice answered from within; the door was slowly opened; and at length the mail-bags were deposited in Her Majesty's mail-coach. I have heard that there are many strange vehicles employed by the post-office in England to convey letters about, including hand and wheel-barrows, with the royal arms on them; but I do not think that in all Her Majesty's dominions there was a conveyance in 1843 that would have more surprised the royal lady herself, had she seen it starting, than the Galle and Colombo mail-coach.

Portuguese mop-head was right. There *was* another start; and again was the entire force of the mail coach-office put in requisition—aided by sundry volunteers from the post-office—to set us in motion, and again with the same triumphant success. We rattled under the gate of the Fort, and were gone. I looked round, but grooms, Portuguese, and coolies had disappeared. Their morning's duty was performed, and they were doubtless retiring to sleep off the fatigue of the exertion. What amused me most was the perfect gravity with which the whole operation was gone through. There was no smiling, no loud laughter, no jest or answer. It seemed to be regarded by all as far other than a laughing matter. The scientific precision with which the horses' ears were grasped—the grim determined air with which the spokes of the wheels were handled—the dogmatic sternness with which the horses were flagellated—all showed that it was an accustomed affair, too common to be at all amusing—rather, indeed, the reverse to all parties.

The Portuguese coachman, a native groom, and myself constituted the entire occupants of the vehicle; and right glad was I when I saw the sun rising over the forests and hills on our right, as we made our way rapidly along a beautiful road, lined on either side by masses of cocoa-nut trees—their graceful stems and the delicate tracery of their foliage becoming every moment more distinct. Occasionally we were near the sea, its waves breaking into foam on one side, whilst thick vegetation bounded our path upon the other.

The road, throughout the entire distance, was beautifully variegated by wild and cultivated scenery, and yet it was completely level, scarcely a hill to compare even with Ludgate, throughout the entire journey of more than seventy miles. Occasionally we caught glimpses of fishing-boats making their way out to sea or returning to shore, whilst on land, as we passed the various villages, the people seemed to be employed principally in the expressing of oil from the cocoa-nut by a rude species of machinery, turned by the most diminutive of bullocks. Women were to be seen occasionally pounding rice in a wooden mortar with a large iron-shod stick for a pestle, labour that seemed to be by far the most active and energetic in which any portion of the people were employed. Three or four times during the journey, a priest of Budha passed us by—to me one of the most interesting of objects, anxious as I was to learn something of the strange faith which the Budhists professed. The yellow robes of these priests, encircling the body and legs, and thrown over the right shoulder, whilst the left remained bare—the small leaf-fan which they held in their hands—their abstracted air, so befitting those who professed to have higher thoughts than "of the earth, earthy"—all tended to invest them with an interest in my mind far superior to that with which I regarded any other class of the inhabitants. Generally speaking, they passed us by, without so much as lifting their eyes to the carriage, making one almost believe that they had succeeded in effecting what appears to be the great object of their philosophy and religion—the detachment of the mind from all cleaving to external objects, and the fixing of it on itself, and on higher subjects of meditation.

I was as yet by no means reconciled to the colour of the Singhalese, and therefore regarded, more with disgust than benevolence, the troops of naked children whom we saw playing in every village or in the neighbourhood of the cottages. Occasionally the little imps treated us to a friendly cheer as we passed, and there was so much that was human in the honest sound that I felt it open my heart to them; but, for the most part, they contented themselves with a quiet, silent stare, and then a short run after the vehicle. As for the women, I do not believe it would be possible for female humanity to dress itself more unbecomingly than the majority of the Singhalese do. Some, indeed, I remarked who dispensed with all covering above the loins, but they were chiefly old withered hags, engaged in beating the coir which surrounds the cocoa-nut. Those who were more respectable wore a white jacket, closed in front, loosely dangling over their shoulders and breast—no attempt whatever being made to fit it to the shape, or to confine it at the waist. A piece of cloth wrapped round the lower part of the person, resembling scanty petticoats, and similar to what the men wear, formed their nether habiliments, whilst between the two a dreadful hiatus was often left, disclosing a considerable portion of the chest or stomach, over which the white jacket above projects ungracefully, the further in proportion to the fulness of the bust, thereby casting a shadow on the exposed skin below, that renders the contrast between it and the white jacket all the greater. Altogether, a more unbecoming and a more ungraceful dress it would not be easy for women to adopt; and yet I found that this abominable style was general throughout the island amongst the middle classes. The higher classes show some attention to elegance, by fitting the vest, to a certain extent, to the figure; but such women are only to be seen in the interior, or in remote villages, where the chiefs have taken up their abodes.

As we made our way briskly to the north, occasionally impeded by the difficulty of getting some fresh horses to start, and sometimes crossing wide rivers or small arms of the sea in large flat-bottomed boats prepared for the purpose, I was joined by two gentlemen from some of the stations in the neighbourhood, who were likewise on their way to Colombo. We stopped at a village called Bentotte, about half-way between Galle and our destination, for breakfast. The village is celebrated for its fresh and salt water fish; and a more palatable or more excellent breakfast, of its kind, it would not be easy to get anywhere than the hospitable little rest-house at Bentotte afforded us. The light curry and rice, or fish and rice breakfasts usually partaken of in India and Ceylon, are admirably adapted to the climate, and to the European constitution—far more so, I believe, than the extensive and heterogeneous collections of viands with which Anglo-Indians load their tables at dinner.

The views afforded by the wider river-estuaries on the road from Galle to Colombo particularly as one approaches the latter town, are strikingly beautiful, as examples of what might be called landscape-garden scenery. The broad expanse of water closely hemmed in by thick foliage nodding over the banks of the stream, and stretching far up into the country in winding, luxurious, and graceful curves, wants but the light skiff of the West, with its glistening white sails, to render it picturesque as well as beautiful. At Caltura, one of these outlets, the wild loveliness of the scene is enhanced by the ruins of an old Dutch fort, situated on the only hill near the mouth of the river, and as the traveller is wafted slowly across the broad and placid sheet of water, he must have a quiet imagination indeed, if he does not associate traditions and tales of bravery, and war, and love, with the old moss-covered walls that look down so silently and sad upon the variegated landscape below.

CHAPTER II.

COLOMBO AND THE CINNAMON GARDENS.

" In Ephesus I am but two hours old,
As strange unto your town, as to your talk."
Comedy of Errors, act ii., sc. 2.

BUT few, even of oriental towns, are built in so scattered a manner as the capital of Ceylon. The old Dutch fort forms the nucleus, on all sides of which stretch the European and native suburbs. Due north and south, lining the sea-shore, are situated detachments of neat white houses, with picturesque verandahs, occupied by the European community, whilst in an island formed by the Colombo lake—a flat, unvariegated island, by no means of a picturesque character—others of the same fraternity, particularly military, have taken up their quarters. From these different stations, the drive into the fort, the great centre of Governmental and mercantile business, is a pleasant one—the roads, for the most part, skirting the sea or the lake. East from the fort lies the native town or *pettah,* as they call it, a collection of narrow intricate streets, in which Singhalese, Malabars, Portuguese and Dutch descendants, Moormen and Parsees, are all to be found in close proximity to each other, professing as many different kinds of faith, and speaking as many different languages. The main street of this district is entirely occupied by shops and warehouses, where the native merchants and shopkeepers carry on their business, and it would not be easy to find elsewhere, a collection of goods so various and miscellaneous, as some of these shops contain. Chandeliers, plate, dressing-cases, crockery, cloth, shawls, haberdashery, cigars, harness, saddlery, and perfumery, are all to be found in the well-stored warehouse of Neine Mereker for instance, a celebrated Mohammedan shopkeeper of this street. Neine Mereker is a small instalment of the name of the owner—the only portion of it known to Europeans—for the entire appellation is lengthier than that of a Portuguese princess.

"Well, Sir, what you want to-day?" asks Neine, as your buggy draws up before the door, making his portly way carefully through a crowd more plebeian purchasers—that is, of purchasers who do not drive buggies.

"I want some cheroots, Neine," is the answer.

"Aha, you know I got plenty good cheroots in the other day, Sir, fresh from Singapore?" says Neine, as he again makes his way through the crowd—"you not seen these new dressing-cases I got from Paris, day before yesterday?"

"No, I have not," says the complaisant visitor, "they're very pretty. But they make these in Birmingham, Neine."

"No, no, no—ha, ha!—no, no, Sir, they not make that kind in Birmingham, I know. They make plenty good in Birmingham, but not that kind. All from Paris. Now look at these *papier mâché* things. You think that come from Birmingham. I know, no. All Paris, all Paris. See, plenty pretty pictures, eh! The ladies do like them so much. There was Mrs. Cubb," whispers Neine confidentially, mentioning the *belle* of Colombo, "did want to make her husband buy one, she wanted it so much. But he's all the same as one black bear—he turns his back to her, to look at his watch, and says he is plenty time to go home." So saying, Neine leads the way to the glass case in which a tempting display of patent leather boots and shoes is presented to the eye of the visitor.

"Hoby's boots, Sir," he mutters, as he points to the glistening collection. Saddlery comes next. Neine points to a specimen—"same kind Prince Albert rides on," he insinuates, "all London made, Christy's, plenty good." The visitor, still taciturn, is next swept past a case of harness, and so Neine would take him all round his shop, certain of finding something he would buy ultimately, did not the impatient visitor speak of "cheroots" again.

"Ah, ah, I know," says Neine, disappointed, and opening a large chest, in the immediate vicinity of the spot whence they had set out, displays a tempting array of boxes of five hundred and a thousand, Nos. 2, 3 and 4—all fresh from Manilla, he declares, for Neine is well aware that the Manillas, unlike the Havannahs, do not improve with age.

If it be a lady that he thus escorts, Neine has a whole host of articles to show her fresh from London, from Paris, from Canton. Silks, shawls, bonnets, and flowers, all, strange to say, obtained within the last few days; not an article a week old in his shop by his own account; nor do I doubt that he will often show to the fair purchasers the very counterpart of the last bonnet worn by Her Majesty herself. Shopping may be a pleasant thing for ladies in London, and doubtless pleasant it is to judge by the quantity of time devoted to it, but I doubt if it can be considered pleasant under any circumstances in India or Ceylon. The intense heat, and the unpleasant close smell of any collection of new goods, of whatever kind, rendering the shops almost unsupportable.

The Fort of Colombo is a very large and a very badly constructed one. I have heard military men say that it would take five thousand men to garrison it properly. At the time of which I speak, there were seventeen gunners in it, and two companies of a European regiment. It is situated on a rocky projection, nearly in the middle of the western coast, washed partially by the sea on three sides, and with a lake stretching away to the south-east. There are several small streets in it, lined with low houses on either side, some occupied by merchants as offices and warehouses, others by European shopkeepers, and a few used as dwelling-houses by subaltern military officers and others. Government house, where the Governor resides, a large public library, two churches, a bank, the principal offices of Government, together with a small esplanade, and barracks, are all likewise contained within its walls. From all sides in the morning, may be seen buggies and dog-carts, and palanquin-carriages (with grooms running at the horses' heads, or flying behind like the tail to a boy's kite, attached by one arm to the vehicle,) making their way vigorously into the Fort. Its drawbridges, and covered ways, and embankments and gates, however useless against an enemy, forming formidable obstacles to the unlucky driver who happens to have a spirited horse. Merchants, military and commissariat officers, and those employed by the local Government, keep perpetually rolling in from nine to eleven in the morning, in the whitest possible habiliments—white pantaloons, white waistcoat, and white jacket, surmounted but too frequently by as white a face, out of which the heat and the musquitoes have sucked every trace of colour and of blood. Towards evening again, between three and six, the same stream makes its way, through the only two gates available for the purpose, back to the suburbs, the grooms running at the horses' heads, or flying behind the buggies and dog-carts in the same wild style as in the morning. A few ride from the Fort in the evening, but this exercise is generally reserved for a later hour, when a large piece of unoccupied ground south of the Fort, and by the sea shore, called the Galle Face, is crowded by carriages and equestrians, some seeking the cool breeze from the sea, others exhibiting their horses and new liveries, and others their fine dresses and habits, just as on the Strand in Calcutta—the only difference of importance being that whilst a carriage with two horses is the exception in Colombo, it is the rule in the City of Palaces, where a far larger number of barouches and chariots make their appearance than of any other description of vehicle.

The library is the principal resort in the daytime for those in the Fort who have leisure or desire to read the periodicals. An admirable institution it is, well supplied with the current and standard literature of England, and containing many valuable classical and foreign works of travels. The principal newspapers and periodicals of England and the Presidencies are to be found on its tables, and although the character of the literature monthly added to its shelves, is principally popular or light, there are but few valuable works published in England respecting the East, which do not find their way into it. To the expatriated Briton there can be no greater pleasure than to be able to visit, when he pleases, an institution in which he finds himself surrounded by the old familiar magazines and reviews, and newspapers, from which he daily received instruction or amusement when at home—yes, at home—for, let him go where he will, home means, not his dwelling-place or temporary residence, but the country he has left, and to which he hopes some day to return.

The trees with which the Dutch bordered the roads and streets in the Fort, form an agreeable contrast to the glistening white and red-tiled houses, and an agreeable shade to the pedestrian who makes his way under so tropical a sun as that of Colombo, from one part of the curious old fortification to another. These trees, however, are fast disappearing under the innovating reformations of John Bull, and he does not see the propriety of planting new ones as fast as the old are removed. In fact, he does not consider them business-like enough, and hence his aversion to what is merely intended to adorn and to gratify.

A canal, of which no one knows the use apparently, and which is so seldom filled with water that it might be correctly styled "the dry canal," divides the barracks and parade-ground from the business portion of the Fort, and as the visitor looks across it, he may see numbers of sturdy warriors, doomed, perhaps for their sins in a former birth, a native would say, to dress themselves daily in heavy red cloth coats, as unfitted for wear in such a climate as the constitution of the wearers for exposure to such a sun—some leaning over the railing of their verandah to watch and remark upon the native idlers below, others lying passively on mats, engaged in the meditative process of smoking, but all listless and quiet, as if unable or unwilling to exert themselves in any way in such an atmosphere.

The cinnamon gardens in the vicinity of Colombo, form one of its chief attractions, both to the occasional visitor and to the resident. My buggy has been left at the library—we will drive to them. The horse-keeper is dozing as he sits on his heels right in front of the horse's head, doubtless under the conviction that it will be impossible for the vehicle to go on very far without awakening him. A word or two recalls him to himself, although he is not always so easily awoke, and we are off. Government house is left on our right—a building of little pretension—too low to be grand, and too Dutch-like, in its broad massive expansion on either side, to be mistaken for the erection of any other people. The banks—for there were two in those days of coffee-planting and enterprize, although only one remains—are on our left; one of them a fine three-storied building, well-built, and remarkable amidst the architectural poverty around. The post-office we pass rapidly on our right, and find ourselves between two avenues of trees leading down to the gate of the Fort. Here we plunge into danger and gloom under a dark tortuous archway, where any enemy might be easily arrested by half a score of brave determined fellows, if the said enemy would be but polite enough to make his way into the fort that way, and leave untried the far easier road over the battlements. Emerging from this subterranean defile,—invented, some say, by a coach-builder, who had become by accident Governor of Colombo, when the Fort was being built—emerging from it, without having taken off the wheel at the sharp angle in the midst of the Tartarean passage, or dislocated the hood against the envious projecting buttress a little further on, we find ourselves on a narrow level road skirted by what ought to be a ditch I believe, but is a green level plot of grass, leading down to a draw-bridge outside another gateway, at which a second sharp angle invites buggies, palanquin-carriages, and dog-carts to destruction. The sea is before us—a narrow strand only broad enough for a road, separates the frowning walls and muddy ditch of the Fort from the glorious ocean beyond. On our right the surf is dashing against the huge rocks incessantly, and then scattering it in showers of spray over the ramparts, whilst before us, in all its magnificent grandeur and sublime vastness, stretches the placid bosom of the deep, meeting, in a distinct line beyond, the overarching blue.

We are now approaching the Galle Face—the favoured haunt of the beauties and beaux of Colombo, when the sun is taking his departure for the day, and precipitating himself into the ocean. Not a cloud obscures the grand luminary at some seasons of the year, whilst he sinks away to the horizon, now touching the water with his reddened disc, anon cloven in two by the clear line that divides earth and sky, and scattering glorious rays lavishly over the ocean and the heavens until the whole western welkin shines with a blood-red glow, which, reflected on the surface of the water, is beautiful to behold.

> "The sun is dying like a cloven king
> In his own blood; the while the distant moon,
> Like a pale prophetess, whom he has wronged,
> Leans, eager forward, with most hungry eyes,
> Watching him bleed to death, and, as he faints,
> She brightens and dilates; revenge complete,
> She walks in lonely triumph thro' the night."

It is only in the tropics that such a scene as the poet pictures here can be seen in all its vivid reality, although of course it may be imagined, in the more cloudy north.

But leaving the contemplation of the grandeur and magnificence of nature, let us turn our attention to the scene which humanity displays on this strip of green that fringes the lake on one side, and the ocean on the other. It is a fine evening, the day has been intensely hot, and all Colombo is on the "Face." By the sea-shore roll quietly lines of carriages of all kinds, drawn by horses as various looking. Some of the vehicles one might almost fancy had left England when Charles the Second reigned, and carriages were becoming for the first time extensively used, so antiquated and dilapidated do they appear to be, whilst the poor horses, labouring along, find it useless to attempt anything more than a solemn walk with them. Others are of the newest cut, and that which is most unsuited to the climate, whilst their occupants seem uneasy if their horses have a moment's breathing-time. I have known a young man, ambitious and eccentric, who disliked being only like other people, and who imported in consequence a London cab into Colombo, with front board, C springs, and tiger's stand complete, cooped up in which, and protected by it from every breath of air, he perspired and smiled amazingly, whilst the light Arab horse to which it was attached, with difficulty tugged it forwards. The equestrians occupy the turf, and if the carriages be outré-looking and absurd, every one must admire the horses and their riders that figure on the "Face." The elegant Arab is in his native element when he has a firm-handed, light rider on his back. The fat pursy Colonel of sixty, whose huge dimensions no other uniform but his own would encase, does not look either picturesque or interesting, mounted on a slightly-built graceful Arab of thirteen hands high, but he is an exception. The majority of the cavaliers are young men and maidens, and, as they sweep over the turf in animated converse or excited emulation, none can deny that the scene is one of striking beauty and great attractiveness. The fine forms of the horses, exhibited to perfection in the bounding canter or more severe gallop—the light airy figures of the female equestrians, bending gracefully over the saddle-bow as they manage their steeds or converse with their companions—the athletic figures of the young military officers, who love to display at once their skill in horsemanship and their red coats—altogether form a scene of a new and exciting character, in which the various colours of the horses, the hues of the flowing riding-habits, the black hats and coats of the civil, and the red jackets of the military, horsemen, all combine and contrast elegantly with each other, and with the green turf beneath. It is doubtful whether even the drawing-rooms of the private houses or the ball-rooms of public assemblies, are more frequently the birth-place of love between youthful members of Colombo society, than the Galle Face. Certain it is that many choose the lonely ride and the confidential companionship which it engenders, for the disclosure of affection and the making of what is so vulgarly called "a proposal." Nor would it be easy perhaps to find a better opportunity for such a purpose than when the warm blood has been set rapidly in motion by the most agreeable of all forms of exercise.

A smart trot through Colpetty—a suburb of Colombo, extending to the south beyond the "Face," and almost exclusively occupied by the English—brings us to the entrance into the cinnamon gardens. Every cultivated spot of ground in Ceylon is called a garden, and therefore in the cinnamon gardens, the visitor will be much disappointed if he expects to see neat walks, trimly laid out, or artificial arrangements intended to heighten or improve the effects of nature. There is nothing of all this here, and yet gardens they undoubtedly are, in the noblest and truest sense of the term. The well-kept road affords us an excellent view of them on either side. The whole place resembles a wilderness of laurel bushes growing out of masses of snow or salt. The fine sand which forms the external coating of the soil is almost purely white, and the bushes thrive in it luxuriantly. They grow in irregular tufts, their perennial green of all hues, varying from the faintest yellow to the most sombre brown, contrasting pleasantly with the glimpses of white sand beneath, which the visitor occasionally gets, as he rides or drives along. Nothing can be more delicate in hue than the first tender leaves of the cinnamon bush, as they shoot forth variously from its branches—half-opening, half-curling up, as if afraid to trust themselves to the broad, garish light of day. Their flavour too is a faint, pleasant, aromatic one, that tempts the early wanderer to pluck them occasionally as he brushes past, and, whilst the dew is rising in vapour from the leaves, caught up by the morning sun, it carries with it a delightful perfume of the spicy shrub, which makes the air peculiarly pleasant. On horseback, or in a buggy, the visitor's eye sweeps unimpeded over the wide extent of the tops of the bushes, which cluster thickly on the ground, here and there a solitary tree arresting his attention, and looking as if it were sorry to have left the agreeable companionship below. In the very centre of the plantation, a noble knot of lofty trees, judiciously planted, afford an agreeable shade, and make the pedestrian sigh for a bench on which to enjoy the scenery and the refreshing air,

It is only in the morning, as I have said, that the cinnamon bush affords a perfume, just when the dew is being evaporated from the young leaves,—at all other times, a strong imagination may conjure up a "spicy breeze," but it is entirely of the character of a "baseless fabric of a vision;" no such breeze blows, no such odour is wafted over sea or land—"the only thing that can ordinarily be smelt about them," as my uncle, old-bachelor like, somewhat cynically observed, "being the rotten leaves, which," he added, "have very much the same perfume in all countries." There certainly are few places in which a ride is more agreeable, or perhaps more beneficial, than in these gardens, and accordingly on every fine evening, that is, on nineteen evenings out of every twenty, they are visited by numbers who have become weary of the constant unchanging round on the Galle Face, and who desire rather to obtain amusement and enjoyment for themselves, than to afford them to others. The morning however is the proper time to visit these gardens—just when the rays of the sun are struggling with the few light misty clouds that impede their progress, just when the dew is beginning to forsake the leaves, and the birds, waking from their night's sleep, are replacing the hoarse murmur of insect life by their own sweet chirping and songs—then it is that the visitor, whether on foot or on horseback, may truly enjoy the gardens, and then it is of course that they are most deserted.

The preparation of the spice from the bush is a very simple operation. Sticks, as straight as possible, three or four feet long, are cut from the bushes in large numbers, the thickest, not much grosser than one's thumb, the thinnest not so small as one's little finger. These sticks are held by the operator in his left hand, resting lengthways on his fore-arm, whilst with a sharp knife, prepared for the purpose, he cuts the bark down the entire length of the stick, and then peels it off, endeavouring to retain the pieces of as great a length and breadth as possible. A slip of the knife would of course bury it at once in the hand or arm, but practice makes them quite perfect in the matter, and they seldom injure themselves. To the visitor who sees the stick pressing into the soft flesh of the arm, or almost imbedded in the muscle of the bare thigh, whilst the knife is brought rapidly along, making a deep incision, the labour appears a highly dangerous one, nor can a spectator witness it at first without a shudder; but to the operators themselves the fear of the novice is merely a subject of amusement —they see no danger in it, and know that carelessness alone can turn off the edge of the keen knife, even at the hardest knot. The strips of bark, so peeled off, are then thoroughly dried in the sun, rolled up into thin cylinders, the smaller being placed within the larger, and packed for exportation.

There was much in my life in Colombo that I enjoyed with a keen relish. True the heat and musquitoes were dreadful, and never was there a greater martyr to the latter than I was. From the moment of my arrival almost, they had evidently marked me as their own, whilst the heat was increased by my constant desire for exertion of some kind. But if the middle of the day was all but unbearable, the mornings and evenings were delightful; and in coursing through the cinnamon gardens or boating on the Colombo lake, I found both employment and exercise of the most agreeable kind. I did not think much of the Governor's dinners, stiff, formal, and unenjoyable as they were, and even a ball at Government House did not appear to me to be the acmé of felicity, but even these were interesting because they were novel, and their very novelty made up for their dulness.

The coffee-estate, which I had left England to manage, was already planted, and in bearing it is true, and there were all the hopes and fears of a new and untried life yet to be entered upon and to be encountered; but these considerations did not trouble me much. There was something piquant in the very idea of life in the jungle which made me wish to be there as soon as possible. My uncle's former partner, whose place I supplied, was dead, and a Portuguese servant, a confidential man, was at present acting as superintendent. He was thoroughly acquainted with coffee-planting practically, and I theoretically, so that I had no doubt we should form between us an admirable estate. In the mean time I learned Singhalese and Anglo-Ceylon customs in Colombo, whilst residing with my relative. He was a kind though eccentric old bachelor, who had lived for fifteen years in the island, and had a profound contempt for everything but commerce and coffee-planting, and for every one except those engaged in them.

On a native holiday, when there was no

business doing in the Fort, he accompanied me to the house of a clergyman, to whom I had recently been introduced, and who had invited us to visit a Budhist temple at the opposite extremity of the lake, by the side of which his house was built. We started very early. Even the morning was oppressively hot, whilst a mist, rising from the ground just preparatory to the sun's appearance, rendered the air heavier and more oppressive than it would otherwise have been. We had a journey of several miles to accomplish in this atmosphere, cooped up in a close palanquin-carriage.

Mr. Padre, our host, was a pious man, an exception to the general rule in India; and as morning prayers were but just beginning on our arrival, we joined the family. I have said that the ground without was steaming; vapours were endeavouring to rise through the loaded air, but ineffectually, for there were other vapours above—not fogs, such as London delights in, but invisible steam, not to be seen, but to be most indubitably felt. The atmosphere within the house was little more tolerable; and as I took my seat I felt two streams coursing down upon either side of my forehead, which it was useless to interrupt by occasional mopping up.

Not a single musquito had remained out of doors on this particular morning. I was a perfect martyr to them. They had been swarming at home when we left; but they were swarming near the lake in still greater abundance. I had scarcely taken my seat to listen with what devotion such an atmosphere and such circumstances would allow, when I felt that my old enemies were upon me. At the knees my pantaloons were of course drawn more tightly than elsewhere, and, as I never could endure drawers in a climate where all dress was superfluous, the larger animals of the musquito kind invariably found out this weak point, and perched upon my knee—insinuatingly inserted their proboscces, as if that knee were their own—and then commenced their depredations. I became painfully conscious in a moment that they were at work, and, looking down, distinguished two monsters already bloated with excessive sucking. I put my hand out quietly, as if intending nothing particular, and allowed it gently to descend upon the smarting, itching knee; but they were gone; the rascals had been too quick for me. I rubbed the wounded member a little, and then placed the other knee upon it, for the pressure was agreeable. Amidst the sonorous reading of the Scriptures there was a constant buz, buz, buz from my bloodthirsty enemies around my ears, longing for a bite. By skilful evolutions of the head and hand I contrived to keep them from settling. The punkah was pulled but lazily, and it would not have done to have shouted out under such circumstances. I directed many an agonized glance at the wretch who was pulling it, but he heeded them not, for he was dozing; his head had sunk upon his breast, and his closed eyes showed that he was utterly oblivious of my woes, and likely to remain so; whilst his hand moved mechanically backwards and forwards, lazily, heavily, and uncertainly. In the mean time a smart of more than ordinary poignancy, caused by some monster musquito I suppose, made me almost jump from my chair. I forgot where I was for an instant, and brought down my hand with terrific force upon my leg, with force enough to have killed a thousand of the insects had they been collected there; but the start had warned the poacher away, and he was quietly performing gyrations round my chair, waiting for the next convenient opportunity. I felt ashamed of myself; all eyes were upon me for an instant; my uncle was grave; and it was quite evident that Mr. Padre's family, consisting of Mrs. Padre and two Misses Padre, looked upon me already as a dissipated character. But, alas! these were but the beginnings of sorrows. I was seated upon a cane chair, and through "the interstices between the intersections" (*vide* Johnson's definition of network), these insatiable bloodsuckers made their way to another portion of my frame, where the pantaloons were equally tight, and where it was impossible for me to get at them. The loud report which my hand had caused in coming down with such force upon my thigh had roused my friend the punkah-puller. I saw a malicious grin upon his countenance, as he fixed his eyes on me, and pulled harder and more regularly. The agitation of the air caused by his vigorous exertions relieved me from the enemies who had been swarming round my head; but, alas! they had only made their way under the chair, where the influence of the punkah was not to be felt. I could sit at ease no longer. It was only by constantly changing my posture that I could detach those who had attacked me from beneath; and what with the pain and the endeavour to prevent fresh assaults, I literally writhed in a species of perpetual motion. It was impossible for mortal man to endure it long. That interminable chapter would apparently never be done; and seeing a chair with a horse-hair seat in my vicinity—(the cane-bottoms are generally preferred for coolness)—I at length mustered up courage to rise, and convey my person to the safer piece of furniture, on which I was at all events secure from such insidious attacks from beneath. Another general stare was the result of this fresh move on my part, and I felt as if I should like very much to be anywhere but where I was. *Mauvaise honte* was my prevailing folly; and I blushed up to my ears first, and then down again to my toes. Punkah-puller was grinning more indecently than ever, almost audibly, in fact, and I felt as if I could with pleasure have vented my accumulated rage and shame and pain upon him. I thought he saw that in my face, for he turned away his eyes when mine met his, and hid his dark features between his knees again. The reading proceeded as before—the temporary interruption caused by my sudden move was at an end—and I now ventured to turn my attention to the chair I had left. From where I sat, at a short distance from it, I could distinctly see numerous musquitoes quickly and regularly revolving round the space enclosed by the feet of the chair beneath, evidently looking for the same consolation which some of their brethren had already received at the expense of my ease and comfort. I chuckled with satisfaction as I thought that they were outwitted now at all events, but was instantaneously recalled to a consideration of my own position by an acute sting upon the exposed knee, and another upon the most prominent portion of the calf of my leg. These assaults had been simultaneous, and all the injury was done before my attention had been called to them. But why linger upon so ticklish and painful a subject? Those who have never experienced the ferocious assaults of an army of musquitoes can have no sympathy with me; those who have, need but few words to recall the image to their mind—an image which,—

> "To those who know it not, no words can paint,
> Whilst those who know it, know all words are faint."

The reading of that chapter, which I had long looked upon as interminable, and which I still think must have been the longest in the

Bible, was at length finished, and we knelt. Any change, I thought, must have been for the better; but I was mistaken. My friend, the punkah-puller, had relapsed into somnolency, and the breeze caused by his exertions was of the most gentle and harmless description possible. I need scarcely say that, as I knelt, my jacket, exactly of the fashion of an English school-boy's, only differing in the material, which was white long-cloth, did not defend me from the assaults of the musquitoes, as a paletot, a frock-coat, nay, even a dress-coat, to some extent, would have done. It was impossible not to become speedily and painfully sensible of this fact, and, whatever my feelings of devotion, the pain to which I was subjected in consequence of the want of any posterior defence, was quite sufficient to have roused a saint from his propriety. To attend to the prayers, under such circumstances, was impossible. One of the Misses Padre was kneeling near me—the mother was fortunately at the opposite side of the study table—and my back was turned towards the reverend gentleman himself. I could not shy a book at the punkah-puller's head, to rouse him to greater exertions. I could not openly rise from my knees and seat myself. I thought of quietly passing my handkerchief round, so as to form a kind of kilt worn on the wrong side, but I knew Mr. Padre must see such a manœuvre, and I knew that these sallow-faced, liver-diseased, old Anglo-Indians never give a young man credit for being so unmercifully persecuted as he sometimes is. He would ascribe it all to a species of irreverent larking, to which I was as little disposed as he was. The evil was every moment becoming more unendurable. I felt that a crisis was at hand, that something must be done; and at the risk of losing the esteem of a highly estimable and worthy family for ever, I did at length muster courage to insinuate my handkerchief as well as I could into the desired position; but this could not be done without noise, and a pause in the worthy clergyman's reading convinced me that he was watching my proceedings. I did not venture to turn my head—the Miss Padre beside me was evidently disturbed in her devotions by my uneasiness—and a sense of these accumulated and unmerited wrongs and sufferings threw me into a heat, to which, what I endured, when the thermometer was at 98° in the shade, was a trifle.

Throughout breakfast I was painfully conscious of the fact that every member of the family regarded me as a reprobate, and although I did all I could to remove the impression, I saw plainly that it was fixed in the minds of Mr. and Mrs. Padre. The young ladies were more just, and, forsaking the parents, I did my best to ingratiate myself with the daughters. Whilst the preparations for departure to the Budhist temple, by boat, were being made, my uncle found an opportunity of addressing me privately.

"I thought you had learned a little more reverence for religion in college," said he, "than to create such a disturbance at prayer-time." The struggling grin which played round his mouth as he spoke, proved to me that he was thoroughly aware both of the extent of my persecution and of its cause.

"There never was a man so beset by those plagues, the musquitoes, as I am," I replied. "I endured enough this morning, both at prayers and at breakfast, to weary out the most imperturbable patience."

"They bite you through your pantaloons, then?" said he.

"They bite me through everything, but my boots," said I.

"A florid complexion," he answered, grinning; "never knew a florid complexion that wasn't a martyr to them."

"Very satisfactory to know that, truly," I replied.

"Oh, but you'll get rid of them on the coffee estate. They don't go up so high—only that the leeches are worse there, a thousand times worse there than the musquitoes here."

"A delightful country," I sighed, as I rubbed my knee, still smarting with the morning's infliction.

"As fine a country as there is under heaven, Sir," was his reply; "and if people will only wear drawers and leech-gaiters, they need not fear either the musquitoes or leeches much."

Mr. Padre joined us at the moment, and I endeavoured to give him some idea of my sufferings, but evidently without success.

We were soon seated in our host's boat, under a comfortable awning, and making our way slowly but pleasantly over the lake, as it glistened brightly in the sun's rays. The cool breeze that played over the surface of the water fanned our faces agreeably, and made the voyage enjoyable. Behind us was the sloping hill on which stood the house we had just left, its white walls and pillars contrasting well with the green lawn that swept down to the edge of the lake, and with green Venetians that guarded the windows. We were rowed by four boatmen belonging to Mr. Padre's establishment, tastefully dressed in his livery of white and blue, and by no means exerting themselves to any dangerous degree to urge the boat too rapidly along. The winding, well-wooded shores of the lake stretched away from us on either side, more resembling those of a river in their form than the extremities of an extensive sheet of water—its broad expanse on the northern side, being shut out from view by the sinuous line of forest. Far away, at the extremity of the water, could be seen the temple to which we were bound, agreeably perched upon the summit of a hill, with its tapering spire pointing heavenwards, whilst behind it rose another, and a loftier hill, that seemed the outer barrier of the extensive valley occupied by the lake and forest.

An hour and a-half's rowing brought us to the landing place, where a somewhat steep path ascended to the temple and its dagobah. I escorted the elder Miss Padre, a demure, imperturbable young lady, very white, and very thoughtful—I doubt if she had ever, in the course of her life, acted once from impulse, even when an infant, so staid and sober, and methodic, and calculating were her words and her actions. She was a valuable companion, however, in the present instance, for she explained much that would have been otherwise incomprehensible to me.

"The Budhist temples consist of two parts," said she, as we ascended; "a *wihare*, in which the priests live, and where they read the sacred books to the people, and a *dagobah*, or monumental, bell-shaped erection, covering some relics, supposed by them to be holy."

"Then it is the *dagobah*, of which I see the spire overtopping the trees yonder," I observed

"It is," said she.

"And the other part, the w——"

"*Wihare*," she suggested.

"*Wihare*," said I, "is a kind of monastery."

"Something resembling a monastery and a chapel, amongst the Roman Catholics. One part of it is devoted to a large image of Gotama Budha, which the people worship, and another to the residence of the priests."

"They lead a quiet, peaceful, happy kind of life, I suppose," said I; "with little to do, save to consume the food the people give them."

"They are not wholly dependent on alms;"

she explained; "there are lands attached to the temple, on which they principally subsist. My papa knows the chief priest of this temple very well; and has often discussions with him; and I have heard pa say, that he believes the priests for the most part lead a moral, useful kind of life."

"How useful?" I asked.

"In teaching the young," was the reply.

By this time we had reached a square enclosure surrounded by low cottages, on one side of which the large massive temple rose,—its stuccoed walls shining like white marble, and making the thatched cottage-looking buildings in its vicinity, appear all the more mean and paltry. Mr. Padre and his younger daughter, a lively, interesting young lady, to whose cheek the exercise had lent a blush that made her look pretty, was close behind us; whilst, as we looked down the path, we saw my uncle and Mrs. Padre labouring along, as well as their size and weight would admit of, for neither of them was of small dimensions.

A yellow-robed priest, with shaven crown, and the usual fan in his hand, soon joined our party, and informed Mr. Padre, that the chief of the temple was absent—offering very politely to escort us round the building himself. He spoke in Singhalese, which I had been studying zealously ever since my arrival, and in which I had now made some proficiency; and from a dark-skinned specimen of humanity, with his left arm and shoulder bare, and without shoes or stockings, shirt, coat, waistcoat, or pantaloons, nothing in fact, but a vast mass of yellow cloth wrapped round his body in voluminous folds, and stretching from his feet to his right shoulder—from such a figure our European prejudices would not have expected the perfect courtesy and good breeding, the gentlemanly suavity and elegance, with which he offered his services. I was surprised and pleased; and the film of prejudice through which, up to this moment, I had regarded the natives, was now torn from my eyes. Conventionalism is the bane of modern society. So little that is natural is left us, so little, indeed, that is not wholly and altogether artificial and unnatural, that even our impressions and feelings, our thoughts and convictions are too often not our own, but those of the society with which we mix, of the limited circle in which we move. Our minds, like our bodies, are so covered with tight trappings, swathing bandages and drapery, that the form and feeling within are almost lost, or at all events, effectually concealed. Custom and society daily make new inroads into our individuality until little or nothing is left us that is our own; but, as in the diamond, the plain form of nature is exchanged for the angularities and caprices of the lapidary—the twinking and sparkling, perhaps, increased, but the gem certainly reduced in size, and the inward light torn from its dwelling, and thrown as much as possible upon the exterior, so it is with us—so is our individuality destroyed. I could not help making a reflection of this kind as I followed our swarthy friend, from the square, well-shaded court-yard in which we stood when he approached us, to the adjacent temple.

We passed a few youths seated on the ground nasally intoning a portion of their sacred books under the direction of a priest, and it was an interesting sight to see how little impression the approach of our party made upon the youthful assembly. Six Europeans, in what to them must have appeared to be holiday or masquerade attire, could not have been a common spectacle for them, yet so well-trained were they, or so apathetic, that there was no lifting of the head, no stoppage of the recitation. The priest in charge of the little body did not once take his eyes from the page as we passed, whilst the youngsters cast but furtive glances now and then, as the ladies' dresses rustled together, or as we spoke. So different is the East from the West; so complete the contrast between the soft, apathetic, indifferent Asiatic, and the rough, energetic, curious, and eager European!

The massive walls of the temple reminded me of the Dutch buildings in the Fort of Colombo; in their thickness and solidity, all the more striking from the flimsy, temporary character of the wood and leaf cottages of the priests' dwellings without. Advancing into the gloomy interior, it was some time before the eye could distinguish objects, so abrupt had been the transition from the bright glare without to the comparative darkness within. At length the large outline of a recumbent figure became clearly perceptible in the surrounding gloom—a gigantic image of Gotama Budha, the man-god of Budhism, reclining on his right side, with his right hand under his head. There was little or nothing in the sculpture of the figure to admire, for all was g aring and exaggerated, but its faults were hidden by the imperfect light; the great fact which impressed itself on my mind, and doubtless which impresses itself powerfully on the minds of thousands of worshippers, being, that there, within two yards of us, was the image of a man worshipped by more votaries than any other man or god, real or pretended, that the world has ever seen or heard of! *That* was the impression that sunk deep into my mind, as I gazed, almost awe-struck with the thought, at the huge uncouth figure. Between three and four hundred millions of the human race are said to be believers in that wonderful being, and as many have been so for ages—believers, not in his goodness, in his holiness, in his wonder-working power merely, but believers in him as above all gods and men; "the most exalted in the universe; the chief of the universe; the most excellent in the universe," at whose conception all the worlds trembled, a preternatural light shining in each, the blind from birth received the power to see, the deaf heard the joyful noise, the dumb burst forth into song, the lame danced, the crooked became straight, those in confinement were released from their bonds, and the fires of all the hells became extinguished;*

* Hardy's "Manual of Budhism," p. 143.

and at whose birth, men, angels, and gods equally confessed their inferiority and his supremacy. The history of the world affords no page more extraordinary than that which records the rise and progress of Budhism ; appearing to us in these material, matter-of-fact days all romance and falsehood, but the living fact exists before our very eyes, and although the successive steps by which it reached its present greatness may be hidden from us, unlike the progress of Mohammedanism, for instance, yet its widespread diffusion from Ceylon to China, from Malacca to the Caspian Sea, proves that it too has strided over the world in grandeur, and its traditions assure us, not with bloody malignity and violence, but mildly, peacefully, and harmlessly. Considerations such as these invest a Budhist temple with a mystery and a significance that cannot but make it interesting to the cultivated observer.

The altar on which the faithful make their simple offerings of flowers stood at a little distance from the image, together with a copper basin, in which their donations of money are received. The walls were entirely covered with paintings, in the stiff hard style of the Egyptians and Assyrians, although with somewhat greater correctness of outline, representing, as the priest informed us, incidents in the life of Gotama, either when on earth as Budha, or in some former state of existence. On the outer wall in a sort of passage that surrounded the inner and sacred apartment were various similarly pictured scenes, intended, according to Miss Padre, who seemed to know all about them, as allegorical representations of the happiness of the blest, the advantages which accrue from embracing the faith of Gotama, and the misery of the damned. Some of these allegorical representations, if such they really were, were not of a kind that a European public would tolerate, but Miss Padre seemed quite innocent of the fact, and it certainly was not for me to hint it. I contented myself with looking at them, as they were described, wondering, at the same time, what the young lady's ideas of indecent pictures might be if she considered these decent—not that I ever asked such a question, or suggested a doubt on the subject—indeed I do not suppose that so imperturbable a soul as hers would have been at all disconcerted at the inquiry, for, I fancy, she never supposed it possible that indecent figures could be drawn.

From the *wihare* we directed our steps to the *dagobah*, a large rounded mass of masonry terminating in a spiral minaret, that glistened brightly in the sun's rays. It was built, my companion informed me, in accordance with Budhistic custom, over some relics esteemed holy—generally over the bones of a saint. There was little about it, save its gigantic size and strange form, to arrest attention, and as I saw much finer samples of the same kind of building subsequently I shall not stop to describe it particularly.

Our inspection of this temple finished, we descended to the beach, where the servants had prepared a luncheon for us under a banian-tree. The repast, which was an agreeable one, concluded, we returned, as we had come, to Mr. Padre's house, delighted with our excursion.

CHAPTER III.

JOURNEY TO KANDY.

"Our haste from hence is of so quick condition,
That it prefers itself, and leaves unquestioned
Matters of needful value."—*Measure for Measure*, act i., sc. 1.

At length it became necessary to think of joining the estate of which I was already part-proprietor, and of which I intended, as soon as possible, to take the entire management into my own hands. My collegiate studies in England, it is true, did not appear to be the best possible preparation for such a new and untried mode of life, but I was mistaken. There was not so much difference after all between a wine-party in college, and a planter's party in the jungle. The former a little rougher, more boisterous and more boyish, the latter a little more intellectual often, and to me more interesting from the variety of character which it displayed. I was certainly as well prepared for coffee-planting life as three-fourths of those who had already embraced it, whilst, by my devotion to active physical exercise and to study, I was far better suited for it than men who had abandoned an apathetic Anglo-Indian existence in the large towns of the East, to engage in it.

I had met, whilst in Colombo, an interesting couple, who, from the contrast which they exhibited with each other, powerfully arrested my attention—Mr. and Mrs. Hofer. Like myself, Mr. Hofer had abandoned an English home to embark his capital and his fortunes in coffee-planting, but whilst I had come to Ceylon to see what was to me the new world of the East as much as to make a fortune, he, on the other hand, had already seen it, was thoroughly disgusted with it, and had resolved to bury himself, as he expressed it, on a coffee-estate for ten years. He had been all over Europe, and had seen much of Asia and America already. I regarded him with an interest which I could not explain when I heard him discoursing, from personal knowledge, of Broadway, New York, and of Chowinghee, Calcutta. He seemed equally familiar with Trafalgar Square in London, the Place de la Concord in Paris, and the Neuer Parade Platz of Vienna. His observations showed that he had gone through the world with his eyes open, and that he had made a good use of the opportunities he had had of studying mankind, and it was therefore with delight I heard of his having purchased land not many miles from Ruminacaddee, the nearest post town to our estate.

I had a few opportunities of studying Hofer's character in Colombo, and many subsequently. A brilliant fancy, a luxuriant imagination, acuteness of perception, warm but regulated benevolence, and an abiding sense of justice, had all been lavished upon him by nature or developed by cultivation, yet it appeared to me that the key-stone of the arch was wanting. The mind may be compared to the horse, the will to the rider. It avails nothing that we boast of the powers of our steed, of his swiftness, of his endurance, of his sure-footed paces, if we cannot guide and control him. The animal that runs away with his rider may travel over the most ground at the swiftest rate, but the slower-paced obeyer of the rein is still the more valuable of the two. And so of the mind. If the will cannot control and direct the other faculties, their luxuriant growth and power become sources of irregular enjoyment, but often too of inconvenience, and result in a want of force of character. He had spent some months in Jamaica to learn the art of coffee-planting, and he had now arrived in Ceylon to turn his practical knowledge to account. I was interested so much, both in him and in his wife, that it was with extreme pleasure I accepted his offer to journey with them to Kandy.

Mr. and Mrs. Hofer had been but four months married. Their wedding trip was the overland journey from England to Ceylon, and the freshness of the first months of matrimony between the truly loving had not as yet worn off. A more complete contrast between two beings, notwithstanding their fitness for each other, scarcely ever existed. She had never left England before, except to pay a flying visit to the Continent, one of those hurried roving excursions which disgust even the oldest traveller, and implant indelible dislike to the noblest countries and cities, in the breast of the youngest. Thus was it with the fair Emma Morley. She was hurried from place to place, from city to city, from novelty to novelty, until the absorbing wish of her heart was to return at once to her peaceful home in England again; and when she did so return, nothing but the strong bond of love could have succeeded in once more dragging her from her beloved country. Hofer, then on his way from Jamaica to Ceylon, saw, and wooed, and won her. He, the cosmopolitan, to whom all countries were equally indifferent, and she, the thoroughly-English maiden, shrinking from all but English habits, alive to every English virtue, nurtured from infancy in a love and admiration of every English characteristic, had come together to live in the wilderness, surrounded by rude semi-civilized mountaineers, whose dark skin is not more different from ours than are the constitution of their minds and the peculiarities of their habits!

The road from Colombo to Kandy leads, for half its length, over the even lowlands of the coast, exhibiting to the traveller on either side the usual aspects of tropical nature. Rice-fields deluged with water, and neatly divided by thin little mounds from each other, plantations of cocoa-nut and areca-nut trees with thin graceful stems and umbrella-like waving branches at the top—long strips of land in cultivation here and there amidst these, loaded with various vegetables unknown to temperate regions, some protected partially from the sun by coverings, others wooing its fiery rays; and above them all, the great luminary himself, small, of a white heat, fierce in his scorching vigour, and casting a glow over the whole sky, blue though it was, which rendered it almost impossible to turn the eye upward in any direction. Although the forms of the vegetation and the aspect of the country were equally new, yet there was a monotony about this first day's journey, in consequence of the level character of the district, which we did not subsequently experience. Now and then a group of natives, naked generally to the waist, variegated the scene, their dark skins, and the bright colours of the handkerchiefs worn on their heads, or as girdles, being in vivid contrast to each other, whilst men, women, and children, as they proceeded, seemed all equally at a loss for time to say all that they had to say, so rapid and incessant was their talking.

We stopped for the night at a bungalow, half-way between Colombo and Kandy, beautifully situated in a valley, formed by a semicircular group of hills, amongst which the road wound on to the east in its uninterrupted course. As the sun sank, large, clear and unclouded in the west, the full moon rose with a splendour peculiarly her own in the clear air of the tropics, upon the east. I know not how to give an idea of the loveliness of that night, as we enjoyed it, walking in the verandah of the bungalow, and bathing as it were in the flood of silver glory poured down so profusely by the pale queen of night upon the earth? Not even upon the ocean have I witnessed a splendour equal to that! The stars twinkled dimly here and there, obscured by the more powerful beams of the moon, whilst the whole earth seemed lit up with intensely burnished silver mirrors, reflecting floods of light in every direction. The dark shadows on the hill sides were rendered still darker by the soft glow which diffused itself equally upon all the salient points of the landscape. If one could choose, where all was loveliness, perhaps the palm trees presented the most strikingly new and bewitching aspect. Their long graceful leaves, wet with dew, shone with a mild radiance as the flood of light was poured down upon them, whilst, between their ever moving branches, the rays of the moon made their way timidly as it were to the earth, where an exact impression of the graceful tracery above was pictured out upon the grass in black and silver, never at rest, but always lovely. All nature seemed to enjoy the glorious spectacle.—"Most glorious night," I involuntarily exclaimed with the poet, "thou wert not sent for slumber." From the minutest insects in the air to the hugest denizens of the forest, all seemed equally impressed with the same idea, that it were treason to the majesty of nature not to enjoy such a scene. The air was filled at intervals with the various noises that a luxuriant tropical fauna alone can produce; bellowing from the woods, the wild shriek or shrill cry of the monkeys mingling there with the trumpeting of the elephant; croakings from the river and marshes; loud buzzings from the trees and air; whilst birds called to and answered each other with incessant rapidity: all intermingled and alternated with each other at intervals, between which a silence as of universal awe or death, crept over the landscape—the nearer and sharper sounds ceased, the silent circle widened, and gradually the more distant reverberations ended, and then there was a perfect calm for a time, holy, pure, and exciting in its peacefulness so different from the tumult which preceded and succeeded it. The scene is stamped upon my mind still, and will probably never be effaced. And yet I have not mentioned the most exquisite of all the scenes of that bright evening! It was love that lent its charm to the whole. I was the witness of the happiness of two noble specimens of our race, as they reflected love from each other's eyes, drinking in deep draughts of the intoxicating sentiment with every glance. It would have been a sin on such an evening not to be grateful and happy, and no shade of jealousy darkened my heart as I rejoiced with them in that glorious prospect. I had never seen the lady otherwise than as the companion of her husband, and therefore I looked upon their love and relationship as a natural thing, which did not interfere with me, and which, if wise, I too could afar off, participate in, or, at all events, sympathize with. When I saw her face shining in the pale moonbeams, her sparkling eyes and black hair, contrasting vividly with the pure whiteness of her brow, and of her neck, and whilst I felt her warm hand resting on my thinly covered arm, I looked upon her as I looked upon the landscape, as an object of loveliness, on which my eyes might feast, and which memory might treasure in my heart, but which nearer approach would probably but sully or disturb. As I saw her gaze directed towards the stars, and heard her sigh, saying, that she was sorry she had not studied astrology, yes, sigh in the very wantonness of happiness, and as I saw the clear intelligent eye and brow of her husband turned towards her, whilst a good-humoured smile played around his lips, I felt that we require but a sensitive heart to enjoy the happiness of others, and that he must have a bad one who cannot see that happiness without envy.

"My husband smiles at the idea of astrology, do you not think there is more in that 'poetry of heaven,'" said she, turning to me, "than he is willing to admit?"

"You are too polite, I am sure, to say there is nothing in it, after such an appeal," said he, quickly; "but, Emma, I am equally sure your own reason declares to you the folly and absurdity of the pretended science."

"My reason, as it has been cultivated, may," was her reply, "but my heart, my dear Ernest, wishes it were otherwise, and often tells me that it is so."

"The heart is an erring guide in matters of science," said he.

"Why should it be so?" she asked. "Is there, then, an opposition between the two? if so, God grant I may ever follow the dictates of the heart, and leave the reason, with its cold, selfish, calculating wisdom, behind me. The heart is everywhere the same, whilst reason differs everywhere. The heart prompted a thousand years ago as it prompts now; reason, a thousand years ago, taught a hundred things which it laughs at now. I, at all events, will cherish the unchangeable."

"Your German philosophy, my dear Emma," he urged, "has misled you. There is no opposition between the two—the cultivated heart and cultivated reason say one and the same thing—at least, the more they are cultivated the more nearly they assimilate."

"What do you think on the subject?" he added, turning to me.

Thus directly appealed to, I could not avoid the discussion further, although I feared it might lead to dangerous ground.

"I am inclined to agree with Mrs. Hofer's German philosophy, as you call it," said I, "that where the heart and the head differ, the former is to be preferred. The impulses of the heart, eminently subjective as they are, are more likely to be true than the reasonings, purely objective, for the most part, of the head. But both certainly require cultivation, and the due cultivation of the heart appears to me to be a far more difficult thing than that of the head. As to astrology, there is something fascinating and poetical in the supposition that our destinies are written in the everlasting firmament; but is it not making ourselves of too much, and the stars of too little importance, to conceive such a thing possible?"

"Like my husband," Mrs. Hofer replied, "you are a sceptic, with reference to man's higher and nobler nature; you have no belief in that inner world which shadows forth so truly the outer. Did I assert that the stars were there—there, in that glorious canopy," said she, disengaging her hand from my arm, and stopping to point to them, "merely that man might read his destiny in them, there would be truth in your objection—but no, I believe they are there for other and infinitely holier and higher purposes. Is it not, however, consistent with the divine economy of nature, that one thing should serve many ends, and do we not see a thousand examples of such on earth?"

"There is much ingenuity, but little logic in your observation," replied Hofer. "Astronomy reveals too much of the stars to permit astrology to be true, and if astrology be true, all our modern science is false."

"And that same modern science," I observed, "I fear Mrs. Hofer will regard as destroying all the poetry of life."

"Yes," she replied, "material science goes far to do so, but not mental. I fear it is too often forgotten, however, that astrology was once the universal belief of mankind, and is still believed in by a majority of the human race."

"That," said her husband, "cannot be allowed to be an argument in favour of its truth. A thousand bubbles float over the heads of mankind for centuries, are admired, examined, believed in, sung, and praised enthusiastically, and at last, burst to be seen no more;—nay, men have fought, strangling each other with death-grips, to seize such bubbles, and lo! when they touch them, they dissolve into thin air, and leave not a wrack behind."

"Well," said his fair partner, gaily, "the Budhists are astrologers; I will learn the science of them, at all events, during my residence in the jungle, and then I shall be better able to contest the point. In the meantime, although our hearts would prompt us to remain here all night, basking in this lovely moonlight, yet our heads tell us, if we are to journey early to-morrow, we had better retire. There is no opposition, you see, between them; shall we obey both?"

"A truly feminine method of concluding the argument," said her husband, as they bid me adieu, leaving me to meditate a little longer in the moonlight.

The road, from the bungalow at which we passed the night, to Kandy, lay through some of the wildest and noblest mountain scenes in the East. Indeed the difficulties in the way of its construction, presented by the nature of the country, were such that it has been justly styled the "Simplon of the East." We were amply repaid for the monotony of the previous day's travel, and as we got deeper and deeper amongst "the everlasting hills," our spirits became invigorated and our bodies refreshed, by the cooler air and more variegated landscape. Such was the steepness of the way in some places, that we preferred leaving our carriage, and proceeding on foot, often gaining the brow of an eminence in this way, from which an extensive view could be obtained on every side. From this eminence, the plains we had left became gradually more and more apparent, stretching far to the west, in an ever-widening prospect, whilst, before us, the rugged and confused mountain masses rose, more and more irregularly and with greater vastness and wildness. "There is more of the stern reality of nature here than one sees in Jamaica," said Hofer, "where cultivation, at least along the ordinary highways, is more extended and universal than in Ceylon." Now and then we skirted the edge of a primeval forest that stretched far away amongst the hills and valleys, presenting a rich contrast, in its gorgeous green livery, to the naked rocks and bleak mountain sides, with which it was often associated. In many places the mountain rose almost perpendicularly upon the left, whilst on the right, from the edge of the road on which we stood, it descended, bleak, fearful, and precipitous, to the valley beneath; not even a rail, nothing but a few scanty bushes, sown and nurtured by nature on the hill-side, intervening between the traveller and destruction. It is a grand sight to see the mountain torrents, in such situations, rushing impetuously down the sides of the hills, foaming on their way as if chafed by the opposition of the rocks and the vegetation which impede their progress. Roaring here over a stony bed, there leaping indignantly from one crag to another, as if determined on success—at one time cooped up in a deep, narrow gorge hoarsely complaining, but still struggling onwards,—at another, spreading out into a wider reservoir, as if peace had been attained at last, and it were content. But, no, ever restless, ever changing, like the world of which it forms a part, it finds a vent somewhere, and resumes its brawling, struggling, character, until lost in the river or the ocean. What an illustration, I have often thought, of the headlong career of passion?

The pass of Kaduganava is one of the great engineering feats of the road. So rocky and precipitous were the mountains on either side, —so narrow, rugged, and uncompromising the deep dells between them—that it was only by continued blasting, a way could be torn out of the sides of the hills. Indeed, in one place, a complete tunnel was thus formed through a mass of rock, that reminds one of the side of a gigantic elephant, and which now stretches over the road, joining the almost perpendicular heights above, with the equally precipitous declivities below. "The nation that can make a road from Colombo to Kandy, through the Kaduganava pass," said an old Singhalese proverb, "will ever be the rulers of Ceylon." The road is made, and its makers *are* the rulers of the fair island,—"the pearl drop on the brow of India," as its people delight to call it,—but all that is contained in that little word "ever," can never, as long as time lasts, be fulfilled. Fearful is it to stand on the edge of the fairy-like road that creeps so modestly along the hill side, and look down into the awful chasm below. The tops of a few bushes present themselves at a considerable depth, deeper down a few rocks, and the indistinctly-seen form of a torrent, making its way below—deeper still a dun, dark haze, impenetrable to the sight, in which all distinct vision is lost, but from the depths of that vast chasm come up the confused sounds of the strife of elements waged there incessantly—water and rocks in never-ending conflict, battling with each other, the weaker ever eating into and wearing away the stronger in its persevering flow. One shudders while fancying the sensations that would accompany a fall into that deep dell—

the headlong passing by the quivering tops of the bushes seen far beneath—the rapid gyrations, as whirling downwards to destruction, rocks, trees, chasms, and smooth mountain sides would be passed—the blind plunging into the depths, beneath which the eye cannot pierce, and in which imagination is almost lost; a fitting emblem of the grave which would assuredly be found at the bottom, wherever that may be, or if bottom there be to it at all.

On the sides of this celebrated pass, as well as upon its summit, there are several valuable coffee estates, on one of which we were hospitably entertained during the heat of the day; and as the drive thence to Kandy was short and easy, we prolonged our stay with its kind inmates far into the evening. Mr. Massey, the proprietor and superintendent of the estate at which we stopped, gave us a hearty welcome; and as the Hofers had met him and his wife in Colombo, the greeting between them was like that of old friends rather than of only casual acquaintances. Out of Europe Englishmen appear to me to form friendships sooner than any other portion of mankind. Aware, probably, that they differ from every other class of the human species in many notable respects, they who would frown at each other without knowing why in England, will cordially extend the hand, and welcome with a bright smile their compatriots in the far East or West. So it was in the present instance. Hofer and Massey had little in common, except that they were coffee-planters; yet their greeting was of the most cordial character. Mrs. Hofer and Mrs. Massey were still more dissimilar; but they were both Englishwomen in Ceylon, and this appeared a sufficient reason for their intimacy and friendship.

The bungalow of the Parahara estate, as Mr. Massey's was called, was well situated on the side of the hill, a deep mass of the primeval forest rising behind it, and the estate stretching on each side and below, in a wide amphitheatre. From the opposite hill, as we approached, the effect was extremely picturesque; and one could scarcely help thinking, on looking at it, that, with a suitable companion, any man alive to the beauties of nature might spend his life happily there, did not experience too probably cut short the reflection by asking whether happiness depended upon external circumstances in any great, or even more trivial, degree?

As we drove up to the verandah, three fair-haired children, their looks telling of northern lands and more bracing climates, were playing in it, watched and attended by as many native servants. One female and two males, at all events, we saw paying the usual attention of *bonnes* to their little charges, by laughing and chatting in the corner, whilst "Misse Mary" was on the point of poking out little "Masse Henry's" eye with a pair of scissors she had picked up somewhere, in vainly essaying to clip his somewhat redundant locks. Our arrival created, of course, a general sensation, and a dispersion of the verandah group. The ayah, or native female servant (catching up "little Masse Henry" just as he was on the point of shrilly screaming forth his disapprobation of his sister's scissors' performance), went to inform her mistress of our arrival. The two well-bearded and moustached guardians of the other pledges gazed intently on the equipage, on the coachman, on the foreign *mahathmas*,* on the servants that brought up the rear, whilst

* The Singhalese *saheb* or Mr.

they talked incessantly to each other, the one stroking his fine black beard, the other vigorously engaged in scratching his head, and then examining his nails.

Mrs. Massey soon made her appearance, and welcomed us. She was one of those women who at thirty contrive to look as if they were between forty and fifty, and then often retain precisely the same expression of countenance for thirty years more.

"I knew you would be here about this time," said she, "and I told William so; but he would go to look after the new sowings: men, but particularly coffee-planters, are so obstinate."

"Especially when there are new sowings to look after, I fancy," said Hofer, bowing.

"O, they are never without excuses, Mr. Hofer, as Mrs. Hofer will one day find," said our hostess, leading the lady off, and giving directions to the servants respecting our entertainment.

Mr. Massey, a plain burly man of about fifty, shortly after made his appearance, in the orthodox plantation dress of a Ceylon coffee-planter; that is to say, with coarse canvas shoes, and leech gaiters tied over the checked pantaloons at the knee, a short coat of a similar check, a black belt at the waist, and a pith hat that defied the sun. There is much to be said for the comfort of this dress and its adaptation to jungle wear; but much certainly could not be said for its appearance on the person of our friend Massey. A rotund stomach of large dimensions loomed still larger over the tightly-fitting gaiters, and made a ridiculous contrast —"a barrel balanced on a pair of tongs," was the simile by which Hofer subsequently described it, although I willingly confess there was much exaggeration in the comparison.

"Well, Mr. Massey," said his spouse, on first observing him, "did I not tell you they would be here this morning? Yet you would go out."

"You are always right, my love," he prudently answered, whilst Hofer and his wife exchanged amused glances. "You are always right, my love. I trust dinner is nearly ready."

The fair dame was mollified by her husband's prudent submission, and calling a servant, Jayatillike by name, told him to tell the *appoo,** or butler, to hurry the dinner as much as possible.

As good a dinner as a well-kept estate in the jungle could afford was speedily provided, and we attacked it with appetites such as a mountain journey can alone supply. After it had been discussed, the conversation turned on our estate, and on my uncle's measures respecting it, which met with but qualified praise.

"I was there," said our host to me, "when your uncle's partner, Mr. Roquelaire, the Frenchman, died; and a more melancholy scene it has never been my lot to witness."

"I heard that it was, indeed, a lamentable occurrence," said I, "although I have not been able to arrive at all the particulars."

"Mr. Roquelaire," said our host, "had been in the island for many years. He was an experienced Java planter, and, like all of us, had hoped to make enough to enable him to return to his native land, and settle there, in the prime of life. His first speculation in Ceylon, however, was a failure, owing to the caprice which directed the making of roads in the neighbourhood. He spent much money upon an extensive piece of forest land; and had it

* The Appoo corresponds to the Indian *Khansamah.*

been made accessible by a high-road running near it, as he and every one else expected, for the estimates had been already prepared, and Government had announced its intention of prosecuting the work, it would have been a most valuable possession. The engineer had advised the construction of the road as I have said—the estimates were sent in—nay, a commencement had actually been made in its formation—when the Colonial Secretary, unfortunately for poor Roquelaire, bought a piece of land, at a distance of fifteen miles from his, and the road suddenly diverged in that direction, forsaking the neighbourhood of Roquelaire's property, and the valley in which it was situated, altogether. Others were equally aggrieved with himself. The case was brought before the Legislative Council, but the Government majority carried the day against the planters, and there was no redress. A private road was then talked of, but was only talked of; and as it would have been too extensive for Roquelaire alone to have undertaken, he entered into partnership with your uncle, and opened the estate for him; and a more flourishing plantation, up to the period of his death, did not exist in Ceylon."

"Resolved, then, to settle in the island, he wrote to France, asking a young lady, to whom he had, from her infancy almost, been attached, to link her lot with his, and she consented. Louise Morin was a Parisienne, delicate, finely-formed, and *spirituelle*. Having made acquaintance with an English family going to Bombay, she accompanied them overland. Roquelaire was counting the days that would intervene before he could lead his bride from Colombo to the estate, where he had fitted up his bungalow with exquisite taste for her reception. Ere it came near the time for the arrival of our little island steamer with the mails and passengers from Bombay, he had prepared everything for his departure to Colombo to meet her. It was on a Monday that he was to have left the estate; on the Saturday previous, with two friends who had joined him for the purpose, as it was an idle period of the year, he went out elephant-shooting, a sport of which he was particularly fond. One of his companions was a rash young fellow, a countryman of his, who unnecessarily exposed himself to danger. The elephants were being driven up the hill by the beaters, near the summit of which stood Roquelaire and his companions, at some distance from each other. Roquelaire brought one down in a moment with the two barrels of his never-failing rifle, and having leaped upon a crag to avoid the death-rush of his huge foe, he saw his young friend in imminent danger. He had awaited, like his more experienced companions, the approach of an elephant, and had fired, but without their precision, and a large tusker was rapidly approaching him, mad with pain and rage. Some rocks were near, amongst which the inexperienced youth clambered; but the elephant was intent on pursuit, and, had it not been for Roquelaire's devotion and heroism, he would probably have lost his life. As it was, the immediate advance of Roquelaire, with a fresh rifle, turned the attention of the monster upon himself, and, as the broad forehead of the enraged animal was turned directly towards him, the experienced sportsman felt no fears for himself. The unerring rifle was raised, and a zinc bullet was sent directly into the brain. Roquelaire turned to avoid the dying struggles and convulsive rush forward of the wounded animal, but an unobserved creeper caught his foot, and he fell directly in the elephant's path. He had no time to raise himself again, for the tottering monster advanced with wonderful rapidity, and fell dead directly upon the body of his destroyer.

"It was some time ere poor Roquelaire could be released from his terrible situation; he was perfectly insensible, and his companions believed him dead as they carried him to the bungalow; but it was not so. The natives speedily succeeded in restoring symptoms of life, and a medical man was procured, with as little delay as possible, from Kandy. But irreparable injury had been done—some of the bones of the chest were broken—and no hopes were held out of ultimate recovery, although no idea could be given as to when death would actually occur.

"The bodily torture which Roquelaire endured was nothing compared with his mental anxiety, and this mental anxiety, the surgeon assured me, hastened his death. Knowing that his bride was now near Ceylon, he was maddened at the idea of her landing alone in Colombo, and of her probably being left, by his death, without a friend in the island. The name of Louise Morin was ever on his lips, and the idea of her, doubtless, filled his heart.

"Your uncle received the bride on her arrival in Colombo, and broke the intelligence to her as delicately as possible. What a revulsion must it have caused in her mind! She had been looking out for Colombo with high hopes of seeing her affianced lover anxiously awaiting her, of meeting with a bride's welcome, when alas! that of the widow was in store for her. She called here on her way to the estate, and I accompanied her during the rest of her journey."

"Leaving me at a very critical period, I must add," said Mrs. Massey, "but then Mademoiselle Morin was really very enchanting, every one said."

"The poor girl was bathed in tears almost the whole way," continued the imperturbable Massey, unheeding the interruption; "at Kandy we heard that Roquelaire was better, and as no one could venture to tell her that there was no chance of permanent recovery, she passed at once from the extreme depths of dejection to all the wildness of unbridled hope.

"It was towards evening when we arrived at your estate on horseback, for the road was impassable for a carriage—we dismounted at some distance from the bungalow that the patient might not be excited by the sound of the horses' feet. As we entered his bed-room softly, the surgeon was sitting by his side—Roquclaire's face was turned from us, as he gazed at the setting sun, now half concealed by the forest—he looked round, and saw his bride who had just completed her long journey from Paris to Ceylon to be his! 'My Louise, my Louise!' he exclaimed in French, as she bent over him, hot tears dropping from her eyes as she kissed his flushed cheek. 'I am happy now, very happy,' said he, faintly, 'and, doubtless, all will yet be well.' She could not say a single word, but contented herself with pressing his hand in her own. 'Have you seen the bungalow?' he asked. 'Do you like Ceylon? Shall we not be happy, very happy here? O my Louise,' —the lips faintly moved further, and she bent down to hear his words—there was a pause—she lifted her head, and, with a terrible calmness, said to us—'he is dead.' It was even so! The conflict was over, the joy of seeing her had been too much for him; but nothing, the surgeon assured us, could possibly have saved him, even had this meeting never taken place, as every moment threatened death. Who that had seen that fair and elegant form leaning over the dead body of her betrothed one—who that had thought of the thousands of miles she had traversed to embrace a dead lover, could help weeping like a child as I did, with her?"

"But what became of her, Mr. Massey?" asked Mrs. Hofer, earnestly, her eyes bedewed with tears.

"She returned with me," he answered, "and, before we got to Kandy, she was seized with a brain fever, which was on the point of uniting again those whom fate had so cruelly separated. But she recovered slowly—her maid, whom she had left in Colombo, tended her, affectionately, and I was seldom absent from the house. On her recovery, she spent a few weeks with us here."

"My Henry was born whilst Mr. Massey was waiting upon her," said his aggrieved spouse.

"She returned to Paris, shortly after, and has taken the veil, I am informed," concluded the worthy husband.

"She could not have done better. One, whose heart is dead to the world, will still find consolation and interest in religious exercises and benevolent offices," said Mrs. Hofer. "Would that Protestantism afforded a similar refuge to the weary in soul and the broken in heart!"

"Bless me, Mrs. Hofer," exclaimed Mrs. Massey, "do you wish that we had nunneries in our Protestant religion?"

"I do," replied the fair enthusiast, stoutly. "I do, because I think there are thousands, who, like Louise Morin, are so sick of the world and so sorrow-laden, that they would find the only alleviation their woes admitted of, in a religious house, and amongst companions suited to their tastes and dispositions—companions similarly prostrated in mind or body with themselves."

"Well, I have always looked upon them as dreadful places," replied the amazed Mrs. Massey, "and I thought all Protestants did so too."

"We are often nurtured in such a belief from infancy in England, and thus look at these, as at many other things, through false glasses that distort the objects regarded," observed Mrs. Hofer; "but ignore the good, reject anything merely because it has been abused sometimes, and what, on the face of this fair earth will you retain? Not Christianity, certainly, for have not its holy precepts, preaching love and benevolence, been made the pretexts for torturing and slaughtering thousands of our race —thousands who were better, nobler far, than the millions who were spared, or the few who have been applauded at other times for virtues that involved neither sacrifice nor self-denial in their practice?"

"I am content to accept my religion as our ancestors handed it down to us," replied Mrs. Massey, "and should be sorry to see any steps taken that would lead us nearer to Popery, and probably land us there at last."

Here the conversation ended. Mrs. Massey was content as she had had the last word. Her husband looked approbation of what Mrs. Hofer said, but did not venture to express it openly. Time and experience had taught him prudence, and Hofer and I abstained from joining in the discussion, as it was peculiarly a topic for the ladies, and the temper of one of them could not be depended upon.

Strangely are we affected by the woes of others, even of those whom we have little or no chance of ever seeing or becoming acquainted with! The story of poor Louise Morin and the unfortunate Roquelaire made a deep impression on our hearts. The Parahara estate was sacred to us from that hour, and was ever afterwards associated with it in our minds. We could scarcely endure the ordinary tattle of the table after the rehearsal of this melancholy drama of real life, and were all equally anxious to pursue our journey. Mrs. Massey's eloquence in describing the woes of her existence was powerless to arrest our attention, nor could Massey himself say anything of coffee or the coolies that did not appear to grate upon our feelings.

By moonlight that evening we drove into Kandy—our journey was, for the most part, a silent one; nor, indeed, was there much to excite our admiration or interest in the way. We descended into the large valley which encloses the hills that surround Kandy; and after passing a few inequalities of ground, trifling in comparison with what we had already gone over, we approached the great bridge which leads across the principal river of Ceylon—the Mahaweli—directly into Kandy. This bridge is of sandal wood, and crosses the river in one wide span of two hundred and five feet; an interesting and imposing object in the variegated landscape of which it forms a part.

Arrived in Kandy we separated. I found

Mr. Pinto, my uncle's Portuguese agent from the estate, awaiting me at the "rest-house," or hotel, where I spent the night; and, next morning, rode off in company with him, anxious to inspect the property of which, for the future, I was to be master—the scene of the tragical death of poor Roquelaire, and of the first keen agony of his bride. The Hofers remained in Kandy, partly to cultivate the society which it afforded, and partly to give time for the erection of a substantial bungalow on their property, which they designated the "Lanka Estate"—Lanka having been the ancient native name of Ceylon.

CHAPTER IV.

THE ESTATE—COFFEE.

"This drink, Sir——
—— it takes away the performance."
Macbeth, act ii. sc. 3.

SEEN from a distance there is little to recommend a coffee-estate that has been but a short time in cultivation. During the greater part of the year, the long charred trunks of trees that have been felled to clear the land, and have lain ever since in the furrows between the coffee-bushes, are but too conspicuous. When the plant is in flower, however, there is a beauty in the general aspect that makes up for the monotonous ugliness of the rest of the season. The unsightly trunks are lost in the delicate white blossom, whilst a delightful perfume sweeps over the hill side, borne far away into the valleys by the wind. Nothing can be more grateful to the sight than the pure white colour of the blossom nestling amid the bright green of the leaves. It has been truly said, that "although it is an evergreen, few plants exhibit a greater variety of appearance throughout the year than the coffee-shrub."*

It does not grow well in low situations, and is therefore cultivated on the sides of the mountains, between fifteen hundred and four thousand feet above the level of the sea. Nor will it thrive on table-lands, although they may be of the requisite elevation, as it requires shade and shelter, both from sun and wind, in order thoroughly to develope its best qualities, and to bring it to perfection. In Ceylon, indeed, scientific considerations, and, in many instances, the experience of all other countries, have been so completely ignored and neglected that the qualities of the berry produced are as various as the situations in which the plant is reared, and the amount of attention paid to its

* The Coffea is a genus of Cinchonaceous plants, containing many species, and known by its tubular corolla, with four or five spreading divisions; stamens arising from the naked throat of the corolla, and either extending beyond it or enclosed within it; and a succulent berry containing two cells lined with a cartilaginous membrane, like parchment, in each of which cells there is a single seed, convex at the back and deeply furrowed in front, in consequence of the albumen being rolled inwards.

wants and requirements. The best and the worst descriptions that find their way into the English market have been equally shipped from Ceylon, when a little care and attention on the part of the cultivators would have removed the bad specimens altogether, and thus given the island a better name as a coffee-producing country.

In opening an estate, the situation of the land, the directions of the monsoon winds, the amount of shade available, and the probable supply of moisture from the neighbouring heights, should all be taken into consideration—the best estates having been invariably those which, well sheltered and shaded, are situated in such an amphitheatre-like depression on the side of a lofty mountain, as insures a rich soil—the accumulations of ages washed down from the hills above—and a plentiful supply of moisture even in the dryest part of the year. This moisture may not always consist of streams or mountain torrents, but merely of the dews or of the clouds condensed on the hill-top, and constantly percolating through the hill-side to the soil beneath. Much have Ceylon planters been laughed at for asserting that abundance of rocks was almost indispensable to the proper growth of the shrub, and that no plantations should be formed where rocks do not abound; yet there is truth in the observation when properly understood. The soil between the large rocks, so plentiful on some hill-sides, is of the richest possible description, and plants placed in it are sure to thrive, just as the forest did before, if in other respects the situation be favourable. But when people couple their observation about the rocks with another, that the coffee-shrub loves a poor soil, they are altogether mistaken, as experience, all over the world, proves.

Clearing the ground of the forest is an arduous undertaking, requiring the most unremitting care on the part of the superintendent to have it properly done. The trees on being felled are not lopped into convenient lengths for burning as in America, but are merely deprived of their branches, allowed to dry for some time and then set fire to, the large charred stems being subsequently laid in convenient rows, between which the young plants taken from the nursery are planted. When the hill-side is steep and a large mass of the forest thickly fills the air, it is sometimes sufficient to notch the trees half through on the side turned away from the valley beneath. This done, a few of the largest trees at the top are simultaneously cut through and allowed to fall with all their weight on those half-notched immediately below them. These fall with the momentum of the others, and in their turn weigh down the line immediately below, and so it proceeds until the entire vegetation of the hill-side lies shattered and fallen in the most frightful confusion. This operation is accompanied by quick rapid reports from the crashing timber that reverberate round the hills and valleys like the irregular discharge of cannon; the neighbouring echoes taking up the sound, till it is lost in the distance, when all is again still for a time.

When the berry is ripe, indicated by its rich red colour, every one on the estate is in a constant state of activity—men, women, and children conveying, in hot haste, baskets of the berries to the pulping-house, there to be separated from the pulp, which surrounds the coffee-bean within, just as the rich juicy fruit surrounds the "stone" in the cherry. This pulp is of little or no use, although occasionally given to animals that are not fastidious in their diet; whilst the berry, still surrounded by a horny coating resembling parchment, is dried a little in the sun to admit of this covering being the more easily removed. The "parchment," as it is called, stripped off, the berry is fit for packing. The different descriptions are sorted, the finer being labelled "Mocha," and the whole sent in canvas bags to the coast for exportation. The pulper and a mill for removing the parchment are the only machinery required for the working of an estate, even of large dimensions, all the rest being done by hand, or with the assistance of the diminutive bullocks of the natives.

Even the coarsest-grained native coffee is by no means so inferior in flavour to the finest peaberry as people in England suppose. The great difference generally consists in the way in which the beverage is prepared. As soon as the operation of roasting is completed—an operation which requires care and attention not to have it overdone—the coffee should be ground at once and diluted. The subtle aroma which resides in the essential oil of the berry is gradually dissipated after roasting, and of course still more after being ground. In order to enjoy the full flavour in perfection, the berry should pass at once from the roasting-pan to the mill, and thence to the coffee-pot; and again, after having been made, should be mixed, when almost at a boiling heat, with the hot milk. It must be very bad coffee indeed which, if these precautions be taken, will not afford an agreeable and exhilarating drink. Two great evils are constantly perpetrated in England in its preparation, which are more guarded against in almost all other countries, and which materially impair its flavour and strength—keeping the coffee a considerable time after roasting or grinding, by which its strength is diminished, and its delicate and volatile aroma lost; and mixing the milk with it after it has been allowed partially to cool. Experience taught us to avoid these errors in the jungle; and it was not till Mr. Pinto had repeatedly made both kinds in perfection that I began to discover the difference between the exquisitely delicate flavour of the peaberry, or finest description, and the coarser, equally strong, but less delicate taste of the larger, rougher, and more unsightly qualities.

Our estate was situated on the side of a lofty mountain, stretching down to a rivulet that wound about its base; beyond which a wide extent of level land opened out to the

East, sheltered on three sides by lofty l'ed a The bungalow was built on a level projecting portion of the hill's side, in the very centre o.; the cultivated part of the property, for as yet but a fourth of the land which it comprised had been cleared and planted. Further down the mountain, and concealed by thick forest from the bungalow, lay the coolies' "lines"—the residence of the native labourers—miserable sheds, low, filthy, and stifling, in which they and their families were all huddled together without decency or comfort. To this method of life they had been accustomed; and Mr. Pinto informed me that any attempt on my part to alter it would but be attended with discontent and desertion. Certain I am that were these labourers slaves, it would be for their owner's interest to afford them better-ventilated, loftier, and more comfortable abodes; yet they were quite contented with them—peals of laughter bursting from these "lines" at night, and during Sundays and holidays, proved that their occupants did not lead what they considered a miserable or hopeless life. Nor were they worse off with us than with others; but, on the contrary, rather better, as the rivulet was in the immediate vicinity, and there was, therefore, no want of water, did any desire to render their habitations at all cleanlier. I subsequently made the trial I intended, notwithstanding Mr. Pinto's advice, by dividing one of the sheds into compartments for the families; but I found it worse than useless. It abridged the space allotted to them, without any corresponding advantage, for the undivided portion assigned to the bachelors soon became crowded with both companies, so that the evil, instead of being diminished, was increased, whilst my *cānganies,* or head-workmen, informed me, that they had compared the rooms to cattle-stalls, and that those were laughed at who occupied them. Perseverance might perhaps have overcome their prejudices, but I had not the necessary time for it, and gave up the trial in disgust.

An amazing amount of sympathy has been lately wasted by the British public on the condition of the slaves in America—that public has but to turn to a portion of the world with which it is more intimately connected, in order to discover abuses as gross, methods of life as repulsive, tyranny as flagrant, as any that exists on the other side of the Atlantic. In India all these are to be found, if the inquiry be but made. As a class, I believe the Ceylon coffee-planters were kind and humane, as I have no doubt the Carolina and Mississippi cotton-planters are, but there were Legrees and Haleys amongst them too, and always will be as long as human nature continues as it is. What redress could the poor coolie, for instance, have against his European master who illtreated him, miles away in the jungle, far from a magistrate or a court, with all his fellows up in arms against him, lest they should lose their employment, and his wife and family almost at the complete mercy of his persecutor, or of that persecutor's assistants? In such circumstances there must be despotism on a small scale, and, wherever that exists, there will occasionally be cruelty and injustice.

The following burlesque account of a pretended paper, supposed to have been read by a member before the Ceylon Agricultural Society, notwithstanding its gross exaggeration, proves the extent to which the unfortunate coolie is at the mercy of his European employer, even in the matter of wages, how much more then in personal ill-treatment, when his companions cannot be expected to take part with him, lest they should thereby endanger their situations, and lose their only means of livelihood.

"A member of the name of Squeery next read a very clear composition, treating upon an improved system of working a coffee or sugar estate, with the least possible amount of funds. His plan was to keep a well-paid agent in the low-country, to offer high wages to labourers, and of course secure great numbers at all times. By the end of the month great fault is to be found with the coolies, which ends in their being discharged, minus their pay, and a fresh lot is sent up by the Colombo agent. As a matter of course the blackguards go to the District Judge, and he issues summonses which must be attended to; in the mean time fresh labour is secured, which, in due course, is disposed of as the last; so that cases multiply exceedingly. But mark the result! By a wise law of nature, it takes an ordinary District Judge at least three years to decide a case of this kind; should he, however, be so foolish as to settle the thing in two, you can appeal, which will give you two more. Now by the time the first of these cases is decided, you are getting in a crop, and the proceeds of it enables you to meet the many claims against the whole for labour in past years. So that the sum actually required to be spent in the first instance, need be but trifling, if these practical hints are acted upon."*

It is amusing, when contemplating the almost universal use of coffee at present, to turn one's attention to the storm which its first introduction into England created. In the time of the Commonwealth, and under Charles the Second, coffee-houses seem to have been first opened in London, and this "Turkish drink," as it was called, to have become a general favourite with their frequenters—the beaux, and idlers, and newsmongers of the metropolis. Great was the wrath, however, of those whose trades or employments were endangered by the use of the new beverage, and a storm of indignation arose against the innocent shrub, which threatened to drive it for ever from our shores, or to bury it under a load of falsehood and abuse. The pamphlets which appeared at the time on the subject, prove the violence of the opposing parties. Poetry and prose were exhausted in depicting the evil effects of the habitual use of coffee, in language such as

* "Life in the Jungle, by Sampson Brown," p. 90. Colombo, Herald Press, 1845.

cannot now be quoted; nay the very head and front of its supposed offending seems to have been of such a character, that modern refinement or modern affectation would scarcely permit the subject to be hinted at at present, much less openly canvassed. The following were the titles of a few of the broad sheets which were devoted to the vituperation or expulsion of the obnoxious drink: "Bacchinalia Cœlestia—a Poem in praise of Punch," published in Charles the Second's time, for he is named in it, but without date, in which the various gods and goddesses introduced, do not hesitate to speak their minds openly on the subject—all lauding, of course, the good old Punch, which coffee threatened to dethrone. "Rebellion's Antidote" was another pamphlet on the subject, being "a Dialogue between Coffee and Tea." "Printed by George Croom, at the sign of the Blue Bell, Thames Street, over against Baynard's Castle, 1685." "A Broadside against Coffee, or the Marriage of the Turk. Printed for J. L. 1672," was, as its title imports, a fierce diatribe, far too coarse, although amusing, for modern "ears polite"—the following lines, however, which are almost the only ones I could quote without censure, will give some idea of its animus—

"Bold Asian brat! with speed our confines flee,
Water, tho' common, is too good for thee."

"This canting Coffee has his crew enricht,
And both the water and the men bewitcht."

"But to cure Drunkards it has got great Fame,
Posset or Porridge, will 't not do the same?
Confusion huddles all into one scene,
Like Noah's ark, the clean and the unclean.
But now, alas! the Drench has credit got,
And he's no Gentleman that drinks it not.
That such a Dwarf should rise to such a stature!
But Custom is but a remove from Nature;
A little Dish, and a large Coffee-house,
What is it, but a Mountain and a Mouse?"

But enough of J. L.'s doggerel—useful, however, in two respects, to prove at once the abuse still lavished on coffee in 1672, and also its common use at that time in London; for "he's no Gentleman that drinks it not," according to J. L.'s own confession.

A few years before, in 1663, an anonymous writer had similarly railed against it in good set terms, under the title of "A Cup of Coffee; or, Coffee in its true Colors." The following is quoted from this "Cup:"—

"Fie, friends to the gross Turkey-shore, shall then
These less than Coffee's self, these Coffee-men,
These sons of nothing, that can hardly make
Their broth, for laughing how the jest does take,
Yet grin, and give you for the Vine 's pure Blood
A loathsome Potion, not yet understood,
Syrrup of Soot, or Essence of Old Shoes,
Dasht with Diurnals and the Books of News?"

"News from the Coffe-House. Printed by E. Crooch, for Thomas Vere, at the Cock, in St. John's St., London, 1667, with Alowance" —was equally severe.

"The Maiden's Complaint against Coffee" was certainly not written by a maiden, nor calculated to be read by such. It must have appeared during or before 1663, although without date. More able, but not more decent, was "The Women's Petition against Coffee; representing to Public Consideration the grand Inconveniences accruing to their Sex from the Excessive Use of that Drying, Enfeebling Liquor. 1674."

Under such a load of abuse, and such torrents of hostile verse and prose, it might be supposed that the much-hated berry would have lost ground, but such was not the case; its advocates were up in arms in its defence, and were probably quite as disinterested in their praise of it, as its adversaries in their hostility. Whilst, on the one side, there was scarcely an evil under which humanity laboured that was not, in some form or other, attributed by its enemies to the use of coffee; so, on the other, there was not a disease which it was incapable of curing—so rife were assertions of the boldest and the most absurd character. Perhaps the earliest defence of it, although unfortunately without date, was "The Vertue of Coffee Drink, first publiquely made and sold in England, by Pasqua Rósee." "Made and sold in St. Michael's Alley, in Cornhill, by Pasqua Rósee, at the signe of his own head."

"The Vertues of Coffee," a long panegyric of the new beverage in verse, appeared in 1663, but was far inferior, both in wit and in point, to the tirades which it professed to answer.

A more interesting and more able production was—"The Coffee-Man's Granado, discharged upon the Maiden's Complaint against Coffee, wherein is discovered several strange, wonderful, and miraculous cures performed by COFFEE (the like never heard of since the Creation). Written by Don Bellicosgo Armuthaz, to confute the Author of that lying pamphlet," wherein the valorous knight stoutly denied the evils said to be produced upon the frame by the use of coffee, and challenged investigation, asserting, furthermore, that rheumatism, gout, stone, quinsy, and a host of other diseases, were curable by its use. Don Bellicosgo Armuthaz's warlike production made its appearance likewise in 1663.

"The Men's Answer to the Women's Petition against Coffee," was not a whit more delicate or refined, than the pamphlet to which it professed to reply. It bears the date of 1674.

In the same year appeared a far more temperate production on the subject, although equally extravagant in its broad and unqualified assertions, entitled, "A brief Description of the excellent Virtues of that sober and wholesome Drink called Coffee, and its incomparable Effects in preventing or curing most Diseases incident to Human Bodies. London, printed for Paul Greenwood, and are to be sold at the sign of the Coffee-Mill and Tobacco Roll, in Cloth Fair, near West Smithfield, who selleth the best Arabian Coffee-Powder and Chocolate made in Cake or Roll after the Spanish fashion, &c."

"The Natural History of Coffee, printed for Christopher Wilkinson, at the Black Boy, over against St. Dunstan's Church, in Fleet Street," in 1682, professed to be a scientific treatise on the subject, exhibiting a caricature of a coffee-bush as a frontispiece, but was in reality nothing more or less than a preposterous panegyric of the drink, which, by that time, had doubtless firmly established itself as a common article of consumption in London.

There is something at once interesting and humiliating in now looking back at the struggle which ensued upon the introduction of the harmless berry—interesting in the proofs which it affords of the frequency with which, even then, the press was appealed to, and humiliating when we consider the character of the struggle and the way in which it was carried on. Some interested in its abuse and disuse, others in its more extensive diffusion, but both employing the same weapons—wit, lying, and obscenity—to sustain their assertions, and give piquancy and attractiveness to their effusions. In a survey of the entire struggle it is almost impossible to discover the simple truth from a consideration of the opposite statements, and is not the same true at present of all discussions in which unlimited and unbounded assertion can be hazarded?

CHAPTER V.

A NATIVE CHIEF, MARANDHAN.

"I cannot hide what I am; I must be sad when I have cause, and smile at no man's jests; eat when I have stomach, and wait for no man's leisure; sleep when I am drowsy, and tend on no man's business; laugh when I am merry, and claw no man in his humour."

Much Ado About Nothing, act i., sc. 3.

SHORTLY after my arrival on the estate, which I found in a flourishing condition, under Mr. Pinto's management, I made acquaintance with some of the European and native gentry of the vicinity. Of the latter I was particularly struck with the appearance and intelligence of a Modliar, or Kandian Colonel, named Marandhan. My first visit to him made such an impression upon my mind, that I have never forgotten it, notwithstanding the friendship which subsequently sprang up between us.

The sloping mountain's side which formed the most accessible portion of our estate, and on which the bungalow was situated, stretched, as I have said, to a rivulet in the valley beneath. Crossing the rivulet, I made my way through a patch of forest, abruptly terminated by a mass of overhanging rocks of the most wild, irregular, and desolate description. Stretching for five miles from east to west, this natural barrier formed the boundary of our property—its weather-beaten summits exhibiting forms the most fantastical and picturesque that can be imagined. In some places covered with moss or some species of tropical lichen, in others bare and bleached with the constant exposure, these rocks reminded me forcibly of the similar groups upon the sides of the mountains in Dove Dale, in Derbyshire, resembling—

> "Temples like those amongst the Hindoos,
> Churches, spires and abbey windows,
> And turrets all with ivy green."

To find a way for one's horse through this strange natural barrier, was by no means an easy matter, but, once through, my further progress was unimpeded, although it was some time before I met with a road. The ground was uncultivated, even, and covered, for the most part, with long tufted grass—such land as is in Ceylon called "patua"—resembling, I suppose, the prairies of the far West.

Dashing then through this tufted grass, with a salutary dread of snakes and serpents, I make my way rapidly along; keeping on either side and ahead, what the sailors would call a bright look-out for some wild adversary, or more subtle assailant, for the leopards and tic-polongas are equally fond of the open grass land at some seasons of the year. At length there are symptoms of cultivation in the neighbourhood. A large open plot of ground, saturated with water, bears traces of having borne a recent crop, and "Uncle Toby," my redoubted steed, covers his fetlocks at every plunge, as he flounders through it. There is a hard bank at one side, however, which has evidently served the purpose of a road, and, making my way to this, "Uncle Toby" is more contented and snorts forth his approbation. A little further on we meet a labourer apparently going forth to plough, or more probably, passing from one field to another for that purpose. His plough, a miserable piece of wood with a crooked stick fastened on the end, (one extremity of which he holds whilst the other scratches the ground when actually "ploughing," as they designate that operation), is, for the present, thrown over his shoulder, whilst two diminutive bullocks creep on, at a snail's pace, before him. They go quickly enough for him, however, for he is in no hurry whatever. My appearance on the bank has evidently disconcerted him, and, putting his plough on the ground, he stares vacantly at me—eyes, mouth, and nose, all dilated to their utmost; for a white man on a horse is not an every-day sight in this out-of-the-way district. The bullocks calmly crop what little vegetation they can, whilst their master thus enjoys his stare.

"Is that Marandhan Modliar's house?" I shout to him in my best Singhalese.

"It is, my lord," is the reply wafted to me after a little, and I pass on.

The house to which I pointed, a white-walled, thatched, and somewhat extensive cottage-looking tenement, surrounded by numerous mud cabins, stood right before me in a kind of hollow formed by the undulating ground. "Uncle Toby" seemed perfectly aware of the state of the case, for he pushed on bravely and briskly, whilst, looking over my shoulder, I saw my friend the ploughman slowly picking up his plough and creeping on again after his cattle, as I disappeared from his gaze round the corner.

Having met Marandhan at the magistrate's in our post town of Ruminacaddee, I had informed him of my intention of calling on him on this particular day. He was therefore prepared for my approach, and I found him hospitably awaiting me in the verandah as I rode up. Except for the group of poor cottages which surrounded his tenement, and for the amazing numbers of little darkies all jabbering Singhalese, and running hither and thither, for the most part in a state of complete nudity, there was not much to distinguish his house from that of a European, externally. Amongst the smaller fry, the children doubtless of the dependants on this small feudal lord, (for I could not believe that he was the father of the mall,) my arrival created a great sensation, and many of them whispered comments to each other on my white face, which, had I caught them, would not probably have been considered by me as very flattering, for they have an ugly habit, these Singhalese, to us perfectly unnatural, of painting their devils white instead of black. Many of these little ones, those especially who kept carefully at a respectable distance, and peeped from behind a wooden pillar, or over the shoulder of a braver companion, or from behind their mother's scanty drapery, had never seen a white man before, although the aforesaid paintings in their temples were familiar to them, and there is, therefore, no necessity to indicate further for whom they probably took me. Even a few pice which I scattered amongst them did not seem to relieve their minds on this point; yet some of the bolder, those who had remained nearest, bravely laughed at their fears, and advanced one step nearer, to show that they, at all events, were not afraid.

Rising from his chair, Marandhan saluted me with a hearty shake of the hand, and expressed fluently in English his pleasure at this the first visit with which a European gentleman had ever deigned to honour him. He was a fine specimen of his class. Let me try and bring him before the reader, as he stood before me at that moment. Imagine, then, a middle-sized man, with a darkish face, not by any means black, scarcely approaching to black by any conceivable degrees;—the colour of well-milked coffee, is the simile that naturally suggests itself to me; a variegated silk handkerchief, tied, turban-fashion, round his head; a close-fitting vest covering the upper, and a roll of muslin, forming an ample girdle, the middle, whilst full petticoats, looped up between the legs, giving the appearance of wide trousers, concealed the lower portion of his person, his feet being thrust into a pair of Chinese-looking slippers, peaked and turned up at the toes. In such a guise, his hand extended to grasp mine, Marandhan was a noticeable object, such as no one could pass by, whose eyes and mind were active, without feeling an impression that it was a living, breathing man, of some mark and likelihood, that was thus tricked out externally—as we all are, according to the fashion of our time and country.

The reader is disposed to smile at the looped-up petticoats, the ample muslin girdle, and the rings which adorned his ears. Nay, let us not smile; let us begin to judge men by other than tailors' eyes, and to think more of the furniture within the cranium than of its external ornaments; for whether a man wears a silk handkerchief tied round it, or a beaver hat a foot high above it, makes little matter in the long run; nor to the world within is it of the slightest consequence whether the hair be long, lank, tied in a knot behind, as Marandhan wears his, or more artistically disposed in well-cared ringlets on the reflecting European's head. Noble thoughts and grand ideas may have occupied both internally, and doubtless both are seeking ardently, as all thinking men do seek, to solve this strange enigma of a nineteenth-century world, with such lights and helps as Europe and Asia respectively can afford for that purpose.

Having conducted me to an apartment within, ornamented with several elaborately-carved articles of Singhalese workmanship, and the walls of which were hung with various trophies of the Marandhan family—a family once of great note in the island—my host pointed to a chair, and we seated ourselves. A servant shortly after entered with fruits, sweetmeats, and wine, which I found pleasant and refreshing after my long ride. Cigars were subsequently introduced, and we smoked in concert till the conclusion of my stay; an energetic and interesting conversation being maintained between us during the whole time. Of this conversation I noted down shortly after a few fragments.

"So many of my countrymen," I began, "have assured me that the native chiefs desire to withdraw themselves from European society, that I fear I may have been rude in visiting you as I have done."

"Far from it," said he; "we of the Kandian provinces do not certainly desire to be measured by the standard of our coast fellow-countrymen, whose meanness and sycophancy we, for the most part, despise; and, as European gentlemen know little of the distinction between the Singhalese of the coast and the Kandians of the mountains, we shun that supercilious contempt to which the others subject themselves. You are certainly the first European gentleman that has taken the trouble to find out my poor abode and to visit it; but I have all my life lived in intimacy with some or other of your countrymen, either here or in Kandy."

"You do not, then, regard the natives of the coast as being equal to those of the interior?" I observed, surprised.

"I regard them as being as much our inferiors in intellectual and moral qualities as they certainly are in physical," said Marandhan, firmly.

"I am inclined to agree with you," said I, "short as has been my acquaintance with either. Of their physical inferiority there cannot be a doubt—and to this the bracing air of your mountains and table-lands, doubtless, much conduces, whilst their lives are spent amid the heat and enervating tropical luxuriance of the lower coast district. But this fact seems generally understood by Englishmen, so far as my experience goes—they invariably rank the Kandian far above the lowland Singhalese."

"They do, I believe, in words," he answered, "but not always in act. Accustomed to the servility and debasement of the coast, they treat, too frequently, with supercilious injustice, the claims of the Kandian to be recognised as a man, and not to be cuffed and petted alternately, as a spaniel of the tamest character. Hence, frequently, our shyness. I have always remarked, however, that those who have but lately left England have less of this intolerable hauteur than those long resident on the coast."

"Your words, Modliar, convey a quiet sarcasm, which I fear we too often deserve," said I. "We are all creatures of habit, indeed, and if a man has been brought up, or has even only associated for years, with 'spaniels of the tamest character,' he is likely to becamc somewhat overbearing."

"It is erroneous to suppose, however, that the contrast between the Kandian and the Singhalese is solely the result of physical circumstances or conditions, or, indeed, chiefly so," continued mine host; "the history of our country, which few Englishmen know anything about, shows plainly that other causes besides temperature and situation have been at work to produce this contrast."

"I fear I too must plead ignorance of the history to which you allude," I observed.

"It would be well for us, Sir," he continued, "if, indeed, it can at all be well with slaves such as we are, did all Englishmen know something of our history, ere they came to govern or to dwell amongst us; they would respect us more, believe me—if, as I said, any lingering remnants of respect can anywhere be fished out of deep human contempt for slaves. Our royal and noble families can trace back their pedigrees through lines of statesmen and warriors to the time of your era and before. A noble whose family only boasted of such antiquity as your Howards and Stanleys, would, amongst us, be considered 'a new man.' You smile at these comparisons, doubtless, if not externally, at least internally; you may so; yet, what your Howards and Stanleys are now, and have been in days gone by, our Molligoddes and Kapittipolas, with similar lights and influences, might have been. Nor are we without our Agincourts and Cressys, our Blenheims and Waterloos, although on a smaller scale. There was a time, Sir, when Ceylonese arms conquered all Southern India, the country of our natural enemies—our France, in fact. There were invasions on both sides frequently, and the Gulf of Manaar has as often been covered by warlike armaments as the English Channel; for years our superiority was confessed—our kings carried all before them, extending their arms from India to the Eastern peninsula, where our religion was permanently planted, a living monument of our former prowess. Not very long after William the Conqueror destroyed Saxon liberty in England, Prackrama, our king, was successfully carrying the arms and warriors of Ceylon into Burmah and Cambodia, which he thoroughly subdued.* Pardon me, Sir, but I love to linger over these deeds of other years,

* In the Appendix will be found an account of the reign of Prackrama.

when the title I bear* was the symbol of command over a thousand men, and not an almost unmeaning civic distinction. Miserable is the nation that can but boast of the deeds of its ancestors, whilst it mourns existing debasement, without the faintest hope of eradicating it!

"I intended to show you why, as history tells us, the Singhalese of the coast and the Kandian of the mountains are not like fellow-countrymen, nay, are most unlike. It was early in the sixteenth century, as you count centuries, although in our twenty-second, that the Portuguese first landed in this island. Their guns and ships equally astonished the degenerate men of the day, for civil wars and inhuman tyranny had accomplished their usual feat of destroying the spirit of the nation.

"The coast was speedily conquered by them, but all their attempts upon the mountainous interior, defended as it was by Kandian valour, miserably failed, and, for one hundred and fifty years, the heart of our island beat as freely and as manlike as ever, although the extremities had been trained to obey their new masters. The Dutch came, and, aided by Kandian arms, they drove out the Portuguese,

* That of *Modliar*.

under the promise of liberating the island, but the forts were strong upon the coast, its wealth was enticing, and they seized for themselves that, of which they had succeeded, by our help, in depriving their enemies. Violent were the efforts to dislodge them—the low-lands continued theirs notwithstanding—and for nearly one hundred and fifty years more seemed contented with its new masters. Thus you see our coast-Singhalese fellow-countrymen have served three sets of sovereigns in succession, whilst *our* bondage, I mean that of the Kandian provinces, is but as that of yesterday in comparison; free for more than two thousand years, we have been slaves for thirty, and what are thirty years in the life-time of a nation? Is it any wonder then that there should be a contrast between the two?"

"Yes," I replied, "this does indeed sufficiently account for the wide difference between the Kandians and the Singhalese, but it appears to me that, with a very pardonable national vanity, you attribute the long independence of the Kandians to a different motive from the true one. Surely the natural features of the country would be sufficient to repel any invaders. Do not mistake me. My object is not to prove that the Kandians are not brave—all allow that fact—but where natural difficulties of an almost insuperable character presented themselves, surely we need not look for any other cause of defeat. The immense superiority of European over Asiatic arms, and the perfection to which the science of slaughtering man has been brought in the West, puts the consideration of personal bravery almost out of the question."

"The rugged mountains," replied Marandhan, "which encircle, like the quills on the porcupine, the heart of our island, doubtless did much to protect us, but these difficulties were again and again surmounted by the enterprising Portuguese. Their armies frequently made their way to Kandy, but were always ultimately expelled. They took advantage to the utmost of the disputes of the princes, and always added new elements of discord when they could, in disputed successions or contests for the throne; but without ultimate success. Nay so far from assured success of any kind, that often, of all their coast possessions, a fort or two was alone left to them—the hard walls of which formed impenetrable obstacles to unscientific Asiatic valour. Yet there were they cooped up for months, sometimes for years, by a blockading army of Kandians, which, without artillery and the command of the sea, could do nothing effectual, till in their despair and famine, whilst still looking anxiously sea-ward for supplies, they actually began to eat one another! This is no romance, Sir, nor the coinage of an overheated brain, but these are the words of sober history and truth, as the Portuguese chroniclers and your own, avouch, for I have taken some pains to make myself acquainted with their works."

"You are right, Modliar. These facts are but little known, I fear, to Europeans generally, and it would probably be well for her children, if the history of Ceylon were more studied by all who make her rich low-lands, or her rugged mountain sides, their home."

"The study of that history would, I believe," said he, somewhat bitterly, "make your countrymen think something more of us—spaniels though we may appear to be upon the coast—at the same time that it must make the Englishman think more of himself, and of his country; for must not the reflection occur to him—what the Portuguese and Dutch, whilst living in the island for three hundred years, could not accomplish by force or fraud, we, before we had been twenty, had fully effected?"

"But were not the British invited into the interior to aid in dethroning some inhuman monster, and then forced to extend their dominion by breach of treaty on the part of the Kandian authorities, involving the massacre of some British troops?" I asked. "I retain some confused images of this kind, dimly floating over the surface of my memory, from what little I have read of these matters."

"A people in possession of the coast," replied the Modliar, "all powerful by sea, and completely masters of the adjoining continent, would find little difficulty in getting invitations into the interior; nor was there an Eastern despot, I suppose, that ever lived that might not be made to appear inhuman when his actions were properly coloured to horrify an European audience. I know nothing of the secrets of cabinets, or of the working of that political machine, a Court, but I can easily conceive a disappointed or discarded minister wishing to embarrass his successor in every possible way, and little scrupulous of the means, when passion or interest urged him on; such a minister, we are told, fled to Colombo, and asked the assistance of a British force against the tyrant who would employ him no longer, and against the stability of whose throne he had been plotting. I have known some who were intimately acquainted with the private life of the last King of Kandy, and they accused him of weakness of intellect, and of headlong fits of passion, but of nothing worse. Certainly not of worse things than sovereigns now upheld in India at Hyderabad and Lucknow, by the British authorities, and whose throne, in fact, rests upon British bayonets, are constantly guilty of. But the nation that has not the spirit to die in the struggle for freedom deserves its abasement, and it is useless to extenuate the circumstances on either side; the result is palpable—on all sides we have but to half open our eyes to see it too. A country enslaved—a nobility falling into the depths of servility—a religion tottering under the incessant attacks, open and secret, of that patronized by our rulers. Altogether as miserable and lamentable a spectacle as the eye of man probably ever witnessed."

"The theme is a melancholy one for you, who feel so acutely, Modliar," said I; "but, believe me, I did not introduce it from any evil motives, or even from a vain curiosity. If it be any consolation to you to know that you have made one European think better of you and of Ceylon, you have that consolation; and it will be long indeed ere I forget the eloquence, both of tongue and eye, with which you assert your country's claims to respect. But surely there are lights as well as shadows in this grand historic painting. Is there not social improvement visible? Is not education spreading amongst the people? Are not war and bloodshed put an end to in the island? No more disputes, their history written in characters of blood, for the throne; no more warring of coast with hills, or hills with coast; no more foreign invasion or domestic disturbance." *

"Thanks for your kind words," said he. "They, like cool draughts for the fevered blood, have their value and their use. As to the present state of things, we, in our Oriental palm-leaf books, have a fable, often referred to, that illustrates it. A company of ants had collected, with long toil and incessant labour, a great heap of corn. 'Now,' said they, 'we

* It must be remembered that this conversation was held some years before the late rebellion under Lord Torrington's administration.

have worked enough, let us enjoy.' Hereupon violent disputes arose amongst them as to the division of their store. Some would have too much for the present; others wanted their whole portion at once; others declared they should feed in common. At length they decided that a venerable grey-beard, assisted by able diplomatists, should decide the disputes, having authority to enforce his decisions. A big burly fellow, with an excellent appetite, got a good round share, and professed himself contented, but, in the night, tried notwithstanding to steal some more. He was brought before the grey-beard. 'Let his portion be taken from him,' said the judge, 'and distributed amongst others. Nevertheless, he shall be fed daily, if he works hard, and must not starve; and if he, by repentance, proves his sorrow, he shall be restored to our favour, and get a share at last nearly equal to that which he has forfeited.' The big burly fellow was discontented however, and stealing off, like a thief as he was, came to a sparrow who had found great difficulty in providing for her numerous young ones. Her he told of the store, and of the weak point of the ant-hill. Collecting her little ones, she flew directly to the neighbourhood, and conveyed them all there in safety, one by one. Then speedily making an entry into the ant-hill—'My friends,' said she, 'you are all quarrelling here; brethren should live in peace and amity. These stores of corn are the cause of all your troubles. I wish to make you happier, and therefore I shall relieve you of what is to you a serious annoyance.' So saying, she called her brood, and the corn stores were speedily demolished—all that could not then and there be eaten, being conveyed to her nest. 'And *my* share,' whispered the big burly fellow that had brought her. 'Traitor, you do well to remind me of your treachery to your relations,' she exclaimed, as she picked him up in her bill, and he disappeared. All that remained of the ants, from that moment, were on a footing of equality—there was no fear of any further disputes respecting the division of property amongst them."

"Your apologue is amusing, Modliar, at all events," said I, smiling, "if not very apt; but it does appear to me that you take the gloomiest view of things. You surely will allow that the civilization of the West, with its world-traversing ships and engines of every kind to diminish human toil, is a superior thing to that of the East, with its empty despotic shows, and stand-still-do-nothingness. Progress is the law of humanity as established by nature; immobility was the law of Eastern despotism, and hence it was unnatural; and, like all unnatural things, was destined to speedy destruction, root and branch."

"I am not by any means insensible to the grand facts of European civilization," replied Marandhan; "but whether they lead, with their restless uneasy change, to heaven or to hell, I am not aware. No paradise of man, it appears to me, is to be found in this ever-rolling, never-stopping whirl of frothy commotion. Far otherwise. Ships capable of traversing the ocean in all directions, and journeying from pole to pole, and from antipodes to antipodes, are grand facts in this new civilization of the West; but we, in times past, have had the like, although by no means equal—far inferior, doubtless, to yours: but these very ships are themselves an element in that ever-whirling frothy change. They make men look to change, and not to permanence, as their greatest happiness; and that is, in my mind, a lie. And then, as to your engines, that diminish human labour, do your people work less, or require to work less, now than before? nay, if the accounts I see in books, be true, the labouring poor of England find it difficult to keep ragged or naked starvation from their very doors. Indeed, I have heard gentlemen from England say, that the poor of Ceylon are infinitely better off than those of their own country. In God's name then, may we not ask, if not for the benefit and happiness of your own people, for whose do you come and make India and Ceylon subject, the Cape, America, and innumerable islands here and there? Strange advance that leaves more misery at home than it finds abroad! strange glory that cannot even hide hunger, destitution, and want of all things, in its ample cloak!"

"The very superabundance of the population of England proves the prosperity of the country," said I.

"Then so did that of Bengal under its worst tyrants—tyrants, at whose doings virtuous England has held up her hands in horror," was his reply.

"The cases are not analogous," I argued.

"Tropical luxuriance supplies that food in the one case, which, in the other, must be wrung hardly from a scanty soil. But it is not so much in physical, as in moral and mental respects, that European civilization stands so pre-eminent. The science, the philosophy of Europe, is of the highest character that this earth has yet seen. Man, with a hammer in his hand, breaks the rocks, and finds the handwriting of ages on them; from which handwriting he decyphers the history of his planet, thousands, perhaps millions, of years before he appeared on it. He shapes a tube, and wanders in the immensity of space, through other systems and other suns, and sees wide universes on every side. Surely, Modliar, there is a nobility in such thoughts, which even the meanest may conceive, that tells well for our European civilization in this much abused nineteenth century?"

"You are younger than I am," said he, quietly, "and have higher and brighter hopes. Thoughts such as you have hinted at, wonderfully feed our vanity, and are, in my mind, extremely deceitful. Man, as you say, finds out everything about everything, except about himself; and that knowledge about himself is precisely of the most importance to him. Whether he knows more of himself, with all those pyrotechnic flashes, that dazzle, but do not illumine some of us, at all events, I cannot pretend absolutely to determine. But I shall bring in the testimony of a man who, for fifty years I have heard, was at the head of European literature, and who was an ardent cultivator, and successful explorer in that field of science you praise so much. What says he, with all his modern lights, pyrotechnic and otherwise?

> 'Stars silent roll over us,
> Graves under us silent.'

Profoundly significant appear to me these few words, meaning, among other things, that he, for his part, had not learned much of the origin or destiny of humanity from all his researches."

"I am amazed," I replied, "at your depreciation of these ennobling thoughts. To me they appear to be of practical importance the most extraordinary, inasmuch as they cultivate the soul, and make it look something further than the eye can see. They give it a tone it cannot otherwise acquire—an elevation, a superiority, a power and vigour unattainable in any other way. Nor did I conceive it possible that an enlightened mind like yours should for a moment uphold Eastern in preference to Western civilization."

"Let us talk over the matter then," replied mine host, bringing his chair nearer to mine, "quietly and argumentatively. Take another cigar; it conduces to thought. Yes, I must confess, I look upon these noble thoughts as so many air balloons, yielding mighty rumblings when struck and wonderful to gaze at, but difficult of practical application to any useful purpose on this earth. To ask me to prefer Western to Eastern civilization is to ask me to prefer Christianity to Budhism, which I cannot do. The civilization of Ceylon, of Tartary, of Chin-India is Budhistic—that of Europe is Christian; and retaining my prejudices, if you will—convictions, I should have said—in favour of Budhism, I must prefer its influence in most ways. But I am ready to talk over the matter quietly with you."

"At some other time, then,"* said I. "I have already trespassed too much on your goodness, and am deeply grateful for the in-

* My subsequent conversations with Marandhan on the subject of Budhism and Christianity will be found in the Appendix to the second volume.

formation you have given me, and the pleasure I have received in conversing with you."

So saying, I took my leave, my stock of knowledge increased, my eyes very considerably opened on many points, by this conversation.

CHAPTER VI.

A DAY AT A FRIEND'S—SNAKES AND MONKEYS.

"There was more foolery yet, if I could remember it."
Julius Cæsar, act i., sc. 2.

THE incidents of the planter's life are not generally of a very strange or exciting character. The felling of a new piece of forest; the planting of the newly-cleared ground; the engaging of a new gang of coolies or labourers, and their subsequent dismission, when the picking and manufacturing periods are over; the occasional starting of a leopard or bear in the uncleared land; the destruction caused by some wild elephant, banished from his herd, and an outcast from society generally; the happy anticipations of a heavy crop, or the gloomy forebodings of a more than ordinarily light one; these, with an occasional journey to some friends in the neighbourhood, to Kandy or to Colombo, form the staple of the varieties of his existence. To these must be added the arrival of his letters, and particularly of the English mail. That is, indeed, a joyous time! How he luxuriates in the well-known address that heads the letter from home, telling, probably, of boyish days, raising happy associations, recalling a host of incidents that the cobwebs of memory have been gradually rendering dim and dingy in his mind. The old familiar handwriting, too—it is dear to the banished exile, nay, beloved by him. But how much more the quaint old thoughts, the remarks on his letters, so full of home and simplicity—it is breathing English air again to read them! The same stereotyped advice that a fond mother has been inculcating from the day he first left her watchful eye—the same anxious exhortations of sisters and maiden aunts to be careful, and not to expose himself heedlessly or rashly to danger from wild animals, and by no means to associate much with that horrid Mr. A., that reckless Mr. B., or that plausible, but dangerous, Mr. C. The sly hints of the more "knowing ones," that it would be well to avoid exaggeration of all kinds, are equally amusing, as an exhibition of self-satisfied humanity, that would show itself so much above the common, gently hinting many things, openly asserting few or none — qualification built on qualification, until the entire epistle grows into one gigantic "if" and "but."

The fact is, no man can live long in the jungle without encountering many adventures, which the aforesaid "knowing ones" would deem highly problematical, if not absolutely false; brought into constant contact, in some way or other, with the wild denizens of the forest, he must either be a witness to, or hear of, dangers, escapes, struggles, and accidents, that many would doubt, and some absolutely reject as untrue. Unlimited scepticism leads, perhaps, to more errors than unlimited credulity; and there can be no doubt that the latter is the happier quality of the two. Every one has heard of the sagacity of that good old Scotch dame, whose son, an apprentice on board a West Indian ship, returned to her, brimful of news, from his first voyage. "Flying fish, Jock," said she, with a wise shake of the head; "na, na, lad, ye'se no get me to believe that. Sich-a-like monsters I never heerd tell on before; and dootless, Jock, an' ther' war sich the Bible would say someat aboot them." "Oh, then," said Jock, "I suppose, mither, there's no use in telling you of the sugar-mountains and the rum-river in Jamaica? But you speer't at me, mither, about what I saw, and sae I tell't you." "Noo, Jock," said the old dame, smiling sagaciously—"noo, Jock, your talkin' the words of truth and soberness, I ken weel, for a' the sugar and the rum, I heerd your father often say, comes from that part, and sae I see nae reason why they should na have their mountains of sugar there weel eneugh, ay and their rivers of rum tae."

We had been very busy getting in our crops—every hand hard at work—every corner of the plantation alive with men from earliest dawn to the latest glimpse of light, picking the berry or bringing it by bullocks or by hand to the pulping machine or to the drying platform. New coolies at work to be looked after, much of every kind of work requiring to be done, and but little time to do it in—the manager's eyes required everywhere, whilst he, heated and excited, moves rapidly from place to place, now inspecting the pickers, and anon galloping off to the machinery, forming all the way abstruse calculations as to the probable result of the season. All bustle and excitement, healthy hopeful work too that year—the "out-turn," as we called it, rather above the average.

At such a period, there was no time for calling, and, for some months, I saw little or nothing of the Hofers. At length, when the bags of coffee were almost all despatched on the road to Colombo, and a little breathing time allowed, a servant from Lanka brought me a note from Hofer, asking me to come and spend the following day with them. I joyfully assented.

Starting early I reached their estate in time for breakfast. Their bungalow was situated on the levelled top of a round and gently sloping hill—a small round hill, about twice the size of that Primrose, which reminds the true Londoner of the Alps, surrounded on all sides by lofty mountains; a vast amphitheatre, in fact, from the centre of which rose this Lanka hill, and on the flattened summit stood their bungalow. A strange situation, and picturesque, but not more so than that of many other bungalows in the district; highly convenient, moreover, inasmuch as the sides of the surrounding mountains, on which the cultivation was chiefly carried on, were all more or less distinctly visible from its verandas. As I crested the southern hill, and turned "Uncle Toby's" head downwards into the valley, now intervening between me and the Lanka bungalow, I had a beautiful bird's eye view of the entire estate—the sides of the gigantic mountains contrasting strangely with the little artificial-like mound in the centre, on the summit of which the bungalow and works seemed like those little painted toy-houses of which children are so fond. A small stream completely encircled the central hills, entering "the happy valley," as we planters called it, from the west, and dividing, so as to encircle the mound, before it made its exit, brawling and foaming through a chasm on the east. Here and there on the sides of the amphitheatre by which I was surrounded, patches of the forest remained in the narrow chinks or chasms with which the hills abound, affording to the eye a pleasant relief in the dull uniformity of the lines of fallen trees, with the small coffee bushes just beginning to be visible at a little distance between them. On the northern side, that facing me as I rode downwards, the jungle was untouched, and still waved in its primeval luxuriance.

Arrived at the little stream, over which a substantial bridge led the way to the bungalow above, I passed the "lines," or dwellings of the coolies, situated behind a clump of mangoe trees, through which the eager occupants inspected the strange *mahathma* and his horse, both, to the uncultivated natives, equal objects of interest.

On reaching the summit of the hill, on which the bungalow stood, I found the breakfast-table most invitingly laid out on the western or shaded side of the verandah, whilst the tall graceful figure of mine hostess, garnished with a broad-brimmed Spanish hat, tended the flowers bordering the road. A servant having held my bridle and stirrups, I dismounted and advanced to salute Mrs. Hofer, who was now standing at the edge of the verandah to receive me. The Spanish hat added a new charm to her lovely countenance, which was flushed with heat and toil, whilst her hair fell in thick, massive, black ringlets over her shoulders. Her form was well set off in a tasteful dressing-gown, tied round the waist with cords from which depended two tassels. Altogether there was a bizarre, and yet an exquisitely graceful, air about her, which heightened the charm of her purely feminine beauty.

"Ernest, like yourself," said she, as I shook

hands with her, "has been taking a long ride this morning, and would have gone to meet you had not business taken him in another direction. But you would like to wash your hands—Mamdeli!" Mamdeli appeared. "Take the *mahathma* into Mr. Hofer's dressing-room."

Hofer soon after made his appearance, and we sat down to breakfast.

We were seated in the open verandah, thoroughly shaded from the sun, with a view to the west of the most striking character. There were the two gigantic hills opposite and at some little distance, whilst through the valley between, the Paloya flowed into this happy region, as if lovingly to embrace the bungalow-crowned hill on the summit of which we sat. Nearer to us was a garden tended by Mrs. Hofer herself, the walks and flowers of which ended in the thick brushwood and mightier forest vegetation stretching down to the little stream. It was a scene to make any man's heart glad who could find gladness anywhere in nature. Yet I thought I could distinguish a shade of melancholy pass over my fair hostess' features, as the joyous laugh of children was borne faintly on the breeze from the labourers' cottages below. It might possibly have been fancy on my part, but it certainly left the impression on my mind that she would be happier had she a little one to rear tenderly and wisely amid this profusion of natural beauty. Hofer was in excellent spirits, and seemed to be ignorant of, or to ignore, this feeling, if any such existed, on his wife's part. Our conversation, as might be supposed, was principally of the crops, of our late bustle and hurry and hard work, of his felling and planting, of his nursery, of the laziness of the coolies, and the cunning falsehoods of the *cangānies,** of the miserable bullocks, and the difficulty of getting an adequate supply, of the comparative excellences and defects of the various pulping machines in use, and of the various measures which we severally adopted in many matters—all interesting themes to each of us, but by no means so to others. Nor did the state of the market escape our astute observations, the last mercantile circulars and private advices being frequently referred to, as we discussed that point.

Breakfast concluded, Hofer took me to see a

* Each gang of coolies has a head-man to watch over and direct it, and he is called its *cangūny.*

new piece of machinery, lately contrived and erected by himself, which he had found, but for one or two accidents caused by the excessive stupidity of the coolies, as he said, work admirably well. He had adopted too a new method of preserving the roads on his plantation during the rains, with which, at present, he was very busy, but, as this new method had not yet been tested by our tropical deluges, I did not feel much anxiety to witness it.

About twelve o'clock, Mrs. Hofer being ready, we started eastward for a ride, for she was an excellent horsewoman, and fond of the exercise. Hofer accompanied us for a short distance, and then darted off in another direction to see what success had attended the fishing in the Paloya, which he had ordered in the morning. Crossing the stream, we commenced the ascent of the hill on the other side, which we performed leisurely and cautiously, the road not being of the best. Here we had an opportunity for some conversation.

"You seem to have resigned yourself completely to a jungle life," said I, "and to have determined to make yourself content with it."

"There is much in it," she replied, "that I like exceedingly. I was always passionately fond of the country and of a country life, and the beauty of nature here charms me—the want of society is not very distressing, but I should be happier if the natives were more improvable—they look upon me with suspicion, and do not seem capable of believing that I can wish to assist them from a benevolent motive. There is a little village at the other side of this hill to which I have frequently ridden, in the hope of being of service to some of its inhabitants, but there is only one woman in it that seems at all disposed to be grateful, or even to like my approach, and she, poor thing, finds a relief in my visits only probably because she is miserable."

"The Kandians are naturally shy, I fancy," was my reply, "presenting, in this respect, a striking contrast with the frank confidence of the coolies from Malabar."

"I do not know much of these coolies," said she, "being totally ignorant of their language, but what little I do know of them is far from favourable. They seem deceitful, mercenary, and lost to all sense of decency and propriety."

"If you judge Asiatics by your English standard, you will certainly find them wanting sadly," I remarked, smiling. "You must remember these are the poorest and least civilized of their class, who travel hundreds of miles to work for a season on our plantations, starving themselves the while, in order to return with their paltry savings (to them, valuable hoards) to their country and families. This alone is, in my mind, a redeeming characteristic—they slave here, not so much for present, as for future, advantage, and very often, to share their little pittance ultimately with starving relations at home. Such is the result of a superabundance of population, the greatest evil, I am beginning to think, whatever political economists may say to the contrary, that can afflict a nation."

"There is doubtless much reason in what you say in their favour," she replied, after a pause, "but with all the shyness of the Kandians, I prefer them."

"The hardships these Malabar coolies undergo, in travelling on foot through the jungles of southern India and those of northern Ceylon, are but little known," I added. "They must arrive, within a certain limited period, in the plantation district, for their supply of food is small, or otherwise they would perish in the forests—hence accidents of a comparatively trivial kind are often death to them, for their comrades cannot wait; the race is for life, and they must sacrifice one, or run the risk of being all destroyed. Hence the disabled member of the gang is necessarily abandoned, and deep in the recesses of the forests, amid wild beasts and serpents, the poor sufferers are left with a handful of rice and a shell of water to meet death, all alone under the most horrible of all possible forms. Can any picture that the most highly-coloured romance ever presented, be more terrible? The outcast is stretched perhaps beneath a tree by the side of the seldom-trodden path in that cheerless waste—rich vegetation in ample profusion all around him, but no hope! He begs and intreats, but the other members of his gang are inexorable. It is his life or theirs! They have carried him ten or twenty miles already, they can do no more—he seems to become worse instead of better, and now lying helplessly at the foot of that tree, he sees them leave the little bowl of rice, the little shell of water, by his side. His outstretched hands, his agonizing wailings are disregarded; he sees them making their way, one by one, through the thick vegetation in front, the long line ever pressing onwards — hope before, misery, despair, and death, behind. At length they are all gone, and in the heaven or on the earth, there seems for him no comfort, no ray of light. Think of night gradually approaching under such circumstances—another human being will probably not approach the spot for days or weeks, and he knows that well. Fancy the slimy snake or wilder leopard stealing towards him, glaring on him, whilst he sees the fiery eyes or the forked tongue gradually approaching, without a chance of avoiding the intended slaughter."

"O, it is too horrible to think of," exclaimed my fair companion, shuddering, "and yet I know that not a season approaches without some such scenes occurring in the recesses of the jungle."

"Some such," I repeated, "many such. Have you ever questioned your *cangānies* about them?"

"Never," said she, "nor is it a pleasant task to probe the recesses of human misery. But now that you have brought the matter so vividly before me, I shall look upon them more pitifully than I have done."

"Such a scene only described to you, believe

me, Mrs. Hofer," I replied, "makes *you* feel more deeply than its enactment before their eyes, affects *them*. The most feeling of God's creatures on earth, women, are almost daily witnesses to such scenes, and they survive them; nay, not merely survive them, but are as merry as though they had been witnesses of joy all their lives, a week after."

"A fact which certainly does not say much for their 'feeling,'" she replied.

"Nay, we must not judge them by too high a standard," I urged. "It is a mercy to these women that their feelings are not acute, in our acceptation of the word, for acute they certainly are, even amongst them, when compared with those of the men."

"All which, in my mind, amounts to this," she answered, "that the women are unfeeling enough, the men absolute brutes."

I did not argue the point further, for the road here improved, and we cantered on.

Arrived at the little village Mrs. Hofer had spoken of, the poor woman whose gratitude had been excited by her kindness, came forth from her cottage to bless and praise her in the most glowing terms. A few inquiries respecting the prospects of the little piece of land her son and she were now cultivating, enabled so to do by my companion's liberality, were asked and answered, and we proceeded on our ride to a waterfall in the neighbourhood, a favourite resort of the excursionists from Lanka. It was a beautifully-secluded spot—one of those natural scenes of surpassing loveliness with which the magnificent island abounds. Two vast rocks, with almost perpendicular faces, covered with moss, or something resembling it, met at right angles, and stretched far apart on either side at their extremities. The stream, a tributary of the Paloya, darted from the corner at the summit, in one unbroken sheet, into an abyss below, a depth of eighty or ninety feet, whilst a grassy knoll, covering a rocky base, directly in front, afforded an excellent platform for witnessing it. This grassy knoll was bordered by bushes which fringed the base of the huge masses of rock on either side, and behind it was bounded by a thick forest; altogether, a spot more completely sheltered from the rays of the sun, or affording a more beautiful view, it would not be easy to discover anywhere. It owed its suitability for a pic-nic party partly to nature, and partly to Mrs. Hofer's judicious improvements—improvements which consisted alone in repressing the luxuriant vegetation, which, if allowed, would have encroached again, as it had done before, upon the table-like plot of grass so admirably adapted for accommodating a party.

Servants, who had arrived before us, by a shorter path through the hills, were here in attendance to take our horses, and we found a carpet spread upon the turf, ready for our reception, with an inviting-looking basket in its midst. Seating ourselves in oriental fashion (after the manner of tailors, as a European would say), *sans cérémonie,* we dived into the recesses of the aforesaid basket, in which we found some sandwiches, a cold fowl, and—greatest luxury of all, after our fatiguing ride of an hour and a-half—some bottles of deliciously cool beer. I fear when the genuine Cockney so carelessly reads the words, "Allsopp's Pale Ale," or "Bass's India Ale," in going through the streets of London, he seldom realises to himself the delight with which the weary traveller in India or Ceylon sees these words on the outside of a full bottle—I say a full bottle, for your planter has as little affection for an empty one as Falstaff had for an "unfilled can"—champaign is an excellent drink, if you don't anticipate a dinner after it, but for a breakfast after a hard ride, or a luncheon in the jungle, there is nothing equal to the sparkling glass of cool Bass or Allsopp. The frame is, perhaps, on fire, this is the condiment to extinguish the flames; exhausted with physical or mental fatigue, with a thermometer ranging between 80° and 90°, nothing half so gently-inspiriting as the white-capped draught of pale India ale; but then it must be of the right description, not opened a month too early or too late—a gentle simmer of white foam on the top, not breaking out into a deluge of froth, which proves it over-ripe, nor having to be coaxed into a little foam, which proves it too flat. They say George the Fourth could take a longer time to drink a glass of generous wine than any other man, thereby enjoying it to the utmost; but such Epicurism will not do with our genuine pale India; it must be quaffed, not hurriedly, but without pause—be the quantity large or small, it should not remain in the glass a minute.

"This jungle-life has a strange tendency to develope Epicureanism in the male portion of humanity," observed Mrs. Hofer, as I made some of these remarks to her, on her putting down her glass of ale, half-finished only.

"If Epicureanism mean the making the best of the circumstances in which we are placed, your remark is a very just one," I answered; "there is so little of accustomed comfort and luxury here—I mean that comfort and luxury to which every Englishman above actual want is used—that it is incumbent on us to make the most of the circumstances in which we are placed, and of the few enjoyments left."

"You remind me of Hudibras," answered my companion.

> "He was in logic a great critic,
> Profoundly skill'd in analytic;
> He could distinguish and divide
> A hair 'twixt south and south-west side."

"Nor was he unlike you in being able to give reasons for everything,

> "For when he happened to break off,
> In th' middle of his speech, or cough,
> H' had hard words ready to show why,
> And tell what rules he did it by."

"Laugh at me if you will," was my reply, "but to me the making the most of the circumstances in which we are placed appears the truest philosophy."

"As an abstract truth nothing can be more certain," quickly rejoined my fair antagonist, "but when your dictum is applied to the proper method of quaffing glasses of ale, methinks it has little to do with philosophy."

"Here comes Hofer," said I, "we will refer the point to him."

Hofer had scarcely taken his place beside us, and given us the best possible illustration of how glasses of ale should be drunk, when a servant, who had been in attendance at a little distance, came towards us with the startling intelligence that a snake at that moment was making its way into the folds of Mrs. Hofer's riding-habit. He was a judicious fellow, that servant, cool and cautious, prefacing his information with the remark that he was not himself aware whether it was a venomous one or not, but that if it was, our only chance of safety lay in not disturbing it at that moment! It was a frightful state of things—the joy and hilarity which had beamed on our countenances a moment before, were changed, as by the wand of a magician, into anxiety and terror. Mrs. Hofer turned deadly pale, but maintained her position heroically, feeling or fancying she felt —at that moment the same thing—the gliding of the slimy reptile over the folds of her dress, fortunately voluminous and thick. But what was to be done? To attack it as it lay, was fraught with the most imminent danger to the lady, whose marble-like features sufficiently attested the agony she endured.

"I have sent one of the grooms for a little milk to a cottage not far off, where they keep goats," coolly observed the servant, "the snake will come out to the milk, and, as long as it is undisturbed, there is nothing to fear, it will bite no one." I know not at this moment which of us endured the most suffering for those few brief minutes. The milk came in an open saucer-like vessel, and, advancing as near as he considered judicious, the servant, deliberately, as if about to feed a favourite kitten, put down the bait which was to lure the enemy to its destruction, whilst he departed into the forest for a bamboo. Our riding whips were near us, and these Hofer and I grasped with grim resolution. For another minute all was silence and anxious expectation. At length, as Hofer subsequently informed me, for sitting nearly opposite as I was to the lady, I could not see it—at length the head of the snake, its forked tongue playing over its jaws, emerged from the folds of the riding-habit, and gradually approached the milk, gradually but too slowly, for Mrs. Hofer could endure no more. Seeing by her husband's face that the crisis had arrived, her nerves failed at the moment, and, with a loud shriek, she threw herself forward. I caught her in my arms, and she almost immediately became insensible, whilst the snake retreating into the folds of the dress, which was not yet sufficiently extended to discover the disgusting animal completely, remained motionless.

One would scarcely believe it, but as long as the reptile remained quiet, I cared not at that moment how long it might so continue. There was an enjoyment in feeling that lovely head upon my shoulder, the mouth almost touching my cheek, and in grasping that exquisite form round the waist, awkward though our attitude, half-standing, half-kneeling, was, that rendered me oblivious, for the time being, of the danger, and whilst Hofer and servants were engaged with the snake in the tail of the dress, I was occupied solely with the statue-like head. I poured out a glass of brandy, and tried to get her to swallow a mouthful, and I bathed her temples with the same liquid immediately after. At length —I cannot tell how long afterwards, her eyes gradually, languishingly, opened and looked up at me.

No remedy could more effectually have roused her, than the position in which she found herself on recovering—the eyes, half-shut before, opened at once, a faint frown contracting the brow—the head was raised, and whispering, in a terrified way, "the snake," she stood up, as well as the disarranged habit would permit. The snake thought I, ay truly, the snake! what of it? Why the poor animal was on the grass, at no great distance, and they were all belabouring it vigorously—the servants with bamboos, Hofer with his riding whip. It had been dead long ago doubtless. I felt certain of that fact, and laughed at them heartily.

"And after all," said I, approaching them, "it's perfectly harmless."

"Is it?" said Hofer, turning quickly round, his whole face, grim and determined before, relaxing at once into a smile—"Is it?"

"Of course it is," said I, taking a hold of the head (for I felt morally certain it could not have endured one-half that it had endured and retain a spark of life); "of course it is. You see there are no fangs here," and I boldly opened the mouth. Whether it was a venomous snake or not, I was and am profoundly ignorant, but not a tenth of the snakes in the world are venomous, they say; so the probability is I was right. The natives said nothing. They are wonderfully judicious people. Hofer and I laughed long and heartily at the transaction, and even the lady herself, after sipping a little brandy and water, condescended to smile; so that we rode back in the best possible spirits. I thought she rather avoided my eyes during the rest of the day, but her manner was as kind as ever; so I suppose it was all fancy on my part. One is so fond of flattering oneself!

We spent a wonderfully pleasant evening after this little adventure; the incident itself, indeed, lending a zest to our enjoyment, and affording an ample theme for conversation. The waterfall lost, from that day, however, a kind patron in our hostess, but such a result was natural, and could not possibly be averted.

The party which assembled at Hofer's to dinner consisted of the magistrate of Ruminacaddee and his wife, Mr. and Mrs. Mouat by name, Captain Lister of the Ceylon Rifles, and Mr. Fowler a coffee-planter of the vicinity. How instinctive are not our first likings and dislikings of strangers! I had met Mr. Mouat on joining the estate; he had visited me two or three times since, proved himself an admirable companion, full of life and anecdote and humour, and yet I felt an antipathy to him. He was a small muscular man, with an intelligent face, surmounted by an ample forehead, shaded on either side by straight black hair. Detracting from these advantages, however, and neutralizing their effect on the observer's mind, were two cold, lack-lustre eyes, ever staring, or if twinkling, the twinkle seemed one of malice rather than of benevolence or humour. Not his pleasant manner, nor his racy stories, nor his keen enjoyment of a pleasant party, could remove the impression which his eyes first made upon my mind; and I found in the course of conversation with mine hostess before his arrival, that Mrs. Hofer's impression was similar to my own. He had evidently observed this, and took the most assiduous pains to remove that impression, at all events from the mind of our fair hostess, and doubtless had taken such pains before. Mrs. Mouat, his wife, was a fat pursy little body, whose impression seemed constantly to be that she was always in somebody's way. She would look round the room, as if to find some hole or corner where she would certainly not incommode any one. With an overwhelming sense of her own nonentity, as far as importance went, she amused, or vexed, or distressed those around her, according to their temper and disposition. Twitching her chair the half-quarter of an inch to one side, she hoped she was not incommoding you. You assured her not in the least—quite the contrary, and would fancy it was all over; but, no! a minute after she begs you will forgive her for shaking the table, or spilling the salt, or scattering the pepper about, or some other delinquency which you would never have noticed had not she herself called your attention to it. Her conversation consisted principally of yes!—no!—ah!—indeed!—very! and such like monosyllables, expressive of anything or nothing at will. Nor was she particular as to the way in which these interesting monosyllables were applied. After a pleasant narration that would make Saturn himself, the gloomiest of men and gods, break forth into a smile, she would merely salute you with an unmeaning and insipid "indeed!" casting a furtive glance under the sideboard opposite, at the same time, as if the reflection crossed her mind at the instant that, safely ensconced under that, she would be in nobody's way. I sometimes felt tempted to assure her that it would be well to try some of these holes and corners, in order to relieve her mind; but I refrained. She had three children, and how she ever contrived to get through life with them I never could discover, for she was precisely the same at home as abroad, at least on two or three occasions that I happened to call. Seated uneasily on the corner of an ottoman or the edge of a chair, she stroked her dear boy's head, and simpered out, yes!—no!—ah!—indeed!—very! just as usual, until I felt strongly tempted to smash the pier-glass with a chair, to see if I could not get anything else out of her.

Captain Lister was an excellent elephant-hunter—one of those fine sportsmen with whom Ceylon abounds. And yet to look at him one would not fancy he was a likely person for such sport. Tall and corpulent, he was the oiliest of living men. His hair, which had a slight tinge of yellow in it, otherwise one would call it white, was scanty, whilst his whiskers of the same hue, were abundant. Constantly mopping his forehead with his handkerchief, he seemed to have worn the hair away above it, and hence its great height. He was fond of a good dinner; and the time which he could spare from military duties and elephant shooting (a sport, of which his success in it probably made him inordinately fond) was devoted, according to his friend Mouat, to experimentalizing in sauces. Although somewhat heavy, Lister was a decidedly good fellow, with an amazing fund of anecdote and story, chiefly relating to his favourite pursuit and his own exploits in it; not that I would insinuate that he was vain or ostentatious—quite the reverse—no one who who had ever looked upon his glowing, mild, and benevolent countenance could fancy so for a moment. Circumstances threw him and Mouat much together, on their first arrival in the island, and they maintained a friendly intercourse up to this time, although meeting but seldom. Lister, I suppose, was not always so corpulent as at the time of which I write, and having been successful in early life as a mighty hunter, had been thus led on to consider the sport an essential employment for him—the slaughtering of elephants in fact, one of those things he was sent into the world to do, and which must be done.

Our conversation at dinner turned chiefly upon snakes in general, and *the* snake in particular, on which subject Lister and Mouat both gave us much information, long since forgotten. I have a distinct recollection, however, of having been complimented on the discovery that our adversary of the morning was a harmless one; and of having borne my budding honours with all possible modesty. The conversation subsequently turned, how I know not, upon native duplicity *v.* native honesty; Hofer maintaining that the Kandians were not a whit worse than other people in similar positions elsewhere.

"I quite agree with you," said the magistrate; "duplicity is the rule all over the world, honesty the exception."

"I should be very sorry to adopt your estimate of humanity, Mr. Mouat," said Mrs. Hofer, ever ready to do battle for the noble, the virtuous, and the true.

"If you judge mankind by yourself, you will certainly think honesty the invariable rule, and duplicity an impossibility," answered he; "but alas! it is a truth, that men in my position particularly, and all men, I fancy, in every position, who have seen much of life, must sooner or later discover, that men, when they are honest, are so from habit, interest, or fear, not from principle—that falsehood and dishonesty are natural to the nine hundred and ninety-nine; truth and honesty to the thousandth only."

"I cannot, in your presence," said she, "speak of my experience in Ceylon; but during the entire course of my life in England I was brought much into connexion with the country people, in Bedfordshire, and truth and honesty, I can truly assert, amongst them at least, are a hundred-fold more common than you would lead us to suppose. Nay, truth and honesty are, amongst them, the rule, whatever you may fancy to the contrary."

"My experience," was his reply, "has lain principally with the town-people and the natives of Ceylon, and that may perhaps be the cause of our difference."

"I do not adopt Mr. Mouat's opinion in its widest acceptation; but you must remember, Emma," said Hofer, "that you saw the country people of Bedfordshire under the most favourable circumstances. Your family was known in the neighbourhood, and had been stationary there a long time—the poor around were grateful for assistance received from it, and the worst features of their characters would be hidden from the view of a young lady with some pretensions to refinement."

"Under what circumstances then, would you judge of mankind?" boldly argued the fair enthusiast; "if those who have lived in the midst of a certain population, constantly seeing, and being seen by, them, are not to judge of the virtue or vice they daily exhibit, who shall do so? You object, and probably Mr. Mouat also objects, to my experience, but I have a more weighty objection to bring against his—the experience of a magistrate lies amongst the worst, not amongst the best, of mankind, no, nor even amongst the average, and if such experience is to be accounted that most fit for forming the foundation of a judgment, the dweller in a hospital might be excused for considering all mankind diseased. Do you not agree with me, Mrs. Mouat?"

"Yes," said that interesting lady, casting her eyes furtively behind the door.

Both the gentlemen were silent.

"In my opinion," said Fowler, "your experience is the most valuable of the three, Mrs. Hofer, for, as you say, Mr. Mouat sees more of the knavery than of the excellence of man, and my friend Hofer has spent his life in moving so rapidly from place to place, and country to country, that he cannot have obtained that intimate acquaintance with any one district or population, necessary to form an opinion of this kind. Those who remain long in one locality alone, mingling much amongst the various classes of people resident there, appear to me to be the only people capable of forming, or likely to form, a correct estimate."

"There is, doubtless, much truth in your observation, so far as I am concerned," said the magistrate; "but it must also be remembered that much, very much depends upon the point of view from which we regard the world. If influenced, like our hostess, by benevolence and philanthropy alone, we shall shut our eyes to the vices, and open them to the virtues, of those around us."

"Precisely in the same way," said Captain Lister, "as a planter judges a horse—that is, he has a point of view, as Mouat calls it, of his own; he doesn't care for points or pedigree, all he wants is go—go of all kinds, up hills and down hills, and over rocks and through marshes, without any reference to paces or appearance."

"Undoubtedly," said Mrs. Hofer, always strenuous and earnest in upholding her convictions—"Undoubtedly, the aspect of anything is modified by the subjective bias and idiosyncrasy, the strength and cultivation of the mind that considers it, as well as by the circumstances in which the individual is placed, hence the impossibility of making all, or even a majority of, mankind think alike on any one subject; but if we find around us in the world, self-denial and benevolence, a firm adherence to virtue and religion, honour and integrity, even under the most unfavourable circumstances, are we not bound to raise our voices against the monstrous doctrine, that all virtue is hypocrisy, all excellence selfishness, all honesty disguised interest!"

"I probably expressed myself too unguardedly," said the magistrate, his cold, inanimate eyes lighting up for an instant, as he looked on the warm and animated face of our chivalrous hostess, —"I certainly did not mean to go so far in my assertions. I meant merely that it appeared to me that vice was more common than virtue; but even in that I may be mistaken—I should not at all wonder if I were."

This conversation, trivial as it may be considered, left a deep impression upon my mind; I could not help contrasting the honest, hearty, open convictions, openly expressed, of the lady, with the half-implied, half-asserted hesitations and retractations of the worthy magistrate—the one symbolic of the daring confidence of youthful ardour in the pursuit of the noble and the true; the other typical of the doubt, hesitation, uncertainty, and craft, which an extended acquaintance with mankind but too often fosters in the minds of the irresolute or the vicious.

"What of astrology?" I asked of Mrs. Hofer, before she and her automaton-like guest left the table—"You talked at Ambepusse of studying it when you got into the jungle."

"I have begun the study," she replied, "and like it well. An old priest from the wihare at Mirrepolla, comes to me thrice a-week, and from him I get lessons in Singhalese and in astrology."

"You don't mean to say you believe in astrology?" asked Lister, bluntly.

"No," she replied—"I do not yet know enough of it to believe or disbelieve it, but my impression is, that there must be more in a science, once so universally admitted as truth, than men now-a-days are willing to acknowledge."

"That there is some great or leading truth at the bottom which the mystifications of ages have but enveloped in a mass of absurdity and no-meaning verbiage, appears probable enough," said Mouat.

"If you can arrive at that truth," said Hofer, "you may be recompensed for the trouble and toil of the investigation, but my impression is, that you will indignantly thrust the whole study from you some day soon, as a vast lie."

"I do not think so," she replied, and then turning to Mrs. Mouat, she added—"your husband and I, I am happy to discover, are likely to find some points of agreement in our various opinions."

"Very," replied the fat little lady, for she had just emerged from a long-protracted yawn, and was now feeling her jaws perhaps to make sure that there was no dislocation—the probability was, therefore, that she had not heard the observation addressed to her, but had only a vague idea that a word was required, and thought "very" the safest. The ladies soon after left the table.

"You hinted at dinner, Mouat," said Hofer to him, after a pause, "that our friend Captain Lister had a peculiar antipathy to monkeys. Am I right in supposing that thereby hangs a tale?"

"You are," replied the little man, his eyes absolutely twinkling with malicious wit, as he turned them upon the Captain, who had moved uneasily in his chair when he heard Hofer's question.

"An absurd story," said Lister; "but yet one that Mouat is fond of relating—why, I could never discover, for really it does not appear to me worthy of the flourish of trumpets with which he introduces it."

"But you will let us hear it, Captain," I urged.

"Why Mouat will be sure to tell it to you some time or other, and therefore I had rather he told it now, as I can point out his exaggerations and misstatements as he proceeds."

"It was a simple enough matter in itself," began Mouat; "and really I do not see why Lister fears exaggerations on my part. As an illustration of the accidents that one is liable to in this 'garden of the East,' it is right that you griffins should be made acquainted with it, for it is only by the misfortunes of ourselves or others that we can learn experience. There are two things that Lister is fond of—a good dinner and a fair encounter with an elephant. He is not more delicate in carving his haunch of venison than in striking a tusker; and he is equally good in making away with both. Mrs. Mouat, you are aware, keeps her own sheep, and I always try and have a supply of good claret in the house, in the hope of alluring him occasionally to Ruminacaddee. No man should come to Ceylon to satisfy his gastronomic propensities; and Lister has been heard to say that the tough beef and scraggy mutton of Ceylon had required an amount of patience and endurance on his part during the days of the years of his pilgrimage in the island, to which that of Job only could be advantageously compared."

"You see what a long-winded peroration he comes out with," said Lister, interrupting him. "I may have made some remark of that kind at a time when execrable food only was to be got; but what has that to do with the monkeys?"

"Softly, Lister, softly," was the reply; "I am coming to them. The preliminary circumstances require explanation. I was on the bench one afternoon, about three o'clock, when a servant made his way to me with a scrap of paper, on which were written a few lines in pencil, intimating that Lister was in the neighbourhood; that, being on duty not far from Ruminacaddee, he had determined on paying us a visit, and that he had sent his horse-keeper on before with his horse, whilst he took a bath in the little lake which the Paloya forms about a mile from our house, in the Sreepah valley. I sent the note to Mrs. Mouat, in order that she might take care that our reputation for hospitality should not suffer on the occasion. About half an hour afterwards I left the bench, expecting to find Lister at home; but he had not arrived. Having waited for some time longer, and still seeing no sign of our guest, I proposed to Mrs. Mouat that we should take a walk towards the valley, and meet Lister on his route to our bungalow. She assented, and we set off in the direction of the pleasant little lake, through which the Paloya flows so quietly. You have seen it, I suppose?"

Hofer and I intimated together that we had not. Fowler had.

"Have you not?" he continued. "It's a

remarkably nice place for swimming, and perfectly safe."

"A remarkably nice place, and perfectly safe!" echoed Lister, with a groan.

"The hills rise gently on all sides of it," continued Mouat, "but particularly so on that leading to our bungalow, from which it is separated by a dense forest, through which I have had a path constructed. The jungle does not extend to the water's edge, for there is a pleasant shingly beach on all sides, sloping gradually down to the water. Clear as crystal is the lake itself, and uninfested either by snakes or alligators.

"Advancing towards the valley along the path, Mrs. Mouat and myself were equally surprised at not seeing anything of our portly friend. At length, we approached a little ridge, on the side of the hill, from which the whole lake could be discovered, and, feeling firmly convinced that no man could have been so long bathing, I insisted on my wife's advancing with me, which she did rather reluctantly. Standing on this little ridge, to our astonishment, we saw Lister upright in the middle of the miniature lake, with his hat on his head, and the water up to his neck. 'Why,

Lister,' I shouted out, 'in the name of all that is wonderful, what are you doing there in the middle of the water, dressed?' 'Ahem,' said he, 'I heard you coming—I'm not exactly dressed; in fact—' and as he spoke he took off his hat, disclosing in the action a bare arm and shoulder. My wife returned precipitately to the bungalow, and I advanced. 'In fact,' continued Lister, as he walked deliberately to the shore, 'I've lost all my clothes, and as you're magistrate here, I trust you'll investigate the matter. It does not speak much for the vigilance with which justice is executed in Ruminacaddee, that a man cannot bathe a mile from the magistrate's bungalow, without having all his clothes stolen.' "

"A very natural reflection on my part," interposed Lister, interrupting Mouat's recital, "considering the circumstances I was placed in, and ignorant as I was—"

"'All your clothes!' said I," continued Mouat, 'all, except your hat! and, let me see, why you've got one stocking on.' That was the entire stock of clothing with which he made his exit from the lake, and sat down upon a large smooth stone to talk about it. His hat and one stocking! It was all that I could do to keep my countenance; but in spite of the most vigorous resolutions to that effect, a grin would occasionally distend my mouth and disclose my teeth, as I contemplated the portly figure before me, sitting on a stone, the hat and one stocking forming his entire available wardrobe. 'It's no laughing matter,' said Lister, indignantly; 'the suit of clothes I have lost is a jungle suit of checked cloth, and, anticipating a ride back to our quarters early to-morrow, I did not bring any others, and now, as you see, they are all gone. I cannot dine at your house, or ride to Neapla in this condition.' 'Certainly not,' said I. 'You can neither do the one nor the other—as magistrate it is my duty to see that decency is not outraged in my district.' 'I suppose, then, it is your duty likewise to see that robberies of this nefarious kind are not committed with impunity,' said he. 'Where did you put your clothes?' I asked, mustering up all the gravity possible under the circumstances, in order to investigate the matter judicially. 'I put them all on this stone,' he answered, 'on which I am now sitting, together with two bathing sheets, left by my horsekeeper.' 'And where did you find the hat and the odd stocking?' I asked again. 'Finding my clothes gone when I came out of the lake, about an hour ago I suppose, I searched on every side, at first supposing that some one was playing a very unpleasant practical joke upon me; not being able to find them, I returned into the water and took an additional swim, in the hope that they would be restored. Finding them still gone, however, when I again came out, I got annoyed, and shouted out lustily, but no one heard me. I searched vigorously everywhere in the neighbouring jungle, as far as I could safely penetrate in this condition, and at length I found, over there, my hat, and a little further on, one stocking; but more there was not, although I advanced considerably further.' 'I have it,' I exclaimed; 'the monkeys have been here, and have run off with the clothes; they often play pranks of that kind, and, not being able to manage the huge pith hat, they abandoned it; one of them must have dropped the stocking.' 'Hang the monkeys!' exclaimed Lister, energetically; 'but it is only a very slight consolation to know that your sagacity has discovered that fact, if it cannot do more.' 'And your watch?' I asked. 'My watch is, fortunately, safe,' was the reply; 'I put it on the flat branch of that tree, and there it is still.'

"A servant from the bungalow here interrupted our colloquy by informing us, as he stared, open-eyed, at Lister's appearance, that Mrs. Mouat had sent her compliments, and told him to say that dinner was ready.

"'Dinner!' groaned Lister, as he surveyed his forlorn condition, 'dinner ready, dished, perhaps, and I in this state!'

"'Bring down a suit of clothes from the bungalow,' said I to the servant, 'and tell the peons* to search the jungle on that side for the Captain's clothes.'"

"'Bring down a suit of clothes from the bungalow,' re-echoed Lister; 'whose clothes?' 'Why, mine to be sure,' I replied; 'you would not have Mrs. Mouat's, would you?'"

"It's all very laughable, I don't doubt, gentlemen," said Lister, again interrupting Mouat, and rising from his chair, "but, by Jove, I never heard a man tell a simple anecdote with so much verbiage as Mouat. For my part he

* Native police.

gives me a headache, he talks so much. I'll go and join the ladies."

So saying, the Captain left us, and Mouat proceeded with his story—

"'Do you seriously think that I shall ever get your clothes on?' asked Lister, when the servant had gone, not a muscle of his countenance betraying the slighest inclination to a smile. 'I really don't know,' said I, 'but we must try at all events. Something must be done.' 'True; something must be done, as you say,' he repeated; 'and, besides, the dinner's ready,—spoilt by this time, I dare say,' and he brought down his open hand with startling energy upon his bare thigh. I endeavoured to keep my countenance still, but it was useless; the Sreepah valley rung with my laughter as I contemplated the extraordinary picture before me. Would that I were an artist, and I should commit it at once to canvas!

"The peons soon made their appearance, and commenced searching the jungle energetically for the missing garments, whilst I secured the watch. At length the servant returned with the suit of clothes, and, as Lister seized the pantaloons and held them up before him for inspection, I felt convinced at once that they would never encase those herculean limbs or that protuberant form. Lister sighed deeply as he looked at them, and shook his head ominously. 'But the shirt,' I suggested, 'why not put it on first?' 'O, certainly,' said he, 'that must go on.' With some coaxing the shirt was insinuated over his ample shoulders, and his hands were got out at the proper extremities. True, the wrists and collar would not button, and the whole affair scarcely reached beyond his hips, but, as he said, these were minor inconveniences; the important fact was, that he had a shirt on.

"The pantaloons were essayed next. It was not without much insinuation, coaxing, and management that the shirt had been got into its natural position, but what shall I say of the persevering efforts made to drag the pantaloons into their proper places! Could they have spoken they would doubtless have remonstrated, stating that they had never been intended to fit limbs double the size of their owner's, especially when the aforesaid limbs were quite wet, for, in his haste, Lister had forgotten to dry them properly before essaying the nether garments. It was utterly impossible for me to assist him in any way—the stern, grim air of determination with which he tugged and pulled, and writhed and twisted the garment upon his limbs, and his limbs into the garment, would have been too much for the most imperturbable countenance that ever a man possessed. He was too intent upon his exertions, however, to heed me, and when one of the servants gently offered assistance, he knocked him aside. 'Hurra! hur-r-r-ra!' he shouted at length, as he seated himself once more, overcome with his indefatigable exertions, and the big round drops coursing each other from his forehead. He had hallooed, however, before he was out of the wood; true, both his legs, quivering in their tight covering, were encased, and the feet were both apparent at the proper ends, but the unfortunate article of dress, straining almost to bursting in every stitch, was yet to be drawn up over the ample rotundity of the Captain's portly figure, and this I foresaw would be no joke to accomplish, if not absolutely impossible.

"At length, muttering 'dinner' again, he resumed his exertions with a forced air of desperate calmness. This time I endeavoured to assist by dragging the pantaloons up. 'Stop! stop!' shouted Lister; 'easy, Mouat, easy; they're splitting.' They *were* splitting, and scarcely had one thread gone when another followed it, till, notwithstanding the cessation of our exertions, it was very apparent that the two legs of the garment would, in a moment, be entirely separated the one from the other. Such was soon actually the case; and Lister, groaning again, sat himself disconsolately down upon the stone to vent his disappointment and annoyance upon me, the servants, the pantaloons, and the monkeys. 'These must be taken off again,' said I to him, anxious that the whole transaction were ended, for I felt hungry and exhausted with laughter. 'Taken off again!' he growled forth, in no very amiable key; 'yes, I suppose they must; a worse-made pair I never saw; I wonder you wear such clothes.'

"To put them on had been a matter of no little difficulty—to take them off was apparently impossible. The legs not having been properly dried, as I said, the pantaloons stuck to them with a tenacity, increased tenfold by the tightness with which they were stretched over the limbs. There was this in favour of their removal, however, a circumstance not to be undervalued in such a position—that the legs of the pantaloons had now completely parted company, and might therefore be taken off, one at a time. 'Gatchee, pull them off,' said I to the servant, whose exertions to assist Lister before had been so ill-requited. Gatchee squatted down in front of the huge figure on the stone, and catching a hold of one of the legs, attempted to drag its close bandage off it. He tugged and strained, and puffed and pulled, sometimes standing, sometimes kneeling, sometimes squatting again, as Singhalese servant never had done before, but all to no purpose. The tenacious garment, so laboriously fixed in its position, resisted all efforts to be removed with a force and perseverance that completely belied Lister's statement that they were rotten—to this day he maintains that they could not have been a sound pair, or they would not have split as they did!

"Whilst Gatchee was thus pulling and straining to remove what had been got on with so much difficulty, one of the peons returned with the Captain's waistcoat, which he had found in the jungle, informing us at the same time, that the monkeys, knowing they were pursued, were travelling, in an immense herd, rapidly away to the south-east, still obstinately retaining possession of their unwonted booty. 'Why don't you throw something at them, you donkeys, and they will throw the clothes at you?' asked Lister, savagely, as he arrayed himself in the waistcoat which completely hid many of the defects of the shirt, as it buttoned up almost to the throat. 'We tried that *Mahathma*,' said the peon, making sideways for the forest, for he did not like the expression of Lister's face—'we tried that, *Mahathma*, and they would not throw anything down. The waistcoat caught in a branch of the tree by the arm-hole, and the monkey tore it a little in trying to pull it away.' 'Either the monkey that ran away with it, or the donkey that got it off the tree, tore it, I see,' said Lister, 'but I don't believe you pelted the scoundrels well, or else they would throw them all at you.' 'They are far away in the forest, *Mahathma*,' urged the peon, still making silently and stealthily for the jungle, 'and they can travel there faster than we can.' 'I shall put a bullet into every grinning jackanapes of them all that I can catch henceforth,' muttered Lister, sternly, 'I have always spared them hitherto, but I shall not do so for the future—baboons, chimpanzees, orang-otangs, or monkeys, whatever name they may go under, it's all the same to me; I'll pay them off for this, some day.'

"Another servant now made his appearance from the bungalow, bearing a fresh bundle of clothes, which we proceeded to investigate. Mrs. Mouat, doubtless informed of the difficulty which detained us, had discovered the only possible means of overcoming it—she had sent down a pair of my *pyjamas*,* and a dressing gown. It was strange we had not thought of these before, for the pyjamas were wide enough to go round three men of my bulk, and the dressing gown was ample and loose. 'Yes,' said Lister, a ray of light animating his countenance, as I distended the wide pyjamas to their utmost, 'yes,' those look hopeful; but I must have these off first—here Gatchee, pull like a man! and he seated himself for that purpose again. Gatchee pulled again more violently than ever, but as unsuccessfully, and Lister, irritated by these repeated mishaps and annoyances, put his foot against the unfortunate darkey's chest, and sent him headlong into the lake—'there,' said the much-tormented, half-naked Captain, as the turbaned head dis-

* Sleeping trowsers, made full and wide, in Oriental fashion.

appeared in the water,—'there, I'll teach you to grin, you coffee-faced monkey; have you learned nothing better yet, under your worshipful master, than to laugh at his guests, when they get into misfortune?' Gatchee soon emerged from his involuntary bath unhurt, and made his way to the bungalow, not feeling disposed to offer his services to the much persecuted Captain any more. 'Quite right, Lister,' said I, apologetically, seeing there was no harm done, 'the rascal had no right to grin at you—in fact there is nothing to laugh at: but how are we to remove these casings of which your legs seem so tenacious.' 'They must be ripped up,' said Lister, eagerly, the bright thought striking him at the instant, as he hastily surveyed the aspect of affairs. 'Ripped up, certainly,' said I, 'a capital idea,' and I took out my penknife forthwith. A few threads cut down the side, the rest speedily gave way, and a few seconds after we had thus dissected the unfortunate pantaloons, Lister was decently clothed in the pyjamus and dressing gown. 'Can I sit at your table in this condition?' he asked in a lachrymose tone, as he surveyed himself. 'Certainly,' I replied, 'you'll do admirably now. You know we are not over-particular in the jungle.'

"And truly the figure he then presented was a strange one! The dressing-gown, loose and easy as it was for me, was straining in every stitch between the shoulders and down the arms, whilst such was its tightness that it was absolutely impossible for him to put his arms straight down by his sides, so that they curved out like the handles of some of those antique vases—'the ears,' as they classically term them—which jut out semicircularly on either side. The sleeves reached more than half way between the elbow and the wrist, whilst the shirt was apparent an inch further. Round the portly person of the ill-used Captain the dressing-gown would not of course meet by several inches, 'but that,' said he, as he attempted it, 'is of little consequence, seeing that I have my own waistcoat on.' If the upper portion of his person, however, was ludicrous, the lower was infinitely more so. The pyjamas were by no means loose for him, and as they were well hoisted up to conceal the top under the waistcoat, they did not reach very far below the knee, leaving the rest of the leg exposed, for he had discarded the odd stocking, and was now endeavouring to walk in an ample pair of slippers.

"No sooner was the outer man thus encased in the best way that circumstances would permit, than his thoughts, as I anticipated, turned upon dinner. 'The mutton will be done to rags,' said he, as he tramped vigorously towards the bungalow. 'That will be the fault of the monkeys, not of the cook,' said I. 'Monkeys—monkeys,' he repeated, 'I owe them one. Of all the shouting, roaring, jabbering, grinning, crawling, jumping inhabitants of the forest, I hate them most. I always hated them. They're the ugliest and nastiest animals alive.' 'To say nothing of their thieving propensities,' I added. 'Yes, to say nothing of their thieving propensities,' said he, 'but I'll pay them off. Not another reptile of them shall escape me when I have a gun in my hand;' and so saying he brought down his hand vehemently, as is his wont, upon his thigh.

"A few twitches from the shoulder of the dressing-gown warned him that he must not be too energetic, or else the arms would part company, as the legs of the other garment had before. 'Miserably made clothes you do wear in the jungle,' said he, turning his head to try if by any means he could see the threatened danger; and then brooding over his late mishap, and anticipating the coming dinner, he made his way in silence to the bungalow. Mrs. Mouat's gravity was a little upset when she first saw him, but once seated at dinner, all went off well, nor had so much injury been done to the viands as we had feared—the claret at all events, as he triumphantly remarked, would not be spoiled by waiting. His coat, torn almost to shreds, was brought in late in the evening by the peons, but of none of the other articles missing could they discover a trace. Doubtless the monkeys had hidden them on finding themselves pursued. Next morning, therefore, Lister had to ride back to Neapla in my pyjamas, and an odd enough figure he cut in them on horseback."

Mouat's strange narrative concluded, we rose to seek Lister and the ladies, but my imagination was so busy with the various incidents that had been thus recently related, that I could pay but little attention to anything else, and once or twice when Mrs. Hofer was telling us of the sorrows of some poor Singhalese in the neighbourhood, who would have been starved to death had not she assisted them, I found myself grinning egregiously as

I looked at Lister, and thought of his misfortunes, greatly to the astonishment, and sometimes to the indignation, of the fair narrator.

It was late that night ere I turned my horse's head homewards, for our long moonlight ride. For a short distance my route lay with that of the party of Ruminacaddee, which was not much more than three miles from Lanka, and, on leaving them, Fowler and I rode leisurely along conversing of many things, —the adventure of the snake, the misfortunes of Lister, and the worth and amiability of Mrs. Hofer.

CHAPTER VII.

ADAM'S PEAK.

> "These high wild hills, and rough uneven ways,
> Draw out our miles, and make them wearisome."
>
> *Richard II.*, act ii., sc. 3.

THERE is, perhaps, no natural object in Ceylon that so powerfully arrests the attention of the visitor or traveller as the remarkable mountain called Adam's Peak. It can be seen clearly from all the south-western coast, and from a considerable distance at sea, ever pointing with its bare, insulated, cone-shaped summit to the skies—sometimes clear and well-defined on the bright blue, or white, behind it, but more generally cloud-capped, and either altogether enveloped in its watery shroud, or only partially seen here and there, as if battling manfully with its enemies.

It is sacred to every class of the natives.

The Mohammedans, equally with the uneducated and ignorant Christians, believing that the Garden of Eden was situated in Ceylon, further assert that, on the summit of this mountain, Adam stood for a thousand years on one leg, as a penance, leaving behind him an impression of his foot in the granite rock. The Hindus, not to be behind them in absurdity, state that one of their legendary kings or gods —a giant, called Rama, or Siva, for traditions differ—in making his way into India, put one foot on the summit of the peak, whilst he stepped out to Adam's Bridge, in the extreme north of the island, with the other, a distance of about one hundred and thirty miles, and so left the foot-impression on the summit which has been ever since so remarkable an attestation, at once of his power and size. But the Budhists alone crowd to the top to worship there, notwithstanding all the dangers and fatigues of the way; and their story of course connects this strange foot-impression with the legendary history of their own great prophet.

The genius of the place, says their tradition, having heard of Budha's arrival in Ceylon, went to him, and, worshipping, requested him to leave an impression of his foot on the mountain of which he was the guardian, that it might be worshipped during the five thousand years his religion would last on earth. To induce the man-god to comply with his request, the crafty genius repeated at length the praises of the mountain. The flowers on its sides and near the summit, he compared to a magnificent garment and head-dress—the hum of the bees, as they sped through the air, laden with honey, to the music of lutes—the birds, to bells sending forth sweet chimes—the waving trees, agitated by the wind, to a band of dancers. All, he declared, acknowledged the supremacy of Budha. The trees offered fruits and flowers to him.; the reptiles on the marshes, the fish in the streams, the birds on the branches, the elephants, leopards, bears, deer, monkeys, hares, and other animals in the jungle, all worshipped him. Budha consented. He went through the air with his five hundred followers, and great was the concourse, and magnificent the assembly that crowded the mountain in consequence.

The genius of the place, attended by thousands of similar spirits, with their queens, who made music, and carried flags and banners, and scattered about gold and gems, stood by

Budha's right hand. The gods were all there —Sekra and Maha, Brahma and Iswara—all inferior to the Budha—with their attendant trains, were there, "and like the rolling of the great ocean upon Maha Meru, or the Yugandhara rocks, was the sound of their arrival." In the midst of the assembled spirits, Budha, looking towards the east, put his foot on the hard granite, and lo! the impression was made —"a seal to show that Lanka, or Ceylon, is the inheritance of Budha, and that his religion will here flourish for ever."*

I had determined, from the first moment that I saw Adam's Peak, when at Point de Gallê, to ascend it, if the ascent were possible; and, finding that it was so, that several pilgrims yearly went up, although at considerable risk, I was determined, sooner or later, to make my way to the summit. When the idle season had arrived on the estate—all the year's produce bagged and despatched, and nothing but the ordinary routine of weeding to be done, I found myself called off to Colombo by business—Hofer was there too, and we determined together to ascend the Peak, before we returned to the jungle. It was not much out of our

* Abridged from the "Manual of Budhism," by R. S. Hardy.

way, and a delay of a few days on the route would be amply recompensed by the novelty of an ascent, and the pleasure of spending a night upon the summit, to say nothing of the inspection of the far-famed foot-impression itself. True, it was not the time when pilgrims usually made their way to the top from motives of piety; but that did not disconcert us much, rather, perhaps, on the other hand added a zest to our anticipated enjoyment, as we should be alone, far away from all abode of humanity, after plunging into the recesses of the mountain.

It was therefore with considerable pleasure that we made our way together one morning about four o'clock, from the Fort of Colombo, mounted upon horses with which we were thoroughly acquainted, and which were equally well acquainted with us. My steed was the redoubted Uncle Toby, a small, black Arab, strong as an elephant, muscular to excess, and withal enjoying a spirit and energy that would have made him work till he dropped down dead, merely by the incitement of the voice, had any one been barbarous enough to make the trial. His figure reminded me of the portraits of the Godolphin Arabian, whom he resembled in his strange length and breadth of neck, in his glossy black coat, and in the fine curve of his back. Yet he was no racer, far from it; merely a serviceable hack, of great strength and indomitable perseverance; "*go* of all kinds in him," as Captain Lister would have expressed it, "up hill and down hill, in jungle or on cleared land, on an estate or in the streets of Kandy, *go* of every description, and *good* go too, though not absolutely the best, good in safety, in perseverance, in courage, though not the best in speed." Hofer's horse was a well-trained country animal, admirably suited for the jungle, and by no means bad-looking; so that we regarded ourselves as well mounted for the journey. Our few traps and considerable quantity of provisions were carried by ten coolies, headed by a guide, a Singhalese, who had been to the summit before, knew a little English, and was to act as cook during the expedition

The coolies and the guide—the latter delighting in the euphonious appellation of *Poonchy*—had been despatched to the first station the day before, and, on our arrival, we found Poonchy busily engaged in the mysteries of cooking; he and the coolies occupying a large barn-like building, which had been tastefully prepared for our reception by placing two three-legged chairs, obtained from the neighbouring head-man or village chief, near a nondescript board elevated on four sticks stuck into the earthen floor, which contrivance the aforesaid Poonchy dignified by the name and title of a "table." It appeared strange to us that they had put the table-cloths on the chairs instead of the table, but we learned on inquiry, that this was the head-man's contrivance to show "plenty honour to masters," as Poonchy expressed it. Having sufficiently admired these arrangements we washed and then sat down to breakfast, all the time exposed to the wondering or curious gaze of every man, woman, and child the little village contained, who crowded one side of the building on which the architect had forgotten to construct a wall, and pertinaciously remained there, notwithstanding Poonchy's incessant abuse of them. It was useless talking to him; he was one of those hopeless individuals who will have their own way, feeling quite sure that whoever else may be wrong, they must be right.

Breakfast dispatched, we set about making ourselves comfortable, and, for this purpose,

Hofer took two of the chairs, the one to sit upon, the other for his feet, whilst I endeavoured to make myself equally comfortable with a chair and the " table," an additional chair having been added to our stock of furniture by the indefatigable Poonchy, as a " sideboard." The endeavour however, to render ourselves more at ease was unsuccessful; in a moment of thoughtlessness, Hofer, his feet resting on one chair, tilted himself back on the hind legs of the other, a position for which they were evidently not prepared, for, giving way, he and they sought the ground together. Nor did I fare better. The extraordinary contrivance which Poonchy dignified with the name of table, disdained the ignoble duty of supporting my feet, and no sooner did Hofer, who had been leaning against it on the opposite side to me disappear, than it gradually and gracefully descended after him.

Our road, during our journey in the evening, lay through a fine sporting country. A few years have, I believe, made a great change in the district in the way of improvement, but in 1843, the neighbourhood of Sitawaka was as wild as any tiger-hunter could desire. The leopards were more numerous perhaps in other parts of the island, but every other species of game abounded in the country through which we were journeying. Our progress, therefore, it may be easily conceived, was by no means a rapid one, for as we had not very far to go, and had plenty of time in which to accomplish our journey, we indulged in a little straggling shooting by the way. We were now approaching our destination for the evening, and perceiving symptoms in the sky of a coming storm, pushed on our horses to get under shelter as soon as possible. A smart trot, however, brought us speedily up to a company of natives, whom we soon recognized as our guide and coolies. They had started many hours before us, and we fondly anticipated that already preparations for dinner were far advanced. The cause of their detention was speedily made apparent to us in the huge footmarks of an elephant which appeared to have recently passed along the road in the same direction as that in which we were travelling. There were numerous indications around, to prove that it was a *rogue* elephant, and hence their alarm and hesitation. One who has not witnessed it can scarcely have an idea of the dread with which a native of Ceylon is affected when under the impression that a *rogue* elephant is in his vicinity.

A herd of wild elephants is comparatively harmless, and I have frequently passed within a short distance of them unmolested. On horseback the solitary traveller is perfectly safe, though he may accidentally find himself in the middle of a herd; and even the pedestrian runs little chance of molestation under similar circumstances; but with a *rogue* the case is altogether different. Why this particular designation was applied to them I never could discover, it being quite inadequate to convey any idea of the mad and savage fury of the animal. The "rogue" appears to be one banished, for some misdemeanour probably, from his herd—generally, but not invariably, a male—and from that moment devoting himself to the slaughter of all animal life and the destruction of all property that comes within his reach. Hence, whilst the natives have little dread of travelling on a road on which the footmarks of numerous elephants are apparent, they are almost paralyzed by fear when they find the recent traces of a solitary wild prowler on their path. To a European these traces would probably never be perceptible. He might travel across them for days, and never observe them; but to the quick eye of the natives the huge footmark is at once apparent; the direction in which the animal travels is discovered in a moment, and indications at once sought to ascertain the fact of its being alone or in company—a rogue or tame.

The halting of our coolies was, therefore, at once accounted for, although they had no hesitation to advance with us, feeling safe in our horses and rifles. Even a rogue elephant will scarcely attack a man on horseback, unless wounded or greatly enraged, such is the natural antipathy between his species and that of the horse—an antipathy which is quite reciprocal. Having carefully loaded our rifles with zinc bullets—the lead being often too soft for the forehead of the elephant—we proceeded with increased alacrity, neither Hofer nor myself displeased at the prospect of an adventure. Having judiciously made all necessary dispositions and arrangements in case of an attack, and determined on our line of conduct, we pursued the train of thought until we were canvassing what was to be done with the monster's tusks after he had fallen, when the huge footsteps branched off from our path deep into the jungle, whither, at that late hour, it would have been madness to pursue our intended antagonist. Our guide was certain that we had not seen the last of him, declaring that he had only left the road to skirt the village, which we were approaching, and that we should probably hear or see more of him next day.

Nothing particularly interesting occurred at the little village where we passed the night, save that our good humour was not increased by the delay which attended the preparations for dinner—a delay occasioned by the stoppage of the coolies on their road, but which, to our astonishment and indignation, we found was increased by Poonchy's determination to have his own dinner before he provided us with ours—his only excuse being, that such was always "black man's custom."

Next morning we departed in excellent spirits, more anxious than ever for a glimpse at, and an encounter with, our disturber of the previous evening. Nor were our wishes vain. The coolies, with our guide, had as usual gone on ahead in the morning, and we were waging a desultory warfare against the few jackals and hares which we occasionally met, when a remarkably fine spotted deer crossed our path, and rushed into the adjoining forest. Our horses were fresh, the forest was open, and neither of us could resist the temptation of dashing after it, for it had appeared, and disappeared so rapidly as to prevent our having a shot. Five minutes hard riding brought us to the foot of a hill, comparatively destitute of vegetation; up which, straight before us, the deer, which was a large noble one, was rapidly fleeing. We pulled our horses up on a spot commanding a full view of the entire hill side, our rifles, loaded with ball in both barrels, being in our hands. Hofer fired as he sat, whilst I, less confident of my horse's steadiness, jumped from his back, and fired somewhat more leisurely. The animal received both balls—one in his foot, the other close to the spine—and, staggering on a few paces, fell dead under a magnificent mangoe tree. Our grooms were speedily at our heels, and, in company with them, we ascended the hill, near the summit of which the deer had fallen, at once to inspect our prize and to obtain a view of the surrounding country. The animal was a beautiful specimen of the class to which he belonged—large in size, comparatively speaking, that is, about the size of a full-grown goat, and covered with the most variegated and lovely variety of spots upon his glossy coat. As we were not likely to have anything better for dinner at Ratnapoora, we resolved to have him conveyed there, and, for that purpose, ordered the grooms to carry him to the nearest station, where two extra coolies could be pressed into our service.

This matter concluded, we leisurely skirted the hills, proceeding towards the summit, and advancing in the same direction as the road which wound round its base. From our new position we had a fine view of the country around. The coolies were just visible at a considerable distance a-head, fear or laziness evidently preventing them from advancing with any rapidity. We were on the point of mounting to resume our journey, when Hofer called my attention to a strange commotion in the jungle at a little distance from the coolies, who were flying from it in all directions. In another moment we saw a large tusk elephant emerging from the thicket, and making directly for the little party.

A more formidable thing than a charge from an enraged elephant can scarcely be imagined. His trunk elevated in the air, whilst he trumpets forth loudly his rage or hatred, he shuffles his huge carcase along at a pace more rapid than any one would conceive possible when regarding the unwieldy bulk of the animal alone. The bushes bend before him as he advances—the branches of the trees snap off with sharp, rapid reports—the animals in the neigbouring jungle, alarmed at the danger, hoot, whoop, scream, cry, bellow, and roar to the utmost, in alarm or in anger, and the whole welkin rings with the commotion.

Our baggage was of course flung down in all directions by the coolies as they made for the nearest trees. The elephant paused for a moment over the articles strewed in his way, but only for a moment, and hurling a portmanteau high into the air, advanced as before, bellowing madly. The natives are, of course, expert climbers, so that, ere he approached, all the coolies had made their way into the trees, and appeared to be perfectly safe—all but one, who had still a leg within reach of the monster's trunk when he approached the tree in which the unfortunate man, paralyzed by fear, no doubt, was climbing. To the others who surrounded him, and to us from the brow of the neigbouring hill, it appeared that the man was sufficiently high in the tree to prevent his being caught and dragged down by the infuriated animal. Whether he was so caught, however, or was only struck and fell through excessive fear, certain it is we saw him fall backwards on the uplifted head of the elephant! In a moment the body of the unfortunate man was whirling high in the air, and at length descended with a frightful thump upon the ground, only to be trampled immediately afterwards into a shapeless mass!

His success in this instance, which was all the work of a moment or two, appeared but to increase the savage fury of the monster. He rushed at the tree nearest to him, into which two of the little band had climbed, his broad forehead coming with thundering force upon the trunk, and shaking it in every twig—he struck and dug at it with his tusks—he grasped it with his trunk—retreated to a little distance and made another assault with his broad, heavy forehead, butting, as a ram would do against an antagonist—again was the tree shaken, every leaf quivering violently, but no sign of tumbling about it, a slight list to one side was the only perceptible result—its occupants holding on for life all the time, and shouting violently in the extremity of their fear, or in the vain hope of frightening the animal away.

Whilst all this was proceeding we were reloading the discharged barrels of our rifles, and, having mounted, drew off the attention of the elephant from the coolies, by shouting, as we awaited him on our vantage ground, on the brow of the hill. No sooner did the enemy perceive us than he turned away from the tree, which he seemed intent on bringing down, and made directly for the spot on which we were drawn up ready to receive him—our grooms having climbed high into the largest tree in our vicinity. We were aware that firing at random, or at any great distance, was useless, and that our only chance of bringing him down lay in the accuracy of our aim and his proximity when we fired. We therefore awaited his approach with what calmness we could. Before the elephant had come within range, however, "Uncle Toby," my excellent steed, took fright at the dreadful picture before him, and, starting off, bore me, with frightful rapidity, down the steepest part of the hill's side. What became of Hofer I did not then know, although I heard the clear ring of his rifle behind me as I was borne triumphantly down the bank. His horse, as I subsequently learned, had behaved admirably well, never swerving in the least until he had fired. His ball, we afterwards discovered, had entered the left eye, and must have given excruciating pain, but was not fatal. Hofer then wheeled round his horse, and followed me down the declivity, aware that the elephant, from the great weight of its head, is unable to go down a steep hill with any rapidity. There was this difference, however, between us, that whilst Uncle Toby had the bit clenched in his teeth and was perfectly unmanageable from excessive fear, Hofer's horse was completely in hand, and he could do with him what he pleased. The elephant laboured after us, blood streaming from his eye, and his whole appearance indicating excessive fury and intense pain. When I had now nearly reached the base of the hill—our enemy having been left far behind—my horse, in his wild gallop, threw his fore-legs into a little swamp, where they sank deeply. I was thrown far away over his head, whilst he rolled helplessly on his side. . I was not hurt, but the loss of a moment might have been the loss of my life, so, jumping up, I grasped my rifle more firmly than ever, and stood upon the defensive. A moment of intense interest to both of us succeeded—life or death hung upon the issue, for the elephant, having witnessed the accident, left the pursuit of Hofer, and directed his steps towards me. There might have been time to climb into a tree, but I did not make the attempt—my whole mind being on fire with the earnest desire to bring down the monster. Hofer, seeing what had happened, drew up his horse on the hill's side—the elephant, still advancing, soon came in a line with him, his left, and now blind side, being turned towards him. Seeing that he was not observed, Hofer dismounted, and proceeded to take aim immediately behind the shoulder-blade, as the animal laboured heavily along. Precisely at the moment when I discharged both barrels full into the broad forehead, Hofer's ball penetrated his side. A momentary check to the animal's progress seemed the only result of this double fire at the instant—he advanced twenty paces or so further, and then fell headlong to the earth, turning over gradually on his right side, and beating the ground ineffectually with his trunk. Uncle Toby had only just left the spot a few minutes before to scamper wildly away on the road that we had come, where the elephant now lay extended before us, an occasional convulsive twitch of one of his legs or of his trunk the only failing symptoms of life. The huge mass of his body stood higher than my chest as he lay thus helplessly where he had fallen, making an occasional but ineffectual effort to lift his head off the marsh in which it was half imbedded.

Most people, I believe, feel danger affect the nerves to the greatest degree after it has passed. I am sure it was so with me. When the enormous brute was charging rapidly down the hill, when there seemed no chance of escape by flight, and the slightest accident might have been death—under these circumstances my nerves were so strung to their greatest tension that there was no agitation. I was as able then to take advantage of the slightest turn in my favour, as if our sport had been most harmless, and we had been hunting a hare instead of an elephant. But now that the peril was past, now that the body of the huge animal lay extended before me in all the impotence of death, a sense of the danger I had been in rushed upon me with redoubled force, and I was amazingly agitated.

It may be easily imagined with what pleasure we added the tusks to our trophies, and with what self-gratulation and laudation we listened calmly to the tales which Poonchy had collected or invented of the numerous depredations made in the neighbourhood by our slaughtered foe—of the lives lost, of the plantations destroyed, the trees uprooted, the terror inspired, and the dangers to which travellers were exposed—all done or caused, according to Poonchy's account, by the animal of which we had just rid the country. Nor, strange to say, although at other times we regarded Poonchy as an unconscionable liar, did we perceive at the moment anything absurd or unlikely in his assertions—nay, we were quite willing "for that occasion only," to swallow all he gave us, however hard the *pabulum* might subsequently prove of digestion.

At Ratnapoora we were obliged to leave our horses—Uncle Toby having been recovered only after great labour and a day's loss—as the rest of our journey was to be performed on foot. The principal dangers which we anticipated for the future were swollen torrents, precipitous rocks, and the stoppage of the provision supplies, by the accidents to which the coolies were as liable amongst the mountains as ourselves. We were now at the base of the extraordinary mountain hallowed by the superstitions of so many different races and religions, and as its vast sides and conical top were made more apparent by our proximity, and were better defined to the gaze, the desire to attain the summit became all the stronger and more intense. No village can be more picturesquely situated than Ratnapoora, "the city of diamonds," as the name imports. Built on irregular hilly ground, sloping down on one side to a fine river, the Kalany, and on the other into an extensive valley, of which there is an excellent view from almost every portion of the town, it is itself in a very amphitheatre of mountains, large and small. Its principal height crowned by an old fort, long since deserted by the military, and handed over to the district judge for a court, and to the missionaries for a chapel—there is something venerable about its character, at the same time that the extreme beauty of its situation makes that in it remarkable and interesting which elsewhere, perhaps, would be common-place or even ugly.

Unfortunately the day after our arrival at Ratnapoora was a very wet one, and the consequence was that every little stream on our road was considerably swollen. The first we crossed was the Kalany River, that which flows into the sea, near Colombo, and we found it in one part of the ford, near the left bank, much deeper than we had anticipated. Wading through the water was the only method of crossing available, and, for some time after we had left the Ratnapoora side, it was shallow enough, although raging rapidly on, and covered with white foam. When we came into the deepest part of the bed, however, it was with difficulty that we could keep our long sticks fixed at the bottom of the stream to serve as a support and assistance; such was the violence with which the stream rushed on. Our coolies managed to support each other across with admirable tact—their bundles slung on bamboos raised on their heads, each bamboo being carried on the heads of two men, one at each end. We were obliged to put up for the night in a miserable shed, at a wild place called

Ginnemallee, and as it rained during the night we were plentifully bedewed, through our half-thatched roof, whilst, from the open sides, the fine rain beat in too copiously for our comfort.

Nor did the next day's travelling make amends for the discomfort of the preceding night's lodging. We had no sooner set out than we found ourselves assailed on all sides by one of the greatest plagues in Ceylon—the leeches. The previous rain had moistened the soil and brought them out in hundreds on our path. Every portion of the ground, nay even the vegetation was alive with them—they were to be seen leaping from the stones or dried branches in every direction, full of life and vigour. Few who have not practically experienced it can have any idea of the annoyance caused by these disgusting reptiles. The leech-gaiters, made of closely-woven cotton-cloth, and tied over the pantaloons at the knee, defend the feet from their assaults—without these, the legs would be covered with them, for they will penetrate any ordinary description of stocking, and find their way above and beneath any ordinary boot. But on the entire distance between Ginnemallee and Pallabatula, the last-inhabited district on the ascent, they abounded, not on the ground only, as is usual in the coffee estate, but on the bushes and branches of the trees, so that as we brushed past them in the narrow jungle path, we were literally covered with the blood-thirsty vermin. At every little bungalow, by the road-side at which we stopped, we were obliged to make a general inspection of our persons to rid them of the enemy—nor was this inspection a pleasant operation, seeing that it had thrice to be made in the presence of a miscellaneous crowd of men, women, and children, who pertinaciously maintained their positions around the open sheds, dignified on the ascent with the name of "bungalows," and in which we divested ourselves of our clothing and engaged in the disagreeable search. However, it was necessary to do so and there was no help for it; if the female portion of the population in the wild recesses of Adam's Peak were lost to decency, it was not our fault.

Often did we discover six or eight of the leeches forming a radiated circle around a single point, like the spokes of a miniature wheel, all filling amazingly at our expense—at first, thin as fine threads, but gradually distending till the swollen body could scarcely remain attached by the head. Nor was the detaching of them so simple a matter as many would suppose. To have pulled them off might have produced sores, and caused a considerable flow of blood from the wound for a time; we were obliged to sprinkle salt upon them, before they would voluntarily relinquish their hold, and not even then without giving a sharp twitch to the sufferer. Their first bite, on attaching themselves to the skin, was imperceptible, so insinuatingly was the proboscis introduced, so that the individual, honoured by their attentions, was not aware of the attack until the cold clammy body, distended almost to bursting, rolled about heavily on the skin. It is a consolation to know that they do sometimes burst themselves outright, as I have been informed, although I was never a witness of the fact.

It was with delight we found that the so-called "rest-house," at Pallabatula, the last inhabited station on the ascent, was surrounded by a sandy gravel which precluded the leeches from making their way into it, and that but one more search for them under our clothes was required to render us free from this plague for a time. Having refreshed ourselves after our fatigue by a luxurious loll and a dinner of rice and fowl curry, the best that the culinary talent of Poonchy could supply, to which some slices of ham and some bottles of Allsopp gave the necessary European character to render it satisfactory, we determined to recruit our strength and spirits by a day's rest to prepare us for the more arduous task which still awaited us, Poonchy having kindly informed us that the road yet to be travelled, was " plenty more bad " than that which we had come.

A wihara, at Pallabatula, contains the cover of the sacred footstep on the summit, placed there during the period of pilgrimage by the wily priests annually, to prevent the too curious eyes of the faithful from discovering what a humbug the far-famed foot-impression is in reality. It was a large metal lid, something of the shape of a foot, the toes being distinctly marked on it, the whole covered over in a gaudy extravagant manner, with glass diamonds and gilded ornaments, more glittering and glaring than beautiful. The scene, as we surveyed this cover, was one well suited for the artist. In the large, gloomy, half-lighted temple, the monstrous foot-cover (five feet long) lay upon the ground—two priests of

Budha on one side with yellow robes, bare heads, and shaven crowns, reverentially looking down upon it as the great treasure of their temple, and an honour to themselves as its guardians; at the other end, we, the two Europeans, from a far-off isle of North-Western Europe, surveying the same object with far different thoughts and impressions; whilst a crowd of natives gazed in through the open door, obstructing the little light which gained admission there, and regarding the whole scene with religious awe. Not a word was spoken—in silence the priests stood, their eyes fixed on the sacred covering—in silence we stood opposite to them, struck with its great size, and the glitter caused in the obscurity by its numerous ornaments—in silence the people without strained their necks and eyes to catch a glimpse of it. A scene like that, short lived though it was, lives in the memory with a robuster life than a thousand incidents of a more exciting or more animated character. As the period of pilgrimage approaches, this covering is conveyed, with great ceremony, to the summit, where it remains upon the foot-impression till the last batch of pilgrims has departed. For the rest of the year it is kept in the centre of the largest room at the temple of Pallabatula in gloom and silence—the door never opened save to admit a noiseless priest to dust the apartment, or to exhibit, to prying tourists like ourselves, the holy treasure.

The same day that we inspected the celebrated cover, we went out shooting, to provide a few birds for dinner, and, unfortunately for the success of our expedition, whilst Hofer was crossing a little ravine, a splinter of iron-wood penetrated his canvas shoes and leech gaiters, and wounded his foot so severely, that he was obliged to give up all idea of making his way to the summit. The accident was not of so serious a character as to excite alarm in our minds for its ultimate consequences, but it was evident his foot required rest and care to prevent inflammation, and, as it was impossible to have him carried to the summit, greatly to his mortification and my disappointment, it was absolutely necessary for me to proceed alone, if I wished to reach the object of our journey.

The following morning, therefore, we parted, I taking with me six coolies and the guide, for the conveyance of cold ham, bread, curry and rice, a bottle of brandy, some beer, and such warm clothes as I was likely to require, not forgetting of course my trusty old rifle and ammunition. Our road lay directly up the steep side of a bleak-looking hill that towered far above the puny village; two days before it had been the bed of a raging torrent, that had swept away every particle of mould and earth, leaving nothing but the huge rocks, bleak and grim-looking, jutting forth from the mountain's side, whilst the thickest jungle grew on either hand, and was often so interlaced over our heads as to render the path quite dark. Climbing up this "road," for it could not be called walking, was laborious in the extreme; it consisted in incessant clambering over the smooth time and water worn faces of the projecting rocks, sometimes on hands and feet, sometimes by the aid of the overhanging or over-arching boughs above, whilst frequently this very vegetation so useful at one time, was the cause of our greatest difficulties at another; the interlacing foliage being often so near the hill-side as to prevent our progressing, until we had cut or torn away a portion of it. I now discovered why the wary Poonchy had insisted upon each coolie having the smallest possible load, for it was not long before we all exhibited signs of great fatigue, and I began to fear that the coolies might give up in despair. In addition to the difficulties of the way which I have enumerated, it must be remembered that we were constantly exposed to the danger of meeting with wild animals, and had we so encountered a herd of elephants for instance, coming down the mountain in single file, I know not what we should have done, or how indeed we could escape destruction at all, unless we succeeded in driving them from our path. As we proceeded the coolies and guide kept constantly shouting out at the highest pitch of their voices, in the hope of scaring elephants, leopards, bears, and wolves away; especially those in the rear, whose shouts were ever the loudest and shrillest, for those in front had some confidence in my rifle, and as I never lost sight of them whilst I clambered on, they felt comparatively safe. St. Pierre, I thought, might have taken this ascent to Deabetme instead of the black mountain of Bember, as an illustration of misfortune. "Misfortune is like the black mountain of Bember," says he, "at the extremity of the glowing kingdom of Lahore, whilst you are mounting you see nothing before you but sterile rocks, but when you have attained the summit you see the sky over your head and the kingdom of Cashmere at your feet." Bember cannot be worse than Adam's Peak, and I am sure that the skies and valleys of Ceylon will bear comparison with those of Cashmere.

Two hours of this excessive fatigue brought us to a small empty bungalow, only four miles from Pallabatula, situated on a little level plain that lay directly in our way. A herd of wild elephants were amusing themselves on this plain. I did not venture to disturb them for two reasons, first I was very tired, and secondly, I was afraid of another life paying the forfeit of our curiosity. When we had occupied the bungalow, and the guide was busy with the preparation of breakfast, they slowly left the plain one after the other, as if recognizing our superior right to occupy it. Before breakfast was ready, I had fallen into a sound sleep, so overcome was I with the fatigue of the morning's travel, and very shortly after the meal had been dispatched, and I had refreshed myself with a contemplative cheroot, I was again "in the arms of Murphy,"* (as Paddy poetically expressed it.)

Before four o'clock in the afternoon our

* Anglicè—Morpheus.

journey was resumed on a road of a precisely similar description to that we had traversed in the morning—Poonchy having kindly informed me that we were now in the district most noted for leopards. A wilder region, I fancy, could scarcely be found in nature. Steep after steep of rocky acclivities was to be surmounted. To our right, at no very considerable distance, rose the mysterious Peak itself, whilst on its summit could be faintly discerned the wooden temple which Budhistic piety had long ages before erected over the sacred foot-impression. Like a child's Swiss cottage, or a fairy-like toy, did the elegant little structure appear, as we got a glimpse of it occasionally through some natural clearing in the woods. Behind us, spread out a large jungle-filled valley, over which the clouds and their shadows chased each other as a gleam of the sun occasionally broke through the gloom around. Many a cloud did we see floating near us, some above, some beneath, for we were now at an altitude of between four and five thousand feet, and the nimbi were numerous in our vicinity. Here all was nature in her wild, rude, elemental simplicity, no trace of man or of his works within our utmost ken, save the baby-like temple perched on the extreme summit; even the very road itself was scooped out of the eternal hill's side by torrents!

Three miles of this travelling, occupying fully two hours, brought us to Deabetme, where a stone bungalow, without doors, which owed its erection to the piety and benevolence of some early king, received us. Here we were obliged to take up our quarters for the night, and more miserable and thoroughly comfortless quarters could not well be found in Ceylon or out of it. Both Poonchy and the coolies were anxious to push on, regarding the station as unlucky; but as there was no better bungalow to be met with as far as the summit, I overruled their objections. The house which we occupied was situated in the centre of a small piece of cleared land, encompassed by thick jungle, which descended steeply on three sides, and on the fourth spread out into a small irregular plain, through which the road wound to an adjoining ravine. When we reached the station, heavy masses of black clouds were forming round the hill on all sides of us. We were in the very centre of the rain-cloud, and everything about us was damp, cold, and comfortless. The loud "hoo-hoo" of a large species of monkey might be distinctly heard in our vicinity; occasionally the growl of a leopard would reach our ears, shrill, sharp, and threatening; whilst more frequently the call of the elephant would boom forth from the surrounding jungle. These were the great guns amongst the incessant small-arms' fire of birds and jackals.

So dense was the watery vapour around, that all our efforts to kindle a fire were unsuccessful. Poonchy's flint and steel were useless, as, notwithstanding his most strenuous exertions, the tinder would not catch the spark. I speedily secured a light by means of a little gunpowder; but a light was not sufficient. An old newspaper would burn at Deabetme as elsewhere, because it had been in my pocket previously; but the wood seemed to have lost its combustible properties completely. So saturated was everything with the enveloping mist, that dried leaves smoked only, and the wood followed their example; but no bright cheerful blaze could be extracted from either, nor was it possible to warm either the provisions or ourselves by means of the smoke, however dense. We had not taken any wood with us, it being usual for parties stopping in these sheds to leave a few boughs behind them for their successors, after they have used all the store which they find in them. The firewood was there, and the fire obtainable; but after using large quantities of gunpowder and paper to no purpose, we were obliged to give up the attempt in despair. I looked upon our want of success as a matter that bore solely upon our dinner; but Poonchy insisted upon it that our safety was at stake as well, for that, in our doorless edifice, the only security we could have, during the long hours of darkness, against snakes, bears, leopards, or even a rogue elephant, was a bright fire—an object which, when blazing in the darkness, effectually scares away the most daring of them.

The prospect of passing the night, therefore, as we were, was a miserable one enough, to say nothing of the danger; and, however good cold ham and bread and beer may be in their proper places, one feels that, with the air around saturated with moisture, the seats and clothing wet, the wind cold and raw, they are decidedly out of place. Yet pass the night there we must, for darkness had already set in, and it would have been madness to have attempted to travel in either direction under those circumstances.

Nothing remained but to make the best dispositions we could for the night. To block up the numerous doorways was impossible, for we had nothing with which to do so; and, as we examined our involuntary lodging more carefully, we found abundant evidence that the place was frequently visited by wild animals. In one corner I discovered a heap of bones, one of which was so remarkably like a human thigh-bone, that the very handling of it gave me an uncomfortable creeping feeling, as if I already felt by anticipation the gnawing of a leopard, polishing off my own. I fancy it must have originally belonged to a monkey: but at the time I certainly thought it was part of a human skeleton, and with that pleasant conviction I laid myself down for the night.

The coolies crowded into a corner, and lay there huddled together, wet and shivering. I put my rifle at my head, leaning against the wall, and kept a good substantial walking-stick, which had considerably aided my ascent, by my side, to be used in case the rifle hung fire, which, from the state of the atmosphere, was but too likely to take place. My couch consisted of a number of split bamboos, interlaced together by strong creepers taken from the jungle, the whole supported, as usual, upon four posts stuck into the damp floor. Suppose an ordinary table, with a number of sharp grooves running lengthways from end to end, a multitude of cords bound round it, and plenty of water sprinkled over it, recently wiped off, and you have a tolerably accurate idea of my couch. On my person, wrapped up in a warm plaid, I kept my ammunition, and, thus prepared, lay down, not to sleep, but to wait for the morning.

It was almost as dark a night as ever brooded over the heavens. Not a star could be seen in the deep blackness that enveloped us on every side. Opposite to the bamboo couch on which I lay, half-reclining, half-sitting, was a small hole in the wall which fronted me, evidently intended, originally, for a window; there was scarcely light enough abroad to enable me to distinguish this aperture at all. When I had lain down, it was, of course, with the intention of not sleeping—indeed, I had slept so much after the severe fatigue of the morning that I had but little desire for it. In order to aid me, however, in keeping my resolution, I placed my brandy-bottle on the ground, at the head of my couch, having filled it with water, so as to make very stiff grog of the contents. But, notwithstanding all the sleep I had had the previous day; notwithstanding the energy thrown into me by the contents of the bottle; notwithstanding the dangerous position I was in, I found myself soon nodding at the little window opposite. Five or six times had I roused myself, and endeavoured to shake off the sleepy god, who was fast seizing upon me, and as I did so, at long intervals, I found that the little window was each time becoming more and more distinct, and that the stars were beginning to make their way through the thick blackness without. At length I dozed off into a half-waking, half-sleeping condition, in which I must have continued for some time—that state in which the soul does not wholly resign her office, but performs it somewhat heavily.

I was aroused from my lethargy by a scraping, stealthy, crawling sort of sound in my vicinity. It was evidently produced by some animal on the ground—I had little doubt at the moment that it was a leopard, or one of those horrid brown bears, of which I had heard so much, and I began to think that a second life would be lost in this ill-fated expedition. I could not at first determine from the sound in what direction the animal was proceeding, but I concluded, after a little, that he was in the neighbourhood of the coolies, and from their heavy breathing, I further concluded that they were asleep. If one of the party was to lose his life, I certainly should have preferred one of the coolies being the individual to myself. My hand was on my rifle, but to fire into the corner would have been madness, to shout out and wake them, useless or worse, for the animal might then feel himself called on to attack —so I awaited, with what coolness I might, the result. Slowly and stealthily, I heard the animal, with great distinctness, crawling from the coolie-quarter in the direction of the little window opposite me. A thousand thoughts flashed rapidly through my mind as I listened, with every nerve strung to its utmost tension, to the sound, peering eagerly, but fruitlessly, into the gloom within the building. At length he neared the aperture opposite, and, as he passed it, a sudden jerk upwards threw his head full into my field of vision, that is, the window. It was not the head of a leopard, nor of a bear, nor of a monkey, though to this last it bore most resemblance, but the head of a man, and, of course, of one of my own coolies, for there were no other human beings nearer than Pallabatula, seven miles distant. Relinquishing the grasp of my rifle, I seized my walking-stick noiselessly, and awaited the result, as yet perfectly ignorant of the fellow's intentions, and unable, indeed, to form any rational prognostication of them. The certainty that it was a man, and, besides, only a Singhalese! was a great relief, and I breathed more freely. It must be remembered that all this time the usual nocturnal din of the jungle was going on outside with unabated fury, and yet so strangely were the nerves affected, that every movement in the bungalow was perfectly distinct to my ears.

I followed the man's motions as if by instinct, as he slowly and stealthily crawled round my couch, and it was not till I heard the shaking of the fluid in my brandy-bottle, that I became aware of his intentions. I brought my stick down heavily upon his back at the moment, uttering some exclamation as I did so. He roared out lustily, and, *miserabile dictu*, let fall the bottle. His cry, loud and piercing, awoke his brethren. They, doubtless, fancying a dozen rogue elephants were upon them, shouted as loudly in chorus—the whole bungalow rung with cries as they still huddled closely together, their fears, probably, increased a thousand fold by finding one of their number absent. He, for his part, lay where he had fallen, still crying as if a wild beast were devouring him. I shouted out, I spoke in English and in Singhalese, I reasoned, I intreated, demanded, nay, I verily believe, I swore at them; but, for a time, without avail. Those in the corner evidently thought their companion was already a meal for some one, and he who lay near my couch probably conceived that I was threatening him for the loss I had sustained. At length he made his way to his fellows; they shrieked distractedly as he touched them; but, after a little, the tumult subsided, and I was heard. I explained to Poonchy (whose voice had been clearly and distinctly recognisable throughout the entire commotion as one of the loudest of the shouters), the cause of the scene, and he, with many contemptuous allusions to their cowardice, explained the matter to them. The moon was now rising over the top of the peak—the vapoury cloud had passed away—our bungalow was soon full of light—we tried the firewood again, and, after some trouble, succeeded in obtaining a blaze, under the genial influence of which we all slept soundly till the morning; visions of the broken brandy-bottle, as it lay scattered over the ground beside my couch, the precious liquid all spilt, alone troubled my repose.

The journey of the ensuing morning did not greatly differ from that of the preceding day, save that it was of a more varied character. In some places we were descending for a short time, instead of ascending—at others, we were obliged to clamber over the faces of almost perpendicular rocks of great altitude. One of these rocks is between fifty and sixty feet high, and its ascent would be impossible, were it not for steps which some of the early kings caused to be cut over the entire face. At length I stood at the foot of the extraordinary cone which forms the summit of the mountain. It rises from the surrounding range like a huge sugar-loaf, two hundred feet high—rocky, and bleak, and stern, with a few hardy and stunted plants of temperate climates clinging to its sides. The air was delightfully cool and refreshing—the view around was magnificent, and, right in front of us, as we eat our morning's meal on a little grassy plot, by the side of a brawling stream, rose the mass of rock, on the top of which, almost a point, the holy footstep is imprinted, surmounted by the picturesque little temple —the same mass that we had seen and gazed upon with such interest at sea, in Galle, in Colombo; everywhere in the island in fact. I felt delighted at the prospect of satisfying my curiosity at length, and even looked benevolently upon the coolie through whom I had lost my brandy!

The ascent of this cone is by no means easy. The steepness of the sides and the force with which the wind whistles round it, at a height approaching to eight thousand feet, are sufficient in themselves to render it anything but an easy matter to make one's way to the top, and were it not for the chains which are hung in some places to facilitate the ascent of the pilgrims, it would be both difficult and dangerous. The road winds up the western side in a zig-zag direction, like a strung series of Z's, consisting of a narrow pathway, formed partly by jutting rocks, and partly by incisions in the mountain's sides. The scrubby European-looking vegetation affords the adventurous traveller a hold occasionally as he passes some parts of unusual difficulty, whilst in others, the vegetation shuts him in completely, and he clambers along up a kind of ravine. In three or four places a smooth rock is to be ascended, which would be a matter of no little difficulty, if not altogether impossible, were it not for the chains I have mentioned, which are firmly rivetted into the rocks above, and let down over the ascent; even with these, however, strength and agility are both required to get up securely and unassisted. The loss of his hold, or an awkward slip, would precipitate the traveller or pilgrim into eternity. Even women, it is said, annually ascend the Peak, in compliance with the dictates of religious enthusiasm, and there is scarcely a dangerous spot in the ascent, of which the guide will not be able to tell you some story connected with the loss of human life, usually females. The year in which our guide had previously ascended, the second before our expedition, two unfortunate female pilgrims had been blown over the side of the hill at one of those frightful corners on the road, where a square foot of rock alone preserves the traveller from destruction. On looking into the abyss below, I could discern a fragment of cloth waving on the gnarled stem of an oak-like bush, far, far, beneath us.

At length I stepped forth from a little entrance in the small wall, built round the hallowed precincts of the foot-impression. I was on the very summit of Adam's Peak, and, in my joy and triumph, I saluted the holy locality with a hearty "hurrah!"

The wall which had been built round the summit is about three feet high, and confines a quantity of earth, forming a pathway round the huge rock in the centre, over which the little temple is built. The temple itself consists merely of a picturesque roof, Chinese looking, supported on strong wooden pillars, and preserved from being blown down by massive iron chains inserted into the rocks around, reminding one of the cords from the top of a tent pole. On the eastern side the pathway is extensive enough to admit of a small bungalow having been erected, in which the priests reside during the period of pilgrimage. Here of course we took up our quarters, and I then proceeded to examine the great object of reverence, to adore which the enthusiastic natives encounter so many dangers. The sacred footstep is emphatically a humbug—a humbug of humbugs in fact. I had expected to find it something approaching a humbug, but not so egregious a one, as it proved to be. All that exists naturally in the rock, is two oval cavities, about two feet from each other, one of which some vivid Eastern imagination conjured into a heel, the other into the impression of the ball of the foot—all the rest is evidently artificial—too evidently to leave the shadow of a doubt on the subject in the beholder's mind—the toes indeed are made with coarse lime or chunam, and, were it not for a border of the same, the outline of a foot would never be recognized. The extreme length of this "faint exaggeration of a footstep," as it has been happily called, is five feet three inches, its breadth varying from two feet five to two feet nine inches.

Nothing could be more bracing and delightful than the temperature at this great altitude. I felt it cold of course, but the thermometer, which I carried with me, did not descend lower than 47° during the day and night I was on the summit—a sufficient contrast from the 80° and 90° I had been lately experiencing in Colombo. The coolies, having first devoutly worshipped towards the "sri-pada," or holy footstep, but without venturing to examine it too closely, next proceeded to kindle a fire, and in a few minutes a cheerful blaze shone through the thatched walls of the little priest's bungalow. The natives were not accustomed to use a fire for warmth, and, as they crouched before it, they found doubtless to their annoyance that it did not warm their backs equally with the fronts of their bodies, and in order to secure a little of the genial heat for all, to my surprise, on entering, when I had finished my examination of the summit, I found them gyrating on their heels, like so many monkeys being roasted.

The night passed away without any incident of importance, and next morning I witnessed a scene which fully repaid me for all my previous toils—the rising of the sun. It was certainly the most magnificent sight I have ever witnessed. When I rose in the morning all was black below, nothing whatever could be distinguished, except a few streaks of light in the East. Gradually the rays shot further and further over the sky, and at length, standing in the foot-impression, on the highest pinnacle of the summit, I could discern a small portion of the sun himself. Still everything around and beneath was dark—the sky alone glowing with light, but all below like a vast black ocean of the most forbidding character. At length a hill in our vicinity was touched by the rays, and there, in the gloom, it shone and glistened like a piece of burnished gold in a sea of pitch. Another and another mountain top caught the glow and stood prominently forth, shining gorgeously in the surrounding darkness. And so it went on—the shining islands ever increasing in size and becoming more numerous until nothing remained dark but the valleys between the highest hills, whilst the various tints of the clouds that hung on the mountain sides added a peculiar charm to the landscape. I could at length discover the Indian ocean to the west and south, and more than half the island was laid open, as in a vast panorama, to my inspection. To witness the rising of the sun from the summit of Adam's Peak, is a sight worth living and toiling for, and once witnessed, can never be forgotten—the impression, vivid almost as the reality, will live in the memory, however far we may be removed from the mountain in distance, or from the scene itself by time.

In the vast landscape that was thus spread out before me standing on that solitary cone, a mile and a-half in perpendicular height, from the level of the sea, I was particularly struck by the absence of any trace of man. Not a single object which I could discern around or below recalled him or his works—all was nature in its highest and grandest sense. The thick forests that filled the valleys; the rocks, massive, bleak, and stern, that marked the hills' sides; the rivers or streams winding like threads of silver through the green or brown beneath; the clouds white, grey, and black, that dotted the landscape here and there—all was nature, and nature only, without being interfered with or marred by man. The scene reminded me of an eloquent passage in Jouffroy's works, in which he says:—"In the bosom of cities, man appears to be the principal concern of creation; his apparent superiority is there most signally displayed; he there seems to preside over the theatre of the world, or rather to occupy it himself. But when this being, so haughty, so powerful, so absorbed by his own interests in the crowds of cities, and in the midst of his fellows, chances to be brought into a vast and majestic scene of nature in view of the illimitable firmament, surrounded by the works of creation, which overwhelm him, if not by their intelligence at least by their magnitude; when from the summit of a mountain, or under the light of the stars, he beholds petty villages, lost in forests, which themselves are lost in the extent of the prospect, and reflects that these villages are inhabited by frail and imperfect beings like himself; when he compares these beings and their abodes with the magnificent spectacle of external nature: when he compares this with the world, on whose surface it is but a point, and this world, in its turn, with the myriads of worlds that are suspended above him, and before which it is nothing—in the presence of such a spectacle, he views with pity the miserable conflicting passions of his fellow-man."

On returning to Pallabatula I found Hofer anxiously awaiting me. He had prepared a chair for himself, in which he was to be carried back to Ratnapoora—two bamboos being merely attached to it, one at each side of the seat, and thus he hoped to make the journey, hoisted on the shoulders of four coolies. The coolies were relieved every mile or so, and a dozen of them contrived to carry him safely, though slowly, along, so that we arrived at Ratnapoora, where our horses awaited us, without accident.

CHAPTER VIII.

A PLANTER'S PARTY.

> "Which is the villain? Let me see his eyes;
> That when I note another man like him,
> I may avoid him."
>
> *Much Ado About Nothing*, act v., sc. 1.

NOTWITHSTANDING the great distances of the various plantations from each other, the *réunions* of their owners and managers were common and frequent. In the idle season of the year Europeans were to be seen riding about in all directions through the miserable native paths, over districts which, anywhere else, would be declared impassable for horses. But no district was regarded as of this description in Ceylon, save the ascent of the Peak. Some would be encountered making their way to Colombo, for supplies of provisions or money; some on the road to Kandy; others going to visit a friend, or to spend a week on the table-land in the south-east, called Newera Ellia—a delightful retreat amongst the mountains from the heat and monotony of the plains. Between 1843 and 1847 the cultivation of coffee was so rapidly extending on the island, as to promise the happiest results from the large influx of Europeans and of European capital.

Many estates were opened only to be sold again as soon as they came into bearing, to some one of the many capitalists who determined on embarking their money in the speculation, and in this way perhaps, there was more profit made than in any other. When a piece of land judiciously selected, was cleared of forest and planted with coffee, there were always buyers to be found, ready to give a much larger sum for the infant estate than it had cost —men, for the most part, quite ignorant of the details of cultivation themselves, and who preferred trusting the judgment of others, whom they supposed to know something of the matter. The risks attending the culture of the shrub are considerable, and it is not, therefore, to be wondered at that very frequently excellent properties were thus brought into the market, the owners of which preferred realizing a profit at once to running the various risks of blights, coffee bugs, and rats, which often appeared and disappeared unaccountably.

The Parala estate, on which my friend Fowler was situated pretty much in the same way as I on the one which I managed, that is, as superintendent and part proprietor, was nearly twenty miles distant. It consisted of five hundred acres of coffee, and about one thousand of forest land, up to this time untouched. It was a flourishing property, although it had recently been attacked by the rats, in the same unaccountable way as many other estates in the neighbourhood—the vermin having appeared and disappeared without any one being able to explain either where they had come from, or whither they had gone. However, that they had gone was certain, and no one in our district wished for their return merely that the scientific mystery should be cleared up. By nibbling at the new shoots of the stems and branches, they had injured thousands of plants and destroyed several, so that we were quite willing to rest ignorant of their whereabouts, rather than to encounter them again, to have our theories on the subject confirmed or disproved.

Notwithstanding such drawbacks as these,

however, Fowler's estate, like most others in the neighbourhood, was flourishing. The cultivation was everywhere extending, and the future of Ceylon looked bright and cheerful for it was never supposed that the tariff, on the faith of which all this outlay was made, all this capital embarked, would be suddenly, and without warning, altered. It was by the help of the protective duties on colonial produce alone that Ceylon was enabled to compete with Brazil and Java, and the anticipation that those duties would be removed had probably not entered into the head of a single speculator in Ceylon. At the time of which I write all was bright in the prospect, and there can be no doubt that fifty years of such prosperity would have infused the new life and vigour of the West into the oriental lethargy of the island. The trackless forests would have been reclaimed, man taking the place of the wild beast. Happy homes and smiling faces would have been seen where now the elephant and leopard roam undisturbed. The high lands, so admirably adapted to the European constitution, would doubtless be the homes of English farmers and gardeners, and Christian hymns ascend as thank-offerings from Christian hearts in places hitherto trodden only by the wandering savages, who, under the name of Veddahs, lead a kind of wild-beast life in the forests of Ceylon. True, there is little prospect at present of such ultimate results speedily appearing, but then I saw no reason to doubt their complete realization.

Under such circumstances, with increased facilities for rapid communication with England, I could scarcely picture to myself a happier lot than that of the successful planter, living upon and working his own estate, with his family flourishing around him, spending the cooler portion of the year with them on his own property, and the warmer on some of the elevated tablelands of the south-east. But we were only the pioneers, I knew, of whose labours others must reap the advantage in comfort and plenty, and, as things were, it was not to be wondered at that most married men should feel discontented with their Ceylon life, as Hofer evidently soon began to feel, but I doubted not then, that ultimately all that I have shadowed forth, and more, would be accomplished.

Nothing could be more various than the dress and appearance of us, coffee-planters in Ceylon. Every man's clothes were cut after his own fashion; some consulting ease and appearance, but the majority ease alone, in their habiliments. A short coat, not likely to impede or incommode one in the saddle; a black belt to support the pantaloons, and no waistcoat, were the most ordinary forms into which planting *insouciance* moulded its clothes. But, above all, were we distinguished by our diligent eschewing of the ugly black European hat. In Colombo, and indeed in the towns generally, this extraordinary appendage, so unsuited to a tropical climate, still maintained, and doubtless does maintain, its place, but the race of planters was wiser than to incommode itself by any such absurdity. The substitutes for it were as various as the tastes of the wearers, and the ingenuity of the workmen. Of these substitutes, of which the great majority were formed of pith, some resembled copper boilers reversed, in shape, with broad brims, and innumerable air-holes at the top; others, helmet-fashioned, had a peak in front and a wadded apron behind, just (as far as shape is concerned) as if a child's pinafore had been tied behind upon a jockey's cap, the object of this extraordinary curtain being to defend the back of the neck from the sun; others projected from the head outrageously, caldron-fashion, as if the unfortunate individual had fallen, head foremost, into a whitewashed wooden washing basin, and, having made his way half through it, had there been fixed immovably; whilst not a few recalled to one's mind the helmet of Mambrino in Don Quixote. The hirsute faces, for I need scarcely say that few of us took the trouble to disfigure ourselves by shaving—the hirsute faces and strangely-equipped figures which appeared under these extraordinary head-coverings, formed as striking a contrast as can well be conceived, with what the same individuals would present in Rotten Row or Regent Street.

Our host Fowler, with whom Hofer and myself had become quite intimate, was a superior and an estimable man, disguising under a fierce, bushy black beard, of the most warlike appearance, great amiability and benevolence. His acquaintance Siggins, from a neighbouring plantation, was a strange character, one of those extraordinary compounds who affect singularity in the most trivial matters, and who seem to consider it a sufficient reason for doing anything, that no one else would think of doing so, or, for leaving it undone, that other people would do it. His intensely red whiskers and moustaches beautifully harmonised in colour with by far the most prominent and peculiar feature of his countenance—his nose; in shape the organ was a Brougham, but in size and colour it differed materially from the standard of the type, projecting and peering upwards in awful contrast with the glistening glasses of the spectacles which were almost constantly above it. Like its prototype too, Siggins' remarkable nose was never at rest—at one time the observer might suppose it was holding discourse knowingly with one eye, at another that it was setting, in a facial quadrille, to one of the corners of the mouth. Now it was drooping, with melancholy despondency over the fiery moustache and ample lips, and, anon, it was raised twitchingly aloft as if internally singing an "Io triumphe" in gratitude for some recent blessing—depressed or elevated, however, in converse with one side or the other of the mouth, it still twitched convulsively as such a nose only could twitch, its colour at one moment scarcely crimson, whilst during the next it had mounted into an ample purple that threatened the precincts of the eyes with invasion. Long locks of light brown hair, straight as a ship's masts, hung over Siggins' coat collar, and formed an agreeable contrast with the glowing face. Imagine, reader, such a head mounted to a height of six feet two, upon an ungainly awkward body, and you have the individual daguerreotyped in your mind's eye.

Besides these, there were a taciturn merchant from Colombo, Mr. Smith, not long settled in the island, and an officer of the Rifle-corps, a descendant of a Dutch family, Lieut. Vanstrut, who was justly proud of his uniform, which he would not part with, even in the jungle—justly proud I say of his uniform, for he had nothing else to be proud of. He happened to be on a visit to Fowler at the time, who was under some obligations to his family, or he certainly would not have been a member of a convivial jungle party.

These were all strangers to me, and therefore I have taken the trouble to say a word or two respecting each; but, besides these, there were Mouat and Hofer—the latter had quite recovered from the injury done to his foot, when ascending the Peak. I was sorry to see Hofer there—not that I thought married men should eschew bachelor's parties, but that it seemed to me a sort of neglect to his lonely and beautiful wife, to leave her thus constantly by herself in the jungle—as he did at this period indeed, but too frequently. A childless home is, alas! likely to be an unhappy one, even under the most favourable circumstances, how much more so when thus isolated in the midst of the jungle! True she was the first, as I had seen, to urge him to seek enjoyment elsewhere; always cheerful, always apparently happy, and what between her household duties, her studies, her practice of painting and music, and her benevolent journeys, invariably professing her perfect happiness and contentment, whether her husband remained with her or not, but must not the quick eye of love have speedily discovered what was apparent even to the casual glance of the stranger? If Fowler and I could perceive and lament that he was now fonder of absence from home than he had been, how much more keenly must she have felt it! Who shall tell, I thought, as I rode home the next morning with him, how many bitter, salt tears have coursed each other down her cheeks during his absence! how many sighs of regret have burst from that heaving bosom, as thoughts of home and past happiness have moved the heart!

And yet, to all outward seeming, he was still the same affectionate husband he had been, and the few with whom they were intimate, but who did not observe them so closely as we did, would, probably, nay almost certainly, conclude that a happier, more loving, more contented couple than the Hofers did not exist. How false a test outward seeming is of real happiness! How small a portion the outward visible calamity woman has to bear, forms of the sorrow which her heart mourns over! How many a smiling face, particularly in her case, hides an aching heart! How fatal a blessing is not that sensibility, that sentiment, which forms one of her chief charms, and constitutes frequently, at the same time, her greatest source of misery!

It must not be concluded from this that Hofer was gloomy and his wife querulous. By no means! He was still hopeful, full of life, and joy, and vigour, as when I first met him in Colombo. He still paid every attention to his wife, anticipated her wants only to supply them, was tender, affectionate, nay loving in his manner, and she before him, and his friends, and all the world, was still the same bright, cheerful, beautiful model of womanly grace and womanly fondness she had been, when we travelled together from Colombo. But he, unfortunately, wanted determination and a strong will, and, as a necessary consequence, perseverance. Change and variety were cravings of his nature which he had not learned to direct or to subdue. New schemes and new plans were ever luring him on to short bursts of exertion, and to him the greatest of evils was monotony and uniformity. One would have fancied that his wanderings over the world, in Europe, in America, in Asia, would have satisfied this roving, change-loving disposition, but it was not so. With strong intellect, a brilliant imagination, and a cultivated mind, he wanted that resolute will which is necessary to success and happiness—without which, indeed, the most shining qualities are but sources of inconvenience, nay, possibly, causes of unhappiness. Who can over-estimate the importance of this quality, and yet how shamefully is its cultivation neglected in our youthful studies and training? What greater enemy can man have, as an individual or a community, than a restless, ever-acting desire of change? the peevishness of the child who tires of one toy and cries for another, carried into the important business of life and cankering the fair buds of happiness which the sunshine of home and the tender gardening of woman, cause to flourish so luxuriantly around us. The gourd that arrived at maturity in a night perished in a day, as Burke somewhere remarks, but the oak that will last for centuries takes a hundred years of patient persevering growth to arrive at maturity.

Let me turn, however, from these melancholy reflections to what I intended to describe. Our party was at first a right pleasant and merry one, and the fare of the best that the jungle could afford. European condiments here, as indeed all over the East, amongst Englishmen, being the most highly esteemed. A good ham, or a fresh cheese giving exquisite delight to men who would seldom taste either the one or the other at home perhaps, whilst the richest curries and the most luscious tropical fruits, were despised in comparison. I have so frequently seen this the case in India, that I at length ceased to wonder at it; yet surely it was notable! The very difficulty of procuring the most ordinary European articles of food in an eatable condition, seemed to render them luxuries to the epicurean palate, whilst tropical dainties, that would infallibly be luxuries in

England, were neglected because too easily obtained. A type this, I fear, of humanity everywhere. The blessing which costs us little to reach, either of exertion or of wealth, is often thrown aside for the inferior gratification to which a difficulty in procuring it has added a zest.

How many are there not in London, surrounded by comforts and luxuries of the most intensely gratifying character, who regard themselves as miserable because they want some trifle which they cannot obtain! They take up their 'Times' daily, and receive their letters almost every hour, without ever asking themselves how they would do without either for weeks together. They can obtain their dinners in every street almost, and sit down to them grumbling, without ever reflecting that the planter has often to ride twenty miles, and even then perhaps finds his dinner not ready when he requires it. They lounge in their easy chairs before a grateful, cheerful-looking fire, with a magazine or a review, or the last lionized book of the season in their hands, without bestowing a thought on the grilling to which Anglo-Indians are exposed, the hosts of musquitoes they must encounter, or the snakes, scorpions, and centipedes of which they daily and nightly, stand, and walk, and sleep in dread. But there is no use in pursuing the reflection; the Londoner is doubtless already blushing at his ingratitude so I shall e'en spare him.

The more serious business of the dinner dispatched, we almost naturally fell into a conversation about coolies; a comparison between the Malabar coolies from the continent and the native Kandians, forming a point for discussion. All were willing to yield the palm to the Kandians in many respects, but Hofer and myself alone maintained their superior honesty, which the others were inclined to doubt.

"I think the Kandians are stronger and work more like men," said Siggins, the nose rising perceptibly towards the forehead, "that is, with the help of a little looking after, and occasionally feeling a riding-whip or a cane, but although the Malabars are great scoundrels and thieves, I think the Kandians are greater."

"You are complimentary to them," said I, looking at Fowler's Kandian servant, who was in the room at the time, and who perfectly understood English, but, although he had evidently listened to the observation, not a muscle on his countenance, not so much as the involuntary winking of his eyes showed that he had heard it.

"Why I take care not to let them have their own way, and they soon get used to mine," answered Siggins, his nasal organ effecting a bend sinister. "Every man is a magistrate on his own estate, you know," he continued, "and therefore, as long as the man is working for you, you have a right to do what you like with him—that is, anything short of killing."

"A new doctrine, truly," said Mouat, coming as near a laugh as he ever permitted himself, "but one very often acted upon, I believe."

"Always acted on by men of sense, Mr. Mouat," rejoined Siggins. "How are you or any other magistrate to know what goes on on my estate, for instance?"

"Did I know all that goes on, on any estate, even on my benevolent friend Fowler's, I fear it would not be very edifying—what think you, Hofer?" asked the little magistrate.

"I quite agree with you," replied Hofer, "the distinction between *mea* and *tua* I fear, is little recognized on these bachelors' estates, whatever may be said of *meum* and *tuum*."

"That it should be all *mea* and no *tua* would be perhaps Mr. Siggins' idea," said Mouat again.

"I don't remember much of the Latin I learned at school," rejoined Siggins, the nose waxing purple by degrees, "but I think I can understand what you mean. I go by this rule —if a man on my estate tells me yes, I believe he would say no if he dare, and until I look and discover, or find out the truth some other way, I pay no attention to his yes. Now that saves a great deal of trouble."

"You never believe then what one of your labourers says?" I asked.

"Never," said he, "I never believe what any man about the place says until I look at it, and see for myself. They know that now, and they don't venture to tell me the barefaced lies they used, and it is not often that I find any opposition made to anything I wish, but when I do, they smart for it, I assure you."

"Very extraordinary this in an English colony," said Mr. Smith.

"Siggins understands the native character," said Vanstrut, arranging his collar, "and treats the people very properly."

"I cannot say I approve of the principle," said Hofer, "but really it is very hard to keep one's temper with them sometimes."

"Impossible, Sir, quite impossible," said Siggins, eagerly, "they are worthless, thoroughly worthless—the fear of the whip or the cane is the only thing that rouses them to exertion."

"There you are certainly mistaken, Mr. Siggins," said Fowler, firmly, "men who travel hundreds of miles on foot, through the most unfrequented forests and jungles in order to earn their bread honestly by the sweat of their brow, are not thoroughly worthless, and can evidently be driven to exertion by far other motives than the fear of the lash."

You are right, Fowler," said Hofer; "in that point of view they deserve every praise and commendation—they make great sacrifices that they may carry home a trifle to their homes, and instances of the most unselfish and noble devotion are frequent amongst them."

"It was but in the last gang that I hired," said Fowler, "that a wife preferred remaining behind to perish with her sick husband in the depths of the forest, to pushing on for life with the gang."

"Stuff!" said Siggins, "all sham, every bit of it. Just you try kindness, and see how you'll get on with your work. I tried it when I first came here, five years ago, and I got nothing done, I promise you."

"Why you were up before me, and fined three times during the first two years," said Mouat, "do you call that the result of your kindness?"

"Yes," said Siggins, "I was green, and did'nt know what was what. But you'll not catch me up before you, or any one else, for the future. I manage matters better than that now."

"One of my peons told me of some frightful flogging that one of your fellows got on your estate the other day," said Mouat, "but as it did not come before me officially, of course I took no notice of it—planters and magistrates should mutually support and assist each other; but it shows that these things are spoken of."

"Did he," said Siggins, angrily, "I'm glad you told me. It was a simple affair enough. I honoured the rascal's daughter with a little attention—she was a fair, neatly-formed Kandian girl—and he sulked about it, although he had been regularly employed on my place for three years. In fact, he grew at length so insolent, that he came and demanded her out of the bungalow, where she was living infinitely more decently and respectably than ever she had been living before. The servants had particular orders, of course, that she should not leave. I told him his request was absurd, and he then took to crying. I laughed at him as any one else would do, and he then grew angry and swore at me. That was too much, so ordering him up in the verandah, he had two dozen—he should have had four, but the daughter broke away from the servants inside, when she heard him crying out, and, throwing herself at my feet, begged mercy for him, so I let him go. As he left the verandah, however, he turned and swore at me again, talking of the magistrate, so I had him up once more, and whilst he was getting another dozen and his daughter was being locked up again, I sent for the head-man of the village, to whom I gave a few rupees, and told him that if I had any more trouble from that fellow, I should never hire a man from his village again. He promised I should hear no more of him, and took him off."

"Good God," said I, "is it possible that any

man can, not only do such things, but have the hardihood to relate them before the magistrate, whose duty it is to investigate and punish such crimes?"

"If Mr. Siggins has done as he states, I undoubtedly condemn it," said Mouat, turning his cold, impassive eyes on me; "but, at the same time, I am not bound to take advantage of what I hear privately, at my friend's table, to punish one of his guests."

"It is a horrible circumstance," said Hofer; "and had I had the heart to do it, I should have been ashamed to relate it."

"Very possibly," said Siggins, coolly; "you are both comparatively new here—not much more than a twelvemonth in the jungle yet: a few years will make you less nice."

A silence of some minutes succeeded this observation, during which I reasoned within myself whether I should not urge Mouat to take notice of the matter judicially. Hofer evidently guessed my thoughts, for he shook his head in a deprecatory way; and feeling assured that the sense of the party was against the interference, I said no more. Mouat saw the shake of the head, and probably understood its import, saying, "I regard this relation in the light of a private friendly piece of gossip, not serious; but if any one chooses to come to the court-house to-morrow, and swear that such things took place at Pallagolly, I shall investigate the matter fully."

"Bravo! Mouat," said Siggins, laughing heartily.

"It is sometimes a dangerous matter for gentlemen to take to thrashing their servants," said Mouat, continuing, "as our friend Vanstrut can testify."

Vanstrut showed, by the sheepish way in which he played with a gold cable that hung round his neck in lieu of a watch-guard, that he fully understood the allusion, but by no means relished it.

"Ah—a-hem," said he; "I have no sympathy with the Kandians or Malabars at all. They're both equally bad. Siggins was quite right, hang me if he wasn't."

Now considering that it was commonly reported that Vanstrut's grandmother was a Kandian lady of some rank, this remark was intolerable.

"But why can Vanstrut testify as you say?" asked I of Mouat, to the former gentleman's great uneasiness.

"Why really, after Siggins's very *mal-apropos* narrative, I don't think I can do better than show that the tables are sometimes turned," said Mouat, with his peculiar eye-twinkle. "Vanstrut, it appears, when he first joined the Rifles in Colombo, had a big Malabar horse-keeper, Thuru by name—wasn't it Thuru?"

"Yes, Thuru," said Vanstrut, with some slight symptom of energy in his language; "as great a scoundrel as ever rubbed down a horse."

"Doubtless," continued Mouat; "well, his name was Thuru. Vanstrut had, moreover, an unfortunate habit of horsewhipping his offending servants, which, in the more civilized parts of our noble island, often got him into trouble. One day Thuru had neglected something, or, which was nearly the same thing in its consequences, Vanstrut fancied so, and accordingly gave him a harmless horsewhipping, not exceeding, I believe, in the castigation by any means the limits of moderation. Some of the servants were present, however; and Thuru, who was a favourite, and knew what his rights were, went off to the police magistrate's court, and made his deposition; the other servants were summoned as witnesses. The case was clearly proved; and to make an example of the military offender, Vanstrut was fined five pounds—a sum which he would willingly pay any day for a little gratification."

"Certainly," said Vanstrut, proudly; "a mere trifle. Who wouldn't pay as much for a little gratification, as Mouat says?"

"But our friend was not content," continued Mouat; "he thought Thuru had the advantage of him, as the correction given was inadequate to the price paid: so he sent for Thuru, told him it was all forgiven, and hired him again."

The smile which diffused itself over the coxcombical countenance of Vanstrut showed that he rejoiced in the recollection of this clever procedure.

"One day," proceeded Mouat, "Thuru was alone in the kitchen, and Vanstrut, seizing his whip and the opportunity at the same time, marched down from the house. Shutting the door, he advanced to Thuru, brandishing the whip. 'Now, you scoundrel,' said he, 'no one shall see it, and I'll give you a thrashing you'll remember. I've sent all the servants out of the way, and you shall feel somewhat more than you did before.'—'Stop, mahathma,' said Thuru, beseechingly; 'no hit me; master, forgive all.'—'Yes, you scoundrel, till I could get an opportunity, but no longer,' answered Vanstrut, closing up.—'Stop, mahathma,' urged Thuru again, his hands joined in front in the attitude of prayer. 'Master send all servants 'way?'—'Yes, you rascal,' said Vanstrut, bringing his whip down on the bare shoulder of the suppliant. But now came Thuru's turn. Leaping on his master, whom he speedily overpowered, he seized the riding-whip, a remarkably heavy one, and made it come into intimate acquaintance with his master's body. Vanstrut was thrown down amongst black pots and earthenware dishes, and then, for full five minutes, as he himself afterwards related whilst still sore from the thrashing, did Thuru vigorously ply the whip, proving his muscular force and his dexterity at the same time, for he left no marks upon any uncovered portion of our friend's body. At length, wearied with his exertion, or afraid of interruption, for he swore afterwards that the mahathma had roared like a bull—"

"An infernal lie," said Vanstrut.

"Wearied with his exertion, I say," continued Mouat, "or afraid of interruption, Thuru ceased, and was speedily at a considerable distance from his master's house, where he did not again venture to make his appearance. Vanstrut had him arrested, and the case came before the magistrate, greatly to Thuru's consternation; but a little cross-examination brought out the whole story, and Vanstrut got laughed at into the bargain, whilst Thuru escaped with flying colours. Indeed, Lister told me that 'Thuru' is still a standing toast at the Rifle mess."

"No, no," said the gallant officer, quickly; "they do sometimes quiz a little about it, but that's all—not a standing toast, certainly. Do you know," he continued, more solemnly, "I have been very near going out with some of our fellows about this very affair; and when they saw I really did intend it, there was less talking than there used to be."

The former part of the evening had been pleasant and vivacious, but after this the merriment ceased, and the party soon broke up. Siggins' horrible narrative had completely destroyed our pleasure, and Fowler and Hofer, I thought, as well as our Colombo friend, Mr. Smith, shared in the general indignation. I felt a loathing for the man and his coarse humour, such as I do not remember having ever felt before for any person with whom I had been brought into such close connexion, and it was a relief to me when he was gone. I remained at Fowler's that night, who accommodated Hofer and myself with such extempore beds as a coffee-planter's bungalow could afford. I was astonished at Mouat's taking no further measures to punish so detestable a piece of cruelty; but, strange to say, on mentioning my impressions on the subject to Hofer, he did not agree with me. He condemned the transaction as one of wanton cruelty, "but," said he, "it is quite a Quixotic idea to suppose that a magistrate is to be a hunter-out of criminals in his private meetings with his friends. He is, naturally anxious to stand well with the planters, and such a procedure as you advocate on his part, would destroy all confidence between both parties. Looking at it abstractedly, as a question of right and wrong, you are, doubtless, on the safe side; but other things must be taken into consideration. If the head-man and the people in the village have combined to defeat the ends of justice, you would find that Mouat's exertions would be useless, and so he, doubtless, thinks himself." These arguments were by no means satisfactory to me, nor did Mouat, in my mind, stand absolved from a gross dereliction of his duty; but, on subsequently sending to the village, and afterwards going myself, I found that Hofer was partially right. No evidence to convict Siggins of the crime could be collected, nor could I even discover, after the most diligent investigation, the injured Kandian whom Siggins had treated so barbarously. Had Mouat himself, however, armed with all the authority of the law, undertaken the investigation, there can be little doubt that the result would have been very different.

CHAPTER IX.

SPORTING—ELKS AND ELEPHANTS.

"Come, shall we go and kill us venison?
And yet it irks me, the poor dappled fools,
Being native burghers of this desert city,
Should, in their own confines, with forked heads,
Have their round haunches gored."

As You Like It, act ii., sc. 1.

It was some time after the incidents related in the last chapter had occurred, that Hofer assembled a shooting party at his bungalow for a few days' sport. His estate was situated in a fine district for the purpose, as wild and jungly as the most inveterate hunter could desire. The party consisted of Captain Lister, and a young officer he had brought with him, who had only just arrived in Ceylon, of the name of Sparks—Lister as thorough an elephant-killer as any of the most experienced sportsmen in the island, and Sparks as green a griffin as ever landed in Colombo, and that is saying much; Mouat, and Fowler, and myself completed the party—all three pretending to some little skill with the rifle, but all equally willing to give the palm to Lister, and to be guided by his experience.

The day of our arrival was spent in an inspection of the estate, each of us having a separate opinion to offer relative to Hofer's new schemes and improvements. Beaters were sent out to look after the elephants, that is, natives whose duty it was to drive away any herd that they might find towards the neighbourhood in which we intended to shoot on the succeeding day; and in the meantime we sat down to dinner—such a dinner as men among the mountains can alone enjoy. Not that there was any extraordinary delicacy forthcoming, far from it; the meal was but plain and substantial; but the excellent appetite our walks had given us, and the cordiality which prevailed amongst the little party, all tended to make it such a dinner as one does not readily forget. Nor must I omit the perfect grace and elegance with which our hostess played her part—the solitary flower amongst so stubbly a forest. Her influence was happily felt in adding a charm and refinement to the entertainment, which the want of female society in the jungle generally, makes one feel all the more keenly and sensitively. There is something new to planters, accustomed to their own bungalows for years, and their neighbours' bachelor parties, in finding themselves once more seated near the highest form of civilized life, a cultivated woman. There is an insensible charm diffused over the table and through the air by the presence of one whose refinement pervades at once the bungalow itself and the minutest details of the arrangements in it, that must be felt to be understood.

In the course of conversation, after Mrs. Hofer had left the table, I heard Sparks asking our host whether there were any bread-fruit trees near his estate, and expressing his anxiety to see one.

"Certainly," said Hofer; "we passed several of them to-day—if you come out with me early to-morrow morning, we can bring home some fruit for breakfast."

"I shall be delighted," said Sparks; "but you don't mean to say that you eat it instead of bread?"

"You shall judge for yourself whether it can be so eaten," was the reply; "but you must be aware that out in the jungle here we have great difficulty in getting any bread at all, save what we make ourselves, or procure from the tree."

"Is it possible?" asked Sparks.

"A little roasting," continued Hofer, "to put a crust on it is sufficient to convince you that it is really from the oven."

It was evident that poor Sparks had to pay the usual penalty of griffin-hood, in being deceived to the utmost possible extent that the knowing ones could accomplish. Mouat chimed in with Hofer, assuring Sparks, with the greatest coolness, of the superiority of a bread-fruit for breakfast to the best possible loaf from a baker's, "although, indeed," he added, "you new-comers are so prejudiced in your taste that I have seen men declare it was watery and insipid. Of its nutritious qualities, however, there cannot be a question—indeed, you have only to look at our friend Lister for a proof, for every one knows he was as spare as I am when he first came out, and that the diligent use of bread-fruit alone has made him what he is."

Lister was earnestly describing to Fowler, at the moment, some elephant adventure, and Mouat knew, therefore, that he was safe, whilst

Sparks considered the subject too delicate a one to question his superior officer about.

At half past five the next morning I heard Hofer and Mouat bustling about and getting Sparks out. I quickly joined them, to see what would be made of the joke, and we took the road through the estate where the coolies were just commencing work. A quarter of an hour's good walking brought us within sight of a bread-fruit tree, on which I could distinguish some white fruit, new to my eye, and, as I felt assured, to the tree also. Hofer pointed it out to Sparks—"There is the fruit, you see, quite ripe."

"Very extraordinary, indeed," replied the young officer; "it looks from this exactly like bread. I read somewhere or other that the fruit was green; I am sure I did," he added, giving his companions a searching look.

"You have only to look at the tree," said Mouat, "to see the green fruit in abundance; there are only three or four perfectly ripe, and in a few months there won't be a single ripe fruit on it. That's the cause of the mistake, I dare say, You can have no idea," he added confidentially, "of the mistakes people make in writing about Ceylon. Why, there's one author—I forget his name—that mentions Ruminacaddee as being a few miles from Galle."

"Perhaps there's another village there," suggested Sparks, "of the same name."

"Nothing of the kind," was the reply; "but let us have some fruit for breakfast, Hofer; you know I am very fond of it."

A coolie was called, who from his proximity to us, and the distance at which he was working from the rest, had, I suspected, been stationed there for the purpose, and was told to throw us down three of the ripe "loaves."

The coolie brought down three specimens of the extraordinary fruit, as he had been ordered, and I found, on inspecting them, that they were really and truly loaves of bread, the crust having been scraped off, and something of the form of the fruit itself given to them, whilst tender shoots were ingeniously fastened into the end. They were almost saturated with dew, and on this account, differed sufficiently in taste from the ordinary dry loaf of the table to render the deception complete to the senses of so credulous a man as Sparks.

"You don't like the taste, I see," said Mouat to him; "but you must remember they require a little baking, and then you'll enjoy them."

"It is a wonderful production," exclaimed Sparks; "one would scarcely believe it. If one were to tell this in England he would be laughed at."

"Mention it in your next letter home," said Hofer, "and see with what incredulity the information will be received."

The coolie shouldered his little basket, and conveyed the extraordinary fruit to the bungalow.

No sooner had we been seated at breakfast than Mrs. Hofer asked the appoo, or butler, who was waiting at table, what they had been doing with the bread to disfigure it that way, pointing to the "fruit." The appoo was silent, and looked at his master, whilst Sparks, who was sitting near the lady, laughed out at the inquiry, and exclaimed, "I see you don't know the bread-fruit, then, long as you have been here—ha! ha!"

"Bread-fruit!" echoed Mrs. Hofer, whilst her husband and Mouat diligently attended to their breakfast alone. Sparks handed over the plate, and the lady, cutting one of the "fruit," assured him that those were not bread-fruit, but loaves; "although how they came into their present condition," she added, "I cannot tell." The appoo was at the moment out of the room.

"We gathered them from the tree this morning," said Sparks, "and they have only been roasted since."

It was impossible to keep one's countenance, so ludicrous was the contrast between Sparks' self-satisfied confidence and Mrs. Hofer's amazement. Even she laughed, but soon checked herself.

"When people are new to Ceylon, Mr. Sparks," said she, "it is considered quite allowable—nay, commendable—to deceive them in every possible way. Those are not bread-fruit, but loaves that have been partially wetted and then baked again, the crust having first been removed. But you are not singular in being so taken in; I have heard of the joke having been played off before, although I have never been a witness to it. Mr. Mouat, I think, first mentioned it to me."

"Yes," said the worthy magistrate, "such things have been done before, and will again. It is the penalty one pays for griffinage."

"And is the more successful," added the

lady, "the more amiable and confiding the party imposed upon."

"It is well I did not write home and mention the matter," said Sparks, "as I should have done, Mrs. Hofer, had it not been for your goodness in undeceiving me."

Shortly after breakfast we were all in the jungle, and had some good sport with the birds, but, strange to say, not a wild quadruped was to be seen, and there was as yet no news from our elephant-beaters. Hofer and Lister were both equally surprised and disappointed, and proposed returning to the bungalow, for which purpose we commenced ascending a steep hill near us, the native attendants in the rear, and our host in front. He had not proceeded far, when, whispering an "elk," Hofer pointed to two large antlers, which appeared between some bushes above us, and of which a sharp turn in the road gave us an excellent view. We halted, of course, to hold a council of war as to how our innocent neighbour was to be dispatched. Not a single rifle of the party was found to be loaded with ball, and shot would have been useless. Lister, therefore, proceeded, as noiselessly as possible to draw his charge and reload. Whether the animal heard the sound, or was otherwise disturbed, is uncertain, but, bounding up, for he had been lying down previously, he faced us, and snuffed vigorously at the air, his broad forehead and expanding nostrils just visible through the brushwood behind which we were concealed. This was the work of an instant, and then turning round, he began slowly to ascend the hill.

The Captain advanced to the turn of the road whence we had first perceived the animal, with the intention of firing. As it ascended, however, its hind quarters were alone visible occasionally, and it would soon be altogether hid in the thick forest above. He was compelled to fire, therefore, at a disadvantage; the ball lodged in the animal's thigh, and, as we rushed forward we saw the broad antlers disappearing in the jungle. With all possible speed did we set forward, Fowler and I a-head, whilst Hofer and Lister brought up the rear. At length we gained the summit of the hill over which the elk had passed, wounded as he was, with incredible speed, and before I had attained to a small clearing on the other side, I heard Fowler firing from the front and Mouat from the side. A splendid herd of elks was to be seen from this position rushing down the hill's side into the valley, one of which Fowler had knocked over, whilst Mouat had wounded another.

Just as we were on the point of making for the forest again to pursue them straight down the declivity, Fowler's Singhalese attendant whispered something to him, and he turned off, at right angles to our former course, to the left. I did not understand the movement but followed, and as I did so, I saw Lister making in the same direction, whilst Mouat, Sparks, and Hofer continued straight down the hill side. We were now traversing the brow of the mountain, with a ravine on our right, in which the elks were proceeding in a line nearly parallel to us, but not in advance, for we had struck to the left before they had reached the bottom of the valley. It was a noble sight to see a hundred of them, dashing after each other over rocks and through jungle, in mad terror—the two unfortunate wounded ones lagging a little behind their companions. The ground over which we were passing was terribly harassing —thick tufted grass with occasional brushwood, and now and then a thorny bramble creeping along the ground, as if designedly to impede our progress. Fowler outstripped Lister and myself, and pushed on at a tremendous pace, whilst the lighter and less encumbered natives were a-head of him. The valley curved round to the left, and, if the herd could but be arrested at the angle, it might possibly be turned back to Hofer and his companions, if we could gain the proper position in time—at all events, we were sure of excellent sport.

As we made our way impetuously through grass and bushes, we heard our three friends in the valley sending remembrances after the elks, and, on looking again at the herd, I was glad to see that the two wounded ones were brought down, whilst, as Sparks subsequently declared, he had taken an antler off another. On came the herd, however, in mad speed to the angle of the valley, whilst we were rushing down to secure the position. Fowler and I marked the leader, and fired almost together. It fell, and, at the same moment, our Singhalese attendants raised a frightful din behind us. The effect was electric. In a moment confusion worse confounded was to be seen in the ranks of the enemy, and whilst one was rushing here, and another there, Lister brought down one of them with a bullet from his unerring rifle. The indecision of the herd lasted but for a moment however, and, like an animated mass of dusty earth, they bounded up the hill to our right which we had just descended, directly towards our friend Lister. I was alarmed for his safety when I saw this new movement, but he did not seem much alarmed himself. Before I could get my rifle reloaded, he discharged his remaining barrel full into the forehead of an advancing elk. It fell, and, for a moment, the herd was staggered in its course, but the impulse from behind was too strong to admit of a fresh change of direction. On they swept, Lister was thrown down by the rush, and the whole herd bounded directly over him up the hill, but so swiftly and lightly did they tread their way, that, with the exception of a scratch or two, he escaped scatheless. That was the last we saw of them. In a moment they were over the brow of the hill and had disappeared in the jungle on the other side.

I could not then understand why they had not gone straight up the opposite hill—that on the other side of the valley—but I subsequently learned it—Hofer's estate was immediately over the summit, and doubtless the elks were aware, that by taking that direction, they would have fallen into a trap—their turning to the left, however, instead of to the right, in the first instance, was merely the result of accident, although the Singhalese maintained that they always preferred turning to the left as it was the luckiest side. However that may be, certain it is that had they turned to the right, our party, as contra-distinguished from Hofer's, would have had no sport whatever. Our five elks formed by no means a contemptible trophy of the day's work, and when added to the jungle fowl, proved that the accounts we had heard of Ruminacaddee sport were by no means exaggerated. The day's pleasure was wound up by a piece of news which we did not receive till coffee and cheroots had taken the place of the substantial viands of the table—this was, that a herd of elephants had been met with ten miles to the south-east, which was slowly moving in the direction of the estate, and which had not yet been disturbed. The messenger added that they must already be within seven miles of Lanka. This was cheering news, so with an extra glass of claret to our morning's exploits, we separated early to sleep off the fatigues of the day, and to renovate ourselves for those that were to come. It was agréed, before our dispersion, that we should reassemble at five on the ensuing morning.

It was about six, however, before we were all

ready for the road—each man mounted on his steed, and a curious collection of steeds they were, as is generally the case in mounted parties in Ceylon. Hofer rode the same country horse, or tattoo, as they call it in the island, on which he had accompanied me to the Peak. Captain Lister had a strong Cape horse, very like an English hack, although too much out of condition for elegance, whether from the Captain's weight or recent hard work, cannot now be decided. Fowler had a tall powerful animal, as vicious as any horse that was ever sent from Bombay to Ceylon for sale, and that is saying much, for the good folks of Bombay when they have collected a batch of unmanageable steeds, such as they can make nothing of, are convinced that those are "the very horses for the Ceylon market"—and why? you ask—"because Ceylon planters can ride anything." Sparks had a fine-looking charger which he had bought from an Arab in Colombo, an animal that took an inch of spur to make him trot, and had only once been seen by any one to canter. Uncle Toby bore me as usual, and, though small compared with the Cape horse and Fowler's Rozinante, was by no means the worst of the batch.

Thus mounted, and accompanied by numerous coolies, bearing rifles, ammunition, supplies and talipot leaves to construct tents in case of necessity, we sallied forth, eager for the fray, and auguring well from the sport of the previous day of that which was to come. Our road lay through a wild ravine, such as is frequently to be met with in Ceylon, where two huge mountains rise on either side, barely affording room for the torrent which roars through the aperture—

> "It seem'd some mountain, rent and riven,
> A passage to the stream had given,
> So high the cliffs of limestone grey
> Hung beetling o'er the torrent's way."

Beyond the occasional starting of a jungle fowl, or scaring of some apprehensive and light-footed deer, far off on the mountain's sides or summits, there was little in the way of sport, but the scenery on our road was delightful. A succession of mountain landscapes of the most beautiful character, variegated with forest and open land, or patna, as it is here called, lay on our path—occasionally the dark shade of a hill thrown completely over the valley, and half way up the side of the opposite mountain. Glowing in one place on the little brawling rivulet that struggled noiselessly along, the sun's rays sparkled in the water, whilst, in another, the stream looked like ink from the dark shadow of the forest overhanging it, which the light never pierced. There is much in such scenes that powerfully arrests the attention, and prevents the impression from fading away out of the tablets of the memory.

By a circuitous route we arrived at length at the position indicated by the beaters at the rear of the herd, so as to drive them from the estate in the course of our shooting. Here we found a convenient spot for a hurried, but abundant collation, during which the plan of operations was discussed at the same time as the ham. The beaters were dispersed to the right and left of that part of the forest which the herd occupied—the most resolute however being placed on the elephant tracks, immediately in front, so as to turn them back on us when they first started. Captain Lister and Fowler took the path to the right, Mouat and Hofer that to the left, whilst Sparks and myself were left to pursue the tracks running straight up to the herd, those by which the elephants had passed on the previous day. In a few minutes we two were left alone with our ammunition bearers, the others having dived into the forest. We had each two rifles, one double-barrelled and one single, not grooved—the grooved take too long to load in dangerous sport—with a good stock of ounce zinc bullets, and a large quantity of Lister's excellent advice stored in our heads.

On we went in the forest, eagerly listening for some signs of the foe, or for the report of our friends' rifles on the right or left of us. Not a sound was heard, however, for a quarter of an hour, during which time we kept looking anxiously out on all sides. At length this portentous silence was put an end to by a report on our right, only just audible amidst the din of the jungle. A few seconds afterwards, a female elephant of moderate size, without tusks, and accompanied by a young one, appeared in front, making directly towards us. They were at much too great a distance to render firing available, and, whilst I was exhorting Sparks to be patient, we gallantly advanced to meet the foe. The mother limped perceptibly as she made her way heavily through the jungle, wounded in the shoulder, whilst the young one, alarmed and excited, kept close by her side, and ever and anon bellowed forth his fears. The view which she soon obtained of us made her turn directly towards us, as if determined to have some revenge for her misfortunes. Our horses had of course been left at our temporary halting-place—and the moment the attendants perceived the monster approaching, they climbed into the tree, at the foot of which we stood, leaving one rifle in our hands, and the other by our feet. No fairer target could have been presented to a marksman than the broad forehead of the dam, as she thus boldly advanced. At length she was within twenty paces of us, and we fired together. The balls penetrated the head, but were not fatal. They were sufficient, however, to cool down the energy and boldness of her advance, for she immediately struck into another path to avoid us. This we were determined to prevent, and taking up our double-barrels, made across to intercept her. One shoulder was already disabled, and two balls in the other, brought her down heavily upon her fore-legs and head. Before she could rise again, two additional bullets had put an end to her struggles, and turning on her side, her trunk fell heavily to the ground. The young one up to this time had been neglected, but now, seeing his mother down, he rushed violently towards us in attack, and, as our rifles were empty, we were obliged to beat a hasty and inglorious retreat, Sparks and I vieing with each other in the celerity of our flight. But the object of the infant monster was victory, not revenge, so after putting us thus to the right about, he returned to mourn over his mother. Our rifles were soon reloaded, and advancing boldly up to him, he fell almost immediately on the outstretched trunk of his dam.

Our servants now ventured down from the trees, and endeavoured to remove the impression made upon our minds by their cowardice, by assuring us that master was "plenty good shot"—information which we received with all becoming modesty, glancing at the prostrate elephants, however, with no small satisfaction.

We were roused from our inaction by a frightful din in the distance, caused by the beaters endeavouring, by every species of earthly and unearthly noise that they could make or invent, to turn the elephants back and prevent them breaking away into a thick jungle in front, where pursuit would have been impossible. We soon arrived at the highest point of the gently sloping mound we had been ascending, beyond which there was a species of valley ended far away in the distance by a similar elevation to that on which we stood. The herd were at the extremities of this valley, and the object of the beaters was to prevent them making their way into the jungle beyond, which was of the densest and most impenetrable character. There were very few trees on the valley-like expanse before us, the ground being covered by that long wiry description of grass, which I have so often mentioned. In the meantime it was quite evident that the awful noise which the natives were making at the other extremity of the little plain, was staggering the resolution of the elephants. They halted, trumpeted, ran hither and thither, and tried to break away into the forest at either side. There, however, they were met by unerring rifles that dealt death rapidly—Lister and Fowler at one side, Hofer and Mouat on the other, taking care that they did not break off that way.

At length, with loud bellowing at their inglorious retreat, their trunks and tails high in the air, and the tuskers in front, the herd turned completely away from the beaters, who shouted more ferociously than ever, and, as if furies were pursuing them, on came the huge monsters directly towards the point where we were posted. To have met them then on foot would have been madness, as they were evidently paralyzed with fear, and would rush one after the other blindly, even to destruction. I therefore, climbed a tree and chose a convenient bough for popping at them as they passed—my Singhalese servant by my side, ready to load the moment my gun was empty. Sparks could not be induced to follow my example, declaring that he was not afraid; and, notwithstanding all that I could do, insisted on remaining where he was. His attendant deposited the rifle by his side, and was soon securely placed in a large tree in our vicinity. All this was the work of a moment or two. The elephants were about a mile distant when we commenced to make our arrangements, but were getting rapidly over the ground; so, solemnly warning Sparks of the probable result of his folly, I left him to receive the meed of his temerity. It was impossible for me to assist him; and the sacrifice of my own life, even were I disposed to make it, which I was not, would not have improved his chance of escape.

A large tusker came on very much in advance of the rest of the elephants, a quarter of a mile perhaps, before the main body, which straggled here and there on either side; still making after the leader, however. Lister and Hofer, seeing that they were determined on escaping by the way they had come, now left the shelter of the forest and advanced into the open space in the midst, each bringing down a straggler, before the large tusker in front had neared us. He had no sooner commenced the ascent of the rising ground on which our little party was perched than he saw Sparks right before him, but the view neither lessened nor increased his speed—he came doggedly on as before, determined to escape the commotion and destruction in the rear. He was not more than twenty paces distant when I fired full into his forehead; but the wound was not mortal.

He gave a single bellow, stroking his forehead with his trunk, as he still rushed on. In a moment I heard, to my dismay and horror, the click of Spark's rifle-lock, the weapon having hung fire! The next moment Sparks himself had fallen as if pierced through the head by a shower of zinc bullets. The elephant rushed on—in an instant he was by the side of the unfortunate young man, and putting down his trunk, rolled him over on the ground; but there was no sign of life; and, doubtless fancying he was dead, the tusker sped on in his flight, leaving me to attend to him. I was soon by his side, and he raised himself unhurt from the ground. Before the herd had gained the brow of our little hill, we were both safely seated on the same branch that I had just left, Sparks assuring me that his dropping down was a feint to make the tusker fancy he was dead. I strongly suspected, however, it was the result of an overpowering sensation of fear, at seeing himself, to all appearance, irretrievably lost—whichever it was, feint or faint, it stood him in good stead thus, for it was unquestionably the saving of his life.

From the position we occupied on the tree we were able to do great execution as the huge monsters made their way with difficulty up the hill or mound, wearied with their flight, and confused and terrified with the din behind. We succeeded in bringing down two, before they had all passed; one that had been severely wounded by Mouat a little before, and one that had lost an eye from a ball fired early in the fray, by whom was uncertain. In all, eight of the foe were stretched lifeless in various parts of the plain and forest, and of these, three were tuskers. We were completely exhausted. What with the exertion of first making our way through the forest, and then sitting or running, exposed to the full beams of a tropical sun for a considerable period, the exertion was enough to satisfy the most inveterate glutton of sport. A burning thirst consumed us, and I believe copious draughts of strong brandy and water, alone prevented the most serious consequences. I felt completely knocked up before we had regained the station we had left, and yet Sparks and I had had far less exertion than the others. I was glad to find that they all agreed with me on the rashness and folly of Spark's conduct in insisting on awaiting the rush of the whole herd on foot, as fifty beaters would scarcely have been sufficient to turn them again, and although two or even three were brought down by him at first, he must inevitably have been destroyed by the others.

It must not be supposed that, in thus slaughtering these unwieldy, but sagacious animals, the sportsman is causing wanton and useless pain and destruction of life. The elephants so abounded in many districts, that Government offered rewards for their destruction, whilst the injuries they inflicted on the coffee estates were often irreparable. Nor was it easy to make fences that would keep them out—they would walk through an ordinary fence, or destroy it in their gambols, without having the slightest idea that it was a fence at all. Even the huge logs of the fallen timber laid diagonally on each other and kept in their position by perpendicular supports on either side, were often insufficient to withstand them. They seemed to take a mischievous pleasure in showing what they could do with their tusks and trunks when they liked; whilst the wild buffaloes followed their example, and between the two, the strongest fences altogether disappeared but too frequently.

CHAPTER X.

THE PARSEES—ZOROASTER.

"Call all your tribes together, praise the gods,
And make triumphant fires."

Coriolanus, act v., sc. 4.

THERE was no class of the various inhabitants of Ceylon that more interested me than the Parsees. Their peculiar dress and manners strike the most indifferent observer, stamping them at once as a strange and, at the same time, as a superior race. The hat, covered with flowered silk or stuff, sloping gracefully back from the forehead over the head in an arched form, generally surmounts features of great regularity and often of great beauty, whilst the white robe confined at the waist, always scrupulously clean and neat, sets off to advantage figures generally taller than those of the Singhalese, and infinitely more graceful and commanding. There is an interest too excited in the breast of the most indifferent when he is informed that the man who is before him is a fire-worshipper, the descendant of those of old from the banks of the Euphrates and the plains of Chaldea, who first worshipped "all the host of heaven," that makes him long to know something of the man and of those, who, driven like the Jews from their own country, still maintain, like them, their distinctive character as a peculiar people, and the religion bequeathed to them by their ancestors. Like the Jew too, the Parsee in the countries to which he has fled, has often been the object of persecution and ill-treatment by those whom he despised as infidels and unbelievers. Nor has the one clung more pertinaciously to Moses than the other to Zoroaster. Exile, misfortune, political annihilation, persecution and wealth have equally failed to pluck the religion of their forefathers from their breasts and to throw them stranded on the shores of foreign faiths. Strange analogy between these two peculiar people; the one scattered over the East as widely as the other over the West! The one as much persecuted by the followers of Mohammed, of Brahma, and of Gotama, as the other by the pretended followers of Christ, and with precisely the same result! Like the Jews, the Parsees have accumulated wealth by commerce wherever they have gone. In Canton, in Singapore, in Sydney, in Calcutta, in Madras, in Colombo, in Bombay, in Ormuz, they have been equally successful; and whether brought into competition with the crafty Chinese, the revengeful Malays, the polite Hindus, the indifferent Budhists, the money-loving English, or the religion-loving Mussulmans, the result has been the same—dollars or rupees have been accumulated, until their wealth has become almost proverbial; and this, notwithstanding the frowns of power and the hatred of rival creeds. In all these various places too, they have preserved themselves a distinct people, seeking no alliances with foreigners, and maintaining from Australia and China to Arabia, the same peculiar manners and customs with the faith of their forefathers.

The monarchy consolidated by the successes of Cyrus, continued independent and supreme in some part of Persia until the irruption of the Saracens in the seventh century. Rising ever fresh and with renewed energy after the inroads of the Greeks and Romans, the kingdom still maintained its sacred fire, its Zoroastrian faith, and its worship of Ormuzd, to the reign of Yezdejeerd, in the early part of the seventh century.

At the battle of Kadseah, in 638, the Persian

army was completely defeated by the Mohammedans, and the sacred standard lost. It was three years before the Persian monarch Yezdejeerd found himself again able to take the field for a final struggle. His army amounted to 150,000 men, and under a celebrated general named Ferozin, the fire-worshippers hoped not only to gain the victory but to revenge themselves for the losses their country had already sustained. The Saracen forces were commanded by Mazanni, acting under the orders of the Caliph Omar, and religious enthusiasm, together with the energy and zeal inspired by a new faith, soon swelled their ranks until the numbers were nearly equal on both sides.

For two months indecisive skirmishes alone took place between the armies; their leaders restrained equally by prudential motives from making any general assault. The fate of a kingdom hung upon the result of the battle; the religion of multitudes for more than a thousand years, was to be decided by the contest. If Ferozin had gained the victory Zoroaster would still perhaps have been the prophet of Persia, and his followers at the present day, instead of being ennobled by misfortune and rendered more powerful by trials, might have been sinking into the nerveless lassitude of the present followers of

Mohammed. The battle was rather between the rival creeds of the fire-worshipping prophet and him of Mecca, than between the king Yezdejeerd and the Caliph Omar. At length the impatient spirit of Mazanni could be no longer restrained, and, at an obscure village called Nahavand, forty-five miles south of Hamadan, the ancient Ecbatana, the Saracens were precipitately formed in order of battle, and shouting their war-cry, "Allah Akbar," made a furious attack upon the host of Ferozin.

That battle of Nahavand decided the fate of Persia. The Saracens were completely successful, immense numbers of the fire-worshippers were cut down including their general; and Yezdejeerd fled from the field to lead a precarious life amongst the mountains, which, it is said, lasted for ten years, when he was murdered by a miller whom he had offended, eight miles from Mero. Of the remainder of the host of Ferozin, such as embraced the faith of Mohammed were allowed to serve their new masters in peace, the others fled to the fastnesses of the mountains of Khorasan, or wandered away to the desolate plains of the salt desert. About half a century after, the descendants of these faithful Zoroastrians assembled at the island of Ormuz to escape the persecutions of the Mohammedans, and with the intention of ultimately leaving their country.

They seem to have made their appearance in India about the year 717 of our era for the first time; and, in the history of that country, where they took or obtained the name of Parsees, are frequently mixed up as allies of the Hindoos against their old enemies the Mohammedans, although more frequently as the objects of persecution from both. They had conveyed with them, in their wanderings, the sacred fire, the most precious of their possessions; and for the last thousand years the Bombay presidency, or its neighbourhood, has been the head-quarters of this much-persecuted and almost extinct nation. Under British rule, however, they have been treated with the same measure of justice as the Honourable Company deals out to all its native subjects—Mohammedans, Hindoos, and Parsees, the persecutors and persecuted, being alike subject, *nullo discrimine*, to "Company's law." Nor, defective as that law and its administration may be, do I believe that they would prefer to it the old native rule. About 150,000 members of the community reside in the Bombay presidency; but it is impossible to form an estimate of the probable numbers scattered over the shores of the Indian and Pacific Oceans, from Mauritius to

Shanghai, from Sydney to Ormuz, the necessary data being completely unattainable.*

Zoroaster, or Zerdusht, the founder of the faith now held by the Parsees, was born about 589 years before our era, at a town called Urmi, a city of Azerbijan, that province of Persia which lies south-west of the Caspian Sea. He is variously called a Persian, a Mede, and a Perso-Mede by ancient writers, and is said to have been of royal descent. Ahriman, the evil spirit, says tradition, being aware of the future greatness of the prophet, united with the magicians his followers to try and destroy him. They tempted him and attacked him openly; but in both cases without success. He was under the protection of Ormuzd, the spirit of good, and could not be injured. He was thrown into fire, but the fire had no power over him; he was beset by murderers, but miraculously escaped; he endured temptations to which any one else would have succumbed, but did not fall. Before he was thirty years of age he retired to the mountains, leaving his family and his kindred, as he declared, by divine command; and a minute and tedious account of his journey is given to us in the tra-

* In the preceding account I have been much indebted to Mr. G. H. Briggs' little work—"the Pársís, or Modern Zerdushtians, a sketch."

ditions of his life—this account including miraculous displays of the most extraordinary character, such as his walking across the river Araxe on foot, without so much as wetting his feet. This journey to the Elburz mountains, the great chain that skirts the southern shore of the Caspian, is universally called by his disciples his journey to heaven. It was, whilst in retirement here, that he was first introduced personally to Ormuzd, and received from him the sacred book of the faith, the *Zend-Avesta*, and the sacred fire. When the period had arrived when he should be introduced to Ormuzd, says the *Zerdusht-nameh*, or account of his life, Bahman, a spirit radiant as the sun, his head covered with a veil, appeared before him, and asked, "Who art thou? What seekest thou?" Zoroaster answered, "I seek only what is agreeable to Ormuzd, who has created the two worlds; but I know not what he wants with me. O thou, who art pure, show me the way of the law." Bahman was pleased at these words. "Rise," said he, "to go before God; there thou shalt receive the answer to thy request." Zoroaster rose and followed Bahman, who said, "Shut thine eyes; walk swiftly." When Zoroaster opened his eyes, he saw the glory of heaven. The angels came to meet him, and with them he approached Ormuzd, to whom he addressed his prayer. From him and the six Amschaspands (the spirits next to Ormuzd in glory) he received his instructions, Ormuzd himself ordering him: "Teach the nations that my light is hidden under all that shines. Wherever you turn your face towards the light, and follow my counsel, Ahriman, the evil spirit, will flee from you. In this world there is nothing superior to light."

The Zend-Avĕsta gives a particular account of the various instructions given by Ormuzd to Zoroaster, some of them of an eminently puerile character, others more exalted. "Evil does not proceed from me," said he, "but from Ahriman. My intention is not that people should suffer. Bad thoughts and bad actions come from Ahriman. Sinners are punished in hell. Those lie who say that evil comes from me."—"Who is the best of your servants?" asked Zoroaster. The answer was, "He who has a right heart; he who is liberal with respect to justice, and whose eyes do not wander after riches; he who does good to everything—to fire, water, and animals—will be eternally happy. Those who afflict my servants, and disregard my precepts shall be sent to hell." Zoroaster asked immortality of Ormuzd; but was told that were it granted, he would himself be the first to desire death—that immortality on earth would be eternal misery.

He likewise descended to hell and saw Ahriman, the evil spirit. Words fail to convey an idea of the hideousness of the monster, and doubtless the imagination of Zoroaster was tasked to the utmost to give an account of his appearance, horrible and fearful enough. They abused each other roundly, sparing neither epithets of hatred mutually applied, nor assertions; but what the ultimate object of the interview was, does not appear—probably it was recorded only that his followers might know something of the monster to whom they would be introduced if they did not attend to him.

At length, armed with the Zend-avĕsta, the sacred fire, and the instructions given him by Ormuzd, Zoroaster set forth to declare his mission before the King of Persia, Gushtasp—the Darius Hystaspes of the Greeks, according to some authors. Gushtasp listened to the discourse of the new prophet with great patience, for, in that discourse we are told, were some things that could not be understood—in the Zend-avĕsta are many such. The monarch took time to consider the matter, consulted with the magicians and astrologers, and ended his deliberation by throwing Zoroaster into prison. An astounding miracle, according to the traditions of his history, alone relieved the prophet from his perilous situation, for his life was in danger. The favourite black horse of the King, according to these traditions, was found one morning with its legs so sunk and imbedded in its body that they were useless, and the animal could not stand. Physicians and magicians and astrologers were called in, but could do nothing. The king was in despair, for the black steed was a peculiar favourite—he had no other animal that he liked so well. At length a report was brought him that Zoroaster could cure the horse. The sage was brought from prison, and soon restored the charger to his master, as sound and well proportioned as before.

From that time, the teaching of Zoroaster produced a wonderful impression on the King. The magicians and astrologers were forsaken for the new teacher, and disciples multiplied amazingly. In every part of the wide dominions of Gushtasp the new faith was preached and taught with great success—Zoroaster continuing to surprise and astound the court by exhibitions of miraculous power. A magnificent temple was built at Persepolis to hold the sacred fire—priests and high-priests were ordained, and the entire machinery of ceremonial religion set up. Such was the enthusiasm of Gushtasp himself on the subject, that he ordered twelve thousand cow-hides to be tanned fine, that the doctrines of the new faith might be written upon them. These parchments were deposited in a vault hewn out of a rock in Persepolis. "Holy men were appointed to guard the treasures, and the profane were kept at a distance."

Zoroaster was indefatigable in spreading his faith in every direction. He took repeated journeys to Chaldea, and seems to have made many disciples in that direction, and there is even some reason for believing that either he or some of his chief emissaries made their way into India. He was thrice married, but it is said left only one daughter alive on his death. Certain it is that he exerted his influence with Gushtasp to spread his faith by the sword, and that wars were undertaken with the neighbouring sovereigns that apparently had no other object than the spreading of the Zoroastrian religion. He died about the year 512 or 513, B.C., in the 76th or 77th year of his age—nor does there appear to have been anything remarkable or miraculous related in connexion with his death.

The Zend-avĕsta, or "the Word in the Zend language," is a work of the most extraordinary prolixity and verbosity. Much as oriental works generally are distinguished by vain repetitions and useless recapitulations, I believe it is impossible for any to be more remarkable in this respect than the sacred book of the Parsees. It is no uncommon thing to find the same sentence or paragraph repeated a hundred times in the course of a few pages, whilst the accounts of ablutions and ceremonial observances are prolix beyond what those accustomed only to the concise language of the West can conceive.

The distinguishing doctrines of Zoroaster appear to have been his inculcation of the existence of two spirits, both of vast power and influence in the world, the one good, the other bad—light the symbol and manifestation of the one, darkness of the other. These antagonistic principles are constantly opposing and thwarting each other, and, although the good spirit will finally prevail, the struggle between them is of the most violent character. The immortality of the soul and the resurrection of the body were both taught by Zoroaster, and he appears to have believed that this world, in some new and glorified condition, was ultimately destined to be the residence of happy saints. So constant are the references in the Zend-avĕsta to "Time without end," and so earnest the advice to worship it and pay it all honour, that one becomes doubtful at last whether it be merely a title of Ormuzd or a separate intelligence. Mixed up with some sublime truths there is perhaps more absurdity and obscenity in the Zend-avĕsta than in any other work in existence professing to be a divine revelation. It will by no means bear comparison with the discourses of Gotama Budha or the sacred books of the Chinese edited by Confucius. The Brahminical works may perhaps vie with it in the unenviable characteristics I have named, but, if so, they alone.

Some very interesting traces of fire-worship have been discovered by Mr. Layard in his researches at Khorsabad, and generally in the more recent sculptures unearthed by him. In one of these groups, a slender altar is seen surmounted by a cone, which, being painted red, is probably emblematical of fire. Before it stand two eunuchs, side by side, with their right hands elevated—one of them carries in his hand the mysterious basket, which has caused so much conjecture. On the opposite side of the altar is a table covered with a table-cloth, on which altar is laid a bundle of wood, probably fragrant, to feed the flame. Another representation of fire-worship is engraved by Mr. Layard from Kouyunjik. Two eunuchs are again seen worshipping before the sacred fire on a slender altar, while, behind them, a man leads a goat to the sacrifice. In this, as well as in the Khorsabad scene, there is a table behind the altar, on which are placed objects, that look like bowls containing fruit. Behind the table are two poles, from which serpents are suspended by the neck, carrying on their heads an appendage closely resembling the conventional ostrich-feathers, so generally worn by the idols of Egypt. Both scenes occur in the interior of a fortified camp, but that appears to be an accidental circumstance.

The appearance of the Parsee, as I have said, strikes a stranger in the East at once as remarkable. His fine aquiline nose, with well-developed nostrils, his large black eyes, his well-turned chin, his unusual length of ear, together with his heavy eyebrows and sensual lips, all mark him out as different from the other Asiatics by whom he is surrounded, and stamp him with a distinctive character. He is taller, larger, and heavier in physical formation too than the Hindu or Singhalese. When young, the Parsee female is often handsome, but age comes on rapidly, making her somewhat gross in appearance for the most part, and often producing a corpulence that induces a waddling species of gait. Her luxuriant hair is bound with a handkerchief, called a *pewan*, that often forms a becoming and picturesque head-dress. If there be one point in which the women of the East excel their fairer sisters of the West, it is in the silky softness of their hair. Even in the lowest ranks this advantage is apparent, and, doubtless, in the higher, is the more strikingly so; European females too, the daughters of European parents, brought up in early childhood in India, are superior in this respect to their occidental sisters. Doubtless, the result is caused by the greater care taken of the hair in infancy in the East, and the superiority of the Oriental manner of attending to it. The Parsee men, like the Mohammedans of India and Ceylon, shave the head, wearing the moustache universally, a few of them whiskers, and the priesthood only cultivating beards and permitting the hair of the head to remain.

Many of the Parsees are as fair as Europeans, although invariably with the sallow tint which long residence in the East gives to all, instead of the ruddy glow of more temperate regions. In disposition they are inclined to joyfulness, generally sprightly, often jocose; benevolent, and impulsive in their benevolence; fond of entertainments and of good living. Few are more critical respecting curries and other Oriental dishes than the Parsee, and few understand more thoroughly the mysteries of the *cuisine.*

Indeed every form of sensual enjoyment, as is the case with most Asiatics, is dear to the fire-worshippers, although they are, generally speaking, more refined in many respects than the natives by whom they are surrounded.

Parsee ladies are intrusted with the entire economy of the household, nor would it be considered more seemly amongst them, than amongst Europeans, to have the domestic management taken out of their hands. They are said to be thrifty, precise, and provident. For the most part they are better instructed than Asiatic women generally—few of them being unable to read and write one language at least. They are dexterous in embroidery, and are often conversant with working in wool, principally of an ornamental character. They are permitted much more liberty than formerly. Mr. Briggs says, that in Bombay, "they are even permitted to go abroad in open carriages,"* although such is certainly not the case in Ceylon or in Calcutta, but they receive, with pleasure, visits from European ladies, and will return them in close covered carriages, when they are aware that the ladies are careful not to violate their prejudices by bringing them into contact with foreign male humanity.

"The Parsee commences the day by eating a

* The Pársis, or Modern Zurdushtians, p. 19.

light breakfast, often no more than a slice or two of bread, and of several cups of tea, which he drinks off with a handkerchief applied to the piece of pottery (to prevent it touching his lips). His dinner is taken between twelve and two o'clock during the day, and is served in polished plates of brass—large quantities of rice are then consumed with curry, along with a variety of pungent ingredients, ground into *chitni* (chutnee), stews, &c. By tradesfolks and the better classes of the community, a cup or more of tea is partaken of, either at four or five o'clock in the afternoon. The evening meal occurs between eight and ten o'clock, when license is given, not only to beverages of variety and strength, but also to the use of libidinous speech. The *tât* is the great parting draught of the night, not unlike the stirrup-cup of yore, and the more recent Scottish form of auld-lang-syne."

I may conclude this short sketch of the Parsees by remarking, that one wife is believed by most of them to be the correct allowance, but that bigamy nevertheless is often practised, and unlimited concubinage almost universal amongst them.

CHAPTER XI.

HORMANJEE.

"The current that, with gentle murmur, glides,
Thou know'st, being stopp'd, impatiently doth rage;
But when his fair course is not hindered,
He makes sweet music with th' enamell'd stones,
Giving a gentle kiss to every sedge
He overtaketh in his pilgrimage;
And so by many winding nooks he strays,
With willing sport, to the wild ocean.
Then let me go, and hinder not my course;
I'll be as patient as a gentle stream,
And make a pastime of each weary step,
Till the last step have brought me to my love;
And there I'll rest, as, after much turmoil,
A blessed soul doth in Elysium."

Two Gentlemen of Verona, act ii., sc. 7.

DURING my frequent visits to Colombo, I became acquainted with a very estimable Parsee merchant, named Hormanjee—a man so superior even to his own countrymen, in liberality of sentiment and unaffected admiration for everything excellent and praiseworthy, that I felt esteem for him the first time that I met him at my uncle's office. My visits to Colombo enabled me to cultivate his friendship, and whilst I talked to Marandhan of Budhism and its founder, I talked similarly to Hormanjee of Zoroaster and his faith. At length he accepted an invitation I had repeatedly given him to visit me in the jungle, and highly interesting and intellectual were his meetings and discussions with my Budhist friend Marandhan. Never did the neat little bungalow which Roquelaire had fitted up with so much taste, appear so comfortable to me, as when I had my Parsee and my Budhistic friend on either hand—both men of intelligence and of reflection—both men who had seen the world, and thought much of what they saw. Their conversation was an intellectual treat of no ordinary character.

During Hormanjee's stay with me, I persuaded him to give me an account of his life, which I took care shortly afterwards to transcribe.

"I was born in Calcutta," he began; "my father Manuckjee, was a merchant there of some note, and I was early initiated into the mysteries of the counting-house. He saw little of European society, for the Anglo-Indian population of Calcutta, and indeed of India generally, is less condescending to Orientals than their poorer brethren in Ceylon. Our house in the Circular Road, to the east of the town, was a large one with a spacious garden attached, a tank or pond and statuary ornamented the garden, and several beautiful groves of trees. For a time my boyish life was one of great happiness and content, for my mother was a superior woman and early trained me to piety and reflection. As I became acquainted with the various productions of different countries however, and read works describing travels and voyages, my mind began to expand, and I ardently longed to see something of the world of which I heard and read so much. I became discontented with the narrow circle in which I moved, and longed to explore the wonders of the West particularly. My parents, and especially my mother, were by no means prepared to forward my wishes in this respect, and I became gloomy in consequence. At length, with womanly tact, when I had passed my sixteenth year, she endeavoured to divert my mind from ideas of foreign travel by the gentle but all-powerful influence of love.

"One evening as I was walking in a discontented mood, through the groves of our garden, I heard a sweet melodious voice singing a hymn to the sun, accompanied by the lute, the sounds issuing from an alcove at some distance, which was generally set apart for the female portion of our household. I stopped and listened attentively. I had certainly never heard that voice before—it was completely new to me, and whilst its melody enchanted me its novelty equally excited my curiosity. I walked quietly over the grass leading to the bower. A low shrubbery alone intervened between me and the open alcove, in which a party of ladies were seated. My mother and my favourite sister were there, but the majority I had never seen before. The alcove was completely open; several gothic arches were supported by graceful stone pillars made as light as possible, round which fragrant creepers were entwined, until they reached the roof, where they united into a thick mass of leaves and flowers. The party within consisted of five ladies, of whom three were utterly unknown to me. I was surprised at this, as you are aware that we Parsees practise no concealment of our females like the Mohammedans or Hindoos, but, on the contrary, approve of their mingling, to a certain extent, with all of our own creed. I had seen then, I thought, all the Parsee ladies in Calcutta of any pretensions to wealth, and yet here were three, a mother and two daughters apparently, who, to judge by their dress, must have been extremely wealthy, who in fact must have been our equals, or I should never have seen them there.

"In the centre of the alcove stood a small marble

pedestal of no great height, on which it had been originally intended to place a statue, but through some inadvertence or caprice, it had been left unoccupied. Upon this the youthful songstress stood as she addressed the beneficent Ormuzd, with the fervour and grace of youth and purity. Her form, which was but beginning to mould itself into the rich fulness of womanhood, was beautifully displayed by her close-fitting vest and wide trowsers, and as she stood gazing into heaven, it formed a striking contrast with the group seated at her feet. The light fell full upon her delicate face and picturesque head-dress—a head-dress, as you must be aware, equally removed from the clumsiness of the turban and the unmeaning ugliness of the European bonnet. A single feather drooped gracefully upon her shoulder, its unsullied whiteness forming a picturesque contrast with the black shining hair which escaped in rich braids beneath her cap. The lute, leaning lightly on her left arm, which was bare, after our custom, from above the elbow, was of satin-wood inlaid with mother-of-pearl, and as she swept her delicately small fingers over its chords, her voice gave utterance to such sounds as the nightingale warbles when she would attract her mate and call him home from wandering. Such was the position, such were the circumstances under which I first saw Amoosta. Can you wonder then that I should have been smitten with love at once, or that I should have inwardly vowed, with Oriental impetuosity, that she, and she only, should be the wife of Hormanjee? The hymn or invocation ended, she leaped lightly upon the floor, smiling with a bewitching charm that completed in my mind the fascination which her features, her attitude, and her song had commenced. Her sister then attempted a similar piece, but I had no eyes, no ears for any one but Amoosta. She placed herself beside her mother, and as she gazed upwards at the performer, her face caught a new beauty from the shade into which it was now thrown. She had applause and commendation for all—there was no reserve, no lingering jealousy in the hearty plaudits she bestowed upon the performance of her two more youthful companions.

"It would have been rude and impudent to interrupt the ladies' privacy upon such an occasion. So I contented myself with feasting my eyes to the full, until the approach of night drove the fair worshippers into the house; and shortly afterwards I saw a close carriage, such as Parsee ladies are accustomed to use in Calcutta, drive away from the female quarter of our dwelling. I subsequently learned that the wife and daughters of Halbin Kowasjee had just before this become residents of Calcutta, on his transferring thither the head-quarters of his celebrated mercantile house from Canton,—a house as well known in the East, as that of the Rothschilds' in the West. Amoosta was then the daughter of the great Kowasjee, my mother was evidently intimately acquainted with her and with her mother, and I saw no reason why I should not succeed in bearing off this great prize as my bride. I mentioned the matter to my parents. My mother was delighted, and confessed to me that she had hoped for this. The very means she had taken to keep me at home, however, resulted in sending me abroad to see the world.

"The intimacy between the two families ripened into a friendship, and at length the matter was mentioned to the parents of Amoosta. They were well pleased with the proposal, for Amoosta had exhibited a very heretical predilection in favour of Englishmen, and was known to have frequently spoken contemptuously of the young men of her own nation and faith. Her parents hoped, therefore, that her wild ideas would end with her marriage, and that the comparatively cultivated and polite Parsee of Calcutta might be more acceptable to her, than his more unlettered countrymen in China. When her mother mentioned it to the maiden, however, as the marriage which they had decided upon for her, she, with great perverseness, insisted upon regarding it only as a proposition that had nothing definite in it, and was never likely to be realized. At length, when pressed upon the subject, and when she saw that her father and mother had both firmly set their minds upon it, she told them they might sacrifice her, if they so willed, that she was bound to obey their commands, and she would do so, even though she went to certain misery, but that, if she were allowed a private interview with Hormanjee, of only a few minutes duration, he would no longer seek her hand, and yet she should tell him nothing but the truth. 'O Zardusht!' exclaimed old Kowasjee, 'how wilful the maiden is! This comes of teaching girls to read. Rightly does the Zend-avĕsta declare, that *the wild roes of the mountains may be tamed, the mules of Tartary made to bear burdens, the zebras of Africa converted into gentle palfreys, but the wilful heart of a maid who has set her mind on folly, is not to be turned by gentle entreaty or rude opposition.* Hormanjee is a lad of sense, however; I shall prepare him for the interview, and though it somewhat violates etiquette, she shall have her wish, and I will myself present their first-born before the Amschaspands, and the throne.'*

* The throne of Ormuzd; the Amschaspands, according to Zoroaster, are six great spirits surrounding that throne.

"An interview of the kind required by Amoosta, was of an unprecedented character in Parsee life, and it was not without many misgivings that my mother at length consented to it. As for me, nothing could equal my anxiety to know what revelation she had to make to me, nothing could be stronger than my determination, after Kowasjee's lecture, to persevere in making her my wife—nothing, but my love for her. It was before the altar on which we sacrificed to Zoroaster, that the decisive interview took place. Amoosta was radiant as a bride, and the sorrow and shame which contended in her countenance, rendered her only the more enchanting, whilst on my side, I had spared no pains with my toilet, to prove to her that even a Parsee might look well. She saluted me with a low salaam, and I returned it with all the grace of which I was master. Then advancing towards me, and looking me full in the face, as though her large blue eyes would pierce through me, sparkling as they were with excitement; she extended her hand to me, after the manner of you Occidentals. I put it gently to my lips, as I had read gallant men did in the West, and then, to express my love, I faintly pressed and shook it. 'Hormanjee,' said she, smiling, 'I am sure you would not render me wretched.' 'No,' said I, 'by our holy prophet, Amoosta, I would make you happy, rather than anything else in this world.' 'Then do not marry me, Hormanjee,' she said quickly, at the same time taking my hand in both of hers,—'do not marry me, and putting maiden modesty aside, I will kiss you—I will kiss you fondly, Hormanjee.' I knew not what to say. Kowasjee and his admonitions were quite forgotten, and, even when she looked most enchanting, and was taking the very means to make me love her more, I resolved to resign her. 'You hate me then?' I asked. 'Oh, no, no, no, indeed I do not,—I do not, Hormanjee,—indeed I do not,' and as she thus earnestly exclaimed, she burst into a flood of tears. I threw my arm round her slight figure, and pressed her to my bosom. 'You love some one else?' I asked, whilst I kissed her smooth fair forehead, as it reclined upon my shoulder. 'No, Hormanjee,' she replied again, looking into my eyes, from the azure depths of her own,—'no, Hormanjee, indeed I do not.' 'Then why do you not want me to marry you?' 'It is a secret,' she whispered, looking down upon the floor. 'A secret, Amoosta, and may I not know it,—you cannot tell it me, perhaps.' I pitied her much, for she wept bitterly. 'Yes, yes, I can tell you,' she hastily exclaimed; 'but you will never tell my parents, or any one who will, or who may, tell my parents,' she added, after a pause. 'I will never tell it to a living soul. I swear, Amoosta, by Zardusht himself, never shall it be breathed by me, unless you yourself release me from my oath.' So saying, I bent my forehead upon the altar. 'I took a vow,' said she, 'not very long ago, never to wed one who had not crossed the great ocean—who had not seen that wonderful West, whence the strong rulers of the East come; time was, when the East ruled the West, and still it does intellectually, for we have given them a philosophy and a religion, false as both may be, but the West now rules the East with the strong hand, and the man who has not seen these strong men in their own country, who has not crossed the seas as they do, shall never be the husband of Amoosta.' 'Beloved Amoosta,' I exclaimed, 'your desires and my own are identical. I too, have longed to see these rulers of the world in their own homes, to pry into the secret of their power. I have demanded permission to go, times without number. Now your wishes shall be accomplished, and I shall return two years hence to claim my bride. Is it not so, Amoosta?' 'Yes, Hormanjee,' she whispered, 'let it be so, for I love you as woman only can love. But remember, not a word of my vow,' and so, imprinting a kiss upon my hand, before I could anticipate it, she left me alone by the altar of the prophet.

"Kowasjee and my father, were equally anxious to know the result of the unwonted conference. 'Kowasjee, thou art my father,' said I, touching his robe with respect, 'but this marriage may not be for years—for two years at least. At the end of that time I will ask for Amoosta's hand.' 'Did you not say he was near seventeen years of age?' asked Kowasjee. My father assented. 'And she is fifteen,—marvellous truly are the councils of the foolish. To think that at our age we should have been thus duped! We should have wedded and bedded them, and I warrant me there would have been no more talk of putting off. Why did we not remember, that as geese hatch goslings, even so will folly be the result of the conference of a youth and of a maiden,—if, indeed, she be still—.' 'This must surely be some idle whim,' said my father, interrupting him. 'Does Amoosta consent to this postponement?' 'She wishes it like myself,' I replied. 'I warrant it, she does,' said her father, 'were there any wisdom in it, she would oppose it with all her might. Adieu, Manuckjee,—it is like eating sour mangoes, to hear that youth talking. Amoosta shall wed six months hence at furthest, or I shall know why not. I cannot afford to wait three years for a grandson. Adieu, Manuckjee, adieu. As for you, Sir,' he said, turning to me, 'there is a new lunatic asylum, not yet full, I hear, in Sealdah,—you had better enquire about it.'

"In a month, all my preparations for departure to England had been made. I was at length to see that western world I had sighed after and longed to witness so frequently. The parting with my parents and my sister was a melancholy one, for they looked upon me as doomed; they considered it impossible that I should ever return in safety. For my own part, I did not leave them with that equanimity with which I had anticipated I should. My heart was sad, and it was not without a foreboding of disaster and misery that I left my father's roof. The vessel in which I was to sail to Mocha was an English one, consigned to our own house, and in which, therefore, I had every reason to expect attention and as much comfort as a merchant-ship can usually afford. The captain was a good sailor, but, otherwise, uncultivated, and looked upon me more as an extraordinary animal of great value, which he was carefully to deliver up in a sound and safe condition to the agents at Mocha, than as a human being like himself, capable of being an acquaintance or a companion. I had a cabin to myself, my own servant, and every attention was paid to me, in order that I should feel myself as much at home as possible. My meals, differing, of course, slightly as they did from those of the officers and two European passengers, were served separately; but I always joined the party in the saloon after dinner at wine, and found the free conversation which then prevailed both amusing and instructive. On the first night only during which we were actually at sea did I find myself brought into any unpleasant collision with anyone on board; and I mention the incident in order to show the contrast between my ideas and actions on leaving India and those which I insensibly acquired, and became accustomed to, in England. Whilst we were in the river, I generally retired early, getting up equally early in the morning, in order to present my usual adorations to the sun, which I was compelled to offer up on deck, as my cabin was upon the starboard side, and I could not see him rise from it. When we were actually at sea, however, and I could gaze around our vessel upon every side without seeing land, I sat up to write to Amoosta, for my mother had promised to be a medium of communication between us, and I resolved to give her a full account of my journey and my impressions. Ten o'clock, or four bells, had struck, and shortly after a seaman rapped at my door. 'Come in,' said I. 'Ten o'clock, Sir,' said he; 'must put out the lights.' I smiled at his talking so indifferently of what we regard as a heinous crime—to extinguish by any sacrilegious act the very emblem and embodiment of the Deity upon earth. 'My lamp will not burn much longer,' said I; 'but I cannot put it out.' 'It's the rules of the ship, Sir, and the captain's orders. All the lights to be out at ten o'clock. The light *must* be put out, Sir.' 'The light *must not* be put out in my presence, or with my consent,' I replied, with some warmth; 'nor had I any idea the captain would have either urged or permitted such an insult to me as to talk of it.' 'Oh, far from insulting you, Sir, he gave us all orders to do our utmost to make you comfortable, and to show you every respect; but this is the rules of the ship, you know.' 'I have nothing to do with the rules of the ship,' said I, testily. 'Begosh, but you have, Sir, as long as you're in it,' he urged. 'It's contrary to my religion; it would be a crime if I either did it myself, or suffered it to be done in my presence,' said I; 'leave me, and I will talk to the captain about it to-morrow.' A new light seemed to break in upon the honest seaman as I said this, and he muttered something to himself about seeing how it was; he evidently thought I was mad. How strange that it should ever be thus with mankind; that the sincerest and most honest convictions of one portion of the human race should be looked upon as absurdities and madness by another! The seaman, after a moment's hesitation, advanced to the table, and was about to seize the lamp, or to extinguish it, when I prevented him, by putting it quickly aside. 'You shall not put out that light,' said I, 'till you have killed me;' and so saying, I grasped a stout walking-stick which was near, and placed myself in front of it. 'O, well,' said the sailor, 'if you're goin' to be obstropelous like that, I'll send down the officer of the watch.' So saying, he left the cabin. I never heard any more about my light, nor was any attempt made, for the future, to prevent my burning it as I pleased; although I generally contrived so to trim the lamp as that it should expire a little after ten. The sailors, however, from that day forth, regarded me as insane, and many were the whispered conversations I noticed amongst them as I paced the quarter-deck.

"The captain's estimate of me, as a species of curiosity, was not much more flattering than the seamen's idea of my insanity. I frequently went up to the main-top, particularly in the mornings, when that horrid operation of washing the decks rendered any refuge at a distance agreeable; besides that, from the elevation of the main-top, an excellent view could be obtained of the rising sun. On such occasions, I noticed that I was invariably followed by a seaman, who, whilst he pretended to have some employment in my immediate vicinity, kept his eye constantly upon me. For some days I took no notice of this extraordinary Mentor; but at length, when it became quite apparent that the man had really nothing to do but to watch me, I asked him on one occasion whether he always worked in that spot in the mornings. He was an Irishman, and his strange method of speaking, which I could understand with difficulty only, interested me. 'Why thin now, your honour's highness, but it's splicin' a rope I am,' said he. 'But have you a rope to splice here every morning at this time?' I asked. 'Och, shure and there's always a power to do that a way on boord ship, your highness,' he answered, still working away with imperturbable coolness. 'But do the ropes always want splicing *here*, man?' I asked pointedly. 'Are they always breaking about the main-top, and about the main-top only, that you come here regularly every morning when I am here, and only when I'm here?' 'Shure thin now, and your honour's highness is as 'cute as a weasel,' he urged. 'Begor, it 'd be as aisy to bate Banagher himself, as to bate your honour's highness any way; and shure enough we all know who the same Banagher bate.' I could not help smiling at the ingenuity with which he avoided my question; but, determined to explore the matter, I repeated it nearly in the same words. 'Why, thin now,' he began, 'the divil a use it is at all at all to thry and desave your honour's highness; he 'd be a mighty cliver boy intirely that 'd catch your highness dozing, even with one eye shut; but I hope your honour's highness is'nt angry at my comin' here; shure an' now I'll sing you a song, or do anything in rason, to make myself agreeable.' 'You will not tell me, then, why you follow me here?' I asked again, but this time dryly and coldly. 'Why thin, tare an' ages, but to be shure I will, if so be your highness wants it; shure it is'nt goin' to be angry with me you'd be, for obeyin' the capting's own orders.' 'The captain, then, ordered you to follow me whenever I came aloft; and for what purpose?' I asked. 'Why thin, now your highness, but shure you're goin' on at the rate of a hunt. Sorra' one o' me ever said the capting ordered me to follow you; tho' for the matter o' that, purshuin' to the lie it'd be afther all.'

'The captain, then, *did* order you to follow me up here?' I urged. 'O, begor he did, your highness; now that you've found it out, I don't mind tellin' you all about it, an' makin' a clane breast of it, at onst,' he said courageously. A rupee still further opened his lips, and he proceeded. 'Why thin, the long and the short of it's jist this. "Thady," says the capting to me; "Thady," says he. "Ay, ay, your honour," says I. "Thady," says he, "do you see the furrin gintleman that's goin' up aloft?" says he. "It'd be mighty quare if I did'nt, capting," says I; "for I never tuk my eye off him from the minit I seed him a layin' a hould o' the riggin'." "Shure, an' it's a wonder, Thady," says he, "that he can go up at all at all wid them shoes he wears, wid a toppin' at the end of thim, for all the world like the end of a marlin spike curled up." "Thrue for you, Sir," says I; "a more active gintlemin, or a cleverer, Thady never clapt his two eyes on; there's not a man in the ship could go up them rattlins with all that head-gear and thim curled toes, widout bein' in mortial fear of goin' overboord." "Well, Thady," says the capting, says he; "you're a smart fellow, Thady," says he, and begor it was them very words he spoke; "you're a smart fellow, Thady," says he; "jist go up with the prince," says he—"after him," says he—"take a rope up to splice," says he, "and have an eye upon him," says he. "Begor, an' I'll do that, your honour," says I; "tho' I niver seed a gintleman, let alone a prince, that wanted it less," says I, "if it wasn't always barrin' the toes and the head-gear." That's the long and the short of it, your honour's highness, and the divil a lie in it; an' shure if it's angry you do be gettin', I'll make myself scarce at onst.'

"Notwithstanding the difficulty I had in comprehending his extraordinary English, yet I made out sufficient to understand the matter, and to perceive that my friend Thady might be a very agreeable companion; so I said no more about it. Morning after morning, as I took my accustomed place, Thady made his appearance at no great distance, always splicing with praise-worthy diligence, and at the same time 'keeping an eye,' as he would have said, upon me. I sometimes thought they feared I might jump overboard; for if I rose more swiftly or abruptly than usual, Thady was at my side in a moment. He was an amusing companion, however, and I learned much from him respecting the unfortunate country from which he had come.

"At Bombay I was warmly received by the members of our community, who were much interested in my journey, the young envying me the pleasure and excitement I could not fail to enjoy, the old exhorting me to continue stedfast in our holy faith. At length, furnished with abundant letters to Egypt and to England, I embarked for Mocha, the destination of our ship, and which I longed to reach, that I might say I had left India behind me, and had fairly stepped forth into the world. It was not without a feeling of sorrow that I remembered we were leaving the sacred country of our faith on our right hand, swiftly passing it by, and that there was little chance of my seeing the elevated plains of Azerbijan, where Zoroaster had first delivered his message from Ormuzd and the sacred fire, to the custody of the King Gushtasp. Impetuous Mohammedanism had driven our fathers thence with the sword, and their children, instead of uniting to seize the country afresh, were content with their merchandise and their profits, neglecting all besides. Will the day never come when the evils Mohammedans have brought upon Persia, and upon India, shall be expiated in the blood of their descendants!

"Mocha, from the Red Sea, is a picturesque-looking town. It and its neighbourhood form so pleasant a contrast with the bleak shores of Arabia and Africa, that it seems the centre of an oasis in the midst of frightful rocks and desolation. Its white houses and glittering minarets gleam in the sunshine, in beautiful contrast to the green verdure and foliage by which it is surrounded, whilst, far away to the north and south, the uniform yellow line of bare rocks and desert stretches away to the horizon, leaving, upon the mind of the beholder, an idea of vast desolation which oppresses the spirits. A nearer inspection of the town, however, by no means realises the flattering idea one would form of it from the sea—its houses, for the most part white certainly, are low and gloomy-looking, its streets narrow, filthy, and sombre, through which the proud Musselmans stalk silently to prayers or upon their business, their taciturnity only broken by the curse, or the contempt, or the pity which they gratuitously bestow upon the infidel. The followers of Mohammed and of Zoroaster can never be reconciled, and, Orientals though they were, I felt much more lonely and isolated amongst the populace of Mocha than in the crowds of London.

"I lost no time in embarking for Cosseir, in Egypt, between which town and Mocha a very considerable traffic is carried on. If I had disliked Mocha, however, I was still less pleased with the miserable port of Cosseir, where wretchedness of every description delights to expose itself to the broad light of day; where the stranger cannot steal from his house without being surrounded and followed by a motley group of mendicants, all anxious to prove their wretched condition, by exhibiting their disgusting sores and deformities—Abyssinians, Nubians, Kopts, and even the followers of the impostor of Mecca, so proud elsewhere, all vying with each other in ostentatious mendicancy, and in the exhibition of their misery.

"I was more than recompensed however for the discomfort and filth of Mocha and Cosseir by the sail down the Nile from Denderah to Cairo. I had hired a comfortable boat with an ample crew, and as we proceeded leisurely down this celebrated stream, I examined the various works on the antiquities of Egypt, with which English literature abounds, and which I had taken care to provide before leaving Calcutta. It is a strange feeling that one experiences, when brought face to face with the great works of antiquity—it is a feeling not to be easily forgotten, and perhaps there is no greater incentive to glory, or a thirst for glory, than to stand before the ruins of what has long been glorious; the heart expands as though it would embrace the past and pry into the future, in its reveries,—it feels that it is not so much what we do now or what we enjoy now, as what we leave behind us, when our fretful hour of life has ended, that we shall be judged by. Who that has stood before the mounds of Deir Selin, the ruins and tombs of Siout, or the pyramids that strew the left bank of the Nile between Beni-Souef and Jizeh, has not wished that he too might leave something behind him, as a mark to posterity, even though it should only be a monstrous tomb? And yet how strange that all these monuments that stir the soul so deeply should be but sepulchral mounds; everything in Egypt tells of death, its greatness is more apparent in its tombs and catacombs than in any remains that indicate life and action and vigour! Strange that structures, every line of which speaks of repose, of death, of stillness, of eternity, should powerfully rouse the soul to action and make one feel that 'twenty centuries look down' upon him from these mighty monuments.

"You can fancy, from your experience of Ceylon, that a moonlight sail upon the Ganges, the Bhagirati, or the Hooghly, is a delightful thing. After the heat of the day, when the moon has risen in all her silvery splendour, not obscure or dim as in the north, but throwing down floods of light, what can be more pleasant than to watch the dark shadows of the foliage on either side, forming so beautiful a contrast with the glowing water, if it be peaceful and at rest, whilst the boat glides noiselessly downwards with the current.

There is something in a scene like that, which makes one desire solitude to enjoy it thoroughly —it is not a thing that can be talked about at the time. This pleasure is even increased upon the Nile. Small as the stream is in comparison with the gigantic floods of India—at least, small as it was in the dry season when I saw it—it yet presents more striking contrasts, a greater variety of the picturesque, than the rivers of India. The foliage is as various,—the banks are more frequently covered with picturesque villages,—occasionally a glimpse is obtained of apparently illimitable deserts, shining in all the blankness and desolation of solitude far away to the right hand and to the left; one turns from its monotonous sameness to the variety of the river with something of the feeling experienced after having travelled through an interminable forest, when an unexpected glimpse is afforded of cultivated plains, or fruitful valleys. But, more than all this, and adding a charm to such a scene which probably the world cannot supply to the same extent elsewhere, are the monuments of antiquity so thickly studded on every side. Everything in Egypt is grouped on the banks of the river; life and death are there brought into constant and strange juxtaposition — the mud-cabin of to-day beside the venerable ruin of two thousand years ago—the waving of the living trees of yesterday beside the immovable monuments of dead antiquity. I felt, as we glided down the stream, that there were thoughts and feelings lying deep in the heart which travel only could cultivate; which, without travel, would probably for ever remain dormant.

"The mosques and palaces of Cairo and Alexandria did not detain me long. I had seen the past in Egypt, and I now hurried on to inspect the present, in London. Absorbed as I was with anxiety to visit the great metropolis, I felt little interest in Malta and Gibraltar; I rather felt glad, indeed, when the vessel's prow was turned from them, and we plunged onwards towards the island, of which, from the time that I could lisp a syllable, I had heard so much. It is not to be wondered at, that the Oriental, who had been brought up in India, should regard England and London with even greater interest than the Englishman does Greece and Rome. Were they living Greece, and living Rome—the Greece of Pericles, and the Rome of Augustus—they would then but faintly shadow forth in interest to the Englishman, what England is to the Indian.

"At length the dull haze, and overhanging smoke were pointed out to me, as the signs of the great city. As we drew nearer and nearer, I was stupified by the din, and confounded by the bustle, which met my ears, and assailed my eyes on every side. I could see nothing but masses of men and women, and horses, rushing in various directions, as if life or death depended upon the struggle—and truly, life or death does depend upon the struggle in too many instances. Rising amongst the smoke and dimness which enveloped everything, were great spires and domes, monuments and statues, the proportions of which were only faintly discernible; whilst distinctly, amidst the confusion, was to be received this idea, and this only—that an immense mass of humanity was in earnest about something or other; whether guiding horses, or carrying bundles, or torturing minerals and vegetables into new forms, or ploughing up the waters of the unfortunate river, by thousands—whatever they were doing, they all seemed thoroughly in earnest — there was no child's play, no acting of a part—if they would not struggle, they might not live, seemed the law of their existence. Sunday seemed alone the day on which they were not in earnest. Then they were listless and apathetic, or else incapable of being earnest about anything, for the most part. Then the women seemed to have assumed the character the men had put off. They crowded earnestly to the places of worship; the men sauntered indifferently along. I could see no greater contrast than between the man pressing forward on his daily business, or to enjoy some pleasure on a week-day, and the same man on the Sunday, rolling apathetically to church; a female on each arm, perhaps, giving the impetus. It is not so in the East. If Mohammedans or Hindoos are ever in earnest, it is in their worship.

"I was received with the warmest kindness and hospitality by friends of our house to whom I had introductions. Men, high amongst the mercantile community, who, had they been in Calcutta, would feel ashamed of my occupying a seat at their tables, insisted upon having me at their residences — would not hear of my engaging apartments at a hotel. My first residence was at Bayswater—my host driving in every day to the city, whither I generally accompanied him, for I delighted to see the bustle of that extraordinary hive, and loved to roam about in it, merely to observe. The lions of the great metropolis were duly shown to me; but I saw none so marvellous as Fleet Street, Ludgate Hill, Cheapside, and London Bridge. These are the true wonders of London—its paltry parks and gloomy squares cannot be compared with the palaces and gardens of the East; but its incessant toil and bustle, its work, its thronged shops and paths, its myriads of active, busy men, its noble horses, earnest in their avocations as their masters,—these are truly wonders, such as one cannot see elsewhere, and in these is much of the success of Englishmen explained. Steady perseverance is the secret of their wonderful career, and yet that perseverance would probably have effected little, had it not been directed by an energy as indomitable as itself.

"I visited Paris, and there the foundations of my peace of mind were sapped, and the train laid for a long series of subsequent misfortunes. There I saw more splendid buildings, more magnificent galleries, more highly ornamented public ways, but I saw nothing like Fleet Street or the Strand, nothing to compare with Cheapside or London Bridge. Paris is certainly as much more magnificent than London as the Place de la Concorde than Trafalgar Square. London is as much more business-like than Paris as Ludgate Hill is more crowded than the Rue St. Honoré. There is splendour, magnificence, grandeur, and display in the one, there is more homely earnestness and truth, laborious toil and incessant advance, in the other. The fountains of the Place de la Concorde and those of Trafalgar Square may be taken as samples of the two. The former are grand but seldom play, the latter are homely but are daily at work, as though they should say, 'Our duty is to squirt this water to a certain height for so many hours a-day, and witness ye men and gods that we do it, with all our might.'

"I have said that at Paris was laid the foundation of a sea of troubles in which I was long darkly swimming, almost without hope. In order to avoid observation as much as possible, I had completely adopted the European dress, and, however dark I may look in our white *angraka*, in the black broadcloth of England, I looked light enough to be often taken for a Frenchman. The family with which I stopped in Paris was an English one, that had long been resident there. They conducted me to every point of attraction, and I was dazzled and intoxicated by the splendour and gaiety which seemed everywhere to prevail. In an over anxious endeavour not to be singular, I had made it a rule to frequent the table of my hosts, and often were the most sacred principles of my faith outraged in my presence. Yet I would not be singular. I wished to resemble the people who were round me, and said nothing. Pork was consumed by my neighbour, whilst he smilingly addressed me, and the very hand that helped me to something in the vicinity was probably engaged a moment before in cutting up a slice of ham! Nor was this all. Candles and lamps were extinguished with a levity that sent a shudder through my soul! Alas! in putting off my Parsee garments, I was forced to smother, at the expense of my conscience, many Parsee ideas! I knew that I was doing wrong, yet I had not the moral courage to confess my error and retrace my steps.

"I was passionately fond of the theatre. Never had I conceived it possible that mortal voices and mortal frames could produce the enchantment of the opera, and I delighted in constantly attending it. Had I remained in Europe till this hour, I do not think I should have lost my relish for that exquisite amusement. My friends accompanied me frequently, and I took a pleasure in trying the different effects of different seats. On one of these occasions, when I had engaged a pit box for our party, I saw one who, for a time, was the joy and misery of my life. She was leaning from a box at a short distance from ours, and in the same tier, when I first caught a glimpse of her. I too was leaning forward at the time, and, for a second, our eyes met; it was to me as if a flash of lightning had rapidly dazzled my vision. She retired into her box again, and there, hid by an envious curtain, I could see no more of her. Yet I could think of nothing else. The play, the singing, my friends were forgotten, and abruptly quitting my position I made my way into the pit, in order that I might obtain a full view of the face that had produced upon my mind so electrical an effect. I thought I saw a faint smile upon her lips, as she recognised me, and I was delighted at it. It is possible, thought I, that some strange sympathy links our spirits together, and that I may have made an impression upon her mind, as she upon mine. Her hair, which was of the lightest golden colour, waved over her shoulders in long ringlets. She was a complete northern beauty, but with the bright hazel eyes of the south, almost too spiritual and nervous for the glow of health which animated her cheek. A simple wreath of light flowers encircled her head, and formed a pleasing contrast to the bright golden hue of the mass above them and below; her arm, full and delicately white, reposed upon the crimson cushion in front of her, and the thought struck me at the moment that its proportions were perfection itself, and that any deviation from those proportions must be erroneous. My gaze, however, was too full and bold, for, at the close of the act, she changed places with a lady beside her, evidently in order that she might be again hidden from my view by that envious curtain. I saw and acknowledged the reproof, and, returning to the box I had left, apologised, as best I could, for my abrupt departure.

" Twice again, and twice only, in the course of that evening, did I gain a glimpse of my fair charmer, but those glimpses were sufficient to rivet the fetters with which I was already bound. I tried to think of Amoosta, but I could not. The fair northern had usurped her place, and the more classical beauty of the East was, for a time, dethroned. I noted the box in which she had sat, and during all the subsequent day, I made many enquiries, and spent many francs in vain, in order to discover her name and address. I could learn no more than that, to all appearance, it was an English party that had occupied that box the previous evening—where she had come from, whither she had gone to, it was impossible to discover. I went again the next evening that the opera was open, to inspect every box, and every stall, but my fair northern was no where to be seen; the box she had occupied before, was now tenanted by a bevy of French dowagers, as unlike my fair charmer in their then external appearance, as their frames were doubtless that of the Venus de Medici.

" To you, in whom the passions of love and admiration have not been ripened under a tropical sun, it may appear folly or madness in me to confess, that I became melancholy and unhappy from that moment. The theatre was a kind of forlorn hope—she might possibly be there again, and, with this hope, I had buoyed myself up during all that day. The disappointment was misery, and I returned to my home, wretched and disconsolate. In vain did I argue with myself, that my passion was foolish and hopeless; that, allowing I were introduced to her, there was very little chance of her reciprocating my affection, and still less of her parents sanctioning our love; in vain did the image of Amoosta reproach me in my dreams for my forgetfulness; the whole ardour of my soul was monopolized by the fair-haired beauty, I had no time to think of any one else. I sank into a kind of senseless lethargy, from which my friends vainly endeavoured to rouse me by amusements, by bantering, and by argument. I would not, nay, I could not, be wise. My senses and my mind were overpowered. At length, on one occasion, we drove to Versailles. I remember the occurrences of that day, now, as though it had been but yesterday. We were midway between Paris and the superb palace, when a carriage drove past us, going in the opposite direction.

"I had not failed, according to my wont, to peer into it, and there, reclining languidly, apparently overpowered by heat and fatigue, I saw the same fair form that had enchanted me at the opera. She was alone too. I almost screamed with surprise and delight. My companions really thought me mad. I insisted upon being put down where we were, as I could not prevail upon them to pursue the fair stranger. I ran wildly along the road to Paris, looking for some hirer-out of horses and carriages, that I might follow the enchantress. At length, at a miserable inn, I succeeded, after infinite trouble, for my French was by no means of the most fluent, or correct description, in hiring an old calèche, with one wretched horse, but not till the carriage I wished to pursue, had long been out of sight. The big round drops coursed each other rapidly down my forehead, as I waited impatiently for the vehicle to be prepared. The French, however, unlike my English friends, did not think me insane. They are more accustomed to impetuosity and eagerness in the affairs of the heart. At length we started. Had the horse been a Pegasus, and flown rapidly through the air, he could scarcely have gone too fast for my excitement, but he was far from being a Pegasus, and, it was only by dint of the most incessant appliances of the whip, that I could get him to advance at any reasonable rate.

"The chace was an unequal one, however.

The horses of the carriage in which my fair innamoráta had been whirled so rapidly away, were doubtless private ones, in excellent condition, spirited and swift. The miserable hack that drew my calèche was thin and jaded. I had hoped to obtain but a glimpse of the vehicle I was pursuing, that I might afterwards be able to keep it in view, but I was completely disappointed. To the barrier of Paris we advanced at an irregular gallop, my eyes eagerly straining into the road in advance of us, but without success, and it was not until the police at the barrier of *Sainte Marie* had seized my horse's head, and compelled the wild chace to end, that I reflected on the utter inutility of continuing it further. I dismissed the venerable calèche, and entered Paris on foot, a sadder, if not a wiser youth.

"Again and again did I frequent the theatre and the road to Versailles, but without success, and at length my health began to give way under the incessant excitement of my mind. I resolved, therefore, to quit Paris, and to accept of an invitation from an old Anglo-Indian, settled at Cheltenham, who wished me to spend a month with him. Mr. Haughton had been in the Company's Civil Service in Calcutta, and having been under some obligations to my father, was anxious to show, by his hospitality to me, that he had not forgotten them. He was a peculiar, taciturn man, who seldom went into society, but allowed his daughters, and their maiden aunt, his sister, to visit as they pleased. On the evening on which I joined his family he was alone in the house, all the other members of it having departed on a visit to the lions of Cirencester. They were not expected back till late, and being fatigued by my journey, and far from well, I retired at an early hour.

"Next morning, as usual, Mr. Haughton, who was as regular as the hands of the clock that stood in his own dining-room, was the first in the breakfast-parlour, and on my joining him, told me he expected the ladies presently. In a few minutes they made their appearance, and you may fancy, though I cannot describe, my astonishment, pleasure, confusion, and surprise, when I saw in the person of his youngest daughter, Miss Maria Haughton, the very lady who had so powerfully impressed her image on my heart in the Opera at Paris, and whom I had so unsuccessfully pursued on the road from Versailles.

"My confusion, which was very apparent to the aunt and the elder sister, although they probably attributed it to Oriental 'gaucherie,' was quite unobserved by Mr. Haughton, who merely remarked that it was already five minutes past the usual breakfast-hour, as he seated himself at the table. What an extraordinary position was mine! I had fled from the thoughts of the fair Maria at Paris to throw myself into her very presence and society. I could not be deceived in those shining ringlets, those dark hazel eyes, full of light and happiness; that delicate hand and arm. I had noted them all too minutely—they had been too firmly stamped upon my heart to admit of my having been deceived.

"'You have just returned from Paris,' said Miss Haughton, the aunt, to me; 'my nieces have been on a visit there with an uncle, and have been but three weeks at home.' Yes, thought I, whilst I took care to say something else; yes, I knew they had been there very well, I could have sworn it.

"'And did you like Paris?' I asked of Maria. 'Like it,' she replied, 'I was enchanted with it. It was my second visit, but I should never be tired of it.' Her eyes sparkled with pleasure as she spoke. I felt like a partially intoxicated man —too full of happiness.

"I cannot delay upon this unfortunate portion of my career. The very remembrance of it is harrowing to me now, and I have been ever since doing my utmost to forget it; but alas, where the conscience has once been violently outraged, there is little chance of ultimate oblivion of the circumstances. I was madly, violently in love with Maria. My own fondly-attached Amoosta was quite forgotten, or only remembered as an unpleasant *incubus* that must sooner or later be shaken off.

"The sound of Maria's voice, her very foot-fall vibrated through me with an extraordinary degree of power; it was as if I had delivered myself over to an infatuation which was luring me to destruction. She encouraged my attentions; there was ever a winning smile upon her lips, a gracious word to cheer me, when I showed an anxiety to oblige her. She had never been in India, and had therefore not learned to despise the Orientals; she looked upon me merely as a man, and saw no reason why I should not be treated as any other man. Would that she *had* despised me, and my pride would have revolted at her contempt, and been my preserver! Her aunt encouraged, whilst her sister was displeased at my attentions. Mr. Haughton either did not observe them, or treated them as a matter of profound indifference, as long as they did not interfere with his domestic arrangements, or retard the dinner-hour a moment. Often, to please the caprice of my enchantress, did I make my appearance in Parsee costume, and as I spared neither money nor pains to render it imposing, it was universally admired. The aunt, doubtless, looked upon me with a favourable eye on account of the reports which Mr. Haughton had heard of my father's wealth, whilst the sister, as I soon found to my cost, looked upon me with horror as a heathen.

"At length I found a favourable opportunity of declaring my passion. We were quite alone without fear of interruption. Maria heard me with emotion, yet my declaration was evidently expected. 'Hormanjee,' said she, 'why make such an avowal to me? You know I am a Christian.' And so saying, she looked me full in the face, as though she would read what was in my secret thoughts. 'And for thee, Maria—for thee, lovely and adorable Maria—I would become anything,' I passionately exclaimed, 'I too, will be a Christian.' 'Will you! will you indeed?' said she, 'Will you, for my sake become a Christian? Oh, then, I shall be sure you love me! Until then, however, no more of this. When you have indeed become a Christian, I am sure my father will listen to you.' 'And, should he not?' I asked; 'what then, Maria? Remember, I am one of those natives whom he has been accustomed to despise for years. Should he not listen to me, Maria?' I understood her to whisper a faint, 'I will,' as she sobbed upon my shoulder.

"The next Sunday I went with the family to church. It was the first time I had been at the Protestant service, and my conscience did not fail to reproach me, even then, for joining in rites and prayers which I regarded as vain and false. But Maria was in the pew, and beneath the veil which partially concealed her features, I knew that her eyes were frequently turned towards me. I had become too great an adept, however, at dissimulation to allow any portion of my feelings to exhibit themselves in my countenance or my manner. I had learned the fatal European secret of hiding my thoughts. The sermon pleased me much. It was upon the duty of benevolence, and frequently reminded me of one of those extraordinary questions which Zoroaster (as you call him) put to Ormuzd when admitted to the presence. 'Who is the best of your servants?' asked the prophet. And the reply was, 'He who has a right heart. He who fails not in practising justice, whose eyes do not wander after riches. He who does good to everything in the world, will be eternally happy; whilst those who afflict my people, and disregard my precepts shall be sent to hell.'

"At length the time came when our mutual affection must be made known to Maria's father, and, for his verdict we looked as anxiously forward as the criminal for the sentence of the judge. Maria's aunt undertook to mention the matter. He received the announcement more calmly than we had anticipated, for we were in an adjoining room, in breathless expectation. 'Humph,' he exclaimed, 'this, then, is why he was so ready to prolong his visit, notwithstanding his devotion to the Opera, and the great length of time he has already been from India. Manuckjee will not thank me for making his son a Christian. The idea is absurd—in love with a Parsee, forsooth! Pshaw, nonsense—Manuckjee is rich to be sure; but would he leave his wealth to a Christian, do you think? Not a bit of it. And, besides, I won't have any converts about me. I hate converts. If he says he's a Christian, it's all nonsense. He'll laugh at the priest that baptizes him. O don't talk to me, I know them better than you do. I never saw a Parsee become a Christian. I tell you they are as bigoted as—as bigoted as —as—' the old gentleman could not find a better simile, so he said, 'as the very devil. Are they there? This folly must be put an end to, at once.'

"Maria and I entered. Her hand was in my arm; and, although she was deadly pale, yet she declared her fixed determination to persevere. 'Hormanjee,' said Mr. Haughton, 'have you forgotten Manuckjee, your mother, your religion, your nation?' 'For her, Sir,' I replied firmly, 'I can forget all.' 'Now, come, Hormanjee, you're a sensible lad,' he said blandly, but craftily; 'you don't mean to tell me—me, who have been in India—you don't mean to tell me you are a Christian.' 'I do,' said I, feeling more and more convinced that some awful trial was at hand. 'You do; very well, pray be seated.' He then turned to Maria's aunt, and said quietly, 'Order a light here please, to seal a letter.' My nerves shivered at the fearful idea, which now grasped my heart and squeezed the blood from it, as one would water from a sponge:—a light—he wants to see if I am indeed a Christian; O Maria, little do you know the sacrifice I now make for you, thought I, whilst I felt some great change coming over me, that I could not understand. The light was brought, and placed upon the table. 'There,' said Mr. Haughton, with a calm, clear voice, that formed an awful contrast with the turmoil in my mind, with the agony I was enduring—'There,' said he, 'is the Parsee's god. If Hormanjee be indeed a Christian, let him extinguish that light.' Maria looked at me in triumph. To her it seemed an easy feat. To me it was—hell. It was severing the ties that bound me to my nation, to my religion, to my father's house. I felt the room whirling, my head swimming, my brain on fire, as I rose from my chair and advanced to the table.

"I cannot even now think of that fatal moment without shuddering. I *did* extinguish the light, and next day I was in a brain fever; for fourteen days did I lie utterly unconscious of all around me. Maria's aunt tended me with the care of a mother, and I slowly recovered. My first conscious thoughts were of her for whom I had made the sacrifice, and I asked earnestly after her. For days I was lulled with lying assurances, and it was not until I was strong enough to bear further torture, that I found she had abandoned me.

"With the cold calculation of the north, she would make no sacrifice for one who had sacrificed all for her. She had left a note for me, deeply regretting all that had occurred, but she was sure we could never be happy together. I had made evidently a great sacrifice for her, its very extent proved how little I was of a Christian, how much still of a Parsee.

"I tore the letter and flung it from me. Would that I could as easily have torn her image from my heart! I endeavoured to do so however, and I partially succeeded. After six months further residence in London — a gloomy and miserable six months—I felt that I might again venture to meet my Amoosta, and in her love and truthfulness, console myself for the cold falsehood of Maria.

"I sailed in one of the splendid Indian vessels round the Cape to Calcutta. The voyage of four months, tedious and monotonous to others, was to me as a healing medicine—a balm for the wounds my soul had sustained. Gradually the idea of Maria faded from my heart, with all the guilt and reproach which that image called up in my own conscience. I diligently studied the Zend-Avĕsta, and, in its pages, found consolation under my trials; my religious duties were earnestly and unremittingly pursued—I no longer put off my native habit, and, in resuming it, I seemed, now that every breeze was sending me further and further from the scene of my degradation and my fall, to put on my nationality again. It was as if I had been awaking from some horrible and oppressive dream.

"I arrived at Calcutta only to hear, alas! that death had been making sad havoc with my family and my friends. My mother was gone. Amoosta's sister was dead, and she herself lay incapable of the slightest exertion—she was at the very door of the tomb. Our Parsee mausoleums (*dokma*, or towers of silence, as we call them) are peculiar, as are indeed our rites of sepulture and ordinances of every kind. We have no burial-place in this island of the same character as those in the large cities of India. A high circular wall, with a single door, encircles a space, in the centre of which is dug a deep pit. Around the pit and extending to the wall, rises tier above tier of stone benches on which the corpse is laid. There is no roof to this gloomy abode of the dead, and the crow, the hawk, the vulture, and the adjutant plume their wings, as they sit lazily upon the summit of the wall, waiting for their horrible repasts.* The bones, once stripped, are consigned to the pit in the middle of the large enclosure, and when the pit is full, the cemetery is finally closed—its door barred up, and all ingress denied. Such is the Parsee mausoleum of Calcutta.

" The father, Kowasjee, regarding me as the cause of the illness of his beloved Amoosta, would not see me, and had indeed strictly forbidden my visits to his house. She lay at the point of death, yet I could not see her! Her attendant was induced by my sister to grant me an interview, and she assured me that Amoosta spoke but of me when her tongue could perform its office—that her father would not allow the European physicians into his house, declaring that they had killed her sister—and that she was now steeped in a kind of lethargy that seemed the result of the medical

* A model of the Parsee *dokma* may be seen in the Museum of the Royal Asiatic Society, London.

treatment she had experienced. My heart, torn rudely as it had been by the cold treachery of Maria, was now doomed to have its healing wounds reopened to bleed afresh. I implored Kowasjee by letter and by messenger to see me, and to permit me to send a skilful physician, with whom I was acquainted, to Amoosta. I could get no reply to my messages or my notes.

"A week had elapsed since my arrival in Calcutta, and I was walking sorrowfully in the garden where I had walked years ago nurturing boyish dreams. I was still very young, yet the events I had experienced had prematurely developed my mind, and I felt grave and melancholy, as though I had gone through a long and thoughtless career, and was only now beginning to reflect upon it. A servant approached and informed me that a female of the household of the Kowasjee desired an interview. It was the attendant of Amoosta, and her appearance indicated mourning and sorrow for the departed. 'Amoosta is then dead?' I asked. 'So they say, my lord,' was her reply—'for days she has been insensible, but since last night all sign of animation has left her—the *mubed** has pronounced her dead, and she is to be removed to the cemetery this evening.'

* Parsee priest.

"It is possible, thought I, they may be mistaken; this woman seems to hint as much. What an awful thought, to be consigned to the vultures, and the adjutants, and the kites, amid the horrors of a charnel-house, alive! 'See,' said I, 'take care that the body of Amoosta is well wrapped up in the usual clothes, but let not the head be tightly bound—the folds must be ample, and the cerements more abundant than usual.' 'It shall be done as my lord wills. Will not my lord visit his betrothed?' she asked. 'No,' said I, 'I will waive that right, as her father does not look upon me with the eye of love. How does he bear the loss?' 'He is all but mad. O, Zardusht, comfort him!' she exclaimed wildly. 'Go, my friend,' said I, recompensing her for her attention, 'and remember my words. Let the funeral robes be more ample than usual, with abundant folds, and loosely wrapped round the head.' 'It shall be done as my lord wills,' she replied, as she left me.

"I hurried off to the *Nasursalas*, those whose miserable office it was to bear the dead bodies into the cemetery. Their feet alone have trodden its unhallowed precincts; for, whilst the mourners wait without, they leave the body on one of the stone benches prepared for the purpose, and, removing the funeral clothes, which become their perquisites, they hurry from the tomb, that they may not share it with the filthy birds who swarm upon the body in crowds at once. I saw these men. Their very touch is defilement by our law. I bargained with them for the funeral clothes of the fair girl that day to be consigned to the tomb. These funeral clothes, contrary to their wont, they were to leave untouched; and by an ample bounty I removed their scruples, or silenced their consciences, respecting the propriety of this unprecedented procedure.

"I then went to the guardian of the tomb—a priest. Here I had a more difficult task to perform. None but the feet of the body-bearers might, by our law, enter the cemetery—to open it to any others was to violate custom, and what he believed to be his duty. Money is all-powerful on earth, however. I explained my object to him. I implored him to consider the cruelty of allowing a fair and lovely girl to be torn to pieces by ravenous birds, when, perhaps, she was not dead. I solemnly promised to leave her there, if the medical gentleman who accompanied me pronounced her dead; and, finally, I put twenty gold mohurs* into his hand. He weighed my arguments and the gold—both were good—and admission, as soon as it became quite dark, was promised.

"Dr. Wells had been a passenger with me

* A gold mohur is equal to 16 rupees, or 32 shillings.

round the Cape. We had become intimate on the voyage, and he was still in Calcutta, although preparing to join a remote station up the country. I had little difficulty in persuading him to accompany me, and to adopt, for that purpose, a Parsee costume; for the priest would never have admitted an infidel into the mausoleum. The very novelty of the enterprise would probably have been sufficient to have induced him to come, even had he not known that I was rich.

"That evening, about six o'clock, the mournful procession, bearing the body of Amoosta, deposited it upon the stone bier prepared for that purpose, outside the mausoleum. The priest advanced, and sprinkling the usual perfumes, whilst he recited the customary invocations, he opened the door of the mysterious tomb. A cold shudder ran through my veins, for I was near, but disguised, as I saw the bearers emerge, like spirits, from a shed in the vicinity, and noiselessly advance to the corpse. Their well-oiled bodies were half-naked, and not a sound was heard, save the hurried departure of the friends of the deceased, as the *Nasar-salas* lifted her up and bore her into that abode of dead humanity and live birds of prey. In a few minutes they, too, hurried away, and the door was hastily shut. I watched them narrowly —they had kept their promise—the cerements had not been removed.

"I never could have believed that hours were

so long as I found them on that night. The clocks seemed to stand still—the very seconds would not tick with their usual rapidity. At length it was half-past seven, and Dr. Wells and I stepped into the carriage at that moment. We left it near the cemetery, but not within sight, and I had taken the precaution to obtain a European coachman from a livery-stable in Durrumtollah for the evening.

"It was a dark night fortunately for our purpose. We both had lanterns, the light of which was as yet hidden by a slide. The priest silently opened the door of the cemetery as we advanced, and we shudderingly entered. We had no sooner done so than we heard the door shut and locked behind us. All was impenetrably dark, but the horrid effluvia of rotting bones told too plainly where we were. We moved the slides of our lanterns, and two streams of light burst forth into the gloom. There was a dull, flapping sound, overhead—it was a vulture, disturbed by our intrusion, watching us from above. We advanced a step or two cautiously, until our eyes should get accustomed to our position. Wells stumbled over something as he put down his foot. We turned the light of our lanterns upon it. 'It's only a skull,' said he, 'let us get nearer the centre, near the pit you speak of, and we shall probably be able to see the benches around.' He was right, that was the best measure we could adopt. A path led directly from the door to the pit, whilst others, on either hand, ran round between the stone benches on which the bodies were placed. I, too, stumbled over a bone, and putting out my hand to steady myself, it rested for a moment on the ribs of a skeleton, which were stretched in confusion by my side. 'This smell from the pit is overpowering,' said Wells, as we advanced. 'Have you the brandy-flask?' I gave it to him —we both required it.

"Raising our lamps, we allowed the light to gleam round the awful inclosure. Directly opposite to us—one of the first objects we saw—was a head, standing on the edge of the bench, where the birds had doubtless left it; the light from our lanterns gleamed full into its eyeless sockets,—the lower jaw still hung to it, with all its ghastly teeth, by a tendon. A half-consumed body, with its entrails hanging upon the ground, was being devoured by two vultures, whom even the light did not disturb. From hearing the birds in that direction, we had thought for a moment, it was what we were looking for. At length, Wells, who was infinitely more calm and collected than I was, in this abode of death, perceived the garments, surrounding the body we sought, upon a bench at no great distance. To reach it, over bones and filth, was but the work of a moment. The birds had departed, foiled by the voluminous folds of the cerements, the outer of which were torn in various places, by their ravenous bills. I raised the head, and removing the covering, exposed to the full beams of the lantern, the loveliest features they had ever shone upon. Dr. Wells proceeded minutely to examine the body. 'There is life here still,' he said at length, cautiously and slowly, 'but this atmosphere will soon extinguish it. She must be removed at once.' So saying, he moistened the lips with the brandy. I gave him my lantern, and, taking the precious burden in my arms, followed him from that horrid scene of death and decay. The priest was at the door, and would have opposed the departure of the body—but we heeded him not, and, making our way to the carriage, were speedily beyond the reach of his importunities and his resistance.

" By assiduous care and attention, Amoosta revived. For three years she was my wife in Calcutta—for six more in Bombay—and now in Ceylon, you can judge for yourself by what she is, after having borne me six children, and experienced many trials, whether I have exaggerated as to what she was."

APPENDIX.

HISTORY OF CEYLON, 1140–1186, A.D.

THE REIGN OF PRACKRAMA THE GREAT.

NOTHING perhaps can show more forcibly the sameness of the human character, all over the globe, than the fact that the manner in which the princes of the tropical and luxuriant Ceylon were educated in the earliest times, was very similar to that by which a modern English gentleman is fitted for his duties.* Prackrama, we are informed, was first introduced to the literature of his country—or more properly, perhaps, of his religion—by a priest of great literary attainments; remarkable as well for extent of knowledge as for profoundness of intellect. Under his tuition the young prince became a profound master of the Budhist faith, of logic, grammar, poetry, and music. Nor were physical exercises wanting to give strength to his body and decision to his mind. Horsemanship, archery, and the management of elephants, were also cultivated by him with success; and, under the paternal instructions and care of his cousin, he became fit for the station which he was afterwards to fill, but he had yet to complete his education by travelling. For this purpose he set out with a dignified retinue, and as the countries which he visited

* We must not forget, however, that this enlightened education was given in Ceylon when Europe was confined to the *trivium* of the schools.

are not mentioned, we may fairly conclude that they would be the neighbouring shores of the continent, and, perhaps, Burmah.

The mind of Prackrama, however, needed not the excitement of travel to render it active and ambitious. On returning to Ceylon he was unwilling to hold the station of a subordinate, and formed the ungenerous resolution of dethroning Gajabahu the reigning prince of Rohona. What an exemplification of the ingenious remark of Cicero does this afford us: "Veræ amicitiæ rarissime inveniuntur in iis qui *in honoribus reipublicæ* versantur." Respecting the particulars of his enterprize we are left uninformed. It is however stated, that having become by his imposing qualities the favourite of the people, he found little difficulty in obtaining an armament. His first enterprise was against the subordinate governor of a small province, called Badalattaliya. Him he defeated and slew, and next directed his march against Gajabahu, whom he obliged to fly from the capital into Saffragam. The capital was retaken afterwards by Gajabahu, and when both parties were on the eve of a decisive struggle, the priests interposed and brought about an accommodation. By this agreement Prackrama received the sovereignty from his competitor, who voluntarily resigned it A. D. 1153, precisely twenty-seven years subsequent to the death of Wijayabahu, making the 119th prince of the Singha race who mounted the Singhalese throne. In this great number many subordinate princes are of course included, and many whose names we have not mentioned, their reigns affording little but the name.

On the abdication of Gajabahu, Wickramabahu asserted his claim to the supremacy, a claim which Prackrama was by no means prepared to allow. Avoiding as much as possible a contest with his father, the young prince proceeded to reduce some other parts of the kingdom which still resisted his authority. During his absence on this expedition, Wickrama, with an ungenerous treachery, sent an army into his defenceless province, which occupied the principal fortresses. Prackrama hastened back to revenge the injury, and by his presence quickly changed the situation of affairs. Pihitee, the province of which Pollanarua was the capital, was quickly delivered from its enemies, and Prackrama's father was obliged to recross the Mahavelli-ganga as a fugitive. Shortly before his death he sent for his son; mutual forgiveness was exchanged between them, and the aged prince died, at peace with his impetuous offspring.

We must not omit a romantic adventure related of the prince, which would, were it true, entitle him to the appellation "Cœur de Lion" more justly, perhaps, than its ascription to Richard of England. When travelling with a small train of attendants, through an unfrequented part of the country, an enormous lion sprang forward, with open jaws and lashing tail, as though maddened with rage. All the attendants of the prince fled, leaving him alone. He disdained to retreat; and, advancing, grappled with the lion, to such advantage that the monarch of the forest preferred flight to the combat, and left him rejoicing in his prowess. Lions, however, being unheard of in the island, we may reasonably doubt the truth of the story.

Having become undisputed monarch of the island, Prackrama commenced his reign by restoring Budhism to all its ancient magnificence. For this purpose he appointed particular officers to inspect the state of the temples, and report accordingly: he spared no expense in supplying himself with valuable works for these temples, and paid much honour to the priesthood. The leaders by whose assistance he had gained the throne were placed in situations suitable to their merits. Guards were stationed round the coast to give notice of hostile intrusion. Canals and tanks which had become choked were cleared and again made beneficial. Strong fortifications were erected in convenient positions, as places of refuge in case of sudden reverse. Rice-fields were formed of great extent. A rampart of stone was erected round the capital, and, in fact, no means were neglected to render his kingdom prosperous and powerful. Nor were these exertions vain; for we are informed that Ceylon became by them united and powerful as a nation, and its inhabitants happy and flourishing. A palace for himself, and suitable habitations for the higher orders of priesthood, were next erected; and an extensive garden was planned, with a coronation hall in the midst. The wall encompassing Pollanarua, we are informed, was thirty-six miles in length on one side, and sixteen on the other, showing, if this assertion be true, the enormous size of the city itself. Whilst he was thus embellishing his capital, the ancient city of Anuradhapoora was not neglected. A minister was sent there for the express purpose of investigating the state of the buildings, and of having them put into proper repair.

Whilst thus cultivating, with so much success, the arts of peace, Prackrama was suddenly interrupted by a revolt in Rohona. This revolt was instigated by Subhala, the consort of the tributary prince who had been conquered by Prackrama. The resolution to rebel having been taken, she carried on the necessary preparations with great spirit and energy, proving, by her abilities, that she was an enemy not unworthy of Prackrama himself.

Large and deep moats were dug round the fortified places. The roads leading into the province were rendered impassable to the elephants and cavalry by large trees which they had felled, and fixed deeply in the ground by stakes. The plains were covered by the Rohonians with brambles and thorns, and, in short, every means taken for a vigorons defence. Prackrama was not disposed to regard these things with indifference. Rackha, one of his old generals, was placed at the head of a large and well-armed force. Having marched directly against the enemy, he found them determined to defend one of the roads which they had before fortified. An obstinate battle ensued, in which the Rohonians were at last obliged to give way. Their retreat became a flight, their flight a rout; and at the same time the adjoining fort, into which they attempted to throw themselves, was carried in the melée. The hopes of these mountaineers were not to be overcome, however, by the loss of a single battle; and so closely was Rackha beset in the conquered fort, that he was obliged to send to Prackrama for a reinforcement.

Bhutha, another of the generals and friends of Prackrama, was immediately despatched to his aid, and a junction of the two armies was, after some delay, effected. The war was then renewed "with redoubled spirit." Many battles were fought with various success, but, on the whole, so much to the disadvantage of the Rohonians, that they formed the resolution of emigrating in a body with all their goods; and, what was more thought of with many of the relics of Budha. Prackrama having been informed by some of his private emissaries of their intention, sent strict orders to Rackha and Bhutha to leave no exertion untried to prevent its execution. In order to give them the means of obeying his command a fresh reinforcement was despatched under the command of Kierthy. A line of circumvallation was then drawn by the united forces round the principal strongholds of the rebels, and so well arranged were their exertions that no large body could leave the district without their permission. Straitened by the strict blockade which they endured, the Rohonians were at length forced to surrender the relics and submit. Subhala, however, the ambitious woman who had incited the rebellion, was not taken, nor does it appear that the generals of the king insisted, as they ought to have done, on her surrender. Having thus restored the kingdom once more to peace and prosperity, the king resolved to impose upon the vulgar minds of the people by a magnificent procession, as a type of his power and prosperity.

On a fortunate day, appointed by the astrologers, the king appeared before his attending nobles, his courtiers holding an emblazoned canopy over his head. Immediately on his appearance instruments of music were sounded on all sides; banners waved in the air; the people shouted, "like the loud bellowing of the rushing sea," "Long live the king!" whilst the sky was almost clouded by the smoking perfumes of all kinds. The haughty Prackrama having bowed to the multitudes around, then ascended the royal elephant, at the same time that the nobles entered into their carriages. "With great pomp, amidst the noise of the roaring of elephants, neighing and prancing of horses, rattling of carriages, beating of tom-toms, blowing of chanks, and playing of music,"* the procession wended its way along. The queen and Prackrama appeared at its head, in two splendid towers placed on elephants, with golden crowns upon their heads. Next followed the principal leaders of the late rebellion, walking, followed by the officers of state and grandees, whilst innumerable multitudes concluded the imposing show. Such an important ceremony was not allowed, however, to pass over without a miracle. Suddenly, in the midst of their pomp, the sky became overcast, the heavens lowered, and threatened the rejoicers with an inopportune deluge. The thunder then began to roar, the lightning to flash, and a keen wind to

* Mahawanso, ch. 73.

course over the earth. Prackrama was not a man to be frightened with a tempest: the procession went on, regardless of the impending rain, and now behold the miracle! The rain descended in volumes all around, but not a drop upon man or beast engaged in the ceremony. Whilst the neighbouring rivers and tanks were choked with water, they remained perfectly dry. "Behold," exclaims the author of the Mahawanso, "this striking instance of the power of Budha."

But even this instance of Divine favour could not humble the mind of Subhala: the daughter and wife of a king, she still asserted her rights to be a monarch; and scarcely had the rejoicings of Prackrama ended ere intelligence was brought from Rohona of another insurrection. Two battles (in one of which 12,000 Rohonians are said to have fallen) and a siege were the result of this temerity, and the enterprising queen was at length brought as a captive before her rival. Of her future fate we are uninformed; but as her name does not occur again in the annals of her country, we may conclude that her life paid the penalty of her rebellion.

Subsequent to the sixteenth year of Prackrama's reign (A. D. 1169), and probably very shortly after that year, although we are uninformed of the precise period, he formed the resolution of revenging on the king of Cambodia * and Arramana† the injuries he had inflicted on several of the Singhalese subjects. These injuries consisted in plundering merchants, slighting the ambassador of Ceylon, and intercepting some vessels conveying certain women of rank from that island to the continent.

In the Ratnacari and Rajawali, however, the only reason stated for this invasion is, that he slighted and

* This country still retains its ancient appellation.

† Probably that part of the Burmese peninsula between Arrakan and Siam.

dishonoured the religion of Budha, an offence worthy, in their eyes, of the most condign punishment. To avenge himself on this despiser of Budha, and slighter of Ceylon, five hundred vessels, and a great armament of seamen and soldiers, ammunition, and provisions, were equipped in a few months. A Malabar general, named Adikaram, of great and distinguished renown, was put at the head of this expedition, and it was accordingly despatched.

Having first landed on an island called Kakha, they obtained good omens of their future success by gaining the first battle in which they engaged, the consequence of which was the submission of that part of the island and the taking of several prisoners. Encouraged by this success they sailed for Cambodia, and landed at a port called Koosuma, where the enemy appeared drawn up in front of their entrenchments in great force.

Adikaram, having drawn up his forces in line of battle on the beach, advanced against the enemy, and was received with showers of arrows, which the Singhalese returned; but, as the Cambodians seemed unwilling to leave their entrenchments, it was necessary for Adikaram to force them, and this he accomplished by a resolute and determined attack. Sword in hand the Singhalese advanced, disregarding the missiles of the enemy, and, after a short but severe struggle, the entrenchments were forced, the Cambodians routed, and their king slain in the confusion.

Adikaram, like a prudent general, lost no time in following up his advantages by advancing on the capital, where the country was proclaimed tributary to the great and glorious Prackramabahu, king of Ceylon. Tribute was accordingly collected, and a viceroy appointed.

After this signal success, Prackrama turned his arms against the united kingdoms of Pandi and Sollee, in southern India, who, fearing to meet alone so formidable a prince, had prudently joined their forces. Another expedition was fitted out, and proceeded to the enemies' territories. At Madura, where a landing was first attempted, they found the shore so thickly covered with the enemy that they were obliged to proceed up the coast to Talatchilla (probably Tellicherry); there also, however, the enemy had anticipated them, and were assembled in force. The army of Prackrama was not to be twice repulsed; numerous boats were manned with the troops, which, amidst showers of arrows and spears, advanced towards the shore, and, as soon as a convenient station had been gained, the soldiers leaped out: stooping, and covering themselves with their shields, they advanced in a line against their opposers, and fortunately succeeded in putting them to flight. A landing having thus been effected with so much difficulty, the invaders found the remaining part of the country was as obstinately contested as the shore had been. Five pitched battles were fought, in each of which the army of Prackrama was successful, and by which the whole province of Ramisseram came into the possession of the Singhalese. Whilst the invaders were, after these exploits, enjoying the fruits of their victories in their encampments, an army of the enemy hastily attacked them, and had well nigh rendered all their previous victories useless. But the Singhalese were now soldiers in every sense of the word, and quickly revenged the losses they had sustained, so that in the last and most terrible conflict the Pandians sustained a severe defeat; thousands of them were slain, and the remainder was pursued by the whole Singhalese army for a distance of sixteen miles. The consequence of these victories was, that Kulasaikera, the king of Pandi, was dethroned, and his son, Weerapandu, raised in his stead, as a tributary of Prackrama.

Having thus happily terminated his foreign wars, the

attention of the king was next directed to the adornment of Budhism. The religious edifices of Anuradhapoora were enriched with numerous offerings and additions, and Prackrama himself went there to superintend the erection of a golden spire upon the Ruanelli dāgobah. Events of this kind are those upon which the Budhist historians delight to dwell; and, accordingly, we have a particular account of how the city was ornamented, how beautiful the women were, how glittering the flags, and how noble the entire ceremony; whilst his warlike enterprises are rehearsed only by informing us of the number of the battles, and the names of the subdued countries.

Prackrama, however, did not confine himself to the embellishment of a religion already too rich and powerful. Besides erecting new, and adorning old religious edifices, he planted several immense forests of fruit-trees, and turned the courses of several rivers, so that they might replenish the tanks already formed. Canals also were dug by him to conduct the waters of the tanks and lakes to a distance. The following three of this nature are particularly mentioned as extraordinary works: the Goodaiviree Canal to conduct the waters of the Karaganga into a lake, called the Sea of Prackrama, from which the water was conducted by twenty-four channels to all the neighbouring fields; the lake of Minneria he made available for useful purposes, by digging the Kalinda Canal, to conduct its waters to the northward; and, lastly, the Jaya-ganga Canal, by which the Kalaawene tank was rendered serviceable to the inhabitants of Anuradhapoora.

Were we to give a list of one half of the useful buildings attributed to Prackrama, we would completely weary out our readers: dāgobahs, wihares, relic repositaries, offering-houses, caverns, priests'-houses, preaching-halls, image-halls, dancing-saloons, and strangers'-houses, are but a few of the motley collection of edifices recounted with critical accuracy by the zealous Budhists. Amongst these, however, we must remark that several halls of justice, and 128 libraries are particularly enumerated. There appears little reason to doubt the truth of these details. Prackrama was by birth the sovereign of a rich, fertile, and populous country; he had, besides, rendered himself by arms the master of two important and extensive kingdoms, and being of such an active, energetic disposition, it is but natural to suppose that his many years of peace were occupied almost altogether in adorning his country.

In reviewing his character there appears, as in that of most other conquerors, much to praise and much to blame. We cannot commend his evident ingratitude and injustice to Gajabahu, in the early part of his life; at the same time that we must admire the decision and promptitude of all his measures. He appears to have possessed, in an eminent degree, all the qualities of a great commander; a quick apprehension of the difficulties and advantages of his situation on every occasion; great forethought and judgment in the formation of his plans, and no less decision in their execution. He knew eminently well how to gain the affections of his people; how to oppose presumption and to reward merit. Nor was his ability displayed alone in military affairs: he appears to have been equally energetic when at peace; equally anxious to advance his own glory and that of his people. Without one spark of patriotism in his bosom, he was eminently useful to his country, and it is with justice that his reign has been designated as "the most martial, enterprising, and glorious in the Singhalese history."—*Knighton's History of Ceylon*, pp. 134–147.

FOREST LIFE IN CEYLON

FOREST LIFE IN CEYLON

W. KNIGHTON

IN TWO VOLUMES

VOLUME 2

Published by

Facsimile Publisher
12 Pragati Market
Ashok Vihar, Ph-2
Delhi-110052
facsimilepublisher.com

Distribution Network
gyanbooks.com
India, USA, Canada, UK, Australia, France

ISBN : 978-93-5324-489-7 (Set)
ISBN : 978-93-5324-491-0 Vol. 2 (HB)
First Published, London, 1854

2nd Impression 2020

Printed at: Gyan Press, Delhi.

Forest Life in Ceylon
Author: W. Knighton

FOREST LIFE

IN

CEYLON.

BY W. KNIGHTON, M.A.

FORMERLY SECRETARY TO THE CEYLON BRANCH ROYAL ASIATIC SOCIETY.

Second Edition.

IN TWO VOLUMES.

VOL. II.

LONDON:

HURST AND BLACKETT, PUBLISHERS,

SUCCESSORS TO HENRY COLBURN,

13, GREAT MARLBOROUGH STREET.

1854.

CONTENTS OF VOLUME II.

APPENDIX.

FOREST LIFE

IN

CEYLON.

CHAPTER I.

BUDHISM.

"These oracles are hardily attain'd,
And hardly understood."
Second Part Henry VI., act i., sc. 4.

WHEN we consider what overwhelming numbers of the human race are, and have been, for two thousand years, Budhists, it is amazing to reflect how little is known in Europe of the faith which they profess. Indeed it has only been within the last twenty years that any sources of information on the subject, at all accurate and trustworthy, have been opened up to the European reader. People, even well-informed, accustomed to regard Christianity as the pervading religion of mankind, because it embraces them in its folds, have smiled incredulously or superciliously when informed that half the population of the earth, according to some calculations, and more than two hundred millions, according to the lowest, are, and have been for ages, believers in a prophet whose very name is probably unknown to them. Yet such is the case! so imperfectly are the statistics of the vast empires of China and the Eastern Peninsula known that it is impossible to say whether the followers of Gotama Budha are two or four hundred millions in number. Certain it is, however, that no other creed is believed in by so large a portion of the mass of humanity, and that none other, with the exception of Christianity, teaches doctrines so generally benevolent and humanizing.

Various conversations with my enlightened friend, Marandhan, and visits to the chief seats of Budhistic worship in Ceylon, naturally turned my attention to the faith, and it was not until I sought for information and elucidation on the subject that I discovered how difficult it was to get either with accuracy.

The date at which the founder of the faith, Gotama Budha, lived, is differently stated by different nations; some assign the period of his life-time to 1000 B. C. or earlier, and others, including the Ceylonese traditions, which are the most trustworthy, and are followed by a large portion of the Budhistic world, maintain 543 B. C. to have been the date of his birth. Of the actual existence and personality of the founder of the faith, no one, who has investigated the subject, has doubted.* Whether he lived a thousand, or only five hundred years before our Saviour, there can be no doubt that such a man as Gotama Budha actually did live, and that he engaged also in that extraordinary career of preaching and teaching which has resulted in the establishment of a new system of faith, now prevalent from Japan to Ceylon, from Cochin China to the Caspian. According to his own prophecies, strange to say, his faith is to last but 5000 years, when it will become forgotten and defunct.

The names by which he is known in different countries, vary of course, with their different languages. Thus Gotama is Kiu-tan in Chinese, Ghoutam in Tibetan, Goodam in Manchou and Mongol, and Codam in Siamese; whilst Budha, his title or office, rather than his proper name, has been variously met with by European writers as Bood, But, Wud, Pott, Fuh, Fohi, and Fo.

Gotama was the son of a prince who reigned over a district in Northern India, called Maghadha, a portion of the modern Bengal Presidency, and his conception and birth are said to

* Introduction à l'Histoire du Buddhisme Indien, par E. Burnouf.

have been signalized by many remarkable circumstances that portended the future greatness of the infant.* At the period of his miraculous conception by his mother, whose name was Maha Devi, it is said that a preter-natural light shone in every region of the universe at once, that the blind from birth received power to see, the deaf heard, the dumb spake, the lame danced for joy, the diseases of the sick were cured, the crooked were made straight, the prisoners were released, the fires of hell were, for a time, quenched, and many other prodigies occurred, the bare enumeration of which would weary the patience of the most enthusiastic reader.

As may be supposed, the birth following so wonderful a conception, was still more portentous and extraordinary. A visit from the gods and angels to welcome the new-born sage, was added to all the previous miracles. "Rejoice," said Maha Brahma, the greatest of these deities, to Gotama's mother, on presenting to her the infant. "Rejoice, for the son you have brought forth will be the support of the world." Angels too

* "The resemblance between this legend (one relating to the conception of Gotama) and the doctrine of the perpetual virginity of the mother of our Lord, cannot but be remarked." . . . "The tradition inserted by Mahomet in the chapter of the Koran, entitled 'Mary,' bears a considerable resemblance to this part of the history of Budha. Csoma Körösi says, that he does not find any mention in the Tibetan books of 'Maha Devi's' virginity, upon which the Mongol accounts lay so much stress."—*Manual of Budhism, by the Rev. R. S. Hardy*, p. 142, note

made obeisance before the infant, exclaiming, "Thou art the greatest of beings; there is here no one like thee; no one greater than thee; thou art supreme." When the child had received this homage, thoroughly understanding it and weighing well the words, he walked by his own power, looking in various directions, and at length exclaimed, "I am the most exalted in the world. I am chief in the world. I am the most excellent in the world. Hereafter there is to me no other birth." After this display of precocity and vanity we are assured that he quietly returned to his mother's arms and allowed himself to be handled and tended like any ordinary child. Such are the absurd legends connected with his conception and birth, recorded by the chroniclers of his life. In this, however, they but resembled the biographers of Zoroaster and Mohammed, who have also filled the lives of their saints with legends as ridiculous and incredible.

The father of Gotama, Sudhodana, having been made acquainted by his wife and some spiritual intelligence with the extraordinary character of his reputed son, and of the asceticism and trials amid which a large portion of his life should be passed, resolved, if possible, to avert the honour intended for him, and to keep the boy as much as possible away from those who would be likely to give his mind a religious bent; and as years passed on, and the youth became a man, he doubtless concluded that he had been successful, notwithstanding the prognostications of others. It was not till he was twenty-nine years of age that Gotama left his father's house to dive deep into a distant forest, and there for six long years to live a life of voluntary asceticism and solitude, preparatory to issuing forth a reformer and a prophet; and truly, when we regard what his labours have ended in, the history of the world does not present many more striking pages in its many-volumed bulkiness, than that of this young man, giving up the luxury and enjoyment of a court, of his own free will, to acquire a reputation for sanctity by solitary meditation and a hermit's life, and then issuing forth from that forest, at thirty-five, to preach down the most terrible and pernicious of systems—Brahmanism; using no other weapons but those of precept and example, and, like our Saviour himself, wandering fearlessly amongst hosts of enemies, denouncing their wickedness and folly!

In the age in which we live, highly artificial and unnatural as it is, we may scarcely be able to conceive such a thing possible; but so it was, notwithstanding. The yellow-robed priest that appears on the hills and in the valleys of

Ceylon, in the swarming hives of Chinese life, in the peaceful gardens of Japan, and on the frontiers of the great deserts of Central Asia, is a proof of the reality of the thing, and is a living witness in this, our own age of conventional proprieties and heart-rottenness, of what that one man—alone and unaided—accomplished twenty-three centuries ago. But the oriental warmth of imagination of his followers has not been content to allow this grand historic picture to stand forth in the gallery of the universe in all its sublime simplicity for men to wonder at—to censure and admire—as suited their tastes, prejudices, or capacities; they must even colour it highly to make it more gaudy; they must overlay it with ornament to make it more glittering and captivating to small minds. Hence the miraculous machinery with which the account of his life is overburdened. Infancy, youth, manhood, age—according to them—was each miraculous, full of wonders. Let us take a specimen from his infancy.

A ploughing festival was held at the court of Sudhodana, when Gotama was five months old. The sovereign himself, with his nobles, was to make a furrow in the ground, holding the handles of a golden plough. The nobles were to make furrows likewise, and then the ordinary ploughmen were to compete with each other to gain prizes for dexterity, swiftness, and skill. "On the day that the prince went to the field," says the native chronicle, translated by Mr. Hardy, "the sight that presented itself was extremely beautiful, as the ploughmen and drivers of the oxen were dressed in garments of the gayest colours, gold and silver flags were seen, and banners, fans, ornamental vessels, and caskets; so that it seemed like a sky studded with shining stars. The one hundred nurses of the prince went outside the curtain that was placed around him, attracted by the splendour of the sight. When Gotama saw that he was left alone, he arose from his couch and ascended into the air, where he sat at some distance from the ground, self-supported." He sat in ordinary oriental fashion, doubtless; after the manner of tailors, as we should say in the West. "The nurses, on returning, saw him in this position; and running to the king, they said, 'Sire, this is the manner of *your* festival, but come and see the festival that is kept by the prince.' The monarch went to the place, and, as he approached the tree, he perceived that the shadows caused by the sun's rays were not slanting, as they ought to have been from the early hour of the morning, but directly perpendicular, as if the sun were then in the zenith; by which means the spot where the prince sat was shaded. When the king saw his son sitting in the air, he wept with joy, and, placing his son's feet upon his own head, for the second time he worshipped him."

Of tales, equally probable and equally edifying, there is no lack in the legendary life of Gotama. When he was sixteen years of age, he married,—his wife, Yasodhara, being of royal race, was accompanied by a vast crowd of female attendants, who became his concubines, or inferior wives. It was not, however, till many years after, not indeed till his twenty-ninth year, that Yasodhara became the mother of a son, and, after Gotama had taken one glance, and but one, at the infant boy and at his wife, to whom he seems to have been tenderly attached, he left the palace and his father's dominions, to become a voluntary exile and ascetic in the forest of Uruwela.

What were the motives that led him to adopt so extraordinary a course of conduct? to exchange the luxury and magnificence of a court, for the want, privation, and hardships of a wilderness? naturally asks the European reader. He was conscious, reply his biographers, of the exalted dignity for which he was intended. He knew that he was to become a Budha, and the Budha is the greatest of things in heaven, earth, or hell.

To believers in his system of faith, this answer must doubtless be sufficient, but to us who have received a purer and more sublime religion, it is unsatisfactory. Judging from all that I have read of him, and heard of him from others, who have read more, I should be inclined to give the following explanation of the enigma. He saw Brahmanism in active operation around him, and of all creeds, Brahmanism is the most foul and soul-polluting. The frenzied widow, shrieking on the funeral pile of her husband under the scorching influence of the flames, whilst the ministers of hell around, exhort her to endure, thrust her back if she attempts to escape, and command her to keep her thoughts fixed on heaven;—the devotees crackling beneath the wheels of Juggernaut's car, their dying groans drowned in the horrid music of the Brahmans; these,—and of rites as bad as these, there is no lack in Hindooism—these destroy the body, but the teaching and example of the diabolical Brahmans, destroy the soul. Sensuality and cruelty go hand in hand in their creed, the one not more refined, though varied in phase and nature, than the other. Gotama saw all this, and a thousand times more than a European public could be told, or would believe. His mind was strong, active, and imperturbable. 'These Brahmans are not leading us aright,' might he not have said to himself, ' they pretend to lead us to heaven; they are leading us anywhere but to heaven. We are all wrong together, and if no one else will try it, I at least will see whether I cannot set things right. They will oppose me, doubtless. I shall have all the fury of their bigotry, the madness of their hatred to withstand. I may lose my life, but what brave man was ever restrained from doing what he wished by that consideration? I will attempt the reformation at all events, let what will come.' If such *were* the thoughts of Gotama, his actions were in accordance with them. Sanctity, according to the belief of that day, was only to be acquired by asceticism, so he surrendered the court for the jungle. Cruelty, and the shedding of blood, were the characteristic features of Brahmanism,—benevolence, and tenderness for life, were the leading dogmas of Gotama. Once he had proclaimed himself a prophet, and had been accepted as such by thousands; all the wonders of his earlier and later years were easily invented —indefinite rumours of strange or peculiar events in his history, gradually swelled into miracles, and when these events long afterwards, were to be recorded, circumstantiality was easily given to them by over-heated Oriental imaginations.*

* The Rev. R. S. Hardy, who probably knows more of Budhism than

It was by the influence of his own merit, acquired in the course of innumerable ages, and throughout indefinite stages of existence by transmigration, that Gotama attained the high dignity of Budhaship, so Budhism teaches us, six years after he had entered the forest of Uruwela as an ascetic. Previous to the acquisition of this wonderful dignity, however, there were trials and temptations to be endured and to be overcome under which any ordinary mortal would have succumbed. In the course of these preliminary contests, physical and spiritual, we are told that he was reduced to such a state of weakness that he was unable to stand, and fell senseless to the ground, where he remained so long that the various orders of spirits, who were watching the encounters and the trials, fancied he was dead.

It was whilst sitting beneath a bo-tree (the *ficus religiosa* of botanists), a tree ever since sacred to his disciples, that Gotama finally prevailed, and became the greatest of beings. Immediately previous to this consummation he was attacked by a formidable host of demons, but re-

any of its disciples, has arrived at the same conclusion. "Whenever an important event is recorded," says he, "the day of the week, the age of the moon, the month, and the nekata, (whatever that is,) are recorded. *But it is easy to be thus minute when the annalist consults only his imagination.* The Mohammedans have a tradition that Adam was created on Friday afternoon, at the hour of Am, or between noon and evening."—*Manual of Budhism*, p. 146, note.

mained tranquil, to use the figurative language of his biographers, "like a star in the midst of stormy clouds, and the demons, when they had exerted their utmost power without effect, passed away like the thunder-cloud retiring from the orb of the moon, and causing it to appear in greater beauty."

At the tenth hour of the same night he attained the wisdom by which he knew all things, or omniscience; at the twentieth hour he received divine eyes, by which he saw all things, or omnipresence. Omnipotence was subsequently added, and, from beneath the bo-tree, the man rose with all the characteristics of a god.

He issued forth from the forest of Uruwela, proclaiming himself the ruler of the three worlds—higher than the highest, wiser than the wisest. Yet he was prudent enough, notwithstanding his assumption of universal power and universal wisdom, to attach his faith to a system which he declared men had forgotten, but had long ago been conversant with. He was merely one of a long line of Budhas—the latest link of the chain, but by no means the beginning or the end. The line would still "stretch on to the crack of doom" after his faith had disappeared, five thousand years subsequently to his attainment of the high dignity; so that there was not an enthusiastic devotee amongst his disciples that might not some day be a Budha like himself, if he had but merit sufficient, however remote or indefinite the date might be. He had been preceded by other Budhas, and should be similarly succeeded, and thus did he lash his vessel to the shore of the past, and cast its anchors into the sea of the future, to render it more stable and secure. The Christian reader has perhaps no condemnation strong enough for such pretensions and for the mass of deceit and chicanery to which they must have given rise. But let it be remembered that the system he founded was vastly superior to that which he opposed; let it be remembered that he substituted the peaceful, benevolent rites of Budhism, for the barbarian, cruel, and licentious precepts and practices of Brahmanism, and although to us this fact forms no justification of his career,—although *we* know that evil should not be done that good may come,—yet, for a heathen brought up in the worst of creeds, surely it may be allowed to be a palliative and excuse. Supposing him to have formed the resolution of attacking Brahmanism, he would regard craftiness and wile as necessary weapons. 'Open denunciation,' he would say, 'without proposing anything better, would be futile and absurd, it could not but end in failure and consequent ridicule. If I do not hinge my system on the past, and make it the avenue to an illimitable future of bliss, I can have no chance of success. Here is a man, the Brahmans will say, who says we are all wrong, and who would destroy all religion, whilst he can give us nothing better in its place—away with him, away with him.' Surely some such thoughts as these must have passed through his mind during his six long years of seclusion in the forest of Uruwela.

It must be remembered that he issued forth into the world in all the strong odour of sanctity from the hermit's cave. He was recognised as the king's son, who had voluntarily given up pomp, power, and luxury for trial, privation, and solitude. He was recognised as the man who had surrendered his infant son, his wives and concubines, his family and kingdom, for some doubtful spiritual advantage. Men would naturally regard such an individual with interest, and when he assured them that he had discovered all truth, that he had unfolded all the mysteries of being, and could confer the greatest of all possible benefits, their minds were already but too much disposed to give credence to his words and to listen favourably to his instructions. Looking at the matter in this light, there is no great difficulty in supposing that his position, his conduct, and his eloquence, would speedily surround him with a crowd of admirers and a few believers, whilst the intrinsic excellence of his ethical teaching must have impressed favourably any enquiring minds that compared his system with that of the Brahmans. There is, therefore, nothing inexplicable or mysterious in the plain facts of the case to my mind, nor do I see why the rise and spread of such a religion as Gotama's should be looked upon as a moral phenomenon, equally monstrous and unaccountable. The miracles with which the legendary account of his life abounds are to us simply exaggerations and lies, but I cannot see that they were absolutely necessary to the *first* spread of the faith; and, in such an enterprise as Gotama's, it must be evident that the chief difficulty lay in the beginning. The creed once rooted in the hearts of a few zealots would spread in geometrical progression until millions were ready to believe any tale they were told of the early history of their faith. Hence it is that I regard the miraculous narratives as the inventions of later ages and not of the period in which Gotama himself lived.

That the contrast between the mild, benevolent teaching of Gotama and the blood-thirsty precepts of the Brahman, must have been great in the extreme is evident from the traditions of his life, as well as from the beautiful moral dogmas which he taught to his disciples. On one occasion he was reproached by a Brahman for teaching his priests to live on the alms of others. "It would be better for you," continued the angry Brahman, "to plough and sow, as I do, and then you would have food to eat without begging." "Brahman," replied Gotama, "I do both plough and sow; and from my ploughing and sowing, I reap immortal fruit." On hearing this, the Brahman thought that as Gotama had neither plough nor any other instrument of husbandry, he must have spoken falsely; yet favourably impressed by the dignity of the sage, he said, "My Lord Gotama, I see no plough, no oxen, no goad; if you perform the work of the husbandman where are your implements?" In reply to this question, Gotama informed him that his field was truth; the weeds that he plucked out, a love of the world; the plough that he used, wisdom; the seed that he sowed, purity; the harvest that he reaped, *nirwana.**

The benevolent character of Gotama's doctrines is apparent in the advice he often gave to his neophytes. A merchant, on a journey, before returning home, came to Gotama, and told him he

* *Nirwana* is the summum bonum of the Budhists. It is defined to be the cessation from existence, and Gotama calls it a state of "exalted felicity"—many have regarded it as simply annihilation.

was about to become a priest, requesting at the same time, some advice. Gotama said, "Your countrymen are exceedingly violent; if they oppose you, and revile you, what will you do?" "I will make no reply," said the merchant. "If they strike you?" "I will not strike in return." "If they try to take your life?" "I will neither seek death, nor avoid it." For these answers, says the native chronicles, the merchant received the approbation of Budha. In an account of a contest with an evil spirit, in which as usual, of course, Gotama came off victorious, we are told that the evil spirit learned from the contest "that anger must be overcome by kindness, and not by violence."

When he had converted a distinguished opponent, Upali, a man of eminence in an opposing sect called the Tirttakas, Gotama ended his advice to him by telling him, that as his house had been like a pool of water, free to all, so he must continue to assist all as before, even the Tirttakas. When Upali heard this, he worshipped Gotama for the third time, declaring, that when the Tirttakas made a convert, they forbade him to assist any but those of their own sect. There was a philanthropy in the advice of Gotama which must raise him in the estimation of unbiassed minds. It is not often that men, in religious wars, are ready to succour their opponents, however common such conduct may be in the hostile encounters of rival nations.

In a discourse to a subdued enemy, Gotama "told him that they who exercised hatred, however beautiful they may be, will be regarded with aversion; and that their fate will be like that of those who are destroyed by their own weapons. And he further informed him, that they who are cruel will have to suffer much in hell: or if born in this world, will be diseased, one disease following quickly upon another; and that therefore it is better to avoid anger, and love all sentient beings, to have a soft heart, and exercise compassion."

The following translation from the *Milinda Prasna*, a native work, proves the estimate formed by his followers of the native benevolence of Gotama. "The words of Budha were never intended to cause pain. The strongest term of reproach that he ever addressed to any one was, *mogha purisa*, vain man! On one occasion he reproved the priest Kalandaka-putra, but it was as the physician who uses powerful medicine for the curing of his patient, or who may prescribe loathsome medicaments for the same purpose, or it was the parent, who, from affection, chastises the child. A profusion of fine cotton, though in size it were like a rock, might fall upon any one without his being hurt—thus lightly fell the words of Budha upon those whom he addressed."

One of the most extraordinary facts connected with the origin of Budhism is the preservation of the life of its founder to a good old age. That the Brahmans frequently attempted his destruction is recorded, his escape being constantly attributed, as we might suppose, to a miraculous exercise of power, but, although his position as of royal blood, his powerful relations and enthusiastic disciples, would all protect him from danger, yet, as we are assured that he constantly wandered about, that he preached even in Benares itself, the very head-quarters of Hinduism, it does appear extraordinary that he was not, on some occasion, destroyed by open or secret violence.

His system was not one likely to find favour with the Brahmanical caste. He admitted all classes to his priesthood, without distinction of rank or birth, so that he was thus virtually thrusting them from their usurped supremacy. At the same time he did not attempt wholly to overturn their faith or to destroy its foundations —he merely announced himself as a great reformer. He acknowledged Brahma and Shiva and Vishnu to exist, but declared himself, Gotama, greater than them all.* Brahmanism had

* Burnouf's *Introduction*.

the foundations of truth, he allowed, but the Brahmans had built on those foundations a superstructure of error, and his object was to destroy the novel erection and to restore the ancient temple they had destroyed. But besides the open and active enmity of the Brahmans, he had too another formidable evil to encounter. His example was followed by others, who similarly announced themselves as the true Budhas, denouncing him as an impostor, and the legendary history of his life assures us that as many as eighty thousand followers were led astray by some of these impostors, so that it is doubtful whether the unmitigated hostility of the Brahmans was more dangerous to him and his pretensions than the imitators of his conduct and their injurious rivalry. That his wanderings throughout India were extensive is proved by the fact of his having visited Ceylon, an incident recorded by all his disciples in all countries. He is said to have prophesied too that Ceylon would, at a future day, be the head-quarters of his faith.

He died at the age of eighty, in the neighbourhood of Delhi, and, alas for the dignity of this mightiest and most widely-spread of religions, his death was caused, according to tradition, by the eating of pork! He knew it would cause his death, say these traditions, but the time was come for him to leave the earth and attain *nirwana*; so he ate it.

When he perceived his end approaching, he gave a charge to his assembled priests. "Priests," said he in conclusion, "if you have any doubt regarding the doctrines I have taught you for five and forty years, you have permission to declare them now; otherwise you may regret that you had not the opportunity of stating them whilst I was yet in existence; or if you hesitate to make known your doubts to me, make them known to each other." As the priests did not entertain any doubts they held their peace, and Gotama proceeded: "Are there no doubts that you wish to have removed? Then I depart to *nirwana*. I leave with you my ordinances. The elements of the omniscient will pass away, but the truth, the word, and the priesthood will remain." Thus having spoken, he ceased to exist. His body was burnt upon a magnificent funeral pile, and the few bones that survived the cremation were treasured by his disciples as the most precious of earthly objects; they became bones of contention, too, between rival monarchs, and are now scattered widely over Eastern Asia, beneath the immense dome-shaped buildings characteristic of Budhism, and variously called pagodahs, dagobahs, and topes.

The moral sayings and apophthegms of Gotama may vie successfully with those of any uninspired teacher—a few will suffice as samples of the rest:—

"The worldly-minded man who applauds religion, and understands its precepts, but does not practise them, is like the herdsman of another man's cattle—he tends the flock, but does not receive the produce.

"As a man elevated upon a mountain surveys, in calmness, the plains below, so does the virtuous man behold without emotion, the struggles of the sinful multitude.

"As the fletcher makes straight his arrows, so the wise and virtuous man rectifies his mind.

"True nobility is not of one's parentage, but of a virtuous and noble soul.

"The conduit-maker guides the streams of water; the fletcher forms his arrows; the carpenter bends the wood to his purpose; but the wise man performs what is still more difficult—he guides, shapes, and controls his mind.

"As the solid rock stands unshaken by the storm, so the wise man is unmoved by contempt or applause.

"He is a more noble hero who conquers himself, than the warrior who, in the field of battle, overcomes thousands of thousands.

"Nothing is sinful to the pure.

"All the religion of Budha is contained in these three sentences—purify the mind, abstain from vice, practise virtue.

"Conquer anger by mildness, evil by good, covetousness by liberality, and falsehood by truth.

"There is no fire so fierce as lust; nothing has a grasp so pertinacious as hatred; no net can be compared with folly; no flood is so rapid as desire."*

These examples are sufficient to show that the moral duties were insisted upon by Gotama, and that his precepts were often illustrated by the most apt imagery, and the most forcible similes.

The doctrines of the faith are contained in the discourses of its founder collected into three huge tomes called the Pitakas. Of these Pitakas—the first, or *Winaya*, contains the regulations of the priesthood. The second, or *Sutra*, from which the above moral sayings have been extracted, is a collection of discourses devoted to the inculcation and illustration of moral truth. The third, or *Abhidharmma*, was addressed by Budha to the beings of the immaterial world, and is not therefore intended for man. Each of these portions is again subdivided into a number of books or parts, the names of which would but confuse the Eu-

* From the "Damma Padan," or Footsteps of Religion, a portion of the Sutra Pitaka, translated by the Rev. D. J. Gogerly, Ceylon.

ropean reader.* It was at convocations of the priesthood, assembled for the purpose, long after the death of Gotama, that these works were transcribed, and every syllable determined on and settled so as to prevent future uncertainty or change. They are written in the usual rhythmic style of Eastern sacred books, and contain nearly a million of lines, thus far surpassing western compilations in size. The sacred books of the Brahmans, however, are much larger, a portion of them alone extending to two millions of lines. The Pitakas are probably twenty times as voluminous as the Old and New Testament together. The poems of Homer contain about thirty thousand, and Milton's 'Paradise Lost' about ten thousand lines; when these are compared with the million of lines of the Pitakas, some idea may be formed of the amazing extent of the latter. They are written in the Pali, the vernacular language of Gotama's native country Magadha, a language evidently of extreme antiquity but of the precise relation which it bears to Sanscrit, the world is yet ignorant. "There is a language," say the opening lines of the Pali Grammar, "which is the root of all languages. Men and gods at the beginning of

* A full account of the matter may be found in the Introduction to Turnour's *Mahawanso*.

this cycle of existence, who never before heard or uttered a human accent, spoke it. The supreme Budha himself spoke it. It is Pali."

The priesthood founded by Gotama seems to have been the great instrument of the propagation of the faith, and, to the present day, it is distinguished by similar characteristics on the elevated table-lands of Thibet, on the shores of Ceylon and Burmah, amid the thronged cities of China, and the wild tribes of the Manchoos and Mongols, with probably less variation of dress, character, and habits, than any other similar class in the world.

The ten obligations which the Budhist priest must take upon himself are of a very onerous and self-denying character.

1st. He promises never to take animal life of any kind, or in any shape. The killing of an ant, if wilful, is with him a sin, and therefore he must not indulge in animal food unless some one else will take the guilt of the murder.

"Those who take life," said Gotama, "are in fault, but not the persons who eat the flesh. My priests have permission to eat whatever food it is customary to eat in any place or country, so that it be done, not for the indulgence of the appetite or of evil desire. If one uniform law were enforced," he adds, subsequently, "it would be a hindrance in the way of those who are seeking *nirwana*, but it is to reveal that way that the office of the Budha has been assumed by me."

2nd. The priest promises to avoid the taking of that which is not given.

"When any one conceals near the road or in the forest that which belongs to another, breaks into houses, uses false scales, demands too large a share of profit, uses false measures, or utters false money, it is theft. When any one takes more than is due, or extorts a fine larger than is allowed by law, or procures for himself that which belongs to another by the giving of false evidence, it is theft."*

3rd. The priest promises to abstain from sexual intercourse. If this obligation were however beyond his ability to keep, he was at liberty to forsake the priesthood, to put off the yellow robe, and marry.

4th. The priest promises to avoid lying.

"From the time that Gotama became a candidate for the Budhaship, through countless ages, up to his final victory under the bo-tree," says the *Milinda prasna*, "he never told a lie; it were easier for the universe to be blown away than for a supreme Budha to utter an untruth." If such a declaration were ever made in the pre-

* The *Pujawaliya*. Manual of Budhism, p. 466.

sence of Gotama, one would like to know whether he blushed at it or not.

"It is said by the Brahmans," continues the native work quoted above, "that it is not a crime to tell a lie on behalf of a holy devotee, or on account of one's cattle, or to save a person's life, or to gain a victory in an important contest, but all this is contrary to truth." The character of Brahmanical morality is apparent from the quotation.

5th. The use of intoxicating drinks is strictly prohibited to the priesthood, and forms the fifth evil which the devotee solemnly renounces on entering the community. As intoxication was the cause of many other crimes, the individual who wilfully subjected himself to it was regarded as more sinful than he who simply broke one of the other precepts, and rendered himself thereby liable to expulsion. It is evident from the energy with which the sin is denounced, that it must have been of frequent occurrence in the districts in which Gotama preached, yet we often hear that the natives of tropical regions do not feel that craving for stimulating liquors common to those in more northern climes.

6th. The eating of solid food after midday is the next gratification the priest promises to abjure.

7th. Attendance upon dancing festivals, singing, licentious music, and masks, is likewise interdicted, and is still rigidly avoided by the Budhistic, much more than by many other priesthoods.

8th. The adorning of the body with flowers, and the use of perfumes and unguents is renounced by the eighth prohibition.

9th. The use of seats and couches above the prescribed height, or of honourable positions, and costly beds is prohibited, a command which may remind us of the denunciation of the prophet Amos. "Woe to those . . . that lie upon beds of ivory and stretch themselves upon their couches."

10th. Lastly, the priest binds himself, on no account, to receive presents of gold or silver, lest spiritual blessings might be sold for money, an ordinance singularly unavailing when landed property was permitted to be received as gifts to the priesthouse and temple.

A novice wishing to become a Budhist priest must have the consent of his parents, if of tender years. He then attaches himself to a monastery; and becomes the pupil of one of the body, who is expected to instruct him, and fit him for his profession. The relation between the teacher and the scholar in the East, has always been very different from the same connexion in the West, as is amusingly exemplified in the regulations recorded respecting the novice. When the scholar rises in the morning, say these injunctions, he must place his teacher's sandals, robe, and tooth-cleaner, in proper order, present him with water that he may wash, prepare a seat, and give him rice-gruel from a clean vessel. When the teacher approaches he must rise to meet him; if the priest have anything in his hand, he must ask permission to carry it for him: and he must wash his feet. Thrice every day he must go to him and render such assistance as he may require. The novice must not be younger than eight years; but cannot obtain ordination till he has arrived at twenty. He then shaves his head and adopts the yellow robe, the distinguishing badge of the order, unless absolutely rejected, and refused a further trial. As a priest his duties are to collect alms for the monastery to which he belongs—to read the Pitakas to the people in the temple—to keep the temple and the images of Budha in order; and above all to meditate on the vanity of earthly things, and the folly of cleaving to existence. He must not go near or touch a woman. Were his own mother to fall into a ditch, he might not extend his hand for her to grasp, in order that she might regain the bank, although, gracious condescension! he might hold one end of a stick whilst she grasped the other.

"Any woman whatever," said Gotama, "if she have a proper opportunity, and can do it in secret, and be enticed thereto, will do that which is wrong"—so erroneous was his estimate of the female character. The Brahmans, the Greeks, and Romans, and some of the early Christian fathers have spoken with equal dogmatic force on the subject; so that the founder of Budhism is not to be regarded as the only offender in that way. His followers have of course followed up the dictum of their sage by their own similar contributions to misogynic literature. *Matu gamo namo papo*, said one of them, embodying all malice on the subject in a single phrase—"that which is named woman is sin." With such an estimate of the female character, it is strange that Gotama should have admitted them into the sacred order of the priesthood at all. It was not, we are told, until after much importunity on their part that the order of priestesses was founded, his own foster-mother, Maha Prajapati, being the first high priestess. "Women are hasty," said he, "given to quarrelling; they exercise hatred, and are full of evil. If I exalt them to the principal places in this institution, they will become more wilful than before. They will despise my priests; but unto such no benefit can accrue from profession; they cannot attain to *nirwana*. There must, therefore, be eight ordinances of restraint, that they may be kept in, as the waters of a tank by its embankment." These eight ordinances of restraint provided that due reverence should be paid by the priestess to the priest; that she was not to have the liberty of going about at her pleasure, that her noviciate should continue for two years at least; and that she was not to be admitted, save in a full chapter of the clergy of both sexes, who should satisfy themselves of her qualifications.

No ordinances could be more severe or minute than those which regulated the intercourse between the male and female devotees. There are a jealousy and a particularity in the restrictions, which prove how well acquainted Gotama was with the human heart, and that he foresaw the evils that might possibly arise from the new order. Even for a priest to sit on the same seat with a priestess was a sin—to say three words to her without an intelligent witness was a sin; whilst misconduct on either side, drove the offender irrevocably from the sacred profession, into which no subsequent profession or repentance could obtain his or her readmission.

In Ceylon and India the order of priestesses

does not appear ever to have been numerous, and in both countries they are now extinct; but they exist, although not very numerous, in Burmah, Siam and China.

Crawford, in his "Embassy to the Court of Ava," informs us, that the priestesses in Burmah are by no means so numerous as the priests. They are called Thilashen, and consist, for the most part, of old women—the head being shaved, and a particular form of garment, generally of a white colour, worn by them. The younger are quite willing to forsake the order when they can get husbands.

The profession of a priestess, we are informed, is not much respected by the people, either in Burmah, or in China—being, in general, regarded as only a more reputable form of begging. There are a few recluses amongst them, however, commonly widows, of a more reputable class, who have either funds of their own, or are supported by their relatives.

Of the priests of Ceylon, at the present day, every one who has had any extended communication with them, has spoken favourably. In some instances, indeed, they are lamentably ignorant, but are generally distinguished by affability, kindliness of manner, and unbounded hospitality. Intercourse with Europeans, has, of course, diminished that respect for them amongst the people, which they would otherwise undoubtedly feel, yet still some become popular for their medical skill, their attention to their duties, or the sweetness of their voice in reading the sacred books. "In many places, the people stand in awe of them, as they suppose that various calamities may be inflicted on the objects of their wrath; but this fear is by no means universal. In 1839, for instance, some females went with brooms in their hands to a priest-house, near Negombo (a village, fifteen miles north from Colombo), and ordered the occupant to leave the place immediately, threatening, in case of refusal, to use the brooms upon his back. The quarrel arose from an attempt of the priest, to overcome the virtue of a young woman, who had brought some cakes as an offering to Budha.*" The broom-bearers triumphed, and amidst the jeers and reproaches of the population, the offending priest was driven from the village, probably only to fall into the hands of his fellows, who would inflict a severer penalty for the scandal he had brought upon their order.

In China, the Budhistic priesthood seems to have fallen into greater disrepute than elsewhere, probably arising from the fact of their sacred

* Eastern Monachism, p. 319.

books being in a language little understood, and not easily represented by Chinese characters. Amongst a refined literary people, the service, which is repeated, parrot-like, without being understood, must be treated with contempt, whilst the priests who conduct it, are deservedly despised for not making themselves familiar with the sense, as well as with the words, of their doctrines.

The courtesy with which MM. Huc and Gabet were treated, in traversing the vast table-lands of Central Asia, when they had assumed the character of Budhist priests, or *lamas*, as they are there called, proves that the contempt exhibited towards the Chinese priests, is by no means universal, and from many parts of their extraordinary account,* it would further appear, that "the lamas of the western heaven," as they were often called, were generally held in reverence for their learning. In Central Asia, however, which must at present be regarded as the head-quarters of Budhism, there is perhaps more humbug and chicanery mixed up with the practice of the faith, than anywhere else. The very existence of the Grand Lama at Lhassa, in Thibet, is a proof of this, whilst, in imitation of him, similar lamas, although inferior in honour, pretend to be like-

* Travels in Tartary, Thibet, and China, &c.—Hazlitt's translation.

wise incarnations of Gotama on earth, and claim worship and obedience from their votaries, as a natural consequence. Superstition and chicanery are truly rife in Thibet and Mongolia, to judge by M. Huc's account.

Take the following imposition upon the credulity of their votaries as an example. The terrible feats exhibited by our jugglers, when they cut off people's noses, and so cleverly replace them, are here imitated, as the grand feature of a great religious ceremony! Having met an old lama, in distress, whom they had previously relieved, in the country of the Ortous Tartars, on the north-western borders of China, M. Huc proceeds with his narrative,—" 'Brother,' said we, 'we are from the West, and the affairs of your country not being well known to us, we are astonished at finding so many pilgrims here in the desert.' 'We are all going to Ratche-Tchurin,' replied he, in accents full of emotion. 'Doubtless,' said we, 'some grand solemnity calls you together?' 'Yes, to-morrow will be a great day; a Lama Boktè will manifest his power; kill himself, yet not die.' We at once understood what solemnity it was, that thus attracted the Ortous-Tartars. A lama was to cut himself open, take out his entrails, and place them before him, and then resume his previous condition. This spectacle, so cruel and disgusting, is very common in the lamaseries of Tartary. The Boktè, who is to manifest his power, as the Mongols phrase it, prepares himself for the formidable operation, by many days fasting and prayer, pending which, he must abstain from all communication whatever with mankind, and observe the most absolute silence.

"When the appointed day is come, the multitude of pilgrims assemble in the great court of the lamasery, where an altar is raised in front of the temple-gate. At length the Boktè appears, he advances gravely, amid the acclamations of the crowd, seats himself upon the altar, and takes from his girdle a large knife, which he places upon his knees. At his feet, numerous lamas, ranged in a circle, commence the terrible invocations of this frightful ceremony. As the recitation of the prayers proceeds, you see the Boktè trembling in every limb, and gradually working himself up into phrenetic convulsions. The lamas, themselves, become excited; their voices are raised; their song observes no order, and at last becomes a mere confusion of yelling and outcry. Then the Boktè suddenly throws aside the scarf which envelopes him; unfastens his girdle, and seizing the sacred knife, slits open his stomach, in one long cut. While the blood flows in every direction, the multitude prostrate themselves before the terrible spectacle, and the enthusiast is interrogated about all sorts of hidden things, as to future events, as to the destiny of certain personages. The replies of the Boktè to all these questions, are regarded, by everybody, as oracles.

"When the devout curiosity of the numerous pilgrims is satisfied, the lamas resume, but now calmly and gravely, the recitation of their prayers. The Boktè takes, in his right hand, blood from his wound, raises it to his mouth, breathes thrice upon it, and then throws it into the air, with loud cries. He next passes his hand rapidly over his wound, closes it, and everything, after a while, resumes its pristine condition; no trace remaining of the diabolical operation, except extreme prostration. The Boktè once more rolls his scarf round him, recites in a low voice a short prayer, then all is over, and the multitude disperse, with the exception of a few of the especially devout, who remain to contemplate and to adore the blood-stained altar which the saint has quitted.

"These horrible ceremonies are of frequent occurrence in the great lamaseries of Tartary and Thibet, and we do not believe that there is any trick or deception about them; for, from all we have seen and heard among idolatrous nations, we are persuaded that the devil has a great deal to do with the matter; and moreover, our impression that there is no trick in the operation is fortified by the opinion of the most intelligent and most upright Budhists whom we have met in the numerous lamaseries we visited.

"It is not every lama that can perform miraculous operations. Those who have the fearful power to cut themselves open, for example, are never found in the higher ranks of the lama hierarchy. They are generally lay lamas of indifferent character, and little esteemed by their comrades. The regular lamas generally make no scruple of avowing their horror of the spectacle. In their eyes, all these operations are wicked and diabolical. Good lamas, they say, are incapable of performing such acts, and should not even desire to attain the impious talent."—(Vol. i., p. 191.)

When it is remembered that the Boktè is surrounded by the priests of his monastery, that the laity are sedulously kept at a distance, and that the actual operation is performed at a moment of wild excitement, the mystery is solved, I think, without any necessity for calling in the aid of Satanic agency to afford an explanation of the circumstance. The frauds and impositions of the heterodox Budhism of Thibet and Mongolia, however, do not end here. Every department of the faith, every religious exercise of the lamas, or priests, seems to be more or less mixed up with imposition and deceit. Take the following, also from M. Huc's volumes, as an example:—

"Medicine, in Tartary, as we have already observed, is exclusively practised by the lamas. When illness attacks any one, his friends run to the nearest lamasery for a lama, whose first proceeding upon visiting the patient is to run his fingers over the pulse of both wrists simultaneously, as the fingers of a musician run over the strings of an instrument. The Chinese physicians feel both pulses also, but in succession. After due deliberation, the lama pronounces his opinion as to the particular nature of the malady. According to the religious belief of the Tartars, all illness is owing to the visitation of a *Tchutgour*, or demon; but the expulsion of the demon is first a matter of medicine. The lama physician next proceeds, as lama apothecary, to give the specific befitting the case. The Tartar pharmacopœia rejecting all mineral chemistry, the lama remedies consist entirely of vegetables pulverized, and either infused in water or made up into pills. If the lama doctor happens not to have any medicine with him, he is by no means disconcerted; he writes the names of the remedies upon little scraps of paper, moistens the papers with his saliva, and rolls them up into pills, which the patient tosses down with the same perfect confidence as though they were genuine medicaments. To swallow the name of a remedy, or the remedy itself, say the Tartars, comes to precisely the same thing.

"The medical assault of the usurping demon being applied, the lama next proceeds to spiritual artillery, in the form of prayers, adapted to that quality of the demon who has to be dislodged. If the patient is poor, the *Tchutgour* visiting him can evidently be only an inferior *Tchutgour*, requiring merely a brief, off-hand prayer, sometimes merely an interjectional exorcism. If the patient is very poor, the lama troubles himself with neither prayer nor pill, but goes away, recommending the friends to wait with patience until the sick person gets better, or dies, according to the decree of *Hormoustha*. But where the patient is rich, the possessor of large flocks, the proceedings are altogether different. First, it is obvious that a devil who presumes to visit so eminent a personage must be a potent devil, one of the chiefs of the lower world; and it would not be decent for a great *Tchutgour* to travel like a mere sprite; the family, accordingly, are directed to prepare for him a handsome suit of clothes, a pair of rich boots, a fine horse, ready saddled and bridled; otherwise, the devil will never think of going, physic or exorcise him how you may. It is even possible, indeed, that one horse will not suffice; for the demon, in very rich cases, may turn out, upon inquiry, to be so high and mighty a prince, that he has with him a number of courtiers and attendants, all of whom have to be provided with horses.

"Everything being arranged, the ceremony commences. The lama and numerous co-physicians, called in from his own and other adjacent monasteries, offer up prayers in the rich man's tents for a week or a fortnight, until they perceive that the devil is gone—that is to say, until they have exhausted all the disposable tea and sheep. If the patient recovers, it is a clear proof that the prayers have been efficaciously recited; if he dies, it is a still greater proof of the efficaciousness of the prayers, for not only is the devil gone, but the patient has transmigrated to a state far better than that he has quitted."—(Vol. i., p. 74.)

The entire account is amusing in its very absurdity. Equally so is the convenient practice they have adopted of praying by a wooden deputy, and thereby acquiring merit, as M. Huc informs us (in the following paragraphs) is sometimes done:—

"The Budhists have another mode of simplifying pilgrimages and devotional rites. In all the great lamaseries you find, at short intervals, figures in the form of barrels, and turning upon an axle. The material of these figures is a thick board, composed of infinite sheets of paper pasted together, and upon which are written, in Thibetian characters, the prayers most reputed throughout the country. Those who have not the taste, or the zeal, or the strength, to carry huge boards of books on their shoulders, or to prostrate themselves, step after step, in the dust and mire, or to walk round the lamasery in winter's cold or summer's heat, have recourse to the simple and expeditious medium of the prayer-barrel. All they have to do is to set it in motion; it then turns of itself for a long time, the devotees drinking, eating, or sleeping, while the complacent mechanism is turning prayers for them.

"One day, on approaching a prayer-barrel, we found two lamas quarrelling famously, and just on the point of coming to blows; the occasion being the fervour of each for prayer. One of them having set the prayer automaton in motion, had quietly returned to his cell. As he was entering it, he turned his head, doubtless to enjoy the spectacle of the fine prayers he had set to work for himself; but, to his infinite disgust, he saw a colleague stopping his prayers, and about to turn on the barrel on his own account. Indignant at this pious fraud, he ran back, and stopped his competitor's prayers. Thus it went on for some time, the one turning on, the other stopping the barrel, without a word said on either side. At last, however, their patience exhausted, they came to high words; from words they proceeded to menaces; and it would, doubtless, have come to a fight, had not an old lama, attracted by the uproar, interposed words of peace, and himself put the automaton in motion for the joint benefit of both parties."—(Vol. i., p. 203.)

It must be remembered, however, that all these abuses are not integral parts of Budhism proper, but heresies known to Central Asia alone. The priest of Ceylon, of Burmah, of Siam, or of China, is no believer in the Grand Lama of Thibet, and would at once pronounce the practices of the Mongolian lama to be heresy and superstition.

I cannot take leave of M. Huc's interesting volumes without bringing before the reader's notice his account of a wonderful tree that, according to the faith of Mongolia, stands as a living miracle attesting the truth of Budhism. Here is a nut to crack for the savants of the West! Tsong Kaba, a reformer of Budhism, in the fifteenth century, was a miracle-worker. The reformation which he effected, and which M. Huc believes to have principally consisted in the introduction of the robes, ceremonies and discipline of Roman Catholicism into Budhism, prevails in all the regions between the Himalayas, the frontiers of Russia, and the great wall of China, amongst all the worshippers of the Grand Lama, in fact. From this wonderful reformer's hair a tree sprang, says tradition, bearing a Thibetian character, that is a character in the sacred language of Budhism in these regions, on every leaf! Nonsense, says the European reader, politely. But here are two French missionaries, of learning, intelligence, and experience, who saw the tree with their own eyes, who saw the characters, and are unable to explain the matter at all. Surely then it deserves examination. But hear their testimony in their own words:—

" It will here be naturally expected that we say something about this tree itself. Does it exist? Have we seen it? Has it any peculiar attributes? What about its marvellous leaves? All these questions our readers are entitled to put to us. We will endeavour to answer as categorically as possible.

" Yes, this tree does exist, and we had heard of it too often during our journey not to feel somewhat eager to visit it. At the foot of the mountain on which the lamasery stands, and not far from the principal Budhist temple, is a great square enclosure, formed by brick walls. Upon entering this, we were able to examine at leisure the marvellous tree, some of the branches of which had already manifested themselves above the wall. Our eyes were first directed with earnest curiosity to the leaves, and we were filled with an absolute consternation of astonishment at finding that, in point of fact, there were upon each of the leaves, well-formed Thibetian characters all of a green colour, some darker, some lighter, than the leaf itself. Our first impression was a suspicion of fraud on the part of the lamas; but after a minute examination of every detail, *we could not discover the least deception.* The characters all appeared to us portions of the leaf itself, equally with its veins and nerves; the position was not the same in all; in one leaf they would be at the top of the leaf; in another, in the middle; in a third, at the base, or at the side; the younger leaves represented the characters only in a partial state of formation. The bark of the tree and its branches, which resemble that of the plane tree, are also covered with these characters. When you remove a piece of old bark, the young bark under it exhibits the indistinct outlines of characters in a germinating state, and what is very singular, these new characters are not unfrequently different from those which they replace. *We examined everything with the closest attention, in order to detect some trace of trickery, but we could discern nothing of the sort, and the perspiration absolutely trickled down our faces under the influence of the sensations which this most amazing spectacle created.* More profound intellects than ours may, perhaps, be able to supply a satisfactory explanation of the mysteries of this singular tree; but as to us, we altogether give it up. Our readers possibly may smile at our ignorance; but we care not, so that the sincerity and truth of our statement be not doubted.

"The Tree of the Ten Thousand Images seemed to us of great age. Its trunk, which three men could scarcely embrace with outstretched arms, is not more than eight feet high; the branches, instead of shooting up, spread out in the shape of a plume of feathers, and are extremely bushy; few of them are dead. The leaves are always green, and the wood, which is of a reddish tint, has an exquisite odour, something like that of cinnamon. The lamas informed us that in summer, towards the eighth moon, the tree produces large red flowers of an extremely beautiful character. They informed us also that there nowhere else exists another such tree; that many attempts have been made in various lamaseries of Tartary and Thibet to propagate it by seeds and cuttings, but that all these attempts have been fruitless." (Vol. ii., chap. 2, p. 53.)

Unable to throw any light on the matter, I must leave it here, as one of the most extraordinary accounts the world has ever heard, and yet, strange to say, its publication seems to have produced little or no sensation! An existing miracle to attest the truth of a system of belief that acknowledges half mankind as its votaries!—a miracle that may be seen and examined by any one that chooses to go there! And yet the world is not moved by it, passes it by, and pooh poohs it, as an ordinary, twice-told tale! Verily there is something strange in all this. We surely have a right to expect some explanation of the circumstance. Why did not the reverend travellers bring home a leaf with them to submit it to the learned acumen of the West? Why do not some of our plethoric societies send off a mission specially to examine and report upon this *lusus naturæ?*

But it is time that we should pass from M. Huc's strange narrative of the peculiarities and wonders of heterodox Budhism to an account of what the founder of the faith really taught.

According to Gotama there are innumerable

systems of worlds, all constantly going through cycles of existence, produced by causes constantly operating and inherent in matter, gradually attaining their prime, hastening on to decay and destruction, and finally reproduced as before. Thus he attempted to obviate the necessity for a supreme first cause,—almighty power constantly operating without the Almighty himself to guide, direct, and control it! All the various orders of spirits, men and inferior animals, with the exception of some of the gods, who appear to be eternal, are constantly changing places, from their different degrees of merit. Merit and demerit, indeed, according to this strange system, are the controllers of the universe. A man acquires great merit, and is born again as an angel or a happy spirit or a god; he continues to acquire merit, and ultimately attains *nirwana*, "the bourne whence no traveller returns." He is afflicted with demerit or guilt, on account of his own evil thoughts or actions, and is born as an inferior animal; or, if still worse throughout many ages, in one of the numerous hells. As to the duration of punishment in hell, it is not eternal, but if particulars are asked on the subject, the whole is explained, as usual, by a figure. A man throws a piece of wood into the sea, with a hole in it large enough to receive an ox's head; the wind sends the wood hither and thither at its pleasure. In the same sea there is a blind tortoise, which, after the lapse, say, of a hundred years, rises once to the surface of the water. Will the time ever come when that tortoise will *so* rise that its neck shall enter the hole in the wood? It may, in the course of countless ages, and in the course of as many may the unwise being that has once entered one of the great hells obtain birth again as a man.*

"It is vain," said Gotama, "to seek now for the origin of existence—it cannot be discovered. It is sufficient for us to know that we exist, and that merit and demerit rule the world." Thus he endeavoured to evade the difficulty of introducing a great primeval cause, "by whom are all things, and without whom was not anything made that is made," into his system. The gods whom he has acknowledged are a clumsy part of the machinery of his faith, only adopted because they had been believed in for ages in his country, and he saw no sufficient reason to attempt eradicating the belief. He placed himself above them all, and cheered on his disciples in the pursuit of good, by declaring that any one of them might ultimately become a Budha in the course of future ages, if he had but faith and perseverance sufficient. To us, in our *cui bono* age, it may appear strange that so extraordinary a system

* Manual of Budhism, p. 442.

—a system of negations—should excite enthusiasm in the breast of any, or lead men to surrender any advantage to retain it. Yet numerous are the relations of martyr-like endurance with which the disciples of Gotama bore every evil rather than renounce the faith they had adopted, and there can be no doubt that it was not until after a severe and deadly struggle that Brahmanism ultimately triumphed in India. One example of the spirit which animated the early disciples of the faith will be sufficient to illustrate the matter. A king who reigned at Anuradhapoora, in Ceylon, anxious to test the constancy of a devotee, ordered him to procure a fowl and kill it. He refused. The king threatened; he still refused, whereupon the monarch ordered him to be conducted to the usual place of execution, a fowl to be put into his hands, and, if he still refused, he was to be slain. "I have never broken the precept that forbids the taking of life," said the devotee, "and I am willing to yield my own life, instead of the fowl's, to your cruelty." There was abundant leisure for reconsideration and reflection, as he was being led away to the place of execution. Arrived there, a fowl was thrust into his hand, and the threat reiterated. He threw the animal from him, determined not to shed a drop of its blood, and the executioner would have carried the king's sentence into effect had not the monarch himself interfered.*

Nothing can be more simple and peaceful than the ceremonial observances of orthodox Budhism; for it is to be remembered that the bloody chicanery of Tartary and Mongolia is alike foreign to the precepts of Gotama himself and of the entire tenor of the faith which he established. The people, at the changes of the moon, make their way in crowds to the temples, there to offer up their bloodless sacrifice of flowers and fruit upon the altar of their man-god. They take upon themselves some of the vows of the priesthood, for a shorter or longer time, according to the degree of merit which they wish to acquire, and having repeated the threefold formula of protection, stating that they take refuge in Budha, in his word, and in the priesthood, they return to their dwellings, self-satisfied with their simple and unexciting worship. On other occasions, a building being prepared for the purpose, a priest reads, or rather chaunts, to the assembled crowds, portions of the Pitakas, or sacred books; the people reverently seated on the ground around him. Sometimes two priests officiate, one reading the original Pali, and the other a vernacular translation at intervals. This *bana potha,* as it is

* The *Pujawaliya*, Manual of Budhism, p. 463.

called, or reading of the truth, continues into the night; lamps are lit; the people come and go; some remaining a shorter, some a longer time, according to the degree of merit they wish to acquire; other priests take the place of the former, and so the ceremony continues, without intermission or cessation, "from morn to noon, from noon to dewy eve," and so on throughout the long hours of night till the morning again.

The ethics of Budhism is that part of the system which gives it its highest value in Christian eyes. In its moral aspect, and in the purity which it inculcates—a purity extending to thought and words, as well as to action—it comes nearer the sublimity of Christianity than any other religious system of Asia; and this, too, without endeavouring to lure on its votaries to holiness and piety by any hopes of sensual happiness like Mohammedanism, or denunciations of physical evil in this life, like the faith of Zoroaster. A simple enumeration of the Budhistic catalogue of sins and duties will be sufficient to establish what I have just said of the superiority of this part of the system. Sins are divided into, 1st, those of the body, three in number—murder, theft, and adultery; 2nd, those of the speech, four in number—lying, slander, abuse, unprofitable conversation; 3rd, those of the mind, three in number—covetousness, malice, and scepticism; 4th, those of the general behaviour, five in number—the drinking of intoxicating liquors, gambling, idleness, improper associations, and the frequenting of improper places of amusement. Besides these, there are reciprocal obligations and duties binding upon particular classes; as, for instance, the parent and child, the teacher and scholar, the priest and the householder, the husband and wife, the master and servant, the friend and the friend.* It is amusing, in the particular explanations of the above category, to turn to the crime of scepticism, and to consider its nature and punishment. Those who deny, or doubt, the truth of the doctrines of Budha are to be punished in one or other of these two ways—to be born as a beast on earth, or as a demon in hell. "There are five great crimes, but scepticism is the greatest." When millions of years have rolled away, others may be released from hell, but the sceptic will remain there. Reader, if Gotama was right, you and I are in an uncomfortable position!

* In this brief sketch of Budhistic ethics, as in many other parts of the chapter, I have been most indebted to Mr. R. S. Hardy's works, "Eastern Monachism," and "Manual of Budhism:" works invaluable to every student of this extraordinary faith. It was not therefore without reason that I prefixed York's words to this chapter—"These oracles are *hardily* attained, and hardly understood." (Shakespeare's Henry VI., Second Part.)

CHAPTER II.

THE HOFERS AND MASSEYS—CASTE IN INDIA.

> " I know thou art religious,
> And hast a thing within thee called conscience."
> *Titus Andronicus*, act v., sc. 2.

SITUATED as I was in the immediate neighbourhood of the Hofers, at Lanka, and of my excellent native friend, Marandhan, it was but natural that I should become more and more intimate with both. They and Fowler were, in fact, the only friends I had in the island, who lived within visiting distance, and I therefore cultivated their acquaintance and friendship with assiduity. Fowler, whom I have already mentioned, and whom I esteemed the more, the more I became acquainted with him, as an estimable man and a good planter, was unfortunately too far off to permit of frequent visits on either side; but both Hofer and Marandhan were nearer, and seemed as much pleased when the click of Uncle Toby's iron shoes on the stones, that lay in the roads to their dwellings, announced my approach, as I was when I heard their horses making their way to my silent bungalow. When the monotony of a solitary life, like that of the coffee-planter, is broken in upon by the visit of an agreeable friend, able and willing to talk, the pleasure afforded is as great as the most exciting amusements of crowded cities can yield.

There was a wearisome monotony about this jungle life, however, that made me begin to suspect I had mistaken my vocation, and that, however interesting such a life may appear from a distance, it is, in itself, anything but pleasant to the man whose mind is active, and whose heart is not influenced by ties that bind him to the place. True, the hunting parties were exciting and pleasant: but they were not frequent. The natives might be improved, but they felt no gratitude for favours bestowed on them, which they invariably regarded as bribes, or as the payment of just debts. Besides this, the two languages used by them formed a formidable barrier to the maintainance of familiar relations. The Kandians spoke Singhalese alone; the Malabar coolies, Tamil only; and as most of the work was done by the latter, who were constantly coming and going, whilst the former alone were stationary, there was little chance of doing permanent good, unless one's life was to be devoted to it. I could not regard my position on the estate as a permanent one, but was ever looking forward to the time when I should leave it, without then surmising that the enactments of the British Parliament would not only compel me, but hundreds of other planters, similarly situated, to beat a hasty retreat, and, forsaking the scene of so much labour, where so much capital was embarked, settle down to some new and unaccustomed line of life.

Where men are so much isolated from those with whom they can sympathize and have a fellow-feeling, they naturally take more interest in the joys and sorrows of the few with whom they are in the habit of associating, than could otherwise be possibly the case. Hence, it followed that what shed gladness or gloom over the households of Hofer and Marandhan, similarly affected me. Mouat I did not reckon "on my list of friends," and, therefore, I do not mention him in the same category; but still every little event that affected one, interested the rest of our small community.

The mails from England, towards the end of 1845, had brought bad news to the Hofers, and, whilst all was bustle and excitement on the estate in consequence, there was much gloom and sorrow in the bungalow. Mrs. Hofer's parents had both died within a short period of each other, leaving her sister, Ada, an orphan, without adequate settlement. Homes were offered to her in England, which she refused, resolving to join her sister in Ceylon, and to link her fate with the being whom she loved best in the world, and with whom she had been brought up. The sum of money left to her—a few thousand pounds—she decided on embarking in coffee-planting; and with the approbation of the clergyman of the parish, her guardian, who was, doubtless, blinded by Hofer's glowing accounts of the profits to be made by it, she had already written to him, informing him of her intentions and determination. Hofer was pleased at the resolution to which Miss Mowbray had come, and regarded it as a prudent one. His wife looked on the whole matter as precipitate and ill-advised.

The Masseys, whom we had visited in travelling from Colombo to Kandy, were invited to spend some time with their friends at Lanka. I have already mentioned that Mr. Massey was an honest man and an excellent planter, without much refinement or elegance, whilst his wife, agreeable enough when her husband was away, seemed only to delight in snubbing him when he was present. In the monotony of jungle life any change almost is agreeable, and, therefore, uncongenial as her visitors were to herself, they served, nevertheless, to divert Mrs. Hofer's mind from the thoughts of her own bereavements and her sister's isolation in the world.

I saw at once from the extension of cultivation commenced, the improvements going on in the estate, and the additional buildings in process of erection at the bungalow, that Miss Mowbray's fortune was already in process of investment in Lanka, and, anxious to spare her a pang, for she had said she did not approve at all of the transaction, I asked Mrs. Hofer no questions on the subject. Yet I did not think the less, and on subsequently conversing with Fowler, who was equally intimate with them, on the subject, I found he agreed with me.

"This surely," said he, "is not the way Hofer should have acted. Why this precipitate carrying out of a scheme disapproved by his wife, whom all the world knows to be a sensible woman? Why act thus in accordance with the first impulses of a generous heart, anxious to link her fate with her sister's, when that sister disapproves of the measure, and would probably have succeeded in altering the impetuous girl's mind, had time been allowed? There seems to me to be an indecent haste, a total disregard to the feelings and wishes of his wife in the transaction, which makes me look more coldly upon Hofer than I have ever done before. Surely, so much beauty, so much sense, so much kind-heartedness, deserve more consideration and respect than this; there can be no such haste and precipitancy required as to necessitate such a total disregard for his wife's counsel and wishes."

But Hofer thought otherwise; and his wife uncomplainingly submitted; nor was even Massey aware that she did not yield to the scheme her fullest concurrence. What a contrast between the selfish precipitancy of the one, and the self-denying acquiescence of the other! Not that I would, for a moment insinuate, that any sordid considerations urged Hofer to this conduct. He was infinitely above such. A more liberal, generous-minded man did not exist. A love for bustle and excitement, change and novelty, was the strongest element in his composition, and, whilst flattering himself that he was acting thus, solely from a due regard for Miss Mowbray's interests, the real motive power appeared to Fowler and me to have been a certain uncontrolled impetuosity of disposition which urged him ever from the ordinary and uneventful, into the strange, the new, and the exciting.

"Mrs. Hofer would have had me wait until next year," said he to me, as we went over the estate with Massey; "but only think what the loss of a year is now-a-days. My agents assure me prices must go up; and the loss of a year, under those circumstances is an irreparable misfortune."

"Then Mrs. Hofer does not yet approve of your proceedings?" asked I.

"No; she's positive on the subject. A woman always believes herself very wise about these matters; doesn't she, Massey?" was the reply.

"But suppose Miss Mowbray regrets the speculation, before she has had time to reap the benefit of it?" I suggested.

"She is a young lady of sense and discernment," said he; "and had I not her own strongly expressed wishes, and the consent of her guardian, I should not have so applied the funds."

There was an air of offended friendship about the tone in which he uttered these words that quite prevented me from making any reply; nor, indeed, was it my place to interfere in the matter at all.

The evening passed, on this occasion, most agreeably. There was no martyr-like air of resignation on Mrs. Hofer's face, or in her manner, to show that she considered herself injured. She was gay and lively, anticipating, with almost girlish joy, the arrival of her sister, who was expected by the next mail, and contriving a thousand little surprises for her, intended to exhibit more strikingly the contrast between English and Ceylonese life.

The conversation speedily became general on the lights and shadows of the planter's existence, where opinions at once divided, each having naturally his own ideas on that subject, which were by no means likely to be those of his neighbour.

"For my part," said Massey, in his good, easy, quiet way, "I don't see why people should not be contented with life in the jungle. There are some annoyances, it is true, but so there are everywhere; and, to make up for them, there are many pleasures."

"And few or no comforts," suggested Hofer.

"Well, I don't know that," replied Massey; "one's bungalow may be comfortable enough when the servants and children are kept in order."

"Comfort enough for the body, doubtless," said I; "but look at the want of food for the mind; the isolation, the total exclusion from everything intellectual and elevated. That appears to me its worst feature."

"For you men, that may be the worst; but for us there are sorrows enough, you never feel or even sympathize with," said Mrs. Massey.

"Why, I don't see what moderate men want

more," said Massey, answering my observation, as if his wife had not spoken at all, "you have your papers twice a week, and your letters and news from England once a month. Isn't that enough?"

"O, our friend is a book-worm," said Hofer, gaily, "and is constantly complaining of the Kandy library. Fancy, Mrs. Massey, he actually says there are not books enough in it."

"But it's always the way with you men," answered that lady, "always discontented; never knowing how to value a blessing when you have it. Not books enough in the Kandy library? well, I'm sure! Why how many would you have?"

"The objection to the library," said Mrs. Hofer, laughing at the ludicrous face of her companion, "if I understand it aright, is not so much to the number, as to the quality of the books."

"Ah, that's a different matter," said Mrs. Massey, "I'm sure then I quite agree with him, for Massey has often brought home books from it, that I conceived it my duty to return as soon as I had looked into them. Not that I read a great deal myself,—how can I, with all that I have got to do? but still I consider it my duty to see the character of the books that come into the house."

"How am I to know the kind of books I get until I read them?" said Massey, "I don't read much myself either, but I always like to have a book on hand, just to take up when I have nothing else to do, but I often find it's locked up or sent back to the library before I've half finished it."

Mrs. Massey sat up straighter in her chair, and looked far off through Mr. Massey's head, when he made this statement, but deigned no reply, whilst he, ignorant of offence, in stating what she had confessed only a moment before, poured out a glass of wine for himself, as if he had said nothing particular. But ladies of Mrs. Massey's temperament do not permit their husbands to accuse them of what they will willingly confess themselves guilty, without exhibiting their wounded sensibility, and I could see that a storm was brewing, which, if some accident did not avert it, would infallibly burst over the devoted head of the unconscious Massey. It was with difficulty that we prevented ourselves from laughing outright, but Mrs. Hofer adroitly changed the subject and no offence was given.

"There is one feature of the planter's life that is cheering and refreshing to contemplate," said she, "the material influence he exercises on the coolies, and all who work on his estate, and the consequent improvement he may produce, and the good he may permanently do them."

"You take the most philanthropic view of the matter," said Fowler, "not looking at the planter as a mere money-making machine, as he too often is, but as a human being, with important privileges and influences, which, if he use aright, may be productive of much good; but alas! I fear it is too often the case that the natives learn European vices in addition to their own, instead of learning good from the intercourse."

"Yet there must be a certain civilizing influence," said Hofer, "in the constant intercourse which subsists between the employer and employed, even although the employer be a tyrant like our friend Siggins."

"Can you believe that such a man can be the source of aught save of unmixed evil?" I asked.

"Yes," he replied, "he evidently showed us his worst side, in its worst form, but were we to penetrate more deeply into the man, I doubt not, such is my faith in human nature, that we should find some redeeming traits likely to be beneficial to those under his control, though I freely confess, I think the evil would vastly preponderate."

"I quite agree with you," said Massey, "that must be a very bad European indeed from whom they would not be likely to learn some good. I often think we take too much pains with them, and pay too much attention to them, considering the return we get, and comparing our conduct with that of their own native employers."

"Too much pains with them, pay too much attention to them," echoed Mrs. Massey, looking intently away from Mr. Massey and at Mrs. Hofer, "why there are some men, my dear, that teach their coolies nothing but evil. I should like to know who it is that takes too much pains with them."

"Why I don't mean to say that I take any great pains to improve them," answered Mr. Massey, "it's not my business,—my business is to pay them for their work,—but I don't teach them any evil either, I'am sure; why one would fancy I was a monster."

"I assure you, Mrs. Hofer," said Mrs. Massey, still looking intently at that lady, "I assure you, the amount of swearing that goes on, on some estates, is frightful, and is more than enough to corrupt both the children and the coolies."

"I don't swear in the bungalow, so the children can't hear it," said Massey, "and I don't corrupt the natives by swearing, because they don't understand it, as it's all in English; but Hofer knows right well, Mrs. Hofer, that it's impossible for any man to stand the stupidity and ignorance of these savages without occasionally swearing."

"I must confess," said Hofer, "that it sometimes forms an agreeable vent for ill-humour, however wrong it may be; and then, as you say, of course they don't understand it, and it's harmless."

"I assure you, Mrs. Hofer," said Mrs. Massey, earnestly, "the quantity of swearing that the coolies hear makes them quite familiar with it."

"And the work can be done just as well without it," said Fowler.

"And the work can be done just as well without it," echoed Mrs. Massey. "It's not long ago since I took a sharp little boy from the field-work into the bungalow as a servant," she continued; "he had been living some years with his family on our place, and, would you believe it, he had become so accustomed to swearing, that when I asked him a simple question, suppose only whether the knives were cleaned, he replied with some horrid oath, that made my blood run cold to hear—he never would be content to say simply yes or no—and all that I could do was of no use, to break him off this terrible habit; I threatened, I punished, I scolded, I coaxed, I promised, but all to no purpose; the most dreadful imprecations were constantly breaking out from his lips, and then, with a horrible oath, he would tell you he was sorry, and beg your pardon, until at last I turned him away, although he was an excellent servant, to preserve my children from contamination;—and yet they say the natives don't understand it, because they swear in English."

"I remember reading a missionary's journal, written in Ceylon, in which he mentioned a similar circumstance," said Mrs. Hofer, "only that the boy had been brought up amongst the soldiers, and made it a boast that he knew every oath in English, although he spoke only a few words of the language otherwise. I should think, however, that one such case was a clear proof of the injurious effects of the practice, and ought to be sufficient to induce the gentlemen to abandon such a bad habit altogether."

"Upon my life, Mrs. Hofer," said Massey, eagerly, "I'm by no means so much addicted to the vice, as you might be led to suppose. The boy Mrs. Massey spoke about came from Kandy, and I doubt not had been much amongst the soldiers there, and if such a thing occurred in a missionary's family, it's not so strange that it should have happened in a planter's."

"Did the boy say he had been amongst the

soldiers in Kandy?" asked Mrs. Massey, condescending at length to notice the existence of the criminal before her, and putting the question much in the same tone as the judge who asks the prisoner at the bar, whether he has anything to say why sentence of death should not be passed upon him.

"I don't know whether he ever said it or not," replied Massey, "I never asked him any questions about it."

Mrs. Massey was satisfied, and gathering her clothes, with a full sweep round her, sat up straighter than ever in her chair. Massey was evidently relieved by seeing her leave the table a few minutes afterwards with Mrs. Hofer, and, leaning back comfortably in his seat, he gave, after his custom, a long continued blow from his distended cheeks, as if thus relieving himself of much that had caused him uneasiness before.

"There is much in an Asiatic life generally," observed Hofer, "that tends to unfit a man for active duties in England afterwards; here, and more especially on the continent of India, a man begins naturally to regard himself as one of the aristocracy, however humble his lot at home. He sees the great mass of the population beneath him, its chiefs solicitous for his friendship or notice, and a favoured few of the same rank and class with himself enjoying a monopoly of the advantages of life. It is therefore but natural that he should begin to esteem himself as a very different being from the common herd of humanity around him—as a portion of the china amongst the earthenware of the world."

"Such an idea is more readily imbibed on the continent than here, as you observe, if one is to judge by the samples of Anglo-Indian society, that occasionally make their way to Ceylon, and are sometimes met with at home," said I.

"There is nothing extraordinary in that either," said Hofer; "a Company's magistrate or judge or collector or commissioner goes into a small station, where he is supreme perhaps, or, at all events, never meets any one of much superior rank to his own. For years he is thus constantly flattered with a sense of his own greatness and importance. Natives bow and cringe before him with the most abject humility, native princes even seek his intimacy, and are ready to humiliate themselves to obtain it. If he travels in his district, the whole population is ready to assist him in any way they can—he can do with them as he pleases. It is surely, under such circumstances, only the sturdiest common sense that will not be turned and inflated by such homage and power. Young men, just entering life, often find themselves in this situation—their will is law, and if they act unjustly, there is no efficient means of redress for the poor native; hence the phrase '*Company's justice*' has become a by-word in the East. Yet it could not well be otherwise, considering the position of affairs and the immense extent of territory. Well, a proud *Bahādoor* of the description I have alluded to, one who has been for years nursed in Oriental luxury, flattered into Oriental pride, returns to his native country, and, in walking the streets of London, finds the populace by no means disposed to succumb, as the Asiatics did, to his high mightiness—on the contrary, the porter carrying a basket cares nothing first to strike him with his load, as he stands on the pavement to admire some building opposite, and then to turn round and ask him 'where he's a driving to?' And even if he rides in a cab, the rude charioteer cares nothing to offer his private opinion respecting his gentility, if he only gives him double his proper fare, nor will his footman scruple to tell him, when enraged, that *he* has always been accustomed to serve *gentlemen*, and therefore will wear *his* livery no more. Is it to be wondered at then, that our friend the *Bahādoor* becomes thoroughly disgusted with England and the English, abuses both infinitely more than he abused India and the natives, when in the East, and settles down to spend the remainder of his days in querulous complaint and foolish tyranny over those dependent on him."

"There may be another reason for that too," said I, "that the fortunes made now-a-days in the East, either in the Company's military or civil service, are by no means equal to what they were in times past. The Anglo-Indian, on returning home, finds the successful grocer, the baker, the butcher, all making money as rapidly or more so than he made it in India. Society does not often open its portals to him, excepting under very extraordinary circumstances, either in London or elsewhere, and the consequence is, he is obliged to sink down to a much lower social level than he could have anticipated possible."

"Precisely so," said Massey, "I have seen that the case in England. The old *nabob* is shunned, and perhaps very justly by society, as a querulous, ill-tempered, old fellow, and those who do associate with him are those who expect some advantage, either from his interest or wealth, and such a class is not the most reputable in the world."

"The system of caste, too, as prevalent in India, and partially here," said Hofer, "tends to promote the feeling of self-sufficient superiority on the part of the Company's servant. He sees the natives divided into so many castes, all preserving a strict jealousy from contact with the others—the distinctions even more rigidly maintained than those of the small coteries in English watering and cathedral towns—he sees himself placed above all these gradations, as of an altogether superior grade that is not to be confounded with inferior dust, and it is therefore but natural that he should endeavour to take an aristocratic position when he returns to England, and failing in that, should resign himself to spleen and discontent."

"I thought those distinctions of caste were gradually being obliterated there as here," I remarked.

"By no means," said Hofer, "the people cling to them with the greater tenacity the more the folly of the institution is pointed out. It exhibits itself in its most annoying forms amongst the servants. I had a bearer in Calcutta of the name of Mhadub, who prided himself upon being of a high caste. His office, as is that of all bearers waiting on bachelors in the large lodging-houses of the City of Palaces, consisted in attending to my clothes, assisting me to dress and undress, and occasionally pulling the *punkah*.* One day I had returned from transacting some business in town, a little earlier in the evening than usual. Mhadub

* The large fan suspended from the ceiling in the room, and pulled backwards and forwards by a servant to create an artificial current of air.

was, according to his wont, asleep at the door of my bedroom, on the mat, 'waiting' for me. A gentle touch from my foot awakened him, and, opening the door, he took my hat and whip, and busied himself about the room. I was taking off my coat to wash when I observed that the basin still contained the water I had used in the morning. 'Change that water, Mhadub,' said I; 'you should not have left it there all day.' Mhadub put his head out of the window, and proceeded to shout vociferously for the *mehter*,* whose duty he apparently considered it, to do as I desired. 'Change that water, Mhadub,' said I again; 'you oughtn't to have left it there all day.' Mhadub shouted for the *mehter* louder than ever. 'I don't want the *mehter*,' said I, getting annoyed, and catching Mhadub's eye, as he turned towards me again, 'I don't want the *mehter*; go you and clean the basin.'

"At this moment I was standing near the door, Mhadub at a window opposite, and the basin stood by the door of my bath-room on my left. The only exit from the apartment was by the door near which I stood, and, as Mhadub replied, I saw his eyes furtively wandering to this door, as if preparing for a bolt. 'No, *Codabund*,' said he,

* The servant who sweeps the rooms, and performs all the dirty work about a house.

joining his hands in front, in the attitude of prayer, 'it's not my caste, I can't do it.' 'You can't change the water in that bowl?' said I; 'nonsense, go and do it this instant.' Now, I had observed that when the natives were reasonable and obedient, they always called their master, 'Saheb,' but when obstinate and disobedient, or more than ordinarily extortionate, they used 'Codabund' instead, in addressing their master—a much higher title, I believe, but the honour of which is generally thrown away, not being understood. The very word, therefore, told me that my friend, Mhadub, was preparing to be contumacious; so, planting myself near to the door, and throwing as much force and dignity into the few words as I could, I said, 'Change the water.'

"If you have seen Macready in 'Macbeth,' shouting, 'begone slave,' to the servant, you will have some idea of the tone and attitude I used on this occasion.

"Mhadub was evidently trembling as he saw me getting more annoyed, and I began to fear that he would not comply with my command. I saw at once that it was no ill-timed pleasantry that he was practising. 'Codabund,' said he, the hands still joined in front, and the body bent forwards to me. The word was enough; I saw he was still disobedient, so, making a rapid spring towards him, I caught him by the arm, and drew him towards the door of the bath-room. He talked amazingly during this operation, but the constant 'Codabund' proved that he had no intention of complying with my request, for, if he had, I felt convinced, he would have returned at once to the plain Saheb. He was five feet nothing in his bare feet, and a Bengallee; I six feet one, and an Englishman, so that you may easily conceive I had no difficulty in holding him inside the bath-room with one hand, whilst I emptied the basin, which was the cause of all his woe, with the other. He happened to stand directly under my hand as the basin was reversed; and as he shouted loudly during the descent of the saponaceous shower, I should not be surprised if some of it found its way into his mouth. At length the basin was emptied, and I released him. He bounded down stairs, like a wild deer, and, darting upon the lawn below, in front of the house, he proceeded to vociferate as Bengallee had never vociferated before; the gate-keeper drew near to hear his agonized complaint from one side, and the grooms from the stables upon either hand also approached, whilst Mrs. Curry and her six interesting daughters, the rulers of the establishment, congregated together in the verandah, to witness the wild gestures and listen to the no less wild words of the wet and outraged Mhadub; the Hindoo servants bewailed his fate, assuring him, for his consolation, that his caste was gone; the Mohammedans grinned; Mrs. and the Misses Curry declared that it was a shame, because servants would dislike the house; the lodgers laughed outright; and it was some time before Mhadub talked himself dry, and the commotion caused by his clamour subsided."

"Did he attempt to revenge himself upon you in any way?" I asked.

"He did, in true Bengallee fashion," answered Hofer; "he returned to my service as if nothing had happened, the following morning, and did not refuse to do anything he was told afterwards. About three weeks after the transaction, when I had dined abroad, and returned late to go to bed, in an excellent humour, Mhadub was patiently waiting up for me. 'Codabund,' said he, as he pulled off my boots. 'Never call me that, Mhadub,' said I, smiling benignantly at the recollection of the basin, 'you know I don't like it, ever since —' 'Saheb,' said Mhadub, more discreetly. 'Well,' I asked. 'Saheb knows that his slave's caste is gone,' said he insinuatingly. 'So much the better,' said I; 'it was a very troublesome companion, Mhadub, it prevented you doing your work—you remember.' 'Yes,

Saheb; but I will never refuse anything any more, and I have lost my wife and children with my caste.' 'Have you indeed? that's serious,' said I. 'I have, Saheb,' said Mhadub; 'my wife left me, and took my children; and as long as I'm out of caste, I can't get them back.' 'And can you get into caste again?' I asked. 'O yes, Codabund—Saheb, I mean,' said he quickly; 'but it would cost ten rupees, and where should your slave get ten rupees?'

"Now, it is true his monthly wages were but six rupees; but considering that he cheated me, mensually out of fifteen or twenty besides, in making one little purchase and another, I thought there would be no great difficulty in his paying even the ten rupees. However, I did not like to be hard upon him; and, as I thought of the rueful face with which he had borne the involuntary shower-bath, I considered him entitled to ten rupees for these, as well as for the moral con siderations connected with the affair, and I gave them, adding two, that he might make merry on the occasion, stipulating, however, that whatever I required done for the future must be done willingly and at once, without the slightest hesitation, even although it should be to eat a ham, or drink a bottle of brandy;—at the first he winced, but a bright genial smile diffused itself over his countenance as I mentioned the second condition, which showed that he knew more of the contents of my wine-store than I had anticipated.

"This made the matter completely up, and I experienced no more annoyance from the transaction; Miss Grisi Curry, the youngest but one of the interesting family, smiled upon me with her full and innocent-looking blue eyes as benignly as in times past, nay, even more so. I had often felt, as I accidentally met her so frequently on the stairs, and in the garden, that it would be a delightful thing to have such a companion to meet one, on one's return from office, with such smiles, and to keep one's rooms cheerful. I had been in great disfavour before with the Curry family, on account of this escapade of mine; but now, even I could not help seeing that it was at an end, and that Miss Grisi was quite as willing as heretofore to let me look into her deep blue eyes and rosy mouth, with its well-set teeth. I looked often so, and sighed, and she sighed; and, in fact, how I escaped a formal proposal I know not.

"As the cold weather drew on, I was lying on a couch in my sitting-room, smoking, in the evening, my servants had come up-stairs to wait for me, fancying I had not yet returned, and squatting themselves in oriental fashion on the mat, proceeded to enjoy a quiet chat.

"I listened to their conversation, only separated from them by a thick, red curtain, so that I could hear every word they said. 'I only wish he'd throw a basin of water on me then, if he'd pay so handsomely as that for it,' said the Khitmudgar.* 'I never should have stopped,' replied Mhadub, 'if Grisi Baba† had not sent for me that evening, and told me that the Saheb would pay well for it one day or other—only to watch for some evening when he came home in a good humour, and then to tell him about my wife and children being taken away from me. Grisi Baba knows I havn't got any wife and children, but that's no matter; and then it took five rupees to get my caste again, which she lent me, and I was to ask for ten, that's the way he came to give me twelve. O, he's not a bad Saheb after all, although he said he'd make me eat a ham for dinner one day, but he was only joking, I know; and then, he never examines the accounts too much, and doesn't ask for them too often; now I do like a Saheb that doesn't make a fuss about a few pice—what's a few rupees to people that get hundreds and thousands?' 'Nothing,' said the Khitmudgar earnestly—'nothing. They never miss it; but you're a lucky fellow to have all the money for

* The servant who waits at table during meals.

† All unmarried ladies of all ages are called *Baba* by Hindoo servants.

the grass and grain for the horses go through your hands. I get scarcely anything.' 'But look at my caste,' said Mhadub, proudly. 'Why, I could have taken every Hindoo servant out of the house that time if I had liked, and I would have done it, if it hadn't been for Grisi Baba; but she can do what she likes with Saheb—the sparkle of her eye is a jewel to him.' 'Do you think she'll marry Saheb?' asked the Khitmudgar 'Of course she will,' was the reply. 'Didn't Mrs. Curry tell me, that when Grisi Baba was married I should be kept in Saheb's service, and get my wages raised, if I didn't make a row about that affair.' So you see, caste is still much more thought about than you fancy," he concluded.

"Poor Grisi!" said I, musingly; and here the conversation ended.

CHAPTER III.

THE COOK AND THE MONKEY—A FIRST SHOT.

"I would entreat you to put on
Your boldest suit of mirth, for we have friends
That purpose merriment."
Merchant of Venice, act ii., sc. 2.

THERE was a striking contrast between the animation and bustle which my picturesque bungalow presented when occupied for a time by a few friends, collected for shooting or excursion purposes, and the wearisome silence and monotony of the same building when they had departed, and left me to resume my wonted solitary and unvarying round of life. All was life, noise, and commotion in the one case—the happy, cheerful commotion of good spirits and pleasing excitement; all was silence and gloom in the other—unvarying silence, perpetual gloom. Nature might be lovely without, and the view from the bungalow's verandah was by no means a common one; the estate flourishing, wild mountains and thick forests on all sides, nature on a gigantic scale, and yet beautiful and captivating; but one could not *always* admire the same scene over and over again, one could not silence the heart's cravings for society and sympathy by looking at the scene in a new aspect, and endeavouring to find something fresh to admire in it continually. When, morning after morning, for months together, the same panorama was spread out in unvarying monotony on either side, however beautiful the scene in itself, it could not fail to weary one in the end. But when a visitor made his way to the bungalow, when Marandhan, or Hofer, or Fowler, rode up the hill's side to reach the bungalow, there was a pleasure in the very sound of the companionable voice, and in the hearty greeting, that is unknown where society is more common, and man does not keenly feel the want of it.

Fowler and Lister were, on one occasion, spending a few days with me for sporting purposes, and Hofer and Marandhan joined us in the evening. As usual, when men meet far away in the jungle, all willing to please and be pleased, the party was a pleasant one, and amid tales and descriptions and discussions the hours flew apace. Lister's monkey-adventure, related to us by

Mouat—the adventure in which the thieving prowlers had carried off his clothes, was mentioned, and elicited a tale from Marandhan of what had actually happened in his own bungalow, that amused us much. I have the fullest reliance on Marandhan's veracity, and, as he assured us the incident took place precisely as he related it, I have no hesitation in stating that I believe every word of it to be literally correct and true.

"I was sitting one morning in the verandah at the rear of my house," he began, "when I observed a strange scene passing directly in front of me. The servants' offices extend in two straight lines behind the house, enclosing a court-yard, on one side of which, (the centre being occupied by a tree,) a pole, with a little house on the top, forms the residence of a favourite monkey of mine. The cook, a Mohammedan, being about to prepare a chicken for curry, was standing at the door of the kitchen, a very short distance from the bottom of the pole, on the top of which the monkey lived; the animal above attentively noting his operations below. Squatting himself down at the door, as Singhalese servants will, whenever they can get an opportunity, he dipped the chicken into a vessel of boiling water beside him, in order to remove the feathers more easily, and afterwards commenced to pluck it, after the usual manner of

avoiding the suspicious animal; once more Tambee proceeded to search, this time evidently to see if the chicken were lying anywhere about; he looked into the hot water, into the various vessels near, behind the doors, and generally wherever he thought it probable the chicken might have been hidden, and, at length, not finding it, he called vigorously to his fellow servants, to come and witness the phenomenon. They assembled, and then, with much gesticulation, did Tambee proceed to deliver an oration, intimating that some witchcraft or diabolic influence had been at work to transform the chicken he had left, into the crow he had found, concluding, by begging of them, on no account, to touch the gift of the devil which had thus been left for their confusion and injury—the monkey all the time quietly watching the gesticulation and listening to the address as if he knew nothing of the matter.

"Tambee concluded, and great was the consternation and dismay in the assembly; a wide circle was formed round the innocent cause of all this disturbance, and the question was asked, what was to be done? They at length decided, although not until after much discussion; two sticks were procured and inserted under the board on which the dead crow lay, one at the head and the other at the foot, and by means of these, were the board and crow borne to the Paloya, into which they were thrown amidst the prayers of the assembled servants.

"When I heard of the circumstance afterwards it was as one that seriously compromised the character of the house, nor did I venture to tell them the part my monkey had taken in the transaction, or I might possibly have found him some morning pretty much in the same condition as he had left the unfortunate crow."

We laughed heartily at Marandhan's recital, and some one having remarked that people in England would scarcely believe such a thing to have occurred, he solemnly assured us that it was literally true, that it had occurred precisely as he had related it.

"Mouat is fond of telling that absurd story about the monkeys stealing my clothes," said Lister, "but really after all it was not so ludicrous an affair as his first shot at an elephant, and besides, I was not to blame in that instance, whereas he was, in the case to which I allude. You have never heard the story. I had been in the island some years when he came out, and a rawer youngster scarcely ever made his appearance in Ceylon than Mouat was. As to shooting he did not know the difference between a rifle and a blunderbuss, and had never hit anything but a favourite dog of his mother's and that was by accident. It happened thus—one day he took an old rusty gun out into the garden of her house in Brompton, and resolved to have a shot at something. The gun wouldn't go off for a long time—it had an old flint lock, and might have been used in the battle of Marston Moor, for all he knew—so, leaving the target unmolested, he set himself vigorously to discharge the gun, for he had tried to draw the charge without success. After hammering away at the flint and wasting immense quantities of gunpowder in trying to introduce some into the touch-hole, he at length took up the piece and pulled the trigger. An apoplectic spaniel of his mother's was at the moment walking leisurely along before him, wagging his tail cautiously as such dogs will do—the fowling-piece or gun or blunderbuss, whatever it was, for Mouat has no distinct ideas on the subject, exploded, and the ball, intended for the garden-wall, lodged in the skull of the unfortunate dog who fell dead at once. Mouat was always a lad of quick parts, so seeing what was done, he beat a rapid retreat into the house, first throwing a bough over the dog's body to conceal it, put up the fowling-piece in its accustomed place, and then returned to dispose of the dog's corpse before his mother's return, for the good lady was out. This he accomplished by conveying the carcase into the next garden but one to theirs, whence it was brought in to Mrs. Mouat on the following day. But about the elephant :—

"On arriving in Ceylon, he was appointed Assistant Government Agent at the station of which I was Commandant at the time. Like all men newly arrived in the island, he was anxious to be initiated into the noblest of all possible sports—elephant-shooting, and I promised to be his instructor. I had not then been very often out myself, but had at least such a general knowledge of the way in which the affair was usually managed, and of the best course of procedure in dangerous cases, that my assistance and advice would at all events be valuable to a griff. It was in May that we sallied out, and, as you may suppose, the weather was hot enough to try the strongest constitutions and the most seasoned livers. I had taken care that for Mouat and myself everything should be properly prepared, and had persuaded him to practise daily for a month with the rifle. I had even taken the trouble to show him an elephant's skull, and to point out to him how very small a portion of the forehead was directly in front of the brain, and therefore how accurate the aim must be that brings down the animal with one bullet. A quick eye and a steady hand, the two great requisites for a good elephant hunter, he had, and I felt assured that a little practice would turn him out an excellent jungle-sportsman. Leaving our little station, we went to the south towards a valley where an old Singhalese hermit lived, who delighted to point out the locality of the herds to parties like ours, and whose whole life, and it had already been a long one, had been passed in the neighbourhood. He was a venerable-looking old fellow—the very patriarch of the forest—with a flowing white beard, and a long white stick with which he terrified the most courageous elephants.*

"Some of our party wanted to advance on horseback, but he insisted on our dismounting before he would lead us to the scene of action—the last mounted party having left him to escape from the wounded elephants as best he could. Our beaters were sent up the hill on which he declared the elephants were, in two distinct lines, parallel to each other, and with some distance between, so as to include a considerable space. As soon as the morning dawned we were at the foot of the hill, under the guidance of the old patriarch. Everything was favourable for the

* The beaters sent out to turn a herd, always provide themselves with long white wands, of which they believe the elephants are afraid.

sport, the wind blowing down the hill's side, and I anticipated a day of thorough enjoyment. Mouat was as eager as myself, and all I felt afraid of was, that his anxiety to bring an elephant down would lead him into useless danger. I warned him, therefore, to keep near me, for, although I was only a few years his senior in age, I was a century before him in elephant-shooting.

"We advanced up the side of the hill, keeping well together. In a quarter of an hour we came to the rear of the herd, and, before either Mouat or myself could get a shot at them, two had been brought down by our companions. This was annoying enough. We pushed on, therefore, hastily, I, thinking of nothing but the herd, Mouat, of nothing but the proving of his courage and presence of mind. In a moment we had passed the dead elephants and were separated, nor did we meet again during the day. For my own part, I kept on the trail of the herd watching their marks in the jungle and pushing on with all possible speed, whilst my griffin protégé kept on the path and directly ascended the hill. A run of about ten minutes brought me up with the herd again—at least near enough for a shot, when they turned, which they soon did, repulsed by the beaters. My two barrels were quickly discharged

—their contents lodging in the forehead of the first (a clear waste of powder and ball, but I was not a very experienced sportsman then). He fell, and I seized another gun from my attendant and rushed on. After very considerable difficulty I fell in with a second, quite a cub, and rolled him over. The sun was intolerably hot—there was not high jungle enough to protect us from it, and I was completely exhausted, so much so indeed that I began seriously to fear an attack of brain fever. I returned to our rendezvous, and poured out a tumbler of brandy mixed with a very little water, which I drank off at once. The draught removed the oppression from my head, and I felt quite revived.

" By this time the herd had completely broken away on all sides, and were gone—some over the hill, some forcing their way through the beaters, some scampering down into the valley as fast as their unwieldy carcasses would permit. Seven of them altogether had been dispatched, but not one tusker. I now began to feel anxious about Mouat. During the excitement of the chase, and the subsequent long journey through the sun, I had forgotten him, but now that all was over, I began to fear some harm had befallen him, as he alone of our little party was missing.

" No one had seen him since he had left me.

I sent off natives in every direction, but there was no intelligence to be obtained about him, and so it remained till next morning when he returned unhurt, to our station at the old patriarch's. From himself and some natives I subsequently gathered an account of his exploits and adventures.

"On leaving me he had gone straight up the path to the top of the hill, which path of course the elephants naturally avoided, as is always the case under similar circumstances. From eight o'clock, the hour when we separated, he continued marching straight forward till eleven, his attendant native in vain urging him to return, and at last leaving him altogether to prosecute his romantic journey alone. The fact was, he was ashamed to return till he had done *something*, and on he went, with his gun under his arm, hour after hour in the very middle of the day, under a hot sweltering sun! at length through the jungle he saw a clearing at some distance, and under a tree in the middle of this clearing, a magnificent elephant, a tusker too, enjoying himself in devouring the branches. Here, thought the gallant griffin, is *my* prey—the others have had their sport—now for mine!

"Slowly and cautiously did he creep round to leeward of the noble animal before him, and which he had so unceremoniously dedicated to destruction. The elephant, he thought, once or twice looked round as if he suspected something was wrong, but made no attempt to escape! lucky dog that I am, thought our friend, to get such a chance! On he came, warily, cautiously, silently, scarcely daring to draw a full breath, so anxious and eager was he with expectation. At length the great deed was to be done! within twelve paces of him stood the gigantic animal, his broad forehead right in front, and the monster, as he suspected, looking full in his face, whilst he crouched down behind some thick bushes, that he might be completely hid. But still the elephant did not give over his meal, or relax the energy of his attack on the boughs of the fig-tree beneath which he was stationed! The deadly gun was raised, and silently thrust through the brushwood directly in a line with the brain, as Mouat had learned its position in our anatomical researches. His arm was firm as a rock—his eye true as a hawk's—all the energy of his nature concentrated into one focus, and directed towards the predestined victim's destruction.

"The elephant immediately gave a sort of snort, or blow from his trunk. He is thinking of going, thought Mouat, it's time to fire. The loud report boomed suddenly through the peaceful little valley; the elephant gave a convulsive start, having evidently received the ball full in his forehead,—just where the brain was, as Mouat described it,—and yet stood still. Then followed a sharp piercing cry of pain, whilst the trunk ineffectually beat against the wound. Why the animal neither advanced nor retreated, our friend could not understand, but without waiting to solve the problem he fired again. The second bullet was better directed, and the elephant rolled over on his side. With a chant of triumph, the mighty hunter bounded towards the tree, when, horror of horrors! he saw a chain wrapped several times round the animal's leg, and confining it to the tree! 'Good heavens!' he stammered forth, 'it must be a tame one!' 'Yes, Mahathma,' said a native who had come up unobserved, 'bery tame 'un! him Murtey Mahathma's elephant,' 'Mr. Murtey's elephant,' shouted Mouat—at that time Murtey was Commissioner of Roads, and it immediately struck the ambitious sportsman, that he had been slaughtering a Government elephant employed on the roads—'Mr. Murtey's elephant,' he exclaimed—'ah—very sorry indeed—very sorry—quite a mistake—but I must return—the day's getting advanced.'

"In fact he thought it was time for him to

join our party; but joke or not (and the affair proved afterwards no joke to him,) it was not to end here. Up came Kelly, one of the European subordinates of the Roads Department, formerly a sergeant of the grenadier company of the 54th regiment—up came Kelly, I say, and told Mouat that he must go before the nearest district-judge, twenty-two miles away! 'I must return to my friends now,' said Mouat, with all the dignity he could command for the occasion. 'Faith an' you must come before the joodge first yer honour,' said Kelly stoutly. 'Do you know whom you speak to, Sir?' asked Mouat, magniloquently. 'Upon my conscience I don't,' was the reply, 'but if you won't come pacably and dacently, shure an' I'll be obleeged to carry you—it's Mr. Murtey's own orders, so it is.' 'Well, Sir,' said Mouat, with an awful frown, 'I'm Assistant Government Agent at Killergille, and shall write to Mr. Murtey explaining the circumstance, particularly noticing too your insolence.' 'Arrah thin now Sir, don't be angry, but shure, tare an' ages, I must do what I'm ordered,' said the determined Kelly. 'You shall hear more of this,' said Mouat, walking off proudly. 'O, begor an' this won't do,' said Kelly, 'for come before the joodge you must, an' you war the Guverner's own son, my honey.'

"Mouat walked on unheedingly up the hill—Kelly followed on horse, or rather pony, back. At length seeing that the sportsman was not disposed to be made a prisoner quietly, the sergeant sent the native off privately, and, in a few minutes four sepoys of the Ceylon Rifles came to his assistance. 'Now you see, Misther,' said Kelly, soothingly, 'it's no use in life talkin'—you must come, bekase that's the order, not mine, my honey, not a bit of it, but Mr. Murtey's.' 'I'll tell you what it is,' said Mouat, looking round fiercely, 'if one of these men touches me, I'll blow his brains out.' 'Wid an empty gun, of coorse,' said the fearless sergeant, now beginning to get nettled, 'its aizy to shoot a tame elephant tied to a tree, with a loaded rifle, but it's not so aizy to blow a man's brains out wid an empty one.'

"Seeing that Mouat would not be made a prisoner peaceably, Kelly dismounted and gave his pony to the native. Mouat walked on, never thinking that the sergeant would dare to lay hands on him. Suddenly, however, Kelly sprang on him from behind, and pinioned his arms to his sides, by throwing his own arms tightly round him. Mouat struggled, but Kelly was the more powerful man of the two. 'Saize the jintleman's legs, you black spalpeens,' shouted the sergeant to the sepoys, 'do you think my shins is made of iron?' There was evidently no help for it, so Mouat was obliged to submit, and, protesting against the seizure, and reserving his right to an action for false imprisonment, he marched quietly to the unmanageable sergeant's quarters. Arrived there, he was allowed to remain at liberty on parole, Kelly assuring him, unkindest cut of all! that he might make himself perfectly 'aizy,' for there was no one there to 'laugh at him, barrin' the blacks, an' he'd like to see thim showin' their front teeth in a grin, that was all.'

"In durance vile, Mouat wrote to one of our party, who was Kelly's superior, stating the circumstances and his willingness to pay for the elephant, if necessary. An order was consequently transmitted to Kelly, which he obeyed immediately, and next morning Mouat returned on the sergeant's pony, looking sheepish and crest-fallen enough. Poor Mouat was roasted unmercifully about the transaction—Kelly's account of the capture was obtained by his superior, and was extremely ludicrous. He protested that had he been sure 'the jintleman was tellin' the truth, he'd have let him go at onst, but how was he to tell but he was one of thim planters?'

"When Mouat heard, however, that he had to pay seventy pounds for the elephant, which he had so valorously slain, he declared that it was past a joke, and that a man on a paltry four hundred and fifty a-year ought not to be expected to pay such an amount. He was assured in reply, that had the animal been fully tamed, so as to be available for working on the roads, he should have had to pay a hundred pounds at least. Since this transaction, he has had, I believe, as great an aversion to tame elephants, as I have always had, constitutionally, to monkeys."

CHAPTER IV.

THE CAVE-TEMPLES OF DAMBOOL.*

"——How shall we beguile
The lazy time, if not with some delight."
Midsummer's Night Dream, act v., sc. 1.

The central mass of mountains and table-land that constitutes, as it were, the heart of Ceylon, is surrounded on all sides by a low district, comparatively level, and of very varying extent, that, for the most part, slopes down gently to the sea. On the north, where the island narrows to a point, this level district is of much greater extent than anywhere else, and was, in the olden times of Ceylonese prosperity, the seat of the capital and the residence of the vast majority of the inhabitants. If a pear be taken and cut longitudinally, from the stalk downwards, the core will aptly represent the hilly district in the centre, and the pulp that surrounds it will be no bad illustration of the level region skirting the sea.

When Ceylon was in its prime, a conquering island, issuing forth from its ocean home to spread its arms and its religion in India and the Eastern peninsula, it has been calculated that it contained five millions of inhabitants; now, in the days of its degeneracy and debasement, after Portuguese, Dutch, and British have partially or entirely conquered it in turn, and after centuries of previous civil strife, before Europeans made their appearance at all, it does not contain much more than a fifth of the number. Then the extensive level district, stretching away to the north, was densely populated, its tanks and artificial water-courses fertilizing the ground, and producing, under careful cultivation, abundant crops for the supply of the large masses of the people and for exportation—*now* that level district, with the richest possible soil, is deserted by the natives, part of it has never been explored by Europeans, and the whole is covered with thick, almost impenetrable, jungle; the tanks and water-courses that formerly enabled the inhabitants to irrigate their rice-fields, and surround their abodes with the blessings of plenty and wealth, are now the fruitful sources of miasma and contagion. The artificial mounds and embankments, often of the most gigantic character, are broken or scattered uselessly about, whilst the country is fruitlessly inundated, and thick, tangled masses of aquatic vegetation have taken the places of the flourishing corn and happy abodes of times long gone by. It has been stated, indeed, by men capable of forming an estimate on the subject, that it would exceed the power of the British Government in the island, and be a task beyond its resources, to restore these old-world reservoirs to their former condition, so massive and gigantic were the works.

The cave-temples of Dambool are cut out of a vast mass of primitive rock that rises, rounded and solitary, from the level plain to the height of five or six hundred feet above it. The cave-temples themselves, the traditions connected with them, and the interesting view from the summit, all render the rock of Dambool an interesting object. I had read much of it, I had talked much to Marandhan of it, and was determined to see it. He spoke with raptures of the solemn awe inspired by the first entering into the extensive temples, hewn, as they were, out of the solid rock—an awe felt by the most thoughtless spectator, from the strange and unwonted spectacle they presented; but to him,—acquainted with the history of the caves, knowing how they were mixed up with that of the island from the century preceding the Christian era to the present, —doubly impressive and awe-striking.

Anuradhapoora, too, the former capital of the island, lay in the same direction, fifty miles further on—a veritable buried city. It had been a place of importance long before Rome had first risen to extensive wealth and power. It had been the capital of the island, and celebrated throughout India and China and Chin-India, for its extent and magnificence, when Athens was in its glory and when the Persian monarchy had attained its greatest splendour! its remains attesting, at the present day, its former greatness, and amazing the traveller by their size and often by their preservation. True, the greater part of the city lies buried beneath the all-pervading jungle that attacks within the tropics so unrelentingly every remnant of antiquity, and renders the preservation of old buildings and ruins so difficult a matter, nay, almost an impossibility; but still there was enough to be seen, I was assured, to gratify the most inveterate novelty-hunter—enough to interest, to amaze, and to instruct.

An excursion into these regions was, however, rather a perilous matter. Jungle-fever was often caught from the *miasma* that pervaded the district, and numerous instances had occurred of Europeans having been attacked by it in the course of their exploring expeditions. Not that the danger would have deterred me personally, for I was determined to visit both the cave-temples and the ancient capital, come what might; but I knew that Hofer and his wife were equally anxious to see these places, so famous for their peculiar character, and the interesting associations connected with them; and I hoped, therefore, that, by biding my time, I might travel thither in company with a party, which would add variety to the journey.

I was not deceived. The safest time for making such a trip fortunately coincided with the season of rest and repose, and, too often of idleness, on the coffee-estates, and a large party was ultimately formed to journey northwards, taking Kandy and Matelle * in our way, at both of which places we were to stop for some time, so as to advance leisurely, and prevent the pleasure becoming, as it too often does, a toil. Hofer and his wife, with her newly-arrived sister, Miss Mowbray, Fowler, Marandhan, and myself, were to constitute the party, and a better assorted one could not easily have been formed. Miss Mowbray had not been long in the island, but was eager for any expedition of the kind. She had more buoyancy of spirits, more girlishness in her nature than her more sedate sister, Mrs. Hofer, and was certainly not so handsome; but there was a charm about

* Pronounced Mättelley.

her hearty enjoyment of everything enjoyable that made her society eminently attractive. Fowler, who was somewhat of a book-worm, and a bachelor, like, myself, and an enthusiatic admirer of Mrs. Hofer, was evidently dazzled by Miss Mowbray's attractions, and was now a constant visitor at Lanka. She teazed him, and coquetted with him, as young ladies will sometimes do, and he pouted at it, and made me his confidant. I gave him the best advice I could under the circumstances, although I felt that it was but the blind leading the blind. Courtships and marriages are matters so speedily arranged in the jungle that he seemed astonished that he could not win the fair lady by a *coup-de-main*, and was disgusted at the thoughts of a regular siege. Yet he had "never told his love," in words at least; as yet, his eyes alone had spoken, and he seemed to expect, foolish man, that the lady should have cried out for quarter at once, and surrendered at discretion! So little art do men learn in the jungle, so strangely does a solitary life affect them, when they are surrounded only by books and coffee!

Our intention was to remain a fortnight in Kandy, a friend of Hofer's living there, who had taken his family on a visit to Colombo, having generously placed his house at our disposal. Our next stage was Matelle, where a common friend, well-known to, and esteemed by every member of our party, was anxious to receive us; and thence we purposed making a bold push through the vile jungle path, or "trace" as it is called—a trace at some future time intended to be a road—to Dambool.

At length the day of departure arrived. We all assembled at Mouat's house in Ruminacaddee, it being on the line of march. Mouat had promised to join us; but although his uncle was the Chief Justice, he was unable to leave his station just at the time, as the Supreme Court was to sit in Kandy shortly, and all the neighbouring magistrates and district judges were of course on the alert. Servants had been previously despatched to prepare our temporary abode in Kandy for our reception, and we promised ourselves an agreeable ride and pleasant stay in Kandy. Marandhan was by far the most picturesque object in our cavalcade, with his fine black moustaches and beard, which the hand of time had scarcely yet frosted at all;—his strange head-dress surmounting a pair of sparkling eyes, that spoke eloquently of intelligence and intellect;—he rode a faithful cob or country horse, a hard-working, muscular little fellow, that cared little for an elephant, and had long been used to all the accidents and incidents of jungle wayfaring. The two ladies were well-mounted—Mrs. Hofer on a bay Arab that she had long been used to, and Miss Mowbray on the chestnut Hofer had lately purchased—a steady animal enough, although rather more showy than there was any necessity for in jungle travelling. Both were excellent horsewomen, and in their broad-brimmed straw hats and short riding habits, looked foreign and interesting; both evidently in high spirits, Mrs. Hofer's eye flashing brilliantly as I had not seen it flash for many months; the road, the journey, the exercise, and the scenery, all combining to throw a glow into her cheeks and an hilarity into her heart, that made her, according to Fowler, "perfectly bewitching."

Hofer himself admired her as much as any, and when she cantered along before, or pointed out the interesting objects in the landscapes around, no one could regard another with more love and admiration than he. As to Marandhan, his powers of conversation seemed for a time to fail him altogether, so much were his eyes rivetted by the fine female forms before him, and I was at length obliged to ask whether he had not been taking a lesson from Mrs. Mouat. Miss Mowbray was charming too; but, whatever might have been Fowler's opinion, there was no disputing the superiority of her sister. She sat her fine horse well, managed him admirably, showed off her elegant figure as a graceful lady only can on horseback, and, by her quick-witted remarks and repartees, was the soul of the party. She rather avoided Fowler, poor fellow — rank coquetry thought I two or three times as she stopped for Hofer to come up, when he left Mrs. Hofer with Marandhan and me, and cantered forward to accompany her—rank coquetry, unquestionably!

There was neither stiffness nor formality about the party. For the most part Hofer rode with Miss Mowbray, as she seemed to prefer him, Fowler accompanying, and Marandhan escorted Mrs. Hofer, whilst I joined one party or the other as I listed, occasionally inquiring about objects of interest, or the scenes of remarkable incidents as we proceeded. Marandhan was a living "Murray" for us, and no young lady going down the Rhine, whether making contemptuous remarks about the appearance of Bonn from the river, or lost in admiration of the Drackenfels, ever consulted her Handbook with more assiduity than did we, as we proceeded, consult Marandhan. Not a strange rock, not an oddly-shaped hill, not an ugly tree escaped us. We pumped him almost dry, as we ascended one hill and descended another, for the road from Ruminacaddee to Kandy, if road it can be called, runs straight over everything.

Whether any engineer ever planned it, I do not know—it is impossible to say what engineers in the East, who sometimes survey a district without visiting it, will do, but this I know, that nothing could be more simple than the construction of this attempt at a road. The principles on which it was formed were three in number. Draw a straight line from Ruminacaddee to Kandy. Well, so far so good; that is a great principle in itself to begin with. Now the nearer we can keep to that line the better, principle number two, —diverging from it only to get into the watercourses that sweep down the sides of the hills in the rainy season, which, in the dry weather, will, of course, form admirable roads, principle number three. That is the conclusion, the road is finished, and in due time the same may be said of many poor horses and oxen that have to travel over it.

Where a little level ground permitted—for even in the interior of Ceylon there are some parts level, although I am willing to confess they are quite exceptional—the entire party cantered on briskly, the ladies generally taking the lead, their large hats, their veils and habits fluttering in the most picturesque way in the breeze.

By nine o'clock, when the sun had already attained considerable height and power, we reached Kandy, where Hofer had, of course, as might have been expected, offended all his friends, by occupying the empty house which had been offered to him. As in most other matters, he had consulted his own inclination first, and left others to be pleased or not as suited their fancy. In this instance, however, he was certainly right. We intended to stop a fortnight in the town, and wished to be as independent as possible during our stay—Marandhan promising to show us all the objects of interest in the neighbourhood. Had we been divided, or obliged to consult the convenience and habits of others, as well as those of our own party, much time would of course have been lost, and much entertainment missed. With the exception then of a few ceremonial visits, which were, for the most part, distantly received and as ceremoniously returned, our time was entirely our own—all invitations to dinner being systematically refused—even that of His High Mightiness the Government Agent of the Central Province himself, a circumstance so unprecedented in his life, that it was said, he began to suspect socialism was spreading and the very foundations of society beginning to be shaken; a coffee-planter refusing to dine with him! positively the present state of things, under such circumstances, must be alarming! Nevertheless it was true, and Mr. Bluster was obliged to make the most of it, but, so rank was the offence, that as a matter of course the next time Mrs. Bluster and her amiable daughter met Mrs. Hofer and Miss Mowbray, the former stared very hard at them, as if to ask who *they* were or could possibly be, whilst, by some condescension of which Marandhan and I felt ourselves quite unworthy, we were honoured with a most cordial salute; "and so ends our acquaintance with our dear friends the Blusters," said Mrs. Hofer, as we rode on.

It may be readily conceived what an interest we felt in visiting the lions of Kandy with so admirable a guide as Marandhan. He showed us the ruins of the palace, and took us through the great temple containing the much celebrated tooth of Budha; the temple noteworthy on account of its noble flights of steps, lofty arches, and imposing colonnades. The tooth itself, placed on a silver altar, was covered by a number of conical cases, one fitting over the other, like a juggler's goblets—the outermost five feet high. To me, and indeed to all our party, except Marandhan, the tooth seemed emphatically a humbug. It had not the form of a canine tooth at all; more resembling indeed the top of a small elephant's tusk sawn off. But this we did not hint in Marandhan's hearing, of course. The massive and substantial appearance of the walls of the palace showed us that it was built with the intention of being a permanent structure, not a temporary one as is too often the case in the East, and the carvings on various portions of it are passable.

The lake itself, which forms so interesting a feature of the valley in which Kandy is situated, is a proof of the gigantic character of the works which the old Kandians could undertake and complete. It is quite artificial, fed from the neighbouring hills, is of considerable extent, and, with the road round it, forms a delightful object to contemplate whilst one is walking, riding, or driving at the base, or on the sides, of the hills. This road round it has indeed been constituted the evening promenade of the European inhabitants of Kandy, and I doubt if any city in Europe has a more agreeable one. A house stands in the middle of the lake in a line with the palace, formerly, they say, part of the seraglio of the Kandian kings—such *was* its destiny; but how times are altered! John Bull knows nothing of seraglios; even Mr. Bluster himself would not venture to keep one openly, in all the plenitude of his power, but John Bull knows something of the smell of powder, and the lake-temple, once sacred to women and love, is now a powder magazine! "To what base —" but no, I'll spare the reader the hacknied quotation.

At a distance of about five miles from Kandy we were shown by Marandhan, some rocks which appeared to me to be Druidical remains. I should not have ventured to express such an opinion then, but on inquiring into the matter since, I find these Druidical monuments are much more extensively scattered than I had supposed, not only over Europe, but in Asia also. A complete Druidical circle like Stonehenge exists at Darab, in Persia, described by Sir W. Ouseley, and it has amused me to find that Stonehenge itself has been set down by some savants as a Budhistic remain. The cromlech, which Marandhan showed us—for cromlech I believe it was—somewhat resembled that at Plas Newydd, in Anglesey.

How little, after all our Egyptian and Assyrian discoveries, do we really know of the early history of our race! Who shall tell us where this wide-spread Druidism, extending from Ceylon to Britain, took its rise? when it first propagated its doctrines, and how? whether its progress was from east to west, or from west to east? Whether, like Mohammedanism, its early preachers held the sword in one hand and their religion in the other, and told the unbeliever to take his choice, or, like Budhism, relied upon the force of reason, and the power of persuasion alone? How truly did Göthe write when he exclaimed—

> "To us, my friend, the times that are gone by
> Are as a book, sealed with seven seals.
> That which you call the spirit of ages past
> Is but, in truth, the spirit of some few authors
> In which those ages are beheld reflected,
> With what distortion strange, Heaven only knows."

It was not without a melancholy feeling that we gazed upon "the tombs of the kings" in Kandy, when Marandhan took us to them, and sorrowfully pointed them out. "The tombs of the kings!" there is magic in the very phrase. What text more apt could the preacher desire for his homily, the sentimentalist for his rhapsody? The tombs of the kings, broken, desecrated, and almost destroyed. Goths from England carrying away part, and Vandals in Ceylon seizing the rest—a carving here, and an inscription there picked out, until the pile stands shapeless and disfigured, a monument of what the noblest memorials of greatness, real or fictitious, may ultimately come to. And this race of kings, what is to be said of it?—not much I fear that was great, not much that was good, not much that was noble, yet still something of each—this, at all events, must be allowed, let them have as little praise as they may, the oldest dynasties of modern Europe were new and unvenerable compared with that strange Singha race. Wickrama, whom the British proclamation, in 1815, designated a monster of cruelty, was the last scion of a line that had continued to govern Ceylon for two thousand years! The European monarch that can trace back his pedigree through the one half of that period, whether a Hapsburg or a Hanover, feels proud of the old genealogical tree—Wickrama thrown into a dungeon in India to pine out the rest of his life in misery—Wickrama reviled, insulted, struck, spat upon by the soldiers that took him prisoner, should rebuke the empty boasting resulting from a mere freak of fortune.

We had not nearly exhausted the picturesque rides and rambles in the neighbourhood of Kandy when we left it to continue our journey northward. We crossed the Mahavelliganga, not very far distant from the spot where the massacre of Major Davis's force, by the Singhalese, had taken place —a massacre which Marandhan denounced as quite unjustifiable and cruel, with as much warmth as we could have done.

Our way led through the village of Matelle, where we remained for a few days, to visit some coffee-estates in the neighbourhood, and in compliance with the pressing invitation of the magistrate of the district. No man could live with more patriarchal simplicity than our good friend Mr. Rivers, nor more pleasingly exhibit the noblest patriarchal virtues; his own natural, warm, and unsophisticated benevolence being amiably contrasted with the more cultivated, but not on that account less genuine, goodness of his two daughters. One can have no conception, with his cut-and-dried notions of life in England, of such a family as that of Rivers',—living in the midst of a semi-civilized population, who were attached to them by the ties of affection and gratitude, sure of justice, and looking upon them more as gods upon earth than as men and women —regarding their very house, and all that belongs to them, as sacred;—looking upon it as the abode of every virtue, of power the most unlimited, combined with the most extensive goodness. Did the poor native meet with oppression at the hands of his Singhalese or European employer, he knew that he had but to state his case before "the good mahathma," as he was emphatically called, in order to have it thoroughly and diligently investigated. Had his rice-fields been destroyed, and his only hope of sustenance for the year thus removed, "the good mahathma" was willing to help him for the present, and to direct him to, or to find him, work for the future. Did the father or the daughters walk or ride abroad, through the magnificent valley in which he reigned supreme, the natives crowded around to bless, and even, in their untaught heartfulness, to adore them—to point them out to their children as the righters of the wronged, the stays of the distressed or the oppressed, the bountiful helpers of the helpless.

I can conceive of no situation more gratifying to the well-constituted mind than that of the man who was thus regarded by a whole district as its benefactor and preserver. Yet it is not to be supposed that his situation was altogether without trials. How could it be so in such a world as this? Where did ever the good do battle manfully against the oppressors and the evil-doers, without being exposed to injury and loss, to contumely from some, to obloquy from others, to censure and scorn from many? The habit of ruling with all but absolute sway in their estates, made our class, the coffee-planters, impatient of control, and I have heard men of true hearts and kind dispositions ask the question, "How are we to get on at all, deep in the jungle, surrounded by these half-savages, if we have not the right of flogging them when they deserve it?" and if the more moderate and honest could ask, and ask seriously, too, such a question, what would not the Siggenses be willing to do when they could and dared?

We rode about through Matelle, from one estate to another, in great joyfulness and high spirits, the Misses Rivers forming an agreeable addition to our party. It was an interesting sight to see our various-looking cavalcade, riding, often in single file, up the hill's side, or crossing a rivulet, whilst joyful playfulness suggested, and light-hearted mirth gave expression to, repartees and sallies without number. The more our party became acquainted with Miss Mowbray the more did we value her capacity for enjoyment, and the total abandonment of all that was gloomy and dispiriting, with which she threw her whole energies into the gladness of the moment. As day after day of constant intimacy ripened our friendship, we all became mutually, I believe, better satisfied with each other's society, and more disposed to cultivate it; yet was not our residence at Matelle, sunny and bright as it was, cloudless for poor Fowler.

A Captain Reid, of one of the Queen's regiments, had come out in the same vessel with Miss Mowbray, and now joined our party for a few days. He was accommodated at the bungalow of a coffee-planter of his acquaintance a short distance from Mr. Rivers's residence, and spent usually the entire day with us. He was a dashing sprightly fellow, shallow, according to Fowler's idea, but eminently calculated, at all events, by his benevolent suavity and gentleness, accompanied by a considerable share of fun, to attract a young lady's attention. It was just before he joined us that I had persuaded Fowler to make up his mind to propose to Miss Mowbray, of whom he gradually thought more highly. His esteem and friendship for her had now ripened into love; it was, therefore, not without some chagrin that he saw her begin to listen attentively to Captain Reid's observations, and take evident pleasure in his society; yet he fancied, too, for I was his confidant, that the Captain's attentions, if attentions they were at all, were more directed towards Miss Rivers than towards her, and after his departure he speedily conquered his ill-humour, persuading himself, with the vanity which a young man *will* sometimes feel, that she divined his intentions, and was willing to render her conquest and possession not quite so easy and uninterrupted an achievement as he might possibly have fancied it would be. I say he thought so then, and notwithstanding what subsequently took place during our trip, I think so, too. I do not indeed pretend to fathom the deep mystery of the heart of a playful young lady, or to understand completely the strange levity, on the most momentous of subjects, with which they will sometimes speak, yet I did flatter myself then that I could see as far into the causes of outward actions as most other people. To me it was simply amusing, however, to hear Fowler speak so rapturously of the charming appearance and manner of the young lady in question, of the ineffable grace with which she sat and controlled her chestnut steed—of the beautiful sweep of the head with which she listened to what you had to say, and then raised her eyes to your face to reply; of the happy observations she made, and of the cheerfulness which she diffused everywhere around her. That which to the individual interested is often the most momentous concern of life, to a spectator may be but ludicrous or even absurd.

Captain Reid's stay with us was, however, by no means a prolonged one, and, before we set out for Dambool, still keeping our horses' heads to the north, he had retaken the road to Colombo, and left us to resume our cavalcade journey in the same order as that in which we had originally started from Ruminacaddee.

There is something singularly imposing about the vast mass of rock called by the natives the Damboola-galla, in which the celebrated cave-temples have been excavated. From the surrounding plain it rises majestically in one large, rounded, naked mass—like a gigantic human skull, on the forehead of which the pious zeal of former ages has hollowed out these strange worship-houses. It certainly has a much greater resemblance to a huge skull than the so much vaunted likeness of the rock of Gibraltar to a lion. The summit of it, on which formerly stood some religious erection, is five hundred and fifty feet above the plain beneath, and as the country around is singularly level, a beautiful and extensive view is obtained from it;—a few oddly-shaped rocks dotting the horizon on one side, a rounded hill on another, whilst the distant mountains of the Matelle district are seen dimly and hazily to the south, the intervening spaces filled with tanks and forests, low brushwood in one place and lofty trees in another, monuments of the luxuriant vegetation which pervades the entire district.

Night was fast setting in when we arrived at the large and almost empty building erected here for the use of travellers by government; our servants as usual, however, had been sent on long before us, and we found everything prepared for our reception, and the whole place looking quite comfortable. We were all tired, for our day's journey had been fatiguing, and our rest had been much disturbed at the native house at which we had passed the preceding night. Yet, tired as I was, I was anxious to see something of the far-famed cave-temples that evening. Marandhan and Hofer both regarded my desire as unreasonable, and refused to accompany me, whilst Fowler was by no means disposed to leave the ladies,—so I set off alone. A walk of about a mile, a considerable portion of which consists of vigorous climbing, brought me to the entrance, and, as Marandhan had told me, my attendant found little difficulty in getting a priest to chaperon me, late as it was. A considerable number of the brotherhood reside all about the entrance of the caves, on the sides of the hill which here alone slope more gently than elsewhere. It was quite dark before we arrived at the entrance, and as the priest opened the sacred portal of one of the excavations, he held a flaming torch in his hand to exhibit the interior to my gaze. But it was only a very small portion of it that the red flames could illumine, and as the light flickered about, exhibiting now the head of some gigantic statue, and now the yellow dress and dark features of my guide, the scene struck me as one of an unearthly character. It was as if twenty centuries had been entombed here, and we, for the first time, were violating the sanctity of their catacomb; for twenty centuries have indeed rolled over the world since the hand of man first chiselled out these extraordinary monuments of mistaken piety! Behind us were the stars shining clearly in a sky of a dark-blue ground; on either side and in front was a darkness almost palpable in its intensity; whilst, as the torch flamed here and there, a thousand figures of the

Budhistic man-god seemed to start into existence, and to disappear again in the black night behind, like demons from the tombs. It was a picture, which, once witnessed, could never be forgotten, and in this scene I felt that I, with my rude jungle dress—not quite so rude, however, as it would have been, had I been travelling alone—and my European nineteenth century appliances, must have formed, to any observer, had there been such, not the least extraordinary feature of this striking picture. To me the figures were simply bits of stone or lime, the place in which we stood a simple hole in the rock, large indeed, but artificial; to the priest who stood by my side, these images were idols, this hole in the rock, a sacred temple. What I looked upon as unmeaning symbols or airy superstitions, were to him realities full of deep and holy significance.

A huge recumbent figure of Budha was before us, the vast head, six feet long from the chin to the forehead, was reclining on the outstretched hand beneath, and, as the red glare of the torch waved high and fitfully above, I could faintly discern the gigantic shoulders in proportion—"all," said the priest, as I examined it by the strange glare—"all hewn out of the solid rock around." I doubted the fact, for the face was painted, and, unthinkingly, not for an instant intending to give offence by so doing, I struck the broad forehead before me a smart blow with the stick I had in my hand, to test the truth of his statement. What he said was perfectly correct, but no sooner had I thus violated the sanctity of his idol than he seized me by my arm, and shouted lustily for assistance. My situation was critical—numbers of priests were in the immediate vicinity, and the nearest magistrate was my friend Rivers, at Matelle, thirty-five miles distant. Fortunately, however, my left arm was disengaged, and, taking a few rupees from my pocket, I slipped them noiselessly into my companion's hand. The silver had a magical effect. Even here, in the middle of the jungle, in the very cave-temples of Budha—thirty-five miles away from the nearest magistrate—her majesty's head was all-powerful—the loud bellowing ceased—the storm was lulled, and, as a crowd of anxious monks came rushing into the cave, he informed them that a miracle had been wrought, that a huge bird of some unknown species had suddenly appeared from behind the great statue, and had, as suddenly, flown out at the door, disappearing as strangely as it had appeared, and knocking the torch from his hand in its passage. Some seemed to believe, and looked out anxiously with us after the extraordinary bird, others turned their dark eyes upon us, rolling them from his countenance to mine, and from mine to his, as if they were by no means convinced of the truth of the story; whether they were or not, however, certain I am of this fact that the bird was never again seen, that I did not tell them the cause of the shouts which had thus drawn them together, and it is highly probable that my friend the shouter kept the secret to himself.

It was late when I returned to the rest-house, where our party, wearied out with their day's fatigue, had just retired to rest. The two ladies occupied a pleasant chamber that faced the road, and was more free from insects than those in the rear—it had been comfortably fitted up by the servants sent on before us, and was decidedly, as it ought to have been indeed, the best room in the house. Marandhan and Fowler occupied the other front chamber on the opposite side of the common dining hall, Hofer had taken the room behind Marandhan's in order that he might continue his conversation with him whilst preparing to retire, as a door communicated between the two; and so the chamber behind that occupied by the ladies, fell to my share. Thinking they might probably be already asleep, and aware, from what I had seen in the similar rooms at the other side of the house, that the partition, although apparently substantial, was of the flimsiest possible character, I made no noise, and was the rather induced to act so by hearing none within. In a few minutes I was stretched on my mat-covered bed close to the wall, the musquito curtains carefully tucked all round, and every preparation made for a comfortable night's rest. "Well, I suppose your desire to converse, Ada, is infectious," said a voice that I recognized at once as that of Mrs. Hofer, and which, in the stillness of the house, I heard, through the deceitful partition, most distinctly, "for I too feel more disposed for conversation than for sleep, although I am so tired."

"We shall not allow the antiquarian zeal of Marandhan, or Ernest's love of the picturesque, to wile us up early to-morrow morning," answered the younger lady.

Conscience told me I ought to cough, hem, haw, or in some other way intimate to the unconscious talkers, my proximity, but curiosity said no, and sophistry suggested that besides I really wanted to go to sleep and intended to do so. True, they undoubtedly thought that Hofer was in my place, as had been originally intended, but it was not my fault if he chose to occupy my room instead of his own, so I lay still, and heard distinctly every word, for these thoughts flashed through my mind with the rapidity of lightning.

"I am astonished that you still prefer the younger Miss Rivers to the elder." said Mrs. Hofer, "considering how like the elder is to yourself—a perfect æsthetic character—and considering the more intellectually trained reflection of the younger."

"First impressions carry great weight with me," said Miss Mowbray, "perhaps too much weight. Do you not remember how warmly the younger received us, and the much colder salute of the elder."

"Yes, but you must remember also, that the gentlemen entered just as the elder advanced, and that doubtless disconcerted her a little," argued Mrs. Hofer.

"Captain Reid paid much attention to the elder," said Miss Mowbray.

"It appeared to me that he paid more attention to some one else," was Mrs. Hofer's reply.

"To me?" suggested Miss Mowbray.

"Yes, Ada, to you. There could be no mistaking it. His warmth to Miss Rivers was but a foil to hide a little his greater warmth of manner when addressing you."

"He is a charming man," said the younger lady.

"And Mr. Fowler?"

"An excellent acquaintance or companion," observed Miss Mowbray, "but too solemn for a husband."

"You cannot deny that he is handsome," observed Mrs. Hofer.

"His features are regular enough, and I have no objection to make either to his height or figure, but he wants the gaiety and sprightliness of Captain Reid altogether. His studies have made him too much of a bookworm to please so mercurial a young lady as I confess myself to be."

"I am sorry to hear it, Ada," replied her sister; "I fear he loves you."

"Nay, my dear Emma, do not fear that, he would willingly sell me or any lady alive, I believe, except yourself, for her weight in old books, the mustier and more antiquated the better."

"Except me, Ada?"

"Yes, love, except you. It is not me he loves, nor do I think he means to pretend to love me. I have watched his eye following you, and the brightening of his countenance at your approach—."

"Nay, Ada, no more of this," exclaimed Mrs. Hofer, interrupting her; and then, more seriously than she had yet spoken, she added, "Ada, Mr.

Fowler is a man to make his home happy. Try and regard him with more favour. You are mistaken in your too quick-witted impressions, and have hitherto looked upon him with a prejudiced eye. There is not a man in England or Ceylon that I would more willingly welcome as a brother."

"I am not insensible of his excellences," said Miss Mowbray; "he can ride well, but so can all coffee-planters; he can talk well when he likes, and when *you* are by to hear; and he can quote Greek like a Bœotian. Lastly, he is a quiet, inoffensive man that hurts nobody and no one hurts him. I wonder why Ernest took such a fancy to him, they are so unlike in many respects."

"Better, far better, Ada," said Mrs. Hofer, "than all this. He has a good heart and a clear head. Believe me it is not the sprightliness and the untimed gaiety of a man that makes home happy."

"How seriously you talk, Emma."

"Marriage is a very serious matter, Ada."

"Well, from one who has drawn such a prize in the lottery as you, I am surprised to hear such grave remarks. Are you not happy, Emma?" said Miss Mowbray, and as she said so,

I could hear her throwing her arm round her sister and kissing her.

"Of course I am, Ada," was the reply, after a pause; "you see that with two such beings to love me as Ernest and you, I am and must be happy. But take my advice, my love, and think better and more kindly of Mr. Fowler. Judge him impartially, and not with an eye dazzled by a red coat."

"Dazzled by a red coat!" repeated Miss Mowbray, poutingly.

"Nay, I did not mean that, but merely not to let a pre-occupied mind weigh his sterling qualities against the meretricious advantages of superior dancing and greater gaiety. Tell me, Ada, do you love Captain Reid?"

There was a pause for a moment, after which Miss Mowbray answered with a sigh, "No, O no, I certainly do not love him, but I could do so, if he were to seek my love."

"Well then, my dearest Ada, take my advice," said Mrs. Hofer, fondly, "do not think of him, and look more favourably upon Mr. Fowler. The absence of the one and the presence of the other makes this quite possible. Acquaintance may thus ripen into friendship and friendship into love. It may be more romantic, as in Ernest's case and mine, when both fall in love as it is called, at first sight, but it is not more likely to be enduring."

"Your homily has made me sleepy," said Miss Mowbray.

"One kiss more, and good night then," was the reply, and silence again reigned supreme in the house—the external uproar from the jungle, which always increases as the hour advances towards midnight, being too much an accustomed sound to all of us to prevent our sleeping.

When we visited the cave temples the next day, Marandhan gave us a particular account of their history and object—how a king of Ceylon, Walagambahu by name, who reigned about one hundred years before the Christian era, had taken refuge at the rock, where he had been concealed from some invaders from Malabar, until forces were raised to expel them—how he had subsequently set about the excavation of the largest of three sacred cave-temples, as a pious act of gratitude for his preservation, and had employed the best artists of the island to cut huge figures of Budha out of the solid quartz—how other kings, at various periods, one in the twelfth, one in the fifteenth, and two in the eighteenth centuries, had hewn out or enlarged similar caves at either side of the larger ones but much inferior to them in size and effect, until altogether five temples were the result,—monuments, in this the middle of the nineteenth century, of what the misguided religious zeal of former days was able to accomplish. In the largest of these temples, the second in order from the entrance, called the Maha Wihare, the effect was extremely imposing. It struck me as equally extensive with the largest cave in the Peak Cavern in Derbyshire, that called Pluto's Hall, I believe, but by no means so lofty. One cannot walk through it without feeling involuntary awe. Its great size; the strange echoing of the footsteps; the forty-six gloomy and shadowy-looking statues by which it is partly occupied, stretching away in two long lines; the gentle dropping of the water, regarded as sacred, in the distant corner; the noiseless tread of the yellow-robed priests, with the death-like stillness that pervades the place,—are all calculated to impress upon the visitor a kind of religious or superstitious awe, that one does not like to shake off, and of which it would probably be impossible altogether to divest oneself. In the five caves there are a hundred and twenty-three images of Gotama, varying from sixty feet to one in length.

Our quarters proved so comfortable at Dambool,

there was so much excellent shooting in the neighbourhood for us, and so much sketching for the ladies to do, that we remained there several days; Marandhan pointing out to us various scenes in the neighbourhood connected with the history of the island, and all of considerable interest to the antiquarian; one of these, the remains of an ancient road, struck me as very similar in construction to the great military *viæ*, by which Rome interlaced Italy. About twelve miles from Dambool, he pointed out a flattened mound of earth with stone and rock at the top, at each side of the trace on which we travelled; that was the ancient road, through which the modern engineer has cut, in tracing out a direct way from Kandy to the north of the island. We stopped some time to examine it, Miss Mowbray ironically protesting that it was lovely. A bridge of massive granite, over what was once a rivulet, surprised me by its strength and solidity. It was composed of upright blocks of granite, about eight feet high above their foundation, supporting other similar blocks placed horizontally, each seven feet long, four broad, and one thick. We examined this primitive, but enduring structure with great interest, not even deterred by Miss Mowbray's recommendation to harness all our horses to one of the blocks, and convey it at once to Colombo, for transmission to the British Museum, there to be stuck up for the amusement and instruction of the gazers of all future ages. We make bridges much better now, you will say. So we do, doubtless; but they do not last quite so long. This road ran from Polonaruwa to Kurnegalle, according to Marandhan, and was probably constructed ten or fifteen centuries ago.

CHAPTER VI.

ANURADHAPOORA, THE BURIED CITY.

"—— What seest thou else
In the dark backward and abysm of time?
If thou remember'st aught, ere thou cam'st here;
How thou cam'st here, thou may'st."

Tempest, act i., sc. 2.

ANURADHAPOORA, or the city of Anuradha, was founded by that chieftain five hundred and fifty years before the Christian era. The history of the city is, in fact, coeval with the earliest history of the island, for, previous to that date, little is known regarding the latter, and of that little, nothing with certainty or precision. It was not, however, for more than a century afterwards that it became the capital of Ceylon, one of the distinguished sovereigns of that day, who rejoiced in the euphonious appellation of Pandukabhayo, having removed thither the seat of Government 437 B. C. The accounts of the reforms which he introduced into its municipal government and administration prove that it must have risen, in the course of the century, from an obscure hamlet into a large and populous town. He divided the city into four quarters, each being provided with its own proper governor and conservator—like the quæstor and ædile of ancient Rome. Five hundred men, belonging to the lowest castes, were appointed to keep the streets in order, and to attend to the removal of corpses, and to the cemetery—these men being allotted a distinct region, to the north-west of the city, as their peculiar residence, that they might not mingle, perhaps, with the more refined clay of the superior classes. Thirty years afterwards, a slip of the tree sacred to Budhists, under which Gotamo had attained the exalted dignity of the Budhaship, was transported, with great ceremony and the constant exhibition of miraculous power, to the capital of Ceylon, there to flourish as an object of worship to Budhists, to the present day. The branch was placed in a magnificent vessel, highly ornamented for the purpose, on the loftiest part of the ship that bore it to Ceylon. The vessel bearing it, we are assured, skimmed briskly over the water, impelled by the favour of its protector, and reckless of winds and currents; for twenty miles on every side, the water was hushed to stillness; the most beautiful aquatic flowers sprang up in its path, and ornamented the ocean, whilst the "enchanting strains of heavenly and seraphic music were wafted round the sacred vessel on its course." Tisso, at this time king of the island, received the precious relic with all the honour due to such a miracle-producing object. "At the time when shadows are longest," says the Singhalese historian, "the monarch entered the superbly-decorated capital by the northern gate, in the act of making offerings, and passing in procession through the entire city, and out of the southern gate, he entered the Mahamego garden—the garden which had been hallowed by the presence of four successive Budhas. There, with sixteen princes, his sons, he raised up the bo-tree upon the very spot on which it had been planted in former ages."

During three centuries before, and three centuries after, our era, Anuradhapoora seems to have arrived and continued at its greatest height of prosperity. Within these six centuries are dated the erection of all the buildings in it, the remains of which astonish us, at the present day, by their magnificence or size. Its walls, which were not completed till about the period of the birth of Christ, or a few years after, were sixteen miles square, and were built due north and south, east and west, thus enclosing a space of two hundred and fifty six square miles; that is, about double the extent of ground covered at present by London and its suburbs. "Gross exaggeration!" some sapient Londoner, anxious for the honour of the modern Babylon, exclaims. Pardon me, fiery sir, no exaggeration at all. The foundations of the walls still exist, and have been sufficiently traced to prove that the account is perfectly correct. You may see them with your own eyes, if you will but take the trouble to go to Ceylon, and then journey away to the buried city, through a hundred and fifty miles of jungle. It is to be remembered, however, that these ancient cities contained royal pleasure-grounds and gardens, and vast tanks or artificial lakes, to which the parks of London, with their elegant little ponds, bear no proportion in extent, and that thus, although they covered a vast extent of ground, they were not generally, by any means, so populous as Western cities—probably Anuradhapoora never contained more than half a million of inhabitants, notwithstanding its superficial dimensions.

About the middle of the eighth century it ceased to be any longer the capital of the island, the kings having removed their court to its rival, Pollonaruwa, which rose as rapidly to importance as Anuradhapoora sank to insignificance. Intestine wars, and invasions from the north, completed the desertion which the removal of the court had formerly commenced, and by the twelfth century, little was left of the once proud city but its ruins.

A magistrate holds a court at this ancient city during the healthiest portion of the year, and as he happened to be on a tour of inspection when we arrived, his house was kindly given up to us, and we were extremely comfortable. No spot in the island is more unhealthy, during the rainy season, than Anuradhapoora; but during the dry months there is little to fear, if ordinary caution be observed. A more interesting place it is not easy to imagine; and even Miss Mowbray was brought to confess that there might be food for much thought in old stones.

The ruins are of a character at once to interest and astonish, principally consisting of remains of dagobahs, some of them originally more than four hundred feet high, and all embellished by carvings and pillars, which would not disgrace a much more refined nation. From the base of the largest, for instance, an immense square, five hundred feet long on each side, and composed of enormous blocks of granite, project the heads and shoulders of elephants, strikingly well carved in *alto relievo*, and giving the appearance of the animals issuing from the solid mass into the broad fosse which surrounds it.

The sacred bo-tree is still an object of worship in Anuradhapoora. It is stated by the priests to be two thousand three hundred years old; and it certainly has all the characteristics of extreme age. Here, as everywhere else in the island, the priesthood abound; and as the traveller peers into the secrets of the past, whilst he traverses the wastes formerly trodden by so many thousands, and once ringing with the voices of numerous men, women, and children, and all the hum and bustle of life, he sees now the ghost-like bearers of the yellow robes with their shaven crowns alone gliding about, the very *genii loci*, redolent of buried centuries, of an age and of a faith worn out and exhausted. Noiselessly do they glide along, exhibiting no interest in you, or your white face, or strange attire, as if really dead to all that can excite and influence humanity. What an existence this! How strange and peculiar! How different from the busy, bustling, active life that the same men would lead had their lot been cast in London, Paris, or New York! Yet the very humanity here moulded into passionless quietude, into monotonous apathy, into a kind of breathing statuesque existence, might, under other circumstances, have made the noisy merchant or active sailor, the sensitive city dilettante or the blustering soldier.

In one part of the now almost buried city we

saw immense numbers of square granite blocks peeping through the trees and brushwood by which they were encircled and overgrown. The history of the building which once stood on them is amusing and instructive. It was called the Lowa Maha Paya, or great brazen palace, and was built for, and occupied by, the priesthood. It was erected by a king called Gaimono, who reigned one hundred and fifty years before our era. Long before that, however, its erection had been prophesied, we are told; and, when the priests heard that the king actually intended to commence this great structure, they found the prophecy, till then unheeded or unknown, inscribed on a metal plate, and behold even his name was mentioned in it! *There* was an incitement to an ardent soul to push on the undertaking! Anxious to know the form best suited for the purpose, Gaimono told the priests, who, doubtless, had presented the plate with all becoming gravity, that if they could find out the form and character of the great dwelling of the gods and devos, or angels, on Maha Meru, he would build them a palace like it. Nothing was easier than this. Sending off eight of their number—"all sanctified characters," reverently exclaims the *Mahawanso**—to the other world, they told them to bring back a drawing of the

* The principal native Singhalese history.

palace of the devos. How they travelled, or for how long, we are not told; but back they came, these "sanctified characters" all, with the required drawing upon a large leaf, done in vermilion. The monarch was doubtless too pious to ask any questions, and at once set to work to erect the Lowa Maha Paya.

It was one hundred cubits, or two hundred and twenty-five feet square, and the same in height, being supported on sixteen hundred stone pillars, still for the most part remaining. The building was nine stories in height, and on each story contained one hundred cells for priests, together with common apartments. In the central and largest room was an ivory throne, on one side of which blazed a figure of the sun in gold, to which another of the moon on the other side corresponded, and above, the stars in mother-of-pearl. The building was covered with a metal roof; hence the name, the Brazen Palace. Such was the result of the visit of these eight "all sanctified characters" to the abode of the devos.

The most ancient building, the remains of which still attract the attention of the visitor, is the Thuparamo, a dagobah or pagoda built by the pious Tisso, three hundred years before our era, to enshrine the right collar-bone of Gotama. Considering the immense period of time during which this edifice has stood (upwards of two thousand years) it is in excellent preservation, and the zeal and piety of the existing high priest had restored the small ornamental spire at the top, in its original form, shortly before our visit. The approach to it is along the ancient north and south street of the city, a broad, well-defined road, cleared of jungle by the priests. On each side of this street, once crowded by multitudes, now occasionally trodden by a solitary traveller or devotee, large trees and low brushwood extend, covering the remains of the ruined city, amidst which hundreds of square or round granite pillars lift their heads in lonely desolation, silent witnesses of the desolation and desertion of the once well-thronged streets. Masses of stone cut rudely into the forms of bullocks and lions are also occasionally passed as the visitor makes his way to the Thuparamo dagobah. The building is unquestionably the most elegant ruin in Anuradhapoora. It consists of a semispherical mass of masonry, standing on a square platform of flagged brickwork, and surmounted by a small, tapering granite spire. The entire height is probably not much more than fifty feet, so that in size it cannot be compared with the majority of the other dagobahs that ornamented the city, but in beauty of workmanship and elegance of design it far surpasses them. The columns surrounding it are exceedingly graceful—long, slender, and well-proportioned; they give us a very favourable idea of the taste of the artists, by whom they were designed and executed. They consist of two distinct blocks of granite, one forming a square base and octagonal shaft, both together twenty-two feet long, the upper and smaller one being cut into an elaborately carved capital, ornamented with small human figures, well-cut, standing round the lower part of the projecting ornament, the whole capital about two feet high.

The towering mass of the Ruanwelle dagobah, is a much more conspicuous object than that just described. It rises on the visitor's left as he makes his way to the Thuparamo, like a strange pyramidal hill, overgrown with trees and bushes. The stone platform on which it stands, a gigantic mass of granite masonry, is five hundred feet square.* This massive foundation is surrounded by a fosse, seventy feet broad—the heads and shoulders of elephants being sculptured, as I have already mentioned, as if emerging from the solid mass. On this platform, as on a foundation, the dagobah proper was erected, a semispherical pile of brickwork, nearly solid, that is, with but a small cavity in the centre,—this upper portion being

* The extreme length of St. Paul's Cathedral in London is 500 feet.

two hundred and seventy feet in diameter, and the same in height. The luxuriant growth of vegetation, and the violence of tropical and monsoon rains, have been gradually breaking it up and diminishing its altitude, so that it is not now a hundred and fifty feet high, and is unquestionably diminishing in size and height every year. In consequence of the base of the Ruanwelle dagobah having been shortly before cleared of jungle by the high priest, we got a better view of its vast proportions and elaborate sculptures, than of other similar buildings of still greater extent. Thus the Abhayagiri dagobah stands on a still larger mass of masonry as a foundation; but the whole is so overgrown with jungle that it is impossible to get anything like a good view of it.

To the Abhayagiri dagobah, which was originally four hundred and five feet high, was attached a priest-house and temple, which, for more than four hundred years, was the centre and head-quarters of the Budhistic hierarchy of the island. The dagobah itself was erected a hundred years before our era, but did not attain its greatest splendour and consideration till three centuries later. At that time a schism arose amongst the Budhistic priesthood. The king Mahasen, a wavering, unstable monarch, favoured the heretics, and expelled from the priest-house and temple of the Abhayagiri the orthodox believers. The other dagobahs of Anuradhapoora were stripped of their riches and ornaments to adorn the favorite, which became the head-quarters and rendezvous of the small but powerful heretical sect. But the priesthood were more than a match for the monarch. The minds of the people were soon inflamed against the heretical proceedings of the king, and a serious revolt was the consequence. His position was critical, and he was forced to yield his religious penchant as a sacrifice to policy.

The unfortunate minister who acted by his directions was made the scape-goat of the occasion. On his head Mahasen laid all the iniquity and blame of his proceedings, and, yielding him up to the people, proceeded to alter his principles and conduct, without loss of time. The people were not unreasonable; they were satisfied. They tore the unfortunate minister to pieces; and the king, having promised to reform, became more popular than ever. The unconscious mass of the Abhayagiri suffered from the change. It had been the head-quarters of the heresy, and its glory had passed away. The ornaments and riches so lavishly expended on it, and the spoils of more orthodox structures, were removed, whilst the latter were restored to their former sites. Till the removal of the seat of Government it continued, however, a place of some importance; since then it has gradually been becoming a mere mountain-like mass of vegetation and ruin. Even to the present day the heresy of its adorners, fifteen centuries ago, seems to be remembered, for the labours of the high priest have not been extended to the Abhayagiri! In its present condition it is nearly three hundred feet high, evidence sufficient, that in stating its original elevation to have been four hundred and five feet, the Singhalese historians have not exaggerated. Strange that the loftiest structure of the ancient capital of Ceylon should have been within a foot of the same elevation as the highest building in modern England! *

Great was the interest with which we regarded these remains of the now desolate city, and no one could enter more thoroughly into the antiquarian joys that their inspection yielded than did our party generally. We were yet more impressed with awe and wonder when we visited the vast artificial lakes constructed by the early kings for the purposes of irrigation. Blocks of stone of enormous size were here strewn about on every side, monuments at once of the vast popu-

* The spire of Salisbury Cathedral (the highest structure in England) is 404 feet high.

lation by which the neighbourhood of Anuradhapoora must have been inhabited, of the determined perseverance of its princes, and of the high estimation in which agriculture was held by both sovereign and people. The greatest and most imposing antiquities of Ceylon nearly vie with those of Egypt in age, and were certainly more conducive to the welfare and happiness of mankind than those raised by the great dynasties of that wonderful land. Devoted either to religion or to agriculture, they thus satisfied the two most craving wants of humanity, spiritual and bodily food.

Having spent a very happy fortnight at Anuradhapoora, without finding any of the kind presages of our friends in Kandy realized, as to our taking jungle fever or being eaten by leopards, we now thought of returning, or rather of directing our course to Kurnegalle, an ancient royal residence, by which we could subsequently reach Colombo or Kandy as we pleased. My intention was to proceed to Colombo, where a new career was awaiting me, whilst the rest of the party intended returning to Kandy. At Kurnegalle we were very kindly received by the Government Agent, Mr. Dawson, who, without the pretension of our friend Bluster at Kandy, had infinitely more real dignity. Here Marandhan left us to pay a visit to a native chief, whose residence lay too deep in the recesses of the jungle for us to venture there with our party.

I have already mentioned the fact of my discontent with the solitary exile-like life of the jungle, and of my desire to return to society and civilization. An opportunity was now open to me to do so by becoming editor of a newspaper in Colombo, so that I felt little desire to linger at Kurnegalle, but was rather disposed to push on for Colombo with all possible speed. I left Hofer and his wife, Miss Mowbray, and Mr. Fowler happily quartered at Kurnegalle, enjoying themselves in excursions and antiquarian researches, to which our fortnight at Anuradhapoora had habituated them; even the ladies co-operated with a zeal and devotion from which I augured the best results for the suit of my friend Fowler. I cannot better conclude the chapter than by giving an extract from his letter informing me of his movements subsequent to my departure:—

"We spent together," he wrote, "a very agreeable fortnight at Kurnegalle, and it was here that I first inquired of Miss Mowbray as to her intention of admitting me as a suitor for her hand.

"A moonlight walk on the side of a hill looking down upon a beautiful valley, afforded me an excellent opportunity of sounding the somewhat mercurial young lady's disposition. Mr. Dawson had taken Mrs. Hofer, Mr. Hofer Mrs. Dawson, and so Miss Mowbray fell naturally and inevitably to my share. Now or never, thought I, as we gazed upon the expanse of landscape before us, with its striking variety of light and shade, the glorious moon sailing apparently through silver-edged clouds above. The whole scene reminded me of Homer's description of a moonlight night. Everything was propitious, and as I felt her delicately tapering hand upon my arm, and occasionally her fair form against my elbow, a mesmeric or electric current seemed to flow mutually between us, and I felt as if I loved her devotedly. 'You felt as if you loved her devotedly,' you exclaim, indignantly, and you would ask me, doubtless, if I did not know whether I loved her or not? How can any man, under such circumstances, tell? When he is looking deeply down into a pair of lustrous black eyes, when he sees the fair form in all its wavy outlines, the line of beauty conspicuous in every movement, when he feels the fair fingers on his arm, the warm breath almost on his cheek, and the moon is flooding him with a light full of love from above, how can he tell whether he loves devotedly or not—whether his passion is the holy communing of soul with soul that may endure for ever, or the evanescent whisperings of fancy that lure us on to far other aspirations?

"Now or never, thought I. We were both busy, apparently inspecting the beautiful landscape before us. 'The world is full of beauty, Miss Mowbray,' said I at length, 'and Ceylon has its share of it.' 'It has, indeed,' she replied. 'I can scarcely fancy a more charming scene than the one before us, with its bright lights and dark shadows, the hills opposite, and the brook beneath.' 'I am glad to hear you say so,' said I. 'Then you do not regard Ceylon after all as so very dreadful a place to live in?' 'Why I have no particular affection for snakes,' said she; 'I should rather dispense with scorpions and centipedes, and, as for the mosquitoes, I could kill them by thousands, if I had an opportunity, they torture me so. These are all pretty abundant in Ceylon.' 'But the picture has a bright side,' I suggested. 'Certainly,' said she; 'it would be unendurable were it otherwise.' 'But if your lot were cast in the island you think you could endure it?' I asked. She looked full in my face as she answered quickly, 'My lot *is* cast in the island, so far as I can see, and I am trying to endure it now, and have been doing so for some months. I try to make the best of it.' 'Miss

Mowbray,' said I, seriously, 'you must be aware of my sentiments towards you—my entire conduct, since first we met, must have revealed them, and particularly since fortune has thus thrown us together on this excursion.' 'Certainly,' said she, calmly; although I did feel, I am confident I did, a twitching of the fingers on my arm. Her calm reply, however, disconcerted me.—'Certainly,' said she, with provoking calmness. Good heavens, thought I at the moment, surely she is not going to accept my proposal with the same coolness with which she would allow me to help her to a slice of beef or some curry at dinner!

"'You know my sentiments, then,' I asked warmly; 'and will you not respond to them, dear Ada?'—'Miss Mowbray,' said she, quickly. 'Pardon me if I have offended, Miss Mowbray,' said I; 'but will you make no response?' 'What response would you have me make, Mr. Fowler?' said she, as calmly as ever. 'Does not your own heart, dear Ada?'—'Miss Mowbray,' said she, again, more decisively than before. 'Be it so, then,' said I. 'Does not your own heart, Miss Mowbray, suggest some response, if, as you say, you perfectly understand my sentiments, and if my actions have so clearly revealed them?' 'I am deeply grateful,' she replied, after a pause.

I tried to take her hand, but she firmly resisted, and muttered something about joining her sister. 'Grateful,' said I, at length; 'is that all? Do they deserve no warmer response? Do they touch no deeper chord than gratitude, dear A—' 'Miss Mowbray, Mr. Fowler,' said she, again, authoritatively. 'Miss Mowbray, be it, then,' said I. 'You astonish me,' said she, without expressing much astonishment in her tone. 'I astonish you, Miss Mowbray?' said I. 'What, then, do you suppose my feelings to be, that my actions have for months so plainly declared?' 'That not having much female society in our neighbourhood, you are willing to make yourself agreeable,' said she, 'and even to take some trouble, notwithstanding the absurd affectation of our sex, generally,—you used the words the other day, you remember,—to amuse and instruct an unsophisticated English country girl, who pretends to little refinement and less learning—for this benevolent feeling on your part I am grateful. Will that not suffice?' 'You mistake me much, then,' said I, vexed and annoyed; 'I meant and referred to no such feelings on my part. I alluded to feelings much warmer and more sacred, to the holiest and purest flame that can warm the breast, in a word'—'Mr. Fowler,' said she, interrupting me, 'proceed no further, I beg of you. I am not disposed to listen at present to such language. My residence in Ceylon has been too short to permit me to bind myself for life. You have the friendship, the warm friendship, of my sister and her husband, and I believe you worthy of it. Will you not accept also of mine?' She looked up into my eyes as she spoke so earnestly and bewitchingly, that I forgot she was refusing me, and kissed her hand unresistingly. 'Dearest A'—'Miss Mowbray, Mr. Fowler,' said she, again, still more imperiously. 'I beg pardon, again, Miss Mowbray,' said I, cooling down from the boiling point, 'I shall not offend any more.' 'My object is that we should be really good friends,' said she, in her fascinating way, 'and, for that purpose, will you let me give you a little advice?' 'Most happy,' said I, taking care not to become elevated any more. 'Then it is this,' said she, leaning confidentially on my arm. 'If you really wish to gain my affection in time, do not act so as to make me believe that *you* consider my sister handsomer, wiser, and better than I am, however much she may be so. I sometimes think you forget she is married already.' 'My friendship for Mrs. Hofer,' said I, 'is of old standing, for friendship soon ripens in the jungle, and I know of no lady in the world—

except yourself—for whom I entertain so high a respect and so exalted an esteem. I shall not, however, forget your advice.' We talked of other matters during the remainder of our walk, the subject on which we had already conversed being carefully eschewed."

CHAPTER VI.

FREE TRADE IN ENGLAND, RUIN IN CEYLON—THE HOFERS.

"A wretched soul, bruised with adversity,
We bid be quiet, when we hear it cry;
But were we burdened with like weight of pain
As much or more, we should ourselves complain."
Comedy of Errors, act ii., sc. 1.

For some months rumours had been reaching the island that Sir Robert Peel's Government intended to make alterations in the tariff which would materially depreciate the value of coffee in the market. People were beginning to look anxious and care-worn whose faces before had been the very mirrors of joy and prosperity. Can Ceylon stand the competition? was the question which every one asked. If colonial and foreign coffee are admitted at the same rate into England, the protective duty being removed, what will be the consequence? These were the questions that were in every one's mouth, on every one's lips.

A general anticipation of disaster was the result. a foreboding of coming ruin to many! "We must agitate," said some—"let us meet, and make speeches, and draw up petitions to Parliament and so forth," they cried, as if Parliament or England would care a straw for the complaints or the ruin of a few hundred planters in Ceylon, who could not command a single vote in the House of Commons! The idea was absurd. "But we have planted on the faith of these protective duties; if England now removes them after we have spent our capital and our time in consequence, she owes us compensation," argued some sanguine men. "Pooh, nonsense," said the knowing ones, "compensation indeed! victims of misplaced confidence, that's all! England has nothing to do with us, we are only colonists. What are colonial interests to her, but playthings in the hands of her budding politicians?—You'll get laughed at," these provokingly cool men continued, they themselves, like us, on the very brink of ruin; "you'll get laughed at for your trouble, don't make fools of yourselves." Meetings however *were* held, speeches were made, plain facts and figures were put on paper with the most evident deductions, and were sent to England as petitions. Two lines in the *Times*, one morning, informed the world that Mr. Silent had presented a petition from certain coffee-planters in Ceylon, and no more was heard about the matter.

The fact was simply this: An artificial trade had been fostered by those protective duties; on the faith of them much capital had been spent in Ceylon, much revenue paid to Government too for land, and the opening of the English ports to foreign coffee would be the ruin of those who had embarked their money there and paid that revenue. In Java labour could be got to any extent at three-halfpence a day—in Ceylon we paid fourpence and sixpence a day. In Brazil, again, the slaves were kept by their owners for a mere trifle, and got no wages—it was therefore very plain that if the protective duties were removed, the artificial state of things fostered by British legislation of times past must be at once overthrown, involving, in its fall, the ruin of some hundreds of planters. But coffee is still grown in the island, some one objects—true, the estates were sold for little or nothing at the period of the crash—an estate on which eight thousand pounds, for instance, had been expended, and which, under former conditions, would have been worth from fifteen to twenty thousand in a few years, was sold for six hundred. Clergymen, lawyers, physicians and military officers, who had thrown up their professions, to embark their savings or their fortunes in the speculation, hurried from the scene of disaster, as if the plague had broken out there, many of them having lost their all, some indeed unable to get a bid at all for their estates when they put them up to auction! It was easy for those who had bought the estates for little or nothing, to work them profitably when the prices of everything had fallen in consequence of the crash, and labour was to be got for a mere trifle.

But I am anticipating events. Resident in Colombo, I heard frequently and fully from Fowler, whose letters gave me ample intelligence of the subsequent melancholy history of the Hofers.

"It was two months after I had parted with them in Kandy, before I again saw our friends," he wrote. "Hofer had got letters from England, from parties well acquainted with political affairs, telling him, urging him, to prepare for the worst, for that disaster was impending, and that Ceylon would be ruined—that Sir R. Peel was determined to carry through his free-trade ideas, and that a majority in the Commons would certainly support him—that the consequence must be an immediate fall, to a considerable extent, in the price of coffee, as foreign and colonial would be imported at the same rate, and that it was fully anticipated by those who knew most about it, that Brazil and Java would swamp the market.

"Hofer's all, as you are aware, is embarked in his estate at Lanka, and a considerable portion of Miss Mowbray's little fortune is similarly invested. He was, therefore, dreadfully dismayed at the prospect before him; and doubtless the more so, as his precipitate rashness, contrary to Mrs. Hofer's entreaties and our suggestions, had been the cause of Miss Mowbray's misfortune. His distressed appearance astonished me when I first beheld him, so greatly had two months changed him from the happy, cheerful, hopeful being whom I had left at Kandy, after our trip to the north, into the dejected, care-worn looking man whom I found at Lanka. Yet he was the only one of his little circle who appeared to take it so much to heart. Miss Mowbray still maintained her wonted sprightliness and vivacity, or, at least, if she did not feel it she assumed it; and Mrs. Hofer, although she must have shared the anxiety of her husband, allowed none of that anxiety to appear in her countenance and manner. She was the same contented-looking being she ever appeared, watchful to perform the smallest minutiæ of her duty with the same earnestness and attention that had ever been the characteristics of her nature—if possible, indeed, more attentive, more complying, more anxious to please her husband and lighten his load than she had ever been. I was distressed beyond measure at the time to find or fancy that my appearance was not hailed with that friendly cordiality, by either her or her husband, which I had experienced in times past. Hofer doubtless remembered, with keen regret, that he had not taken my suggestions and yours for delay in the disposal of Miss Mowbray's fortune with that courtesy which he might have shown; and Mrs. Hofer, I thought, rather avoided me than otherwise. Miss Mowbray was still the same; and, although some letters have passed between us, I do not find that my suit makes much progress. Whatever the motives of their conduct, I certainly should have had little encouragement to call again at Lanka, had it not been that Hofer subsequently unbosomed himself, and, in riding part of the way home with me, fully explained his intentions, with his usual friendly confidence and warmth.

"'Fowler,' said he, breaking a long silence, as we rode up the hill at the other side of the Paloya, opposite his bungalow, 'Fowler, I am on the very verge of ruin. All that I had, with the most trifling exception, is invested here, and, if the predictions of my friends are correct, I know not what will become of us. If, therefore, I have been strange or cold to-day, forgive it in considering my position.' 'My dear Hofer,' said I, 'what need of speaking thus? You and I are too intimate to be offended with each other about trifles. But you surely take too gloomy a view of things.' 'No,' he replied, 'I take the true view. I know my position fully. It is not for myself that I grieve so. I can battle with the world bravely, and feel no hurt; but it is for those whom I have led into this misery that my heart bleeds. I do not fear to tell you all, for I look upon you as a sincere friend. When I see the uncomplaining devotion of those who have followed me from their happy English home to this damned island—when I see them still cheerful and contented, acting more like angels than women—I feel as if I were a wretch for having brought them to this ruin. It would be impossible to describe the resignation, the cheerful, happy-looking resignation, with which my wife has set about retrenchment; the firm fortitude with which she anticipates the worst, and is willing to prepare for it. O, Fowler, when I think how I have slighted her, the best and fondest of women—when I think how I have often neglected and injured her, by cruel indifference and want of the most ordinary attention to her wishes—when I think of the resignation, the calm, uncomplaining resignation, with which she has borne all this from me—I feel how great a wretch I have been, how unworthy I have been of such a treasure.' 'I fear, Hofer,' said I, whilst the tears started to my eyes, as I remembered what you and I had often thought and expressed to each other on this subject—'I fear, Hofer, you allow your gloomy forebodings of pecuniary losses to colour your domestic reflections. I do not believe that any woman, in any sphere of life, could exhibit more bravery and resolution than Mrs. Hofer does; and I am sure that her every look and her every action prove her affection for you to be as great as ever—so far is her conduct from encouraging your melancholy reflections.' 'Why that's the very thing,' said he, hastily; 'were she roundly to accuse me of my faults, I should confess them and be satisfied. Were she openly to tell her wrongs and griefs, and point to me as their cause, I could bear it better; but when she acts as if I had all along been the most loving and affectionate of husbands, as if she had nothing to complain of from me, it is that which distresses me most, and makes me feel how inexcusable my conduct has been. I have felt angry with her, God forgive me—yes, I do not mind telling you, unmarried though you be—I have felt angry with her that we are childless. I have left the house gloomily, looking upon it as joyless and hopeless, because the sunlight laugh of infancy was not to be heard in it, and I have returned to it with a sigh, exclaiming that there could be no happiness in a childless home; and she has not complained, but rather exerted herself the more to make that home full of beauty and comfort for me. I have told her that I should bring other children of mine from the neighbouring village to be brought up in our bungalow; and she has declared, with the sweetness of an angel, although not without a tear, that she would be willing to rear any child I might adopt. I have seen all this, and seen it unmoved, as only the heartless can see such things. And now, O God! it is torture to think of it!'

" 'Have you tried to sell Lanka?' I asked, anxious to change the topic, for I felt afraid that he would be angry with himself, and dislike me, subsequently, for having told me all this. 'From the very first intimation of coming disaster, I tried to do so, but without success. Estates became a drug in the market, as you know, the moment the faintest whisper of the coming evil spread.' 'Too true,' said I, 'our house sent out directions from London three months ago to sell Parala, but we have been unable to do so.' 'It is the case with every one,' said he, vehemently, 'ruin stares us all in the face. How strange!

that I should have thought it a misfortune to have no children, when now I think it my greatest blessing that we have none. Nor have I told you all, Fowler, and I will tell you, for you are a true friend, and may one day, if the clouds disperse, be a relation. To her sister, Mrs. Hofer breathed no word of all this. Miss Mowbray has looked upon her ever as the same happy bride she parted with in England, and not a look, not a hint, has intimated to her that she is mistaken. Would that I were worthy of such goodness! Would that good, instead of evil, fortune had made me truly sensible of her worth! However, do not fancy that I have given up hope and am resolved to sit down quietly in despair. Far from it! By the next steamer I go to Bombay, where a relative of mine is high in the civil service—Secretary to Government in fact—and has often professed his desire to serve me, if in his power. I mean to put his professions to the test. He owed his present position partly to my father. It is time for him to repay the obligation.' 'I am glad to hear it,' said I, 'and I trust you may be quite successful. But do you purpose leaving your plantation now, when the busy season is fast approaching?' 'I must,' he replied, 'Plovel goes home, he tells me, at the end of the cold season, and therefore it is time I were there already.' 'And Mrs. Hofer and Miss Mowbray?' I asked. 'They will spend the month, during which I shall be absent, with the Mouats at Ruminacaddee!' 'With the Mouats!' I exclaimed. 'Yes,' said he, 'why not? Mouat has often asked us, and, as I have hired an European, who happened to be idle at Kandy, to look after Lanka, during that period, they could not do better. Perhaps you would not mind riding over occasionally to see how he gets on. It would not be pleasant for them to be living there with a boor in constant proximity, and, at Mouat's they will be near enough to exercise some sort of control over the property.' 'Does Mrs. Hofer approve of stopping with the Mouats?' I asked. 'Why I am sorry to say,' replied he, 'that she has always had a prejudice against Mouat—a most unwarrantable, unfounded prejudice. But Ada and I have laughed her out of it, and she has consented at length.' Shortly after, Hofer turned his horse's head homewards, and left me to pursue my further long and weary ride alone. It appeared all the longer and more wearisome from the heaviness of my heart."

Hofer departed for Bombay. He spent a few days with us in Colombo before the steamer sailed, and even my uncle, placid and unobservant as he was, could not fail to notice the contrast presented by the weary-looking, haggard visage he brought from the jungle, and the joyous, mirthful one, which he had borne there. I had always disliked Mouat, the magistrate at Ruminacaddee—even from the first moment of my acquaintance with him, but particularly since the affair of Siggins, in which his want of humanity and zeal in the performance of his duty, had completely disgusted me. Like every one else too, he was an admirer of Mrs. Hofer—no one indeed could witness her devotion to a cold and unfeeling husband, as Hofer had too long been, or her method of accommodating herself to the position in which she was placed, without feeling at once respect and admiration for her. It was about a fortnight after Hofer's departure for Bombay that Fowler wrote to me as follows:

"The contents of my present letter will amaze you, as much as the circumstances which have occurred have astonished me. I write to you, my dear friend, from Kandy jail, and am here, according to the justest letter of the law, a prisoner. Yet if the thing were to be done again, I should do it. A few days ago I received the following letter from Mrs. Hofer:—

"'My dear Mr. Fowler,

"'I have been subjected to the most gross and unwarrantable insults by Mr. Mouat, during the past two days. Anxious to avoid a rupture between him and my husband, who is, I fear, under some obligations to him, I merely warned him at first that a repetition of his offence would drive me from his roof. He has had the audacity to repeat it, and nothing but his own precipitate retreat prevented the matter being known to the entire household. He is a deep, designing villain, Mr. Fowler, and as such I would proclaim him to the world, were it not that I fear my husband's relations with him are of such a character as to make it possible for him to revenge himself effectually. I have not even informed my sister of the grossness of his conduct, or of the disgraceful and degrading importunity of which I have been the victim. I have merely informed her that Mr. Mouat's conduct is not pleasing to me, and that I am resolved to leave his house. I do not like going to Lanka, as Mr. Hofer desired me not to return thither during his absence, and he might be annoyed if I did so; but the Masseys have importuned me frequently to join them at Kaduganava, and if you will oblige us by bringing in our horses and servants, and by accompanying us to Kandy, we shall feel very grateful.

" 'O, Mr. Fowler, you cannot imagine how miserable this incident has made me, for often have I heard my husband declare that no woman is ever subjected to insult by a gentleman, who does not by some levity of conduct induce it. God knows I have endeavoured to be very careful; but enough of this, you will pardon, I am sure, the repinings of an afflicted soul. If my husband should think ill of me, I am indeed undone! I know I can confide in your prudence and friendship. If ever you have felt a spark of kindly feeling for me or for my husband, or of affection for my sister, let me beg of you to keep this matter secret. I would not, for the world, that it were known. When you come, of course you will appear ignorant of it.

"'Believe me,

"'My dear Mr. Fowler,

"'Your's, very sincerely,

"'EMMA HOFER.'

"My blood boiled as I read this letter. She, the purest and loveliest of womankind, to be subjected to gross ill-treatment! *how* gross and *how* distressing, the fact of her disclosing it to me was sufficient to prove, whilst her resolution to depart, notwithstanding her husband's wishes to the contrary, attested it. How base, mean, cowardly, and unprincipled must have been the wretch, who could thus shamefully violate hospitality; who could take advantage of a husband's absence, and his own accidental power as a host!

Yet this villain I was to meet with a smiling face, as though I did not know him to be the basest specimen of humanity!

"I rode off to Lanka at once, sending a second horse of my own to await my arrival at Ruminacaddee. Yet, with all my speed, three hours had elapsed from the time when I received Mrs. Hofer's letter until I presented myself at Mr. Mouat's house. It was already past two o'clock, and I was fearful they would not leave for Kandy that evening, but I had miscalculated the resolution of the injured lady. She was quite prepared. She had already, indeed, sent off her luggage, and was calmly awaiting my arrival. Mouat met me at the door as I dismounted. 'How do you do?' said he, extending his hand, and looking searchingly into my eyes. I shook his hand, as warmly, God forgive me, as if I had been his best friend, and, at the same time, looked straight in his face, as if I were looking into the face of an honest man. 'You are going to escort the ladies to Kandy,' said he, 'I should have accompanied them, but business is so pressing.' We went into the drawing-room; Mrs. Mouat was there, and exclaimed, 'How! Ah! Indeed!' much oftener than usual. 'We have no time to lose, ladies,' said I, rising, and offering my arm to Mrs. Hofer. Mouat would have given his to Miss Mowbray, but she declined it, and took mine also. With a sidelong glance of surprise, in which I rejoiced at his discomfiture, I saw a dark scowl pass over his face as the young lady joined me; it was almost instantaneously dispelled, however, and, in his blandest voice, he observed, 'the clouds are friendly in keeping the sun away to-day, and, at this season of the year there is no fear of rain.' 'I think we shall have a very pleasant ride,' said I. The ladies shook hands with Mrs. Mouat and her children, and bowed silently to Mouat, as I assisted them into their saddles. My own fresh horse was ready —the servants were far away on the road—and, as Mrs. Mouat muttered 'Adieu!' once more, as if to show that she was still equal to the effort, we struck into the Kandy road, all three abreast.

"For a considerable time no word was spoken on either side, and thinking that it might be expected of me to start some topic of conversation, I mentioned Marandhan and our trip to Anuradhapoora. I was replied to, and, for a time, the conversation was kept up, but gradually the pauses became longer and longer, until silence again prevailed. Each was too busy with the thoughts of each, and so, mournfully and sadly, we made our way to Kandy. Again and again did I start new themes, talking much nonsense to try and make them talk, but, like a candle flickering in its socket, the bursts were all quite temporary, invariably sinking at last to nothing. More than once did I observe large round drops standing in Mrs. Hofer's eyes, or coursing each other down her cheeks; even Miss Mowbray was grave; her light buoyant spirits seemed quite to have deserted her, and to have settled into gloom and melancholy.

"The sun was just setting as we arrived at the southern end of the Kandian lake—the promenaders and equestrians and charioteers were taking their last round. We had resolved upon calling on some friends of the ladies in Kandy, with whom they usually stopped when remaining in the town, but, on arriving at the house, we found the family had left for Colombo, and that strangers were temporarily occupying it. There were many others who had often made offers of rooms and tenders of friendship to Hofer, but Mrs. Hofer was too sensitive to intrude thus unexpectedly upon them, and preferred, therefore, going to the hotel. Here there was ample accommodation, and we found our servants and the luggage awaiting us.

"Dinner was soon ready, and, as we sat down to it—we three alone—I did not feel quite so indignant at the conduct which had thus thrown us together. Miss Mowbray's gloom gradually dissipated, and Mrs. Hofer exerted herself to make her sister less sad, with great success, so that, had a stranger watched us, he would not have believed that our accidental party had been formed by the poignant affliction of one member of it. I made more progress that evening with Miss Mowbray, than I had done in many months before; the clouds gradually opened, I thought, and a ray of sunshine shot into the little room, to which accident and misfortune had driven us. I was in great vein. The confidence that had been reposed in me—the position in which I was placed—the juxtaposition with so much loveliness, at a small table—all conspired to make me joyous and hopeful. The cause which had thus driven us all to Kandy was forgotten, or, at all events, not once alluded to, and, as we chatted and played whist, with much talking, I felt indebted to Mouat for an evening's happiness.

"I had been in the saddle seven hours that day, and yet I keenly regretted the necessity of going to bed, but inexorable time did not delay a moment because I was so happy, and, as the clock struck ten, the ladies vanished.

"The ride to Kaduganava, which we accomplished early next morning, before breakfast, was a pleasanter one than that to Kandy the evening before had been; and having spent the day with the Masseys, who saw nothing extraordinary in our visit, so migratory are we coffee-planters, I returned at night to Kandy, and next day reached Parala again, sincerely hoping that some opportunity would be granted me of giving Mouat a horse-whipping.

"The following day, Pring, a planter in our neighbourhood, and a man for whom I have a great esteem, came over to spend the evening and the night with me, in order to hear what news I had lately received from England. In the course of conversation Mouat was mentioned. I did not of course say a word of Mrs. Hofer's ill-treatment, but I expressed great dislike generally for the magistrate, and my conviction that he was neither honest as a man nor honourable as a gentleman. 'His administration of justice,' said Pring, 'appears to me to be far from impartial; he knows that men can hire witnesses to swear anything they please, and yet, when it suits him, he can declare he must abide by the evidence; at other times, again, he finds no such necessity. Siggins always comes off well at his court, as I found to my cost, the other day. Our estates adjoin, you know.'—'I wish I had a decent excuse for horse-whipping Mouat,' I observed, quietly. Pring laughed: 'Why,' said he, after a little, 'I could give you that excuse. I have a letter in which he speaks of you as "that coxcomb, Fowler;" but no, it would be a serious matter — he is the Chief Justice's cousin or nephew, and you would certainly be put in jail.' 'I don't care for that,' said I; 'have you, indeed, got such a letter? If so, let me have it at once.' 'No, no,' said Pring; 'it would be too serious a matter. Mouat and I were once extremely intimate, but latterly he has taken a greater fancy to Siggins, perhaps because Siggins's brother is rising in the service. At all events, such is the case, and his late decision is a proof of it.' 'Pring,' said I, 'you must positively let me have that letter. I am extremely anxious for it, and you need not fear any dreadful consequence.' 'Well,' said he, at length, 'if you think so to-morrow you can send over to me for it. I preserved it as a curiosity, and in order that, if his predictions were fulfilled, I might remind him of it.' 'What prediction?' I asked. 'O, you will see it when you get the letter,' he replied.

"It was with burning anxiety that I waited for the next day. Scarcely had Pring left ere I dispatched a swift-footed coolie after him for the important document, and it was not without a certain feeling of anxious impatience that I opened it when my messenger had returned. The former portion of it was about business; towards the conclusion, however, I read the following:—' I spent last evening at the Hofers. Mrs. Hofer is decidedly the handsomest woman I have ever seen, and better than that, is sprightly and unaffected, which handsome women seldom are. That coxcomb, Fowler, was there. He thinks himself handsome, too, and if Hofer and he do not fall out some of these days it will be a wonder. I saw enough to suggest consequences. Well, upon my life, I don't wonder at it, for she *is* a fascinating woman, and would turn any man's head, even though it were solider than Fowler's. Adieu, yours, &c.' The lying scoundrel! it was thus that he could write, even when he must have known that the insinuations he penned were unfounded, for no one could have been more correct than I was, as you know, in all that appertained to Mrs. Hofer.

" Putting the letter in my pocket then, I saddled my horse, and made at once for Ruminacaddee—a stout riding whip in my hand, and anger in my breast. Yet it was not so much for the letter as for his insult to Mrs. Hofer, that I was about to punish him. Although my excellent bay tattoo went at a rattling gallop over the uneven trace, he could not go fast enough for my impatience. Mouat was on the bench when I arrived at the court house. This was as I had anticipated. I much preferred chastising him there, to doing it in his own house, to the alarm of his innocent wife and children. I was shown into his office, a small room adjoining the court house. I waited here for a little, and then rising, examined the doors. There were two, one of which closed by a bar and two bolts. That one I shut. The two windows at the opposite ends of the little room, were also open. These I shut and fastened, and then, putting the key inside of the remaining door,—that by which he would enter,—I sat down and wrote a line to him, asking if he would give me an interview for a few minutes. The messenger who had been sitting at the door, and who had watched my movements with surprise, took the note to him, and, mechanically I dare say on his part, perhaps indeed without looking at the signature attentively, Mouat left the court and came into the office. I met him at the door, and shutting it after him, turned the key. 'There is no necessity to lock the door, Mr. Fowler,' said he, turning pale, as he watched my face intently, 'our communication can be perfectly private without that.' 'Did you write that?' said I, handing to him the letter. 'Let me explain,' said he, as he perused the part pointed out to him, his face becoming deadly pale, for villainy and cowardice are ever in conjunction—

he had not time for another word, when my horsewhip descended with force on his shoulder, at the same time that I grasped him firmly by his coat collar. He made no resistance, as the blows descended in showers upon his shoulders, one or two striking him, as I afterwards found, in the face, but he roared lustily, and shouted 'peons,' 'peons!' 'murder,' 'murder!'

"A crowd of natives assembled at the doors and at the windows, and there was infinite talking without, whilst I belaboured the scoundrel soundly. At length they began to attack the outside door, which was the most strongly barred. I had executed my purpose, however, and, as the villain writhed and winced under the infliction, I felt satisfied. We were not far from the door by which he had entered, and, as I saw the outer door yielding, I turned the key and walked boldly into the now deserted court. A moment sufficed to bring me by the side of my faithful horse who was somewhat scared at the uproar, and appeared delighted to see me again. 'Arrest him, arrest him,' I heard the unworthy magistrate shouting after me, and four or five native police darted down the court-yard to obey him. But they were paltry Singhalese, and my English blood was up, boiling in fact. Two of them only dared to lay their hands on me, but I was already in the saddle. One blow to each owner of the hands, one touch of the spur, and we were off, a whole troop of natives shouting wildly and bravely behind. My horse was frightened out of what little stock of wits nature had endued him with, and scarcely subsided from a hard gallop to a canter, even when the estate was in sight.

" 'If any of the police come to arrest me to-day or to-night,' said I to my head *cangāny*, on arriving, 'you must not permit them to reach the bungalow. But if they come to-morrow after breakfast, you may admit them.' '*Bohoma hondhi, mahathma,*' (very good, Sir,) was the reply. I went to bed that night with the pleasing consciousness of having discharged a duty I owed to myself, to Mrs. Hofer, and to society at large.

"No police, however, made their appearance that day, nor the next, to my great surprise. I began to think that Mouat was actually mustering up courage enough to send me a challenge, which would have disconcerted me much more than the police, for I have always condemned duelling on principle. Not that, had he done so, I should have refused to be his target for a shot or two, although I certainly should not fire at any man, and thus run the risk of being a murderer; nor did I indeed fear much what he could do when a pistol was opposite to him, for he was too arrant a knave and coward to fire, under such circumstances, with any precision. I thought much all day about the matter, at the same time that I made every preparation for a prolonged absence from home. I wrote to Marandhan, telling him of the whole of the circumstances, and asking if he had any trustworthy servant who could take my place during my absence, in case I were arrested. He replied, in the most friendly way, that his eldest son Tisso, who was now approaching manhood, and who had just returned from pursuing his studies in Colombo, should take my place, and as he would be able frequently to visit the estate himself, I need be under no apprehensions on that account. The concluding words of his letter struck me much, they were 'You remember what you told me of Siggins, and his barbarity to a Kandian whose daughter he had forcibly retained in his bungalow. In my capacity of Modliar, which still arms me with some legal authority, I sent for the Mohandiram of the village, and examined him on the subject. There was much lying and prevarication. I have sifted the matter thoroughly, however, and my conviction is that the poor man, who died shortly after, did not come by his death fairly. I believe further, and can partially prove, that a considerable sum of money had been paid to the police sergeant at Ruminacaddee to hush up the matter, and, from what I know of other cases, I should not wonder if some of this money found its way into a certain magistrate's hands. Such is the way justice is administered now! but Mouat is a relative of the Chief Justice, and, in order to convince that magnate of his delinquency, the proofs must be perfectly clear.

" 'However this matter terminate, count on me, for any assistance, of any kind, that I can give you, and believe me, when I assure you that I am most sincerely yours,

" 'MARANDHAN.'

" Here was much food for thought and speculation!

" The next morning fifteen mounted police from Kandy appeared from one side, at the same time that Marandhan and Tisso rode up on the other. I was not surprised at the advent of either, although I must confess the number of the police astonished me. What a dangerous character I must have been represented to the honest District Judge of Kandy to have been, before he would have despatched such a force! Or perhaps they anticipated that I intended to call out all the coolies on the estate, and to make a pitched battle of it! But they were mistaken!

It was amusing to see the honest perplexity of the sergeant who commanded the party, anxious to secure my person, on the one hand, and, on the other, to do so as civilly and politely as possible. 'Mr. Fowler will promise to go quietly with you,' said Marandhan. 'You may be perfectly easy, he has no intention whatever of escaping.' 'If the gentleman promises to come quietly, of course he will,' replied the sergeant. 'I know English gentlemen well; when they say they will do a thing, they keep their word.' 'I promise faithfully,' said I.

"That morning I was ushered into the jail at Kandy. My room was by no means uncomfortable,—a fact which I afterwards found I owed to Marandhan's prudent foresight, but the heat was dreadful, and I was obliged to hire two coolies to fan me without intermission, relieving each other every two or three hours. During the entire time that I have been writing this long epistle, a half-naked Kandian has been standing in front of me, moving laboriously a huge fan from side to side, and causing a commotion in the air sufficient to drive every scrap of paper, not properly secured by heavy weights, off the table.

"Brought up before the District Judge, I had the pleasure of seeing Mouat, still smarting from his castigation, and his face bearing evidence that some portion of my blows had not reached their intended destination. I confessed the assault, alleging, as the provocation, a letter in which he had called me a coxcomb, and accused me of attempting seduction, or, at all events, insinuating as much, but the letter I could not produce, although I doubt not Mouat could have done so, had he so willed it, as it was left in his office. Pring confirmed my statement, however. An aggravated account of the affair was given by Mouat's witnesses, and the trial ended by my being fined 50*l.*, and imprisoned for two calendar months, or for six, if the fine were not paid in the interval. Marandhan, who was in court, lent me the money at once, and I now await patiently the expiration of my term of imprisonment. The whole affair will form an interesting article for the *Herald*, which has been rather dull lately, though you must pardon me saying so."

Some time after, Fowler wrote as follows:—

"The following letters from Mrs. Hofer and Miss Mowbray have just arrived, and have afforded me even more consolation than your late kind remarks.

"'MY DEAR MR. FOWLER,

"'WE have heard with mingled pain and pleasure of your trial and imprisonment, with its cause. Believe me, I am grateful, deeply grateful, to you. He deserved all you gave him, and more. Was it on my account *ostensibly*, however, that you horsewhipped him, or on some other? I know full well that it was, *really*, but what was the assigned cause, or was there any? If my sympathy, warm and hearty as it is, can lighten your affliction, be certain that you have it without reserve.

" 'I am sorry to say Captain Reid is here, and is daily making inroads into Miss Mowbray's heart. If this news afflict you, I am sorry for it, but it is better you should know the truth, than that it should be concealed from you. *Her* impression is, however, that your proposal sprung more from friendship for me and my husband, than from affection for her. I trust it may be so. Deep and dark as are the clouds that surround us, your friendship is a bright gleam of sunshine that pierces through and enlightens the gloom. Would that you were as happy as you deserve to be.

" 'Yours, sincerely,

" 'EMMA HOFER.'

" Miss Mowbray's was in a very different style :—

" 'MY DEAR SIR,

" 'I AM glad to see that your fondness for old books does not prevent your acting like a true-hearted cavalier. You have my thanks, small as is their worth, for reminding Mr. Mouat of his duty, even although the hint were somewhat broad. But surely it was not on my sister's account that you horsewhipped him! if so, what will her husband say? Were you not usurping one of his privileges? Ernest Hofer is not the man to be trifled with; besides, the matter has been kept quite secret. I am truly sorry you should have been imprisoned for so long. To one so fond of study, doubtless the confinement and solitude will not be so irksome as it would be to the frivolous portion of man or womankind, like myself. I hope you will visit us at once on your release, that my sister may tell you, with her own fair lips, how grateful she is, a recompense infinitely more valuable to you, than anything you could have from

" 'Yours, faithfully,

" 'Ada Mowbray.'

"There is a contrast between the two letters that jars upon my thoughts and feelings—between the unaffected gratitude and heart-utterance of the one, and the coldly-playful ironical badinage of the other. To Mrs. Hofer the very idea of my having chastised Mouat on her behalf must be dreadful, as inevitably leading to a full discovery of a matter she wishes to conceal from her husband; yet how unselfishly she is willing to submit to it, without the slightest diminution of her friendly feeling for me. I must hasten to assure her that Mouat's insult to her had nothing ostensibly to do with the matter."

About a month after, Fowler wrote fully again:—

"It was about a week after I had despatched my last letter to you before I began to find my imprisonment grow irksome and annoying. Up to that time the pleasure of writing to you and to others, study, reflection, and Marandhan's friendship, all conspired to prevent my feeling the punishment as I might otherwise have done; but as day after day wore on in the same monotonous tediousness and uniformity, as night after night found me restless and unhappy, I began to feel what imprisonment was, and of how much he is deprived who has lost his liberty. Not that reflections about the estate added much to my bitter disquietude—of Tisso's management I heard the most satisfactory accounts from both Pring and Marandhan. Even my relatives, too, had written to say, that, under the circumstances in which I was placed, I could not have done otherwise; yet the full weight of sorrow caused by loss of liberty and want of efficient employment, was pressing heavily upon me, the iron, in fact, was entering into my soul; and yesterday evening, as I was trying to keep my thoughts fixed on some eloquent novel that I had taken up, in the vain hope of being roused and animated by its pictures, I found a full tide of sorrow and repining rushing back upon my mind, and drowning every struggling sentiment of interest in the events, the scenes, and the persons of whom I was reading. I threw the book from me, and putting my hands upon the table, and my head upon my hands, I ordered the servant who was fanning me to leave the room, and gave a full vent to my grief and gloom in melancholy reflections. I had not been long buried thus in the dark waters of affliction, however, when a faint voice, whose slightest breath is exquisite harmony, so musical is every word which it utters, struck my ear, pronouncing distinctly my name—'Mr. Fowler.' I almost feared to look up and dissolve the enchantment, but, as I did so, I saw the noble form of Mrs. Hofer, in all the dignity and grandeur of womanly beauty, standing at the door.

"'Mrs. Hofer,' I exclaimed, as I sprang, delighted from my chair, 'this is indeed kind, very kind and good of you.' 'A poor return,' she answered, 'to one who has suffered, and is suffering, so much on my behalf.' 'A *poor* return,' I reiterated—'the richest the earth could afford.

But are you alone?' 'I am. We are spending the day in Kandy. The whole party have gone to inspect the cromlech that Marandhan showed us, and I preferred remaining behind to visit the modern knight-errant.' I would not have exchanged places with the greatest monarch in Christendom as I listened to the words. 'I must not remain long,' she continued, 'but I determined that the day should not pass without my seeing and thanking you. We expect Mr. Hofer in a few days. The Masseys are going down to Colombo, and we intend accompanying them to meet him; so, this, I felt, was the only opportunity I would be likely to have, and although I fear much my visit is indiscreet, and that my husband would not approve of it, I considered myself bound to make a little sacrifice for one who had perilled so much for me.' I allowed her to talk, as I gazed into her lovely face, animated with the noblest sentiments of humanity—I allowed her to talk, without interruption; there was a music in the sentences, and a felicity in the thoughts, that enchanted me.

"'Believe me, Mrs. Hofer,' said I, 'this visit amply repays me for all, nay, for more than all, I have suffered; indeed I don't know that there was any gratitude at all due to me, for I was revenging my own wrongs at the same time that I punished the scoundrel who insulted you.' 'It is very good of you to lighten the obligation thus,' said she, 'but, believe me, I do not feel it the less. I had another object, too, in calling, and without which I might not possibly have taken all the trouble I did to get admission. Do you really love my sister?' 'I know not what to say,' I replied; 'I fancied for some time I did, but I fear I regarded her as illumined with borrowed light; your perfections I thought your sister must have, and I tried to look upon her as I should have looked upon you were you not already married.' 'Mr. Fowler,' said she, whilst she brushed a tear from her eye, 'do not say anything that we should both regret to think of hereafter. I believe now that in marrying Ernest Hofer I did not marry the man who was destined to find happiness in my smile or to make me happy in his; but I *am* married to him, and even from you, highly as I esteem you, I will not listen to a word unbecoming Ernest Hofer's wife. Enough, or perhaps too much of this,' she continued, after a pause, during which some tears coursed each other down her cheeks. 'What you say of my sister relieves my mind of a great load; it is evident you do *not* love her, and therefore her betrothal to another cannot add to your sorrows. Captain Reid has proposed to her, and by my advice, she delayed her answer till Mr. Hofer's return. Were it not on your account I should have advised her acceptance of him at once, for I know she has much affection for him, which, I fear, she has not for you; indeed she has all along declared that you only proposed to her because you wished to be allied in some way to us.' 'And she was right,' said I, 'perfectly right; being your sister I could not think of her otherwise than as an angel. Nay, do not raise your finger at me—I shall say no word that the most rigid and scrupulous propriety can tremble to hear. I do believe that I have proposed to her only because I wanted to be allied to you. Her woman's quick wit saw at once through the flimsy pretence, and she is quite right. I would, not, therefore, have her marriage delayed on my account; as long as I retain your esteem I care not for any other woman's love.'

"Her hand was upon the table as I spoke, and, as I saw the delicate fingers trembling with emotion, I put my own at the moment upon it. But reflection came to my aid at once, and, with a gentle pressure, scarcely, indeed, a pressure at all, I relinquished it. With a look she reproved my boldness, and with a look she thanked me for my self-denial, 'I have but five minutes more to stay,' said she; 'let us talk of other matters.

Your avowal about Ada has taken a load off a heart but too heavily laden as it is.' 'Have you heard from Hofer?' I asked. 'I have,' was her reply. 'He has been introduced to the Governor at Bombay, and is sanguine of success. Nevertheless he writes despondingly, not apparently from mental so much as from bodily suffering. His anxieties or his late wanderings have induced a low fever, which merely requires, he says, a little rest and attention to shake off.' 'He expects to be successful, then, in his search of an appointment?' 'He says there is no doubt whatever of his success. Mr. Plovel has acted as a true friend; and, by the beginning of the cold season, he hopes to be comfortably settled in Bombay.' 'I am glad to hear of his probable success,' said I, 'although I shall regret deeply the separation. Yet perhaps it is for the best. I could not continue to see you, with the feelings which now animate my breast, without being finally miserable.' 'It is evidently for the best,' she replied, 'for both parties. Letters will be safer between us than spoken words. In fact, it is quite probable that we may not see each other again, for Mr. Hofer writes that, if we meet him at Colombo, it will not be necessary for us to return to Lanka, especially as recent legislation in England has destroyed all prospect of making the estate remunerative.'

'Our last interview!' said I, starting up. 'O, Mrs. Hofer, I had no idea of that when I spoke in so calculating a way of our separation for ever. You will not leave me without some assurance that, although fate has severed us in life, sympathy has united our hearts for ever.' 'I will make no confession,' said she, firmly, 'which I should subsequently regret to remember. Mr. Hofer and I have not been happy at Lanka; we may be more so in Bombay. My coming here is evidence of my gratitude, confidence, and esteem—more I will not say.' 'And you will leave me thus coldly in jail,' said I, 'without a prospect of seeing me again, and yet say no warm words of comfort to my soul, nor give me one fond embrace to remember in later years, as a pledge of the affection which nature, in opposition to art, has nurtured in our souls.' The tears were trickling down her cheeks as I spoke; but, ere I had concluded, she had vanished from the room, and I was again a captive and alone."

Mrs. Hofer and Miss Mowbray came to Colombo with Captain Reid to await Hofer's return from Bombay. I was busily engaged in fulfilling my new duties, but saw them frequently notwithstanding. Mrs. Hofer was looking anxious and careworn, as if years, and not a few months, had been added to her life since I had last seen her.

She had no idea that Fowler had written to me of all that had happened; and I took care to avoid any allusion to him which might awaken suspicion in her mind. At length Hofer arrived. He did not delay more than a day or two in Colombo before proceeding to his estate to wind up affairs previous to his final departure for Bombay, and I had consequently no opportunity of seeing him. A few days after he had left I received from Fowler the following:—

"It was on the very day that I last conversed with Marandhan, who has been unremitting in visiting me, that I received the following letter from Mr. Hofer. I have delayed writing to you for some time, until I had attempted to arrange matters peaceably; but having failed, notwithstanding the most strenuous endeavours on my part, there is no reason why I should not transcribe it for you, in accordance with my promise. It was brought to me exactly a week before the term of my imprisonment expired; and I now again address you as a free, but at the same time as a disheartened, disconsolate man. But the letter—here it is:—

"'Mr. Fowler,

"'By a constant profession of friendship for me you succeeded at first in winning my affection and esteem. The amiability and moral excellence of your nature appeared to me only equalled by your intellectual cultivation and ability. Little did I then conceive that your affected friendship was but a cloak to help you to the seduction of my wife; and that when, at a more recent period, you professed your desire to become allied to us, it was still only that you might be enabled the more craftily to execute your nefarious project. But, Sir, your villany—yes, your villany, I deliberately repeat it—has been unmasked, and I now know you as you are. Your late abduction of Mrs. Hofer and Miss Mowbray from Mr. Mouat's house is but the climax of a series of audacities which my own wilful blindness alone must have prevented my seeing as others have seen them. I do not mean that you forcibly removed them to spend an evening and a night with you at Kandy. Doubtless your fertile brain suggested some excuse which they are now ashamed to own as having deceived them. But this, Sir, is not all. You are aware it is not long since, laying aside all female delicacy and modesty, my wife visited you alone in jail. True, I have these heart-rending tidings from your enemy—from the man whom you horsewhipped for having divined your true character; but I have them further on the oaths of others. Can you deny them? Can you say there is no truth in them? If so, write it, and give the paper to Captain Reid, who will take this to you; and although my wife can never again be to me what she has been, although she and I can never again share the same home or live under the same roof, it will lighten a sorrow-laden heart to read your words, and in spite of myself I will believe them and apologize for my present injustice. But, if you cannot deny these allegations, then how great is not your guilt and hers! after the open-hearted confidence, too, with which I spoke to you of my own feelings! Nay, was it not on that you built rather? I believe so from my soul. You are a villain, Sir—a deep, designing villain—if you cannot deny these charges.

'Ernest Hofer.'

"Captain Reid brought the missive, and politely begged that I would either write the contradiction required, or refer him to a friend. I read the letter twice—my brain was whirling, and, in its excitement, the little room which had been for two months my abode, appeared a boundless expanse. O God! I muttered, as the whole matter flashed through my mind, this is indeed, dreadful! 'Nay, Sir,' said I, aloud, recollecting Captain Reid's presence 'it is not for myself I grieve. Does Mrs. Hofer know of all this?' 'I cannot tell,' said he, calmly, 'she and Miss Mowbray are in Colombo, where Hofer and I left them.' 'This is all that scoundrel Mouat's doings,' said I. 'Then of course you can contradict it all,' said he, 'and in that case I have instructions to hand you this note, which is of a very different character, and to destroy with my own hands that one.' 'Do you know the contents of this letter?' I asked. 'I do not,' was the reply, 'I neither read it nor heard it read, but I can guess its import.' 'I will explain the whole of the circumstances to you —.' 'Pardon me,' said he, interrupting me, 'my instructions are not to demand explanations, but to get the contradiction. Write it, if you please, and give it to me first, and then I will listen to any explanations you please, but only as a matter of private conversation between us.' 'Why, Sir, these allegations are a tissue of falsehood and misrepresentation.' 'I beg you will calm yourself,' said he, again interrupting me, but in the politest manner, 'the contradiction first, and then any observations you please,' and so saying he placed paper and the inkstand before me. 'I cannot actually contradict these assertions,' said I, vehemently, 'but I can explain them.' 'Then if you cannot actually contradict them, Mr.

Fowler,' said he, placidly, 'will you favour me with a reference to a friend?' 'No,' said I, 'I will not be cajoled into this business thus. I must see Hofer and explain all. The happiness of another than myself depends on it.' 'You cannot see Mr. Hofer, Sir,' said he, 'he will not see you. Besides, he is confined to his bungalow by an intermittent fever, accompanied by total nervous derangement, and the doctor declares that he must be kept quiet. He is ready to risk all, however, in defence of his honour, and will meet you when and where you please.' 'He is at Lanka, you say; I will go immediately on leaving this, and a half hour of explanation will set the whole matter right in his mind.' 'He is at Lanka, but you will not be admitted. I know that orders to that effect have already been issued. Your doing so would be infinitely worse than meeting him in the field, as it would inevitably lead to a personal *rencontre*. Be persuaded, Mr. Fowler, either write the contradiction or name your friend.' 'I have no doubt,' said I, 'that Pring would act for me, if need were, but I shall find some means of obviating the necessity yet, believe me.' 'Possibly you will,' said the Captain. 'Well, Sir, adieu! I hope you will succeed.' So saying he left me.

"I sent off at once for Marandhan, and wrote,

at the same time, to Pring, explaining the business, but assuring him that it would ultimately be arranged satisfactorily. The next day Marandhan made his appearance, ever prompt to reply to the call of friendship. I explained the whole matter to him, confessed my own imprudence, but strongly and emphatically declared the perfect innocence and propriety of Mrs. Hofer's conduct in every respect. I told him all about Mouat and his insult to her, and begged him to go to Hofer and explain matters. He promised to do so at once, and, at the same time, resolved to disclose to him all the villany of Mouat, of which he was yet ignorant, in relation to Siggins' case.

"Whilst Marandhan was with me, and we were talking the matter over, it seemed to me impossible that he should not be successful in clearing the clouds from Hofer's mind, and in throwing a flood of light upon the whole transaction, but when he had gone and I reflected calmly on the chain of evidence, by which Mouat had wrought conviction in the unsuspecting breast of his friend, I felt that the mission was fruitless, and that my inability to contradict the assertions would far outweigh all other considerations however reasonable and just.

"I was perfectly right. The next day Marandhan returned, weary with his fruitless journey, dispirited at its result. Hofer would not even hear him speak on the subject, but, in great excitement, ordered him to leave the house, or to speak on some other topic, and this, with such violent passion, that the benevolent peace-maker feared lest injury to the sick man might be the result of his perseverance. He finally offered a written statement of the entire affair, which I had carefully drawn up, but Hofer furiously tore it into pieces and threw them back to him.

"There was no help for it. I **must** stand before him with a pistol in my hand, for he swore, in Marandhan's presence, if I did not meet him like a gentleman, I should be horse-whipped like a dog. I have many conscientious scruples against duelling. I abhor and detest it, but what can I do? Is it not better to run the risk of being shot by him, than to be exposed to a personal assault in which I must defend myself? In his present condition, for Marandhan says he looks miserably ill, the former will be 'satisfaction' for him, and must end harmlessly, so far as he is concerned, unless indeed he should kill me at once,—the latter might cause his sudden death, for it is not in man to stand quietly and unresistingly, whilst an infuriated assailant is showering blows upon him, and, with Hofer's warm and impulsive temperament, there can be no doubt that he would brave any penalty to satisfy his revenge at fancied wrongs of so deep a die. It was thus I was brought to the conviction, sophistical as I may hereafter consider it, that I cannot do better than present myself on the appointed morning at the place of rendezvous. Pring has, in the most friendly way, made all the necessary arrangements for me, and it only remains to receive Hofer's fire as bravely as I may. As to attempting to injure him, I trust you have not so bad an opinion of me as to fancy me capable of it.

"Were I certain that Mrs. Hofer is ignorant of all these matters, I should feel much more contented; depressed, gloomy, and alone as I feel myself at present, the bitterest ingredient in my cup of misery is the reflection that whilst I mourn only a severed friendship, she may be deploring the loss of almost all that she values upon earth. At present her interference would but add fuel to the flame and prevent all subsequent chance of reconciliation. When the duel is over, if duel it can be called when one only will be the fighting party, Marandhan, I feel convinced, will be able to clear my character whether I survive it or not. His testimony and Mrs. Hofer's combined will surely be sufficient, with proofs of

Mouat's villany, to carry conviction to the most unwilling mind. Even should I fall, the consequences will not be so disastrous to Hofer as I had anticipated, for as the affair will be kept strictly private, and the magistrate will be in no hurry to investigate it unless depositions are made before him, and none such will be made on my behalf, the probability is that the whole affair will be hushed up, and made to appear, by Mouat's interference, a case of accidental death—such accidental deaths, Marandhan assures me, are common in the jungle.

" The following note from Pring, which I have just received, will show you in what condition things at present stand, and that this may possibly be the last letter you will get from Harry Fowler. Should such be the case, however, Marandhan will take care to inform you, I doubt not, that I died, with the courage of a brave man, and in the hope of a Christian.

" ' *Krottlo Estate, Monday.*

" ' My dear Fowler,

" ' Captain Reid has just been with me, and informs me, that Mr. Hofer is so much better, the doctor has permitted him to go out to-day. In consequence of this, I have made arrangements for to-morrow morning at six, I shall be with you this evening and explain matters more fully.

" ' Yours, &c.,

" ' ARTHUR PRING.

" ' P.S.—That scoundrel Mouat rode over here the other evening just as if nothing had occurred. I told him if he did not want a repetition of the dose you gave him, he had better turn his horse's head round and be off again. You should have seen how the intimation increased his speed.

" ' A. P.' "

As soon as I had received this letter from Fowler, I called upon Mrs. Hofer in Colombo, and happily discovered that she was ignorant of all that was taking place in the jungle. She was anxious indeed at not having heard for some time from her husband, but Captain Reid's letters to Miss Mowbray reassured her, and she attributed his silence to press of business.

I waited anxiously for a note from Pring or Tisso or Marandhan about the duel, but to my great satisfaction, I soon received the following from Fowler :—

" The duel is over, and I am still alive,—I am obliged however to make use of my friend Tisso's hand and pen, to indite a few lines to you, to assure you of my continued existence in this unfortunate island, and to inform you how things went off.

"Pring came over to Parala as he had promised, the evening before, and great was the hurry next morning to get to the appointed place in time. It is a beautiful spot, and, strange as was our mission, I could not help admiring it as we waited for the other party. It was by the side of the little stream, the Paloya—an overhanging rock, leaving a bare bank beneath, that opened out on either side to the blue sky, the thick jungle foliage being below us, and the hills spreading away in two long oblique lines from the stream. As we walked arm in arm up and down the bare ledge, conversing of everything but of the matter in hand, my thoughts often wandered to the strange causes of all this turmoil and commotion, which had so suddenly ruffled the calm surface of our life in the jungle. Our horses had been sent to the brow of an adjacent hill, where they were to wait for us, if perchance they were wanted again—if not, Pring was aware that Hofer purposed coming in a palanquin belonging to Marandhan, and that the doctor from Kandy, who had been staying with him some time, would accompany him.

"The distant hum of voices gradually drawing

nearer, informed us of the approach of the opposite party. The palanquin had been left with the servants at a distance, and, making their way with difficulty through the jungle, Hofer, Reid, and the doctor, at length made their appearance. The aspect of Hofer, as he was supported on either side by his two friends, surprised and distressed me. The stamp of illness was on his countenance, which looked wasted and haggard—whilst his tall frame, attenuated by fever, was no longer the sturdy, athletic, muscular form it had been. I looked upon him with pity,—there was much in his air and manner to inspire it. But for a moment did our eyes meet, and, in the stern uncompromising gaze with which he regarded me, I saw something of astonishment, that I was not abashed at his presence. 'Mr. Hofer is wearied with his walk from the palanquin hither,' whispered Reid to Pring, 'but a minute or two will revive him—you have been riding too, a little rest will steady Mr. Fowler's hand.' The doctor attended to Hofer, who leaned against the rock; the two seconds walked aside to arrange the pistols, and I continued my peregrination backwards and forwards. I saw that any advance to Hofer would only meet with a rude repulse—enmity was written on his face, and I therefore refrained.

" At length the seconds made their appearance to place us. My own pistols, I found, had been chosen—the same that you and I practised with a day or two before our trip to the North. Did we then conceive to what a use they would be subsequently applied! As I took the offered pistol in my hand, I saw Hofer poising his weapon, as if to try the strength of his arm, and almost immediately letting it fall again. He whispered a word or two to Captain Reid, who spoke to Pring. 'Certainly,' whispered the latter, 'it can make no difference.' I did not ask what it was that could 'make no difference' at the time, but I subsequently found, that Hofer, fearing the strength of his arm might fail, desired that there might be but a single signal, when he would raise it at once and fire. I cannot say that I felt unmoved at the position in which I was placed, yet I was by no means unnerved. I knew that the moment was one on which hung my subsequent life or death, and the very importance of the issue to myself sent a thrill, not of fear, but of anxious expectation, through my frame. I felt as the eager man feels who expects every moment, important news, —whose nerves are intently strung with anxiety and impatience.

" We stood opposite to each other—the signal

was given. I fired high in the air, and as the discharge rang in my ear, another boomed forth from the other side of the cliff, and the sharp whizz of a bullet grated on my senses, as I almost felt it passing my lips. Hofer was gazing intently at me, and as the smoke cleared, and I turned towards him unhurt, he threw the pistol impatiently on the ground, and cried out to Reid, 'My own pistols now at all events—how could you consent to our using these?' Pring muttered something of 'satisfaction.' 'No, Sir, we have had no satisfaction,' cried Hofer vehemently, 'neither he for being called a villain, nor I for the villany.' 'Mr. Hofer,' said Captain Reid, in an injured tone, 'your honour is in my keeping, and I must insist on your holding no communication with Mr. Pring on the subject.'

"'This shot will be final,' said Pring, as he put another pistol into my hand, and placed me. It may be so, in more ways than one, thought I, as I caught Hofer's eager gaze at me. I felt tempted to try my luck too, for you know I am not a bad shot, and the vindictiveness which he appeared to exhibit, somewhat ruffled my temper, but the thought was gone in a moment, and I calmly awaited—more calmly indeed than before—the signal for the fire.

"It was given, and scarcely had I pulled the

trigger when my arm fell bleeding and helpless to my side. His ball had torn through a portion of the muscle at the back of my shoulder, grazing the bone, but fortunately not injuring it. The blood flowed in large quantities, and as the doctor staunched the tide, and Hofer and Reid bade Pring adieu, not far from me, I said to the former, 'You have had satisfaction now, I trust, Mr. Hofer; will you allow me then to explain matters privately to you?' There was no answer, although I saw plainly that Captain Reid was doing his utmost to induce him to return and converse with me, but without success. A moment after Reid made his appearance, and said to me, 'Mr. Hofer acknowledges the satisfaction, Mr. Fowler, but declines the interview. Allow me for myself to say, that, in my opinion, no man could have acted more honourably than you have done. Good bye. I shall order the palanquin down for you, immediately.' 'The wound is not a serious one,' said the doctor, as he bandaged it, 'but will require care and attention, and, above all, rest. You must keep quite quiet for a week or perhaps a fortnight, to prevent inflammation, after that you can go about as usual, if there be no fever, keeping your arm in a sling.'

"Such was the duel.

"Marandhan, Tisso, and Pring, have taken

such excellent care of me that no bad symptoms have resulted from my wound; and such is Marandhan's practical knowledge of surgery and medicine, that I have had no occasion since to trouble a European doctor. But, unremitting as his care of me has been, in this respect, his friendship has exhibited itself in another way still more strikingly and advantageously. He has been to Hofer twice since the duel, and has laid before him such plain proofs of Mouat's treachery and villany, even without referring to his conduct to Mrs. Hofer, that Hofer has refused to see the little magistrate since. Hofer's obligations to Mouat appear to have been by no means of that serious character that Mrs. Hofer supposed, so that, all this penalty of doubt, jealousy, and hatred, he has paid because he did not inform his wife fully of the state of his affairs. Hearing him mention some obligations to Mouat of a pecuniary character she naturally looked upon the latter as having him in his power, an impression strengthened by the rudeness of the magistrate to herself. My first letter, when I am able to write for myself, shall be to Mrs. Hofer, asking permission to mention the whole circumstance to her husband, or rather asking her to state it all, in order that the injurious impressions produced by my conduct on his mind may be removed.

She will have no difficulty in complying with my request when she is informed that Hofer has al-already broken with Mouat, and regards him as a villain; at least, I hope not, when she is further informed of Hofer's misapprehension of me."

Two or three weeks after, I received the following from Fowler, informing me of the melancholy conclusion of Hofer's history:—

"Marandhan came over to me last Friday with the cheering assurance that, although Hofer lay very ill at Kandy, he was now thoroughly convinced of mine, and of Mrs. Hofer's innocence. On hearing of the increase of his fever, you are aware that she and Miss Mowbray came from Colombo to nurse him, and on the first intimation of her husband's suspicions, she fully and frankly explained all to him.

"The long chain of evidence respecting Mouat's venal administration of justice was complete, and Marandhan himself laid it before Mr. Bluster, at Kandy, who transmitted an account of the charges to the Colonial Secretary at Colombo. A secret investigation was held by one of the puisne judges of the Supreme Court, which I believe is not yet concluded. At all events, however, Ruminacaddee has been purged of two scoundrels, for Mouat has been suspended, during the investigation, with a very faint chance of restoration, and an honest upright man has been appointed in his stead; whilst Siggins, whose property was heavily mortgaged, finding the times bad, and his position uncomfortable, made his way secretly to Calcutta, whence, they say he has sailed for Australia, where doubtless, he may expect soon to be joined by his dear friend Mouat, at the expense of Government.

"I got a note on Monday from Mrs. Hofer, stating that her husband was still very ill; but that the doctors had scarcely any fears for the result, although they would not yet advise his removal to the sea, and that both she and Mr. Hofer would be delighted to see me when I could make it convenient to call.

"I lost no time in complying with the invitation, and, as I met Mrs. Hofer in the verandah of their temporary abode in Kandy, she never appeared more cheerful and more animated. A favourable report from the doctor, and a favourable change in the patient, had conspired to give her cheek a glow of happiness to which it had long been a stranger. When I was conducted to the sick man's side, he grasped my hand with all the warmth, although not with the force, of former years, and asked me if I could forgive him for his injurious suspicions. He appeared to me much better than he had looked on the morning of the duel. I told him so; and he said, yet I thought somewhat sadly, that he was glad of it. A moment after, when Mrs. Hofer had left the room, he shook his head mournfully, and said that they were all deceived—he felt that there was something wrong with his heart which the doctors would not admit, and that his recovery was extremely uncertain if not absolutely impossible. 'O Fowler,' he continued, 'I have much to thank you for—very much—in leading me to value the friendship of that inestimable man Marandhan. Were it not for his goodness and his honesty I should now be one of the most miserable of men. He has agreed to rent Lanka from me at two hundred a-year, during the present depression—a melancholy termination to our bright anticipations of fortune! The engagement is to be for ten years; but, should prices rise ten per cent. in England, or the expenses of working the estate, which he will do of course far more economically than we could, fall ten per cent., during that period, we are to have the benefit of it. There is thus some provision—miserable though it be—still something, for Mrs. Hofer; and in leaving her to you and Captain Reid, and Marandhan, I do not fear but that she will be well-cared for.' 'Do not speak thus, Hofer,' said I, 'your case is far—, 'Nay, nay, my good friend, a dying man looks things in the face. I feel I cannot live long. Hear me.'—

"I was glad to hear the rustling of a dress at the door to interrupt the conversation, for there was nothing in his appearance to warrant his gloomy forebodings; but he would not be interrupted—he begged his wife to leave us alone for a few minutes, and she willingly consented. 'Captain Reid's leave of absence will expire in a few days, when he must return to Colombo. He is a man well off in the world, and in giving him Miss Mowbray's hand I am sure I secure, as far as it is possible, the happiness of both. He is a noble character, Fowler—cultivate his friendship, and you will find him such. The poor remains of Miss Mowbray's little fortune—1500*l.*,—he will not accept.' 'Does he know, then, of your own impressions?' I asked. 'He knows all, but, like the rest, will not believe me,' was the reply; 'everything is arranged, however. The 1500*l.* he and she will surrender to Mrs. Hofer in the event of my death. They are gone out now to settle the preliminaries of their marriage, and the day after to-morrow the wedding is to take place, immediately after which they depart for Colombo. Will you have any objection to attend the ceremony?' 'Not the slightest,' said I, without hesitation. 'It is good of you to say so,' he replied, 'and your attendance would be a great comfort to Reid, who thinks, and thinks truly, too ,that we have already injured you sufficiently without giving away Ada contrary to your wishes.'

"He continued, with an effort, 'No one knows more certainly than I how unworthy I have been of the blessings by which I have been surrounded during the past three years and a half in Ceylon. No one can desire to make reparation more ample for the evils they have inflicted than I do now. Could you look into my heart, Fowler, you would find it wayward and impulsive, but not bad—Oh, no, not bad, not altogether bad; and when I am laid in the little cemetery on the other side of that hill, and when you are happy in Ceylon or in England, do not think unkindly of me, Fowler—let the grave cover my faults, and give me credit, at all events, for a good heart at the bottom.' 'Hofer,' said I, seizing his outstretched hand, and struggling with my tears, 'Hofer, do not speak thus. You will yet live to be happy in Bombay, and perhaps we may meet, by and by, in England, when our woes in Ceylon will be but a theme to talk of. But, should you die, there is not a man on earth will think more highly of you than I. I doubt if Mrs. Hofer herself entertains a higher esteem for you, or is more sensible of your virtues.' 'Thank you, Fowler, thank you; you have lightened my heart. Believe me, I did not act differently from what you would have acted had you thought as I did, and who could think otherwise with a false friend whispering jealousy and rage into either ear?' 'I know it, I know it,' said I, earnestly; 'banish such thoughts from your mind, and if you really feel that your stay on earth is to be but short, make peace, not with me, but with One above, who is more ready to forgive than you to ask forgiveness.' 'Fowler,' said he, 'I thank you the more for your thoughtful friendship. Mrs. Hofer and I have prayed earnestly together; and Oh! she is eloquent in prayer, and I feel that I am now gradually becoming prepared to die. Reid is to send me a clergyman this evening when he takes her for a drive. I have told her that I shall not live long, but she will not believe it, for the doctors and my looks belie my words.'

"Shortly afterwards Reid and Miss Mowbray, having returned to the bungalow, entered with Mrs. Hofer. When I looked in the young lady's face, and saw the glow of health and happiness upon her cheek, and the sparkle of wit in her eyes, I felt almost sorry that I had surrendered her so easily; but I turned to her sister, and in the warm smile with which she heard I had consented to be present at the marriage, I had an ample compensation for my former regret. 'Fowler has consented, in the most kind and friendly way, to be present at your wedding, Ada,' said Hofer to her. 'I feel obliged to him,' said she, 'doubtless he will gladly act the papa on the occasion, and give me away.' 'Ada!' said her sister, reprovingly. 'I shall be very happy to do so,' said I, cheerfully, 'if you really wish it.' 'I do,' said she; 'but remember, you will only be a proxy for my guardian in England, the clergyman of the parish in which we were brought up. Yet you will give me away gladly, I know, for you would not like to meet me as Miss Mowbray again, lest I should expect some attention from you.' 'How can you permit your exuberant spirits such licence, Ada?' said Mrs. Hofer, reprovingly. 'Nay, my dear Emma,' she replied, with the most bewitching smile, 'Mr. Fowler and I understand each other; there never was any heart about his attentions to me—ordinary attentions, such as every man in the jungle feels bound to give to any young lady who will receive them—however much I may have felt for him.' We all laughed off the subject, and I positively think now that she was right.

"Marandhan and his wife, with Tisso their eldest son, the Masseys from Kaduganava, the Rivers from Matelle, Mrs. Hofer, and myself, formed almost all the party that attended Captain Reid's marriage with Miss Mowbray—one or two acquaintances from Kandy joining it to inspect the dresses and to comment on the bride's appearance. After the ceremony, Hofer insisted on his wife accompanying the newly-married pair to Kaduganava, whither they were to journey in company with the Masseys, and where they were to obtain breakfast. Her husband looked so much better that morning, that Mrs. Hofer had but little objection to comply with his request, on the understanding that I and Marandhan should spend the day with the invalid.

"When the wedding party had left, all joy and gladness, I read to the sick man, and he dozed. His breakfast was brought in shortly afterwards, on his waking; and he had scarcely concluded it, when one of those frightful spasms of the heart, the cause or consequence of nervous prostration, seized him. He had had no violent return of the attack since he had left Lanka, and the physician, who attended him then, hoped, therefore, that he would suffer no more from them. He felt its approach and seemed aware that it would end fatally, for, whilst I despatched a servant for the doctor, he muttered constantly 'useless, useless.' I returned to his bed-side, 'Fowler, I die,' said he, 'tell Emma that my last thoughts of earthly things were of her. Good bye, my friend; good bye, Marandhan. We shall meet—' A violent spasm prevented his finishing the sentence, but the upturned finger indicated what he meant. Before the doctor had arrived, Ernest Hofer was dead. 'Ah,' said the man of physic, taking the arm which was stretched lifelessly by his side—'ah, dead, I saw how it would be. Aneurism of the heart, of course.' 'Why then did you give the family every reason to believe he would recover, if you foresaw this?' I asked, indignantly. 'Bless me, Mr. Fowler,' said he, astonished, 'every reason to believe he would recover!—so he would had it not been for the spasms. I distinctly said, if there were no more spasms he would certainly recover for the present.'

"I sent off a messenger to Kaduganava at once on my own horse to inform Massey of what had taken place, and to beg of him or his wife to return with Mrs. Hofer."

* * * *

Such were the circumstances attending Ernest Hofer's death. His history was indeed a melancholy one! the history of talents thrown away in ever-changing pursuits—of virtues clouded and obscured by vacillation and want of firmness—of opportunities wasted and unimproved.

Mrs. Hofer joined her sister and Captain Reid shortly after, in Colombo—broken in health and heart by the trials and afflictions she had endured. A few months only had rolled over our heads, when she, too, was numbered with the dead, and we followed her lifeless body in mournful procession to the little cemetery on the Galle Face.

The charges against Mouat were fully proved, after a long and painful investigation; and the consequence was that he was obliged to retire from the service—on his pension. So much for having been Sir ——'s cousin! so much for the administration of justice in the East!*

* It must not be supposed that Mr. Mouat is presented to the reader as a sample of Ceylon magistrates generally—quite the reverse, he was an exception; for, however bad the administration of justice in the Company's territories, in Ceylon the magistrates are, for the most part, active and honest.

CHAPTER VII.

MARANDHAN'S HISTORY—THE SUBJUGATION OF KANDY.

"Why here begins this morning story right."
Comedy of Errors, act v., sc. 1.

IN the course of my intimacy, whilst in the jungle, with Marandhan, my intelligent and honest Kandian friend, I frequently asked him to give me an outline of his life, which, after a little importunity on my part, and reluctance on his, he consented to do, and during my subsequent leisure hours, I put the relation he had given me at various times into order, as a connected narrative.

His father, Baddoola Modliar, was but just past his prime, when the Kandian provinces became subject to England, that is to say, in 1815. A Modliar is a native officer over a thousand men, or rather was so in the times of Kandian independence. Above the Modliars were the Dissauves or governors of districts, then came the Adigars, the first of whom appears to have combined the offices of Prime Minister and Commander-in-chief, and below the Modliars were the Mohandirams, and a host of minor officials. Of the importance of the Modliars as a body, the history of Ceylon affords many proofs—native armies were often commanded, and provinces governed, by individual members of the body; hence the eagerness of the Kandian population to attain to the dignity, and their pride in it when attained, are by no means extraordinary. At present the title is conferred upon those who most faithfully and honestly serve their foreign masters; and the Governor at Colombo—at the time of which I write an old grey-headed Peninsular warrior, Sir Colin Campbell, the very *beau-ideal* of an old soldier—was the fountain of honour.

Baddoola was brought up in the Kandian Court, his family having been ancient and wealthy. Frequent communications with Colombo, both under the Dutch and its more recent masters, the English, had produced a spirit of inquiry amongst the Kandian nobles, which led them to seek information from every available source, and hence accounts of European customs and European politics were eagerly sought and attentively studied by the more active of the native princes. Wickrama Singha, the reigning sovereign from 1798 to the final conquest of the interior, did not encourage such researches, but, without absolutely forbidding them, affected an indifference to everything European, which had its due weight of course, with the sycophants by whom he was surrounded. No despotism was ever more pure and unalloyed than that of Kandy. The will of the monarch was irresistible and uncontrolled—the lives of his courtiers and the property of his subjects were equally at his disposal, and it may therefore be easily imagined, that his example had overpowering weight and influence. Information respecting European science and history was consequently obtained only by stealth or secresy, and the enquiring mind of Baddoola was obliged to resort to stratagem and dissimulation, in order to obtain the wished for enlightenment.

According to Marandhan, Wickrama was not the idiot—the cruel, blood-thirsty monster—he has been represented by English writers. Subject to sudden bursts of ungovernable fury, during which no one near him was safe, he certainly was, and during these fits, he often ordered that to be done, which, at cooler moments, he would repent of, but, did the First Adigar use his authority discreetly, the iniquitous sentence, if the execution were delayed, was generally cancelled in moments of calmness. If the First Adigar himself, however, united with the sovereign, in sudden fury or premeditated malice, against any individual so condemned, there was neither hope of mercy nor humanity. The most barbarous punishments that Oriental ingenuity could invent were exhausted upon the unhappy wretches, and, for weeks and months after some of these horrible executions, a settled gloom pervaded the capital and its neighbourhood, during which men, whispering, asked each other, who would probably be the next victims.

Baddoola was one of the most active in urging the extensive use of European arms by the Kandian soldiers, and the substitution of European military discipline and tactics for those which had previously prevailed amongst his countrymen. In these measures he was thwarted by most of the Adigars, but encouraged by a few of the more influential, until it was insidiously whispered to Wickrama, that the arms and discipline, thus spreading amongst the mountains, and in the provinces, might be used with as much effect against him in Kandy as against the English in Colombo. An order was consequently issued that all such reforms should cease—that those already possessing the musket or pistol were to retain them, but that the further manufacture and importation of either, should be at once discontinued. Marandhan distinctly remembers (for he is still alive) his father's grief at this order which only preceded the final struggle for independence by two years; he can still vividly recall to his recollection the hurried step with which Baddoola paced up and down the court-yard of his Kandian house, the muttered indignation, the prophecy of destruction and ruin, and the final determination to risk his head in an attempt to have the order reversed. But he did not succeed, and the equipment of the army remained half European, half Asiatic, with the defects of both, and without the strength of either—in the condition in which it was subsequently found when the British general advanced upon Kandy.

One incident of those far-off boyish days, seen dimly and indistinctly, through the mists of thirty years, has still dwelt upon Marandhan's memory. His father and he were occupying the usual apartments of the officer of the guard in the palace. The great temple, containing the hallowed relic of the tooth of Budha—"the most precious thing in the world" in Budhistic estimation—rose loftily and heavily, dingy with the ruthless hand of time, which had played with it so long, right opposite to the window of their principal apartment. A court-yard was beneath, between the palace on one side and the temple on the other, and Marandhan, a lively boy of ten years of age, was leaning from the window and looking down upon the flags below, thinking probably of the last game he had enjoyed, the new pony or the young elephant, that had been presented to him, and wondering when his father, whom he expected soon, would return. Occasionally a servant or an officer crossed the court; and their various head-dresses, seen with this bird's-eye view, amused the little idler. At length a thought struck him. He went into the apartment, and taking out a wooden toy, with his name neatly cut upon it, somewhat resembling in shape the smooth rounded top of an umbrella-handle, he stationed himself again at the window and watched the court-yard. At length a figure issued from the door directly beneath, and turning at the threshold to speak to some one following, stood still for a moment. Nothing could be more opportune for Marandhan; it was just what he wanted, so holding the little toy, the *plertah,* as he calls it, over the head of the figure beneath, he let it fall, with mathematical accuracy, into the strange head-dress beneath—strange, even for Kandy, the native place of extraordinary head-dresses—and, seeing that he had been successful, clapped his hands joyfully at the open window. The recipient of this extraordinary donation, looked upwards, and, in a moment, the court-yard was filled with earnest gazers at the window, and at its youthful occupant. "The king!" gasped little Marandhan, as he saw the upturned head—"the king!" There was a quick step on the corridor without, and suddenly his father stood before him—"Unfortunate boy," shouted he, wildly, dragging him at the same time from the window—"unfortunate boy, what have you done? Hurry away, lest you be seized."

But it was too late. Steps were heard too distinctly by both father and son without, and these steps were too rapidly approaching to leave any doubt of the object of the intruders. "In the name of the lofty king of kings, Wickrama-Sree-Hamadhan-Singha," said an officer, putting his hand on Marandhan's shoulder.

"I preceded you to arrest him," said Baddoola, quietly, handing over his son to the officer, "and now I go to call out the guard for the execution."

The father, agonized at heart, but (with that extraordinary self-control on important occasions which Asiatics alone possess in perfection), outwardly calm and unembarrassed, hurried off to the First Adigar to offer his fortune for the substitution of another lad, some unfortunate unloved slave, for his son, but he was again too late, for before he had reached the court below, he heard an officer shouting out, "The lofty king of kings, Wickrama-Sree-Hamadhan-Singha, lord of ten thousand elephants, awaits the criminal in the *Rajāki* hall." Now the Rajaki hall was that where sentences of death were decreed by the Kandian kings, and the very name told Baddoola and Marandhan what sentence, at that moment, was intended.

At the head of this long, blue-covered Rajaki hall Marandhan saw the offended Majesty of Ceylon sitting on his throne. The courtiers stood at some distance, and Marandhan and his guards, as was the wont of Kandian etiquette, advanced on their hands and knees towards the upper end of the apartment.

"Let the youth stand forth," said the king, and bravely did the little hero step into the middle of the open space, regarding himself, and being regarded by all who surrounded him, as doomed.

"You are Marandhan, son of Baddoola Modliar, are you not?" asked the king.

"The words of my lord the king of kings are wise," answered Marandhan, who was an incipient courtier, "I am."

The courtiers regarded each other, as much as

to say, "Behold the wisdom of the one and the audacity of the other."

"That *plertah*, then, is yours," said the king, throwing it to him.

"Wonderful wisdom," whispered the attendants, whilst Marandhan confessed the ownership.

"You dropped it from the window five minutes ago?"

The courtiers opened their eyes, and nodded more than ever. Marandhan assented again.

"Your conduct shows a recklessness of life," said the king, "and a carelessness of consequences, both bad. An assault upon the sacred majesty of my person cannot be overlooked; if, however, you have anything to say in your defence, I will hear you, boy."

"Wonderful clemency," whispered one courtier.

"To think of his throwing it at the king!" said the second.

Marandhan caught the words, and turning quickly round, replied, boy-like, "I did not throw the *plertah* at the king; I dropped it on the funny head-dress."

"Audacious criminal!" said the courtiers, frowning terribly.

"What says he?" asked the king.

The words of the boy were repeated. The king smiled—

"Send for Baddoola Modliar," said he, "*he* shall himself execute my sentence on the youth."

"Very just," muttered a courtier, whose old teethless gums grinned again at the facetious thought of a father cutting off his son's head or chopping his son's body into pieces!

Baddoola came. "That boy of yours, Baddoola," said the king, "is a quick-witted lad. He dropped the *plertah* on me as I was going to the temple, and might have done much hurt; but he says it was not the king, but the funny head-dress he aimed at, and a youth who can make so nice a distinction at his age may do something good when he grows up. Take him away from the court, and bring him up somewhere else. I have no fancy for having *plertahs* dropping from the windows upon me as I pass."

"What wonderful mercy!" exclaimed the courtiers, loudly, as the king retired. "We are truly rejoiced," said one of the oldest to Baddoola; "he is a fine boy." So ended that adventure, and Marandhan saw Wickrama-Singha no more.

In the hilly district of the south-east Marandhan was brought up, upon his father's principal property, for the next two years—two happy, eventless years—during which he learned much of Budhism and the elements of native literature, with much too of the history of his country, from an old priest in the vicinity. Those years were afterwards well remembered; the lull before the storm; subsequent trouble and calamity, rendered their aspect on the memory that of a green oasis in a weary desert. It was near a little village called Kapera that he lived, seeing his father but seldom; of his mother he knew and heard little, for she had been divorced and had died years before. The routine of one day was that of every day. The morning offering in the temple laid upon the altar of Budha, the daily conversation with the aged priest, Gatro, who superintended his studies, and loved the opening intelligence and ripe boyish energy of the youth; the daily meal with two younger brothers, with whom however he associated but little because he was the eldest and aped the man; the evening stroll to Gatro or over the hills in quest of game, or to ponder over some palm-leaf volume recommended to his study or on some lesson learned that day. Such was the even tenor of his way these two years, long afterwards remembered with fondness and regret combined.

It was but seldom that Baddoola made his appearance—events were hastening to a crisis in the capital. A discarded minister fled to the English at Colombo and demanded assistance in the name of the Kandian people and nobles to dethrone a monster. Ever ready to draw their swords in defence of the wretched, and to destroy all tyrants (not of their own creation), the English listened favourably to the Adigar. Benevolence, sympathy, love for a distressed nationality, argued they, urge us onwards to Kandy. We will go and dethrone this monster, whose crimes call to heaven, earth, and us for punishment, and then we will rule the country justly for our sovereign lord King George the Third, if these assisted Kandians will submit to us, and if they will not—they must be made. So, in accordance with the invitation, troops marched to Kandy. Strange to say, the Kandian people, so much tyrannized over and oppressed by this horrid Wickrama, preferred fighting against, instead of with, their protectors, and they fought bravely too, Baddoola showing himself a man in the struggle able to command and do good service in the cause of his country; but English soldiers, and Malays with European discipline and English officers, were more than a match for ill-disciplined Kandian troops however brave. Kandy was occupied—the king fled. A paltry affair, said the English, all over already. They were mistaken. Troops assembled from all the districts, not to join the discarded Adigar and the disinterested protectors of Kandian houses and lives, but to fight against both. Kandy was invested. It lies beautifully in a valley, with an artificial lake to the south—like a glimpse of blue amid heavy clouds in the sky—as seen from the neighbouring heights. These heights were manfully attacked by the Kandians and won. Major Davie, the commandant, hung out the white flag, and spoke of capitulation.

"You have wantonly invaded our country, and we will make you smart for it," said the Kandians, grimly, "if you do not depart at once."

"But our sick and our stores," urged the Major.

"All must be left," said Wickrama, "we will take care of both."

"Our lives—" said the Major.

"Are safe, if you delay not," he replied, "but linger and you die, every man of you, unless indeed I keep one in a cage as a sample of the men that invaded our country in these times."

The Major went, yielding everything, even the unfortunate Adigar whom British protection had brought back to Kandy! The less said of his fate the better. Fiends cannot conceive more diabolical punishments and torture, than Oriental ferocity can execute.

They marched out of the town these downcast, down-looking English soldiers and Malays, Davie at their head—ferocious Kandians, thirsting for their blood, at their rear. They came to the river, the Mahavelli river, a few miles from Kandy, and they stopped there, not liking to cross without boats. "Linger and you die," was forgotten.

"We want boats, go, get us boats," said the Major, greatly relieved as Kandy disappeared in the distance, and the terrible Kandians became less numerous.

"What, you loiter!" urged a friendly native servant, "you had better not. Cross without boats, cross with rafts, with anything, but cross if you would save your lives."

"Impertinence," said the Major, as he used his riding-whip freely on the back of the adviser —"impertinence. There is my lesson, you have given me yours—there, and there, and there."

Such is Marandhan's account of the transaction—his father was in Kandy at the time. What need to linger on such scenes? They were all butchered—every one of them—some on the bank, some in the river, all except the ungallant Major, and he, they say, lived for many years in a remote Kandian village, ashamed to look his countrymen in the face, and despised by his captors.

But Anglo-Saxon breasts do not brook such blows with impunity. That butchery sealed the fate of the Kandian provinces. There was no more irresolution, no more hesitation at Colombo. Troops were marched from all directions upon the capital. It was speedily taken—former disasters were retrieved, and the entire country subdued.

In the recesses of the mountains at Kapera, Marandhan heard of these events, and feared daily intelligence of his father's death, but it came not, nay, in due time, Baddoola himself made his appearance—his king had been taken—the country on all sides had submitted, and there was then no more hope. He had been known as an energetic enemy, however, by the English, and a party of troops was sent by the Commandant of a fort in the neighbourhood, to destroy the Modliar's house and capture himself.

Baddoola was aware of the impending danger. He had some troops so attached to himself personally, with him, that many of them were ready to risk life in the vain attempt to save him from superior power. If they could not bring safety to him, however, they could intelligence, and accordingly he was minutely informed, by messengers, of all that went on in the British quarters. Distinctly does Marandhan remember that dreadful time—the determination of Baddoola to defend his house to the last—the tears and entreaties of his wives and family, and of the venerable Gatro to endeavour to alter his resolution—the devotion with which his followers armed for the sacrifice—all remain deeply and clearly graven upon his retentive memory.

At the rear of the house, its only accessible quarter, a sloping plain stretched down to a mass of irregular rocks, which formed the outworks of the little citadel. The women had been sent away into the jungle, but the three youthful sons had begged to die with their father, and, after much entreaty, had prevailed on him to allow them to remain, yet not until Marandhan had bravely and boyishly declared that he would not leave the house alive. Baddoola, with a chosen band of devoted followers, posted himself on the rocks to attack the advancing foes the moment they should make their appearance—Marandhan, with a pistol he had learned to use, was stationed at a safe upper window, whilst, with silent grim resolution, the warriors took their various places here and there on that fatal day. Everything was prepared. A meal had been eaten in silence—the god of war had been invoked by sacrifice to aid their arms, a rite contrary to Budhistic faith, and only used in extreme cases—and, without noise or confusion, each took his post in the full expectation of speedily meeting death.

The red coats, which make the British soldiers so conspicuous a mark in mountain warfare, at length made their appearance, as expected, in the rear. The house of Baddoola was well known, and they came on rapidly and surely, their officer wisely marching with them as much as possible under the cover of the trees and hills. But at length they were fully exposed to the rifles of the marksmen on the rocks. Baddoola gave the signal, and in a moment eight men, out of a party of fifty, fell, some of them dead, the majority wounded, in the way of their comrades. It was a terrible stroke, but there was no hesitation on the part of the officer. The troops rushed on impetuously, and the Kandians, twelve in number, made precipitately for the house, exposing themselves to the fire of the soldiers as they did so, who took such advantage of the opportunity that nine only reached it, some, even of these, wounded, and, for some time, Marandhan did not know whether his father was one of the fortunate nine or not.

On rushed the troops, now breasting the rocks, and pausing in their shelter for a little. Not a shako made its appearance above them, not a red coat was visible anywhere in a crevice, but an unerring ball found it out, and there was little opportunity for reprisal—an incessant fire it is true was kept up from the rocks upon the windows of the house, a fire which was comparatively harmless, however, for the defenders easily protected themselves behind the jutting cornices and pillars.

At length the officer in command of the troops attempted, and admirably executed, a stratagem of material benefit to his party. Suddenly a wild "hurra" was heard from the rocks, and forty shakos were as suddenly raised) on the bayonet-points only however), above their shelter. A shower of balls from the house, as was expected pattered about in every direction, and then the troops roused themselves with a shout in earnest, and made briskly for the house. Before its defenders could reload their muskets, they had gained the steps, and were completely sheltered in the broad verandah beneath, but not before Baddoola had had time to pick down one more of of the devoted company, he having reserved a number of loaded rifles in readiness for his own use.

With axes, with which the British soldiers were provided, the outer door was soon destroyed—Marandhan from his post above, which he had promised not to leave, hearing fearfully the repeated blows, the loud crash of the falling door, and the hand-to-hand encounter which at once commenced. Baddoola himself was one of the first to fall, although unseen by his companions and supporters, and not being distinguished in his dress from the other Kandians, unknown to the British. The defenders of the house now rushed hurriedly up the stairs of the court-yard, whilst the British soldiers paused beneath, for there were deadly marksmen above, and exposure to their fire was certain death.

At length a voice was heard, ringing like a bell through the house, amid the silence of the moment, interrupted only now and then by a stifled groan, a voice offering, in imperfect Singhalese, quarter to the others if Baddoola were "delivered up to justice, and the fire arms surrendered." Marandhan, from his room above, heard the fatal summons, and missed not a word; whilst he saw determination upon the faces of some of the Kandians, and irresolution upon others. A pause of a few minutes followed, which, to the anxious boy, ignorant of his father's fate, seemed an age. At length a brave follower of the house, whose ancestors for many generations had been retainers in it, stepped from a room above, in the Modliar's coat, and shouted to the officer below, "I surrender then, on condition that the lives of the household be spared."

"We make no conditions with rebels," was the reply; "but our object is to secure Baddoola alone, and the arms—we care not for any thing else."

The brave devotee marched down, and surrendered himself to the soldiers, silence reigning in the house; but its occupants pondering much, and thinking rapidly as men only do think in such trying times.

"Is Baddoola's son in the house?" asked the officer.

"He was not also promised," said the pretended Baddoola.

"No, on the honour of a British officer, he shall be unmolested; but I would speak to him," said the brave commander of the troops.

"He doubts if that is Baddoola—Marandhan, your father's safety depends on you," whispered a voice near the boy.

"Marandhan," called the prisoner from below. "Marandhan, my son, come hither."

"I come, father," was the boy's reply from above, as he bounded down the stairs. No sooner had he reached the hall beneath, than he clung to the fettered prisoner, crying out, "O my father, my father, do not go."

"That is enough," said the officer," I am content," and, as he said so, the quick ears of the dissimulating boy heard a faint voice from the side of the apartment asking, "Who calls me—is that Marandhan, my son?"

A soldier heard the faint gurgling sound, and stooped to put the fallen foe into an easier posture; but he knew not a word of Singhalese, and, amid the trampling of the soldiers' feet on the pavement of the verandah, the further exclamations of the reviving Baddoola were unheeded. He had lain there felled by a blow from a clubbed musket, insensible, from the first irruption of the soldiers into the house, and was only now regaining his lost senses.

Oxen were yoked, by the orders of the pretended Baddoola, and everything likely to expedite the departure of the troops hastened. The wounded and dead, with the fire-arms, were deposited in the rude native carts, with which Singhalese houses of any pretension abound, and in a few minutes, their preparations and search completed, the red coats were wending their way back to the fort, with their heroic prisoner.

Scarcely had they reached the rocks which had been the scene and cause of so much bloodshed, when flames burst from the dwelling, and the cry was raised, "It is on fire;" whether fired by the troops or by accident, Marandhan is still ignorant. The dead and wounded of the Kandians had all been carefully conveyed to remote parts of the building, some for the funeral rites, others to be attended to, and have their injuries treated according to Singhalese science. A scene, therefore, of frightful confusion ensued, during which Marandhan waited on his father, who had been conveyed into the open air and placed under the shade of a fig-tree.

In a few moments the whole house was enveloped in a mass of flames, its peculiarly combustible character hastening, tenfold, the rapidity of its destruction. At length, Baddoola's sufferings soothed, and his burning thirst allayed, Marandhan had time to turn his attention to the blazing house, and, as he did so, the thought of his two little brothers, locked up in a small chamber above, flashed into his mind. He ran wildly towards the house, and would have rushed into the midst of the fire, had he not been violently withheld by some of the servants. A ladder was obtained, and an entry attempted by a window in a room adjoining that in which the youths were confined, for the chamber in which they had thus been locked for safety, looked into the court-yard within—but it was to no purpose that the attempt was made, the flames had gained the complete mastery of the building, and all hope of rescuing them was speedily abandoned.

Baddoola was kept strictly ignorant of the sacrifice which had been made to save his life, until news came from the British fort, that an attempted rescue had failed, and that the prisoner had been immediately shot to prevent any further efforts of the same kind. Then, and then only, did Gatro venture to inform him of the price which had been paid for his life, of the noble heroism which had inspired and carried out so magnanimous a deed. The follower who had thus devoted himself to death for his beloved master, had been standing beside Baddoola when he received the blow of the musket, and knowing him to be insensible, had taken advantage of the incident to offer up his own life as a sacrifice, in place of the more valuable one of his master, a sacrifice which, had Baddoola been made acquainted with it, before it was consummated, he would probably, nay certainly, in Marandhan's opinion, have prevented.

And now commenced a new existence in the chequered life of Marandhan. The wihare, or Budhistic temple, of which Gatro was the chief, and in which Baddoola had been tenderly nursed, was regarded by the British as a hotbed of rebellion and sedition, and, accordingly, a party of soldiers was sent soon after to demolish it. No resistance was made. The more valuable ornaments were carried off by the destroyers, whilst Gatro preserved, at considerable risk to himself, what he regarded as the most precious contents of the building, a few relics and volumes, and with these he laboriously made his way to Kandy, where his learning and piety raised him to a high position amongst the Budhistic hierarchy. Baddoola was then obliged, with his followers and family, to take to the jungle, for information had been given to the British Government, that he was still alive, and his making his appearance in any of the more frequented parts of the island, where he was known, would have been certain death.

A life of hardship and wildness was that which Marandhan now led for two years more, yet one which, to the precocious boy, much nearer manhood than he would have been in the less stimulating climate of temperate regions, was by no means a disagreeable one. He hunted and fished with his father's followers, often encountering the wild beasts of the forest, often obliged to spend the night amid the branches of a tree, whilst Baddoola, apparently absorbed in providing for the scanty wants of his little camp, was really in active correspondence with numerous influential chiefs, organising a general rising—one last blow for the independence of their beloved mountains.

During this portion of his life, Marandhan was often brought into contact with the wild inhabitants of the most rugged portions of Ceylon, called Veddahs; men, whose home is in hollow trees and caves—whose constant companions are serpents, leopards,* and wild elephants—whose occupation is hunting, and who have few of the attributes of humanity, but a language of their own, and bodies similar to those of the lowest and most degraded of mankind. Amongst these outcasts from all refinement and civilisation, even natural affection seems unawaked, except in the maternal bosom. Amongst them, as amongst other inferior animals, not much lower in the scale of animated nature, the father cares little or nothing for his offspring, the mother alone will tend and will fight for it, retaining however but seldom any affection for the father; most probably ignorant indeed where the father of her child is, or whether she shall ever see him again. Here is truly the state of nature, and if European philosophers, who advocate a return to it—if any such there be in these years—would thoroughly understand it, let them study the condition of the wild tribes of South Australia or the Veddahs of Ceylon. Compare the naked

* Properly *cheetahs*—I have called them leopards throughout, that name being more familiar to English readers. They are sometimes called *Ceylon tigers*.

savage that usurps the sacred name of woman, whose matted hair hangs filthily down upon her shoulders full of dirt and vermin; whose flattened nose, and projecting lips, form the greater contrast with the large shining teeth, only to exhibit the dark colour of the skin the more strikingly; whose infant seated on her hip, grasps her coarse rough-skinned body, with its legs, and draws nourishment from the flattened elongated breast —compare such a picture with the monkey whose infant clasps its body with its arms and legs, as she jumps lithely from bough to bough—and then compare it with the civilized woman of Europe or America, whose grace lights up, as with sunshine, her happy home, and whose beauty is a thing for men to worship . . . and deny, if you can, what cultivation can do on the one hand, and how near, on the other, degeneracy can bring the most excellent of created things, to brutehood.

The cultivation which was the result of Gatro's careful training and instruction, was, during these two years, almost eradicated, and little left except a taste merely for more elevated pursuits, when ease or prosperity might give an opportunity to resume the studies thus interrupted, and the course of life thus abruptly ended.

But affairs were now ripening for another

contest between the brave Kandians, and their braver and more disciplined masters. The insurrection broke out, under Baddoola's direction, in his own immediate neighbourhood. The Agent of Government, with a considerable body of troops, rode forth to crush the insurrection by a single well-timed blow, but fell in the attempt, and the troops, having been drawn into an ambuscade by the wary and crafty Kandian, were almost all destroyed. Rebellion at once blazed throughout the land, like the wild fire of the prairie, as it courses over the ground, swift, sure, and dreadful. District after district rose in arms, chief after chief, encouraged by the success of others, or animated with patriotic hopes, put themselves at the head of their retainers and guards, and "hydra-headed rebellion," was seen everywhere, —everywhere rousing itself like a giant, for the struggle. A priest of Budha, a distant relative of Wickrama, threw off his yellow robes, and proclaimed himself King of Kandy, whilst the brother-in-law of the very Adigar who had fled from Wickrama's cruelty, and who had urged the march of the English upon Kandy, put himself at the head of the insurrection.

Kapittipola, for such was the name of this enterprising and courageous chief, was a man formed for such hazardous undertakings. His courage was not that of the cautious, wary general, whose Fabian tactics would destroy his enemy by delay, and whose measures would probably succeed with more persevering people. His disposition was impetuous, and his courage was only redeemed from the imputation of rashness by his well-calculated estimate of the circumstances in which he was placed. Sudden unlooked-for success of some kind, he argued, was the only means likely to bring the country around him with promptitude and energy, and he therefore risked much to attain such success. Nor was he disappointed. The news spread, as such news only can spread amongst an excited people, that a large detachment of British troops had been cut to pieces on their way from Kandy to the South—Kapittipola's name was in every mouth, and the Kandians grasped their weapons and rushed to the combat, in the hope that the star of their unfortunate country was once more in the ascendant, and that independence might be finally achieved.

"During the three following months," writes an English officer at that time (1817) in Ceylon, "our affairs assumed a most melancholy aspect. Our little army was much exhausted and reduced by the enemy, fatigue, privation, and disease. The rebellion was unchecked; all our efforts had been apparently fruitless; not a leader of any consequence had been taken, not a district subdued or tranquillized. Kapittipola's vigilance seemed everywhere in active exercise, Kapittipola's energy equal to every task. This was a melancholy time to those of us on the scene of action, and many began to despond and augur from bad to worse, prophesying, what indeed seemed far from improbable, that the few districts still attached to us would join the enemy; that the communication between Colombo and our head-quarters at Kandy would be cut off, and that we should soon be obliged to evacuate the country and fight our way out of it."

Baddoola was one of the most active and energetic of Kapittipola's generals, and in the species of incessant guerilla warfare which he adopted, was eminently successful. Marandhan accompanied him in his rapid marches over the mountains and across the country, a kind of service for which his previous training in the jungle admirably fitted him.

Two causes, however, combined to render this partial and local success of little ultimate benefit, rather indeed of the most pernicious injury, to the country generally. The first was the want of warlike implements and ammunition on the part of the popular leaders, whose pecuniary resources were by no means equal to their energy and determination. The second was that invariable good fortune, which makes the British advance in the East the march of destiny, which no accident can arrest, no temporary losses retard. The chiefs became jealous of the priest, who was to reap the principal advantage from all these successes. They asked themselves why *he* should assume to be the successor of Wickrama; why they should not appoint a king of their own, who should be responsible only to them, who should look to *them* alone as the supporters of his throne, the causes of his prosperity. Accordingly they chose another sovereign; dissension became rife amongst them. Kapittipola and Baddoola adhered to their first choice, the others would give him no allegiance and yield him no fealty. United the Kandians might possibly at this juncture have succeeded in again achieving independence, although I cannot agree with Marandhan in thinking that such a consummation would have ultimately been for the good of the country, but, distracted by dissension, and divided by clashing interests and pretensions, all hope of ultimate success was foolish.

The leadership of Kapittipola might have been of the most consummate character for prudence and ability; Baddoola's exertions, unwearied and successful, in cutting off detachments and supplies, in harassing, worrying, destroying; but if this leadership and these exertions were not actively seconded by other chiefs, and in other districts, success was impossible. At length things came into such a condition that Kapittipola's defeat was rejoiced in by his opposing fellow-countrymen; many of them sold their neutrality, some their aid, to the British; and, persecuted, distracted, worried, and harassed by domestic treason, defeated by foreign power, he gave up the cause of Kandy as lost, and, in a fit of despair, put an end to his own life. The pretender to the throne, whom he had so bravely supported, was taken, and, with every mark of ignominy, put to death. The sacred tooth of Budha, the precious relic which had been taken from the temple at Kandy by the popular party, at the very outbreak of the rebellion, was recaptured, and, that relic once in the hands of the British, resistance ceased, "for whoever possesses the tooth-relic," said the old Singhalese tradition, "is the master of Ceylon."

Aware of these circumstances and of the futility of the stand which he now almost alone was making, against the foe, Baddoola again retreated into the jungle, where, for the two past years, he had lived, with his family, a nomadic life. Detachments were sent against him from various quarters, it being determined by the General at Kandy that he should be destroyed. Colonel Carroll from the North, and Major Johnstone from the South, with considerable bodies of troops, penetrated into the forest, and aided and directed by Singhalese spies, tracked out the fugitive, who, with a band of one hundred followers, his wives, and his only grown-up son, was retreating deeper and deeper amongst the mountains, into the heart of the jungle. His object was to draw his adversaries into an ambuscade, as he had done before, and to destroy one detachment before the other had time to succour it. The British officers were aware of his intentions, and, indeed, of almost every movement he made, for there were traitors in his little camp, who informed the spies of everything that was going on there, of the very measures which were canvassed and the resolutions taken by him, so far as known to his followers.

At length Baddoola had arrived at the position he sought, a rugged defile, in which a stream had scarcely room to make its way through the valley, so narrow was the steep gorge between the mountains on either side. Through this gorge he ostentatiously marched, giving every facility to the spies of the enemy to discover his route. Colonel Carroll was not far behind, and Major Johnstone was rapidly advancing from the south-west. For a day's journey beyond the defile, in which he hoped to destroy his enemies, did Baddoola march hurriedly on, the trees and jungle bearing the marks of his progress, so as clearly to indicate his route. As evening approached, he called together his little band, and harangued them, telling them that they might all die by their enemies' hands, but they should, at all events, amply revenge their deaths by the slaughter of the foes of their country.

"It wants three hours yet," said he, "to darkness, during these three hours we will repose here—here shall the women and children be left till our return, and ere we have returned, the troops from the North shall be carrion for the vultures and the crows. At the end of the three hours, we march rapidly back to the defile of Horula, and there posting ourselves on the rocks and summits of the mountains on either side, shall hurl down large masses of stone, and balls and arrows upon the red coats below, who will certainly follow us through the defile, for the mountains are impassable on either side, without going very far out of the way."

"Glory to the lion of war, Baddoola Modliar," shouted the wild assembly, as they dispersed, well pleased with the determination. But treason was busy in the little camp. Whilst the rest slept, one crept noiselessly away, and the spies of Colonel Carroll were speedily informed of the intentions of Baddoola. There was time for him to occupy the defile, by a forced march, ere the fugitives could again reach it, and he resolved so to encompass them, at its mouth, that escape would be impossible. They would, on entering it, be cooped up in a narrow space, he was informed, before they separated to occupy their various stations on the hills, and, at that moment, he saw no reason why they should not, every man of them, be destroyed or made prisoners.

Accustomed to this species of warfare, Colonel Carroll was a brave determined officer, quick in decision, and rapid in the execution of his plans. He rode hastily forward, with a single attendant, to reconnoitre the defile, and before his troops arrived, dark as it was, he had decided on the position which each portion should occupy, and on the measures to be adopted by each. Towards midnight, the moon, with a dim faint light, often obscured by clouds, made her appearance. The soldiers were ready, every man behind a rock or hid by vegetation, or in some venerable tree; every musket loaded, every bayonet ready for a charge. A party of Malays formed a portion of

Colonel Carroll's force, and their activity and cat-like nimbleness in jungle warfare, rendered them, at this moment, powerful auxiliaries.

At length, after some hours of anxious expectation, the stealthy guides informed the Colonel that Baddoola and his troop were approaching, and a whispered order was sent round to every part of the concealed force to be on the alert and await the signal. The moon, struggling with the clouds, shone for a moment, lighting up the scene to the east, where already streaks of greyish light were apparent, and as her beams lit up the tops of the trees, and the open brows of the rocks, and glanced upon the little stream, the British officer could doubtless discern the advancing band of Kandians, pressing forward to destruction.

Arrived at the entrance of the gorge, Baddoola, waiting for the laggards, called his men together, and was about to indicate the various positions they should take on the hills, when a pistol shot reverberated through the defile, and quick as lightning, flashes broke from the rocks, and balls whistled about, and struck, and pattered near the Kandians. Marandhan was with the force, his father against his earnest entreaties could not leave him behind, and indeed he was now so expert with the rifle that there was every hope of his giving effectual assistance. He heard the report of the pistol, he saw the numerous flashes, he felt his father, who was beside him on the bank of the stream, sinking down by his side, and thought he heard him say "*waren*" "come," as he sank, he saw the Kandians falling everywhere, he heard a wild "hurra" from the hills, and, as the moon shone fitfully forth, he saw the red coats with gleaming bayonets, leaping from the rocks and charging the Kandians on every side. He felt the cold polished blade of one of these bayonets passing between his naked arm and his side, and saw an officer interfering to save his life. These things were the vision of a moment, and it was not until he found himself a prisoner on his way to Kandy that he felt completely assured they had been realities, and that the band which to him that very day had appeared invincible, was, in a moment shattered, broken, and destroyed.

It was Colonel Carroll himself that had interfered to save his life, when the hunted band of Baddoola had been destroyed in the defile of Horula; Marandhan, unhurt, was standing in the midst, in a kind of stupor, from which the rude thrust of the bayonet, that passed between his naked arm and his side, scarcely roused him. As the mists cleared away from his mind, and the clouds left the face of the moon, he saw the dead bodies of his former companions, lying around him in every direction, each in the position in which it had fallen, when that terrible discharge had burst from the surrounding rocks and trees, so instantaneously changing the life and vigour and hope of the Kandians into the rigid immobility of death. The friendly hand that was placed upon his shoulder, and the benevolent countenance that almost touched his own as it gazed into it intently, disarmed his resentment at once, and, incapable of using it, he threw his light rifle, upon the ground, and told the officer he was the son of Baddoola. Small as was the stock of Singhalese which the officer possessed, he yet knew enough to understand what the boy said, and reiterating the word Baddoola alone, looked earnestly into his face. And then, for the first time, Marandhan began to ask himself what had become of his father—he distinctly remembered, yet with the hazy uncertainty of a dream, that his father, at the first discharge, had sunk down by his side, he thought he had heard him whisper, "come," as he grasped his hand, but the son was stupified and had resisted, whilst the father appeared to vanish into the earth. They had been standing, at that moment, by the bank of the little stream, and Marandhan forgot, that in the subsequent rush of the soldiers, he had been borne onwards a few paces, and had left his former position. He therefore looked around him on the ground, when his father's name was mentioned, and Colonel Carroll concluded that the great "rebel" was dead.

A search was made, however, and no Baddoola was found, whilst on counting the number of the slain and of the prisoners, it appeared that six others were missing. How they had escaped, or whether they had at all escaped, was a mystery and an enigma to the British officer, and to Marandhan was unaccountable. A diligent search was instituted around, and another body that had fallen into the stream was found a little lower down, lying where it had been stopped by some rushes, as the water had borne it along; but it was not the body of his father, Marandhan was rejoiced to see, at the same time that he felt doubtful, whether other corpses might not similarly have been borne much further away, or perhaps were hid beneath the surface of the dark rivulet.

From the first moment that he had seen him, Colonel Carroll appeared to take a fancy to the youthful Kandian, and, sending the other prisoners on with his detachment in front, he procured a pony for the boy, and told him to ride by his side, at the same time intimating to him that any attempt at escape would be certain death. A small body of troops was sent deeper into the forest, to see if any of the missing band had joined the women and children, and if so, to secure them; but, after an interval, during which the Colonel's party, with their prisoners, halted, the detachment returned with the intelligence that the women and children were alone, that they had found them ignorant of the destruction which had so speedily overtaken their defenders, and that they had left them unmolested, as Colonel Carroll had commanded.

Once set forward on the march, the boy speedily found much to occupy his thoughts, and to divert them from the stupor of grief into which he had first been thrown. He made no attempt to escape, nor indeed had he any intention to do so, for, ignorant as he was, whether his father was alive or dead, he had no wish to leave the officer who had treated him so kindly, and from whom he anticipated no evil. Colonel Carroll exerted his utmost powers to keep up a conversation with him in Singhalese, as Marandhan, at this time, was totally ignorant of English, and, although much was said by each that was unintelligible to the other, yet they succeeded sufficiently to feel mutual interest. The wild and stirring life which Marandhan had, for two years, been leading, had completely brushed off all remains of shyness and diffidence which he might have contracted in his retired days previously, and the free and open boldness with which he spoke his thoughts and recounted his history, increased that admiration which Colonel Carroll had previously evinced for his calmness and courage in the most fearful of all positions, with instant death apparently impending over him. He had got credit, indeed, for greater courage than he possessed, for much that was set down to coolness and carelessness of life, was really the result of sudden stupor and confusion.

They were now upwards of fifty miles from Kandy, and it was determined that three days should be allowed for the march thither, in order that the troops might not be overworked, and that they might be enabled to halt sufficiently during the heat of each day. They had been successful enough to raise the spirits both of the officers and men, and although there was an uncertainty about Baddoola's fate, there was every probability that he too had been destroyed, or, if not, there seemed, at all events, little prospect of his being able, in the present peaceable condition of the country, to lure any number of followers together, particularly after the dreadful lesson that had just been taught them.

In the same order as the detachment had set out, did it continue—the soldiers marching with the prisoners first, the bulk of the detachment following, and Colonel Carroll and his youthful companion, the only mounted members of the party, bringing up the rear. On the second day, as they were thus proceeding leisurely, before the heat of the sun became overpowering, their route lay along the side of a steep and precipitous hill, where the path consisted only of a ledge that formed a very insecure footing for their horses, and where even those on foot were obliged to proceed one after the other in long Indian file. The forest rose almost perpendicularly on their right, whilst the deep descent upon their left gave uncomfortable presentiments of the probable consequences of a fall to the shallowest observer. One part of the route, however, was far more dangerous than the rest, unsafe as the rest was. Here a huge rock, jutting from the side of the hill, in a semicircular mass, appeared to preclude all possibility of advance, save at the imminent risk of destruction. By carefully sodding a portion of it, however, more level than the rest, and which had been long used as a path, it was hoped that there would have been little difficulty in getting the horses across, and for that purpose two of the guides, experienced in jungle-life, came to offer their services, and to lead the animals over. But Colonel Carroll anticipated no difficulty, and seeing that the way had been rendered apparently secure, and there was ample footing for his steed, which he looked upon as an extremely safe and steady one, he determined to ride across unassisted, calling out to Marandhan to follow, and ordering the guides to get behind the youth. The horse, trembling at the frightful chasm beneath, which the huge mass of rock completely overhung, advanced cautiously and slowly, step by step, whilst his rider gave him completely the rein, trusting entirely to that sure-footed caution which had often similarly conveyed him out of danger.

Arrived at the centre of the rounded mass, Marandhan carefully and closely following upon his safer pony, and just as the most dangerous part of the route was being passed, a large monkey leaped from a tree above upon the upper part of the rock, directly in front of Col. Carroll's charger. The strange animal, its sudden apparition, and the nervous condition of the horse at the time, all combined to throw the sagacious animal off his guard, and he hastily stepped back, his hind legs slipping over the brow of the precipice, and grating, with their iron shoes, against the hard flint beneath, whilst, agonized in every limb, the poor beast clung, with all the tenacity of despair, to the ledge, with his fore-feet. Another moment and the steed and his rider would have been whirling in the air beneath, and dashing helplessly from rock to rock, to certain destruction, for there was no room between the horse and the rock for the Colonel to throw himself off on that side, and on the other, death stared him in the face.

Marandhan had been an attentive witness of the advance of the Colonel, and had anticipated the probable effect of the sudden appearance of the monkey, so sliding down by the neck of his pony, he had got on the ledge beneath the pony's head, and by the side of the hind legs of the horse which were thus sinking over the brow of the precipice, dragging the animal and the Colonel to destruction. There was not even room for his small body between the sloping rock and the protruded side and shoulder of the poor beast that was struggling for an instant for life, its muscular frame quivering and straining to excess with the violent efforts which the gradually yielding hold of its fore legs caused. Slipping, with the agility of a cat, under the belly of the horse, Marandhan seized the bridle at his head, and pulled with all his might with one hand, as if in the vain attempt to secure the horse's position, whilst with the other hand he grasped a crevice of the rock to his left, and, as he did so, he cried out loudly to the Colonel to seize his hand and throw himself forward over the head of his steed.

The whole incident was the work of less than a minute. The Colonel had shaken his stirrups off at the first alarm, and now, adopting Marandhan's suggestion as the only hope of safety, he threw himself in a moment forward over the horse's head, sliding down the slender form of the youth, whose utmost force was required to withstand the shock, and who, as soon as he saw the Colonel's body clear of the horse, let go the bridle. Even his puny strength had retarded the catastrophe. There was a thump scarcely audible upon the rocks far beneath, a slight rustle heard among the bushes, and the poor animal was gone, doubtless dashed to pieces by the dreadful fall. The Colonel, whose position was still critical, heard the sound, and trembled as he heard it, for had it not been for the bravery of the noble and fearless youth, he too, would have been, at that moment, in the jaws of death. He had slidden down the slight form of the boy, who trembled with his weight, as he clung to the rock, and now, reaching the ledge, there was a dangerous rebound that had almost sent him over, but a friendly crevice, into which he inserted his hand, secured him, and, in a moment, he was standing unharmed by the side of the gallant boy to whom he owed his safety.

"I owe you a life, Marandhan," said he, as they looked shudderingly over the ledge, after the lost steed, "and you will not find me ungrateful."

The pony still stood where the boy had left him a minute before, and seizing his bridle, he now led him across, and insisted on the Colonel's using him during the remainder of the journey, whilst he tramped on by his side, on foot. The guides alone had been witnesses to the transaction, the troops having been hid by the sinuosities of the way; but when the latter heard of the incident, they cheered the young Kandian so boisterously, that he began to feel quite heroic, and marched along with a prouder step and more confident aspect.

CHAPTER VIII.

MARANDHAN'S HISTORY CONTINUED—HIS RESIDENCE IN KANDY.

> " But, my good lord, this boy is forest, born,
> And hath been tutor'd in the rudiments
> Of many desperate studies by his father,
> Whom he reports to be a great magician,
> Obscured in the circle of this forest."
>
> *As you Like It*, act v. sc. 4.

ARRIVED at Kandy, Colonel Carroll, easily obtained Marandhan's release, insisting upon his dwelling with him for a time. In the midst of a quiet, happy, English family, Marandhan exchanged his wild nomadic jungle life for one much better suited to his character and disposition, where he learned something of civilization, and more of that instrument, by the help of which civilization is spreading over the world with gigantic strides—the English language. The fate of his father still haunted him, as an unsolved mystery, and although the Colonel made every inquiry for him, and even Gatro, the aged priest who had been his instructor two years before, exerted himself to procure intelligence, yet neither was for a time successful. The impulsive, impetuous, disposition of youth, however, could not long continue to brood over that or any other misfortune; and before he had been living a month in the midst of this highest product of social civilization, a cultivated domestic circle, his father was forgotten, or, if remembered, only remembered as a kind and loving father should be, after death; whose wild and turbulent career, it was perhaps well for all, had ended as it did.

Of the four estates, in different parts of the island, which Baddoola had possessed, only one, and that the smallest, remained unconfiscated and unappropriated—the one on which Marandhan now lives, in the neighbourhood of Ruminacaddee; and Colonel Carroll at once interested himself to have this property delivered over unreservedly to the youth. When military law pervaded the entire province this was not a very difficult matter to accomplish for one so highly esteemed as the Colonel, and, by putting it under proper management, he hoped that, before Marandhan became of age, a sufficient sum would have accumulated, from its hoarded revenue, to enable him to make extensive additions to it,—the Colonel himself purposing to defray all his expenses up to that period.

And now commenced for Marandhan a peaceful

happy period of his existence. Colonel Carroll's family was an eminently amiable one, and knowing the affection which the Colonel himself felt for the youth, and the obligation he owed him, every member of it vied with each other in showing kindness to the youthful Kandian. As his knowledge of English increased, the opening powers of the boy's mind, dormant for two years, again exhibited themselves in all their lustre, and his European friends were astonished at the ease with which he adapted himself to his new position, at the fondness which he exhibited for books, and at the good use which he made of them. His passion for study indeed, required rather to be checked than incited, and as the Colonel had promised Gatro, as the only condition on which he could be allowed to remain with him, that no attempts should be made to make him a Christian, his reading was rather literary and scientific than religious. Here it was that he laid the foundation of that store of knowledge to which he has since been constantly adding, and which it has been his highest aim, and the great ambition of his life, to perfect. His attention was not, however, to be kept entirely away from religious books; the Bible was neither unknown nor unread in Colonel Carroll's family, and, although no attempts were made to direct his attention into that channel; neither, on the other hand, were any made to restrain his legitimate curiosity.

His native education, however, was not neglected. Gatro had now reached a high position in the Budhistic hierarchy, and superintended the very temple into which the king had intended to go when Marandhan had launched the *plertah* on his head. To this temple did the youth resort, and there he spent many hours daily, poring over palm-leaf books of Budhistic lore, the huge Pitakas, divided into the Winaya or discipline, the Sutra or discourses, and the Abhidharmma or pre-eminent truths, with their voluminous commentaries;—the native histories of his country, too, the surest monuments of its early civilization, the Mahawanso, the Rajavali, and the Raja-ratnacari. There did he imbibe his reverence for Budhism and his love for Ceylon, Gatro taking care to instil into him the former as an antidote to the Christian influences by which he was surrounded, and reminiscences of his father's chequered career and of his own past life impelling him to the latter.

Thus was his mind formed, and hence the character which I admired so much, and studied so constantly as I had opportunities. Surrounded, on the one hand, in his new home, by European comfort and partial luxury, with constant opportunities of consulting European authors of celebrity, and with the humanizing influence of the highest form of civilized womanhood constantly acting upon him, and, on the other hand, acted upon for hours daily by "the old man eloquent," who had first nurtured his opening mind, who gave him deep draughts from Budhistic springs, who fortified his mind against the insidious error by which he and his pupil equally considered him to be surrounded, and who lost no opportunity of pointing out the answers to Budhistic difficulties, or enlarging upon what he believed to be the difficulties of Christianity,—he went to the temple, and there, encompassed by massive walls, and with huge images of the Budhistic man-god all around, with spectral-like priests in their yellow robes and shaven crowns, gliding about him, he opened the venerable-looking tomes which contained the doctrines of his faith—the musty palm-leaves, as he turned them over, one by one, in their perusal, and the straggling characters, all redolent of the East, breathed, as it were, their very spirit into his bosom, whilst the drawling of some youthful student, as he droned over the rythmic pages with nasal intonation, spoke of times long gone by, when men could put their trust for this world and the next in such things, and when form was all, substance and reality little or nothing. The very musty smell, the waving lines of discoloured cloth, hanging, like tattered tapestry, about, the whispered conversation and the dark gloominess of the whole building, all combined to give his soul an impress not of the earth, earthy, which the noon-day glare of the sun, as he emerged into it, speaking, in its bright lustre, so eloquently of the present, could not quite remove. It was the genius of the metaphysical past, entrancing him with its mystical rites and solemn symbolism, stamping him with a character which he was never wholly to lose, and which has ever since been partially the guide and director of his studies and his thoughts.

He returned to his European home, and there, surrounded by the novelties of the West, his situation was wholly changed. The captivating voice of feminine beauty welcomed him, and asked him of his studies; the free bold hand of the western warrior was extended to him in the most friendly way; European appliances accompanied his food, and European furniture occupied his room. He had been reading the *bana-potha* of thirty centuries ago in the old-world temple, with the aged Gatro by his side, at two o'clock, and before it had struck three he was deep in a new novel descriptive of modern refinement and morality on the banks of the Thames, whilst he lounged in an easy chair that might have once occupied a window in Regent-street,—"Blackwood" or "the Gentleman," perhaps, on a table beside him.

Under such influences, leading such a life, is it strange that he should be what he is, and can we wonder that he has grafted on the wild imagery and logical acuteness of the East, the many-sidedness of the West? And yet there was a humanizing influence at work upon his breast, superior to all that I have noted, one that left a more determined stamp behind it than all the solemnities of the temple or the luxuries of Col. Carroll's house. It was the passion of love. So various and manifold are the manifestations of this passion in life, so marked the character which it impresses, that even in the cold North it is generally allowed to be a leading principle of existence, taking its place above the other strongest motive powers in the constitution, but in Ceylon, under the warmer sun of the tropics, it has a pervading, all-embracing power, that totally neutralizes the force of other strong feelings, however apparently uncontrollable. The external heat seems to breathe a warmth into the heart which never leaves it or ceases to influence it; the mind is impelled by it, as by a mystic charm, which lures it ever on and on, making its possessor totally regardless of all other wishes and aspirations.

A love of the noble soldier who had so warmly

interested himself in his behalf first sprang up in the breast of the youthful Kandian. As all hope of ever seeing his father again faded from his mind, and the thought of his death became a certainty and a conviction to him, he transferred that affection he had always felt for the rude and rough but open-hearted Baddoola to the more cultivated but no less brave Colonel, who had thus, in his opinion, so *strangely* befriended him. Nor was Mrs. Carroll less disposed to cultivate an affection for the boy than her husband, looking upon him as she did as the preserver of the life of him who was to her almost all the world. The frank manliness of Marandhan won her esteem, too, and if his want of cultivation at first offended her, the feeling soon wore off, as he so readily embraced refinement. In all the fulness of matronly beauty she tendered her home, and all that it contained, to make him happy, and, as she imprinted a kiss upon his open forehead, or pressed him sometimes warmly to her heart, as the thought of the obligation she owed him rushed into her memory, she little thought perhaps that she was developing in him, for the first time, the filial instinct, and making him feel how happy he would have been with such a mother.

Marandhan felt love for both, an admiring, heroic love for the Colonel, a more boyish and son-like love for his wife; but there was still another in the house for whom he cherished another love, totally different from either of the former.

Belinda Carroll was a little girl of nine or ten years of age, one of those flaxen-haired beauties, with the smooth polished face of a wax figure, so common in England but so extraordinary between the tropics. Full of life and gaiety and animation, she was ever active, and at work or play of some kind—the very spirit of exercise. Delighted with a new plaything or a new game, until she had exhausted her strength in exertion, laughing with eyes and mouth and cheeks and neck all at once, her waving ringlets quivering the while, as though they had been set on wires or agitated by electric agency. Her exuberant animal spirits kept her always gay, always lively, always animated, as long as strength would sustain the exertion, and, when wearied with constant exercise she would throw herself upon a couch and sleep, Marandhan often asked himself whether she was not even more beautiful then than in the midst of her girlish gaiety. Had mortal eyes been able to detect an angel reposing, after being wearied with deeds of mercy, such was the form perhaps, he often thought, in which that angel would be found clothed. For her he felt a pure and holy love, the love which the terrestrial might have for the celestial, a love including the highest appreciation, of which he was yet capable, of all that was beautiful in form and excellent in nature, for Belinda did all she could to make every one around her happy, and took peculiar pleasure in rousing the too frequent abstraction, and sometimes the melancholy gloom of the young Kandian, into life and action. They often wandered together up the hill which rose behind the Colonel's house, and, from the summit of which, there was the finest possible view of the vale in which Kandy is situated, with its picturesque lake and the house in the midst of it. In climbing the hill they would pluck such flowers as pleased each other, and Belinda would teach her dark friend their English names, or, running back to her mamma, seek the information for herself. They would hide amongst the bushes and then call to each other, and in the excitement of the search or the joyous finding of the hidden one, feel a higher satisfaction and a purer joy by far than the huntsman who has descried the flying deer or hare only to goad it on miserably to destruction.

They read together, too; Belinda would read to Marandhan the tales she thought would most interest him, and Marandhan, as his knowledge of English increased, would read poetry to Belinda, with a correctness of intonation, and a propriety of accent, which his Budhistic studies had engrafted upon a naturally fine voice. He would tell her, too, of the strange incidents of his life, of the native kings, of the wars, of the wild forest people whom he had so often met, of the priests and of the temples, and to such accounts she was always ready to listen, imbibing, at the same time, a knowledge of some of the strangest phases of human life, and a sympathy and affection for the narrator.

Colonel Carroll was fond of boating, and during the bright moonlight evenings, bright far beyond anything that we ever experience in our land of fogs and rain, he would take his family upon the lake, he and Marandhan pulling at the oars, and Mrs. Carroll or Belinda steering. Sometimes during these delightful trips, which Marandhan still remembers vividly, though in brighter colours than those of nature, the Colonel would take both the oars, and as the boat glided through the water, now in the black shadow of some gigantic tree at the side, now in the bright beams of the moon which seemed to float around them, the hills rugged with trees and rocks, with light and shadow, rising on all sides, and the clear glassy water of the lake lying, like a mirror, in front of them, as they almost noiselessly stole through it, the lady would tell them of the stars, and of such of the constellations as she had learned to distinguish during her four months' voyage to Ceylon; her knowledge of astronomy might not have been accurate or extensive, but it was amply sufficient to interest her two youthful hearers, as they drank in her words and the moon-beams together. She would ask Marandhan, too, of astrology, and, in order to be prepared for such questions, he studied the pretended science with great assiduity, and talked, as they, ignorant of the subject, supposed, very learnedly of the twelve houses of heaven, and of their different powers; of the lords of these heavenly houses, and of their character and strength; he told them how, in 1815, Gatro had pointed out to Baddoola, that Mars, in the house of death, portended direful disasters by war, and of the malignant influence which Luna and Saturn, in the house of enemies, at the same time, would probably produce; he would remind them that it was in 1815, the very year when these things were noted by Gatro, that the independence of Ceylon was destroyed. and that it was not in Ceylon only that, during that year, death and war had been glutted with victims.

They listened to these accounts with interest, almost with awe, and, as they listened, the youthful Belinda kept her eyes fixed upon the speaker, as though he were uttering the words of inspiration. Nor was the spell broken until Colonel Carroll ceased his rowing to ask what was the subject that interested them so much, and there, in the midst of the lake, with natural beauty all around, would they talk of the self-contradictory character of the pretended science, and of the strange coincidences which sometimes presented themselves between its revelations and subsequent facts. Under such influences, surrounded by such people, Marandhan grew, both in body and mind, for three years, and under the vivifying sun of the tropics was rapidly approaching man's estate, and leaving boyhood behind.

At Colonel Carroll's he was extremely happy, nor did he ever feel uncomfortable there, save when strangers joined the family circle. They could not be expected to sympathise with him, as the members of the household did, and, in their presence only did he feel uncomfortable and strange. The European visitors, indeed, of the Colonel's family, wondered how he could possibly permit a Kandian boy to be treated as his own son, to be on terms of such friendly intimacy with his daughter and his wife; something in their manner showed this to the proud youth, whose sensibility was wounded by it, and he, consequently, exhibited himself under such circumstances as seldom as possible. Even when Belinda was surrounded by youthful companions of her own race, Marandhan kept aloof; she might welcome him as before, and raise her bright eyes, sparkling with joy, to his, as they played together, but they felt very differently—they had no sympathy with the Kandian stranger, they looked down upon him as a member of a conquered race, and he was too proud to succumb to their prejudices, even for her sake. He would regard them from a distance; or, with a book in his hand, keep his eyes fixed on them, rejoicing in Belinda's happiness, glad when he saw her delighted, sorry when she was disappointed, but wishing all the rest of the party at their respective homes.

Such a blissful position as was his, can at best, however, be but an interlude in any man's life, and the retrospect of it is all the more sunny and gladsome, because it did not last long enough to become monotonous and wearisome. Belinda was now arriving at that age when it was necessary she should receive the advantage of an European education,—all the essentials her mother had taught her, but there were graces and accomplishments, which it is supposed in the East can be learned only in an European atmosphere, to be superadded to her stock of knowledge; besides that the warm sun of Kandy was developing, with too much haste and precocity, a form that already promised to be tall. Two little ones also had been added to the household, and Mrs. Carroll's health required change of air, whilst their other children in England had now been so long deprived of parental care that a voyage thither was determined on, at the same time that Colonel Carroll was ordered to Colombo.

The Colonel had become attached to Marandhan during these three years of unreserved confidence and friendship—he had found the boy worthy of his protection, and he now offered to take him to Colombo, in order that they might still live together, whilst he was separated from his family, or during the remainder of his command in Ceylon. Marandhan would have gladly consented. He wanted to see the last of Mrs. Carroll and Belinda, the parting from whom was the second evil that had yet lacerated his young heart; he wanted to see the sea and the mighty ship that was to bear them on its bosom; he wanted, in fact, to linger near them as long as possible, and he was so much attached to Colonel Carroll, that he would willingly have sacrificed Budhism and his Kandian property to share his fortune. But these wishes were doomed to be unfulfilled.

Colonel Carroll had informed Gatro of the intended breaking up of his establishment, of the approaching departure of his family for Europe, and of himself for Colombo, and he gave him the option of sending Marandhan to England, of allowing him to live with him in Colombo, or of withdrawing him altogether from his protection. As the guardian whom Baddoola would probably have chosen for his son, had he lived, he thought it right that Gatro should have the disposal of the boy, with the reservation, however, that if Marandhan vehemently desired to leave Kandy, no force should be used to detain him. Marandhan had heard this intended departure so often spoken of, that he had no fears of its realization; he looked upon it as an event that might possibly occur in the distant future, but, at so great a distance, that it would be foolish for him to look forward to it for years, as probable, much less as certain.

When Gatro therefore informed him in January that the breaking up of the Colonel's household would occur at the beginning of March, he could scarcely bring himself to realize the matter to his own mind. "The family," said Gatro, "is going to England, and the Colonel to Colombo. In either place, my son, you would become quite Christianized and Europeanized, losing, at the same time, your religion and your nationality."

"The family is going to England, my father?" said the youth.

"It is, my son," was the reply.

"I should like much to see England, cannot I go with it?"

"Marandhan," said the old man, solemnly,

shaking his head, "your father, Baddoola, would have brought you up as a Budhist and a Kandian, as your forefathers have been. Would you cast a stigma upon a long line of noble ancestors? Would you declare yourself unworthy of your blood, by becoming a thing for men to point at and to scorn—a semi-Christian, a renegade Budhist, a half European, a despised Kandian—for, believe me, the very men who would do much to Europeanize you, would be the first to scorn you Europeanized, the first to honour you as a consistent Kandian. Be not led away, my son, by smooth tongues and dazzling falsehoods; there is no honour or honesty in this world for the man who has abjured his faith and his country; there can be no respect from his children; there is no hope in futurity! Go, think over my words, boy, the words of age and calmness, of sober forethought and consideration, and remember, Marandhan, son of Baddoola Modliar, that through me, your father commands you to obey, and to remain in Kandy." Marandhan did not go, but sat down where he was, and wept bitterly, when the old man had left the room.

He returned to his English home, and as he entered it, he saw Belinda on her pony, galloping away to the adjoining hills, and, as he threw himself upon his couch, he said—"What right has a dead father to impose commands upon a living son? All has become new with me and with my country—nothing is as it was. I love Budhism, and will maintain it on the ocean or in England as well as here; but Kandy is but a name, it is but a province of that England itself, why should I not leave it? I will go. No earthly power shall keep me here." Having thus formed his resolution, youth-like, he threw down the book he had taken in his hand, and rushing into the stable, prepared his pony for following Belinda.

For a day or two Gatro said nothing more to Marandhan on the subject, and, during that interval, Colonel Carroll asked him what he himself desired on the subject.

"I have long anxiously wished to visit England," replied the young man, his eyes sparkling with pleasure at the very thought, "and though it would give me great happiness to live with my benefactor in Colombo, yet if he would permit me to go to Europe with Mrs. Carroll, I should, in a year or two, return better worthy of the friendship with which he has honoured me."

"You want to see all the fine sights of London," said the Colonel. "Well, there's nothing very extraordinary in that, my boy; few, at your age, would wish otherwise, but what says Gatro Wahanse?"*

* *Wahanse* is a title of honour applied only to sacred things or sacred persons.

"I shall be *so* happy," said Belinda, who had just entered the room, "if Marandhan comes with us. The voyage will be delightful. We shall read books on astronomy together, and you must teach mamma and me astrology, and it will be just like the boat, in fact, only that we shall not have my dear, dear papa."

The Colonel looked at them both for a moment, and then said more gravely to Marandhan, "If you go to England, it must be to study, not to idle—to fit yourself for being a landed proprietor and the head of a noble house in Ceylon. You must, therefore, study in some school or college, and I shall see and make arrangements for your doing so in London, in case you go. Belinda will be at school in Brighton, where her mamma will live, and, as my time of service will soon expire here, I may be ordered away from the island before your return, so that possibly, once arrived in London, you may never see any of us more, although we shall correspond, of course. I want you thoroughly to understand matters before making up your mind. What says Gatro Wahanse?"

"That I must not go," said Marandhan, drooping at the chilling thought of seeing those he loved so well no more.

"Then I am afraid, my boy, you must give up the idea," said the Colonel. "He is your natural guardian, and although he shall not force you to any line of conduct, yet I would advise you to obey him."

Marandhan walked away to conceal the tears that had stolen into his eyes, and Belinda threw her arms round her father's neck, and begged him not to be cruel to poor Marandhan.

The youth heard the prayer of the fair pleader on his behalf as he walked away, endeavouring to commune with himself, and then, as a boy will, he balanced the matter carefully, putting all that his ingenuity could suggest into the scale of his wishes, and shutting his eyes to everything that militated against them,—winding up with the exclamation, "I *will* go. I am determined on it!"

"Well, Marandhan," said Gatro to him next day, "you have pondered my words, I trust, and will not consent to be the laughing-stock of men and devils which you proposed?"

"Gatro Wahanse," said the youth, laying his hand affectionately on the old man's feet, as he sat looking up, with the warm sunlight of youthful eyes, into the cold twilight of age, "Gatro Wahanse, you have been good, very good, to me, and to my father's house, and no youth ever loved a father more, Gatro, than I love you. But the independence of Kandy is ended—it is now but a province of that all-embracing England that is overshadowing Asia year by year, as the branches of the banian spread over the banks of the stream. In seeing England, therefore, I shall be but seeing the lord of Kandy, and I shall return with a juster estimate of my native land, and a greater probability of doing it service. A Budhist, Gatro, my friend and my instructor, you know I am most firmly, nor is there power on earth to shake my convictions on that head. I shall return as good and as devout a follower of the ever-blessed Gotama as I have ever been. Say then, Gatro, that I may go, and bless me when I go."

"O Marandhan, son of Baddoola Modliar, your words pierce my heart and steal the few drops of blood that age has left there still," said Gatro, piteously. "Have my words no sounds for your ears,—my tears, do your eyes not see? Shall I implore my son to stop with me in vain to close my eyes when I am dead, and to see the last rites paid to these limbs when cold? Is it for this I have nurtured you in my bosom, as the mother nurses her sucking child? Is it for this I have made soft your couch and given your thirsty soul the draughts of cold water which have so refreshed it, from the choicest wells of our religion? O my son, my son!"

Marandhan was moved and wept, and his affection urged him to cast his arms round the old man's neck, and promise to remain, but a fair form flitted across his imagination at the moment, and the slightest change in the folds of its drapery was a more eloquent appeal to his heart than the old man's lamentation, so that, whilst he wept, he thought of Belinda, and was silent.

"Enough," said Gatro, after a pause; "I have besought the stony heart and it has remained immovable. I have prayed to the running water and it has heeded me not. Young man, in your father's stead I command you to think no more of England and of those Christian friends who have thus beguiled your young heart to destruction; friends, such as the tiger is to the lamb or the fox to the fowl. You must *not* go."

There was a dignity about the attitude of the old man as he held his finger up whilst he uttered these words that might have awed a more callous breast than Marandhan's, but indignation swelled his bosom and he could not be silent.

"Say not so, old man," said he, impetuously, starting to his feet, "the deer does not more carefully nurture the fawn, nor does the eagle take more pains to instruct its young than my European friends with me. Truth, honesty, and love are written on their breasts, and though the characters in which they are written may not be Singhalese they are not the less there. They found me wild and they have humanized me; naked, and they have clothed me; ignorant, and they have instructed me, and the merit which they have acquired thereby will make them gods in a future birth. Your words were false, Gatro—Carroll shall be now my father, and whatever his wishes are I will obey."

So saying, Marandhan would have rushed from the apartment, but as he reached the door a tall priest, with his yellow robes muffled round his head, stood before him, and beckoned him authoritatively back. The youth involuntarily obeyed, and, as he did so, the stranger shut the door, and advanced into the centre of the apartment. A lamp, suspended from the roof, now afforded the only light to the little group, and placing himself nearly under it, the head of the strange priest, who thus so extraordinarily thrust himself upon Gatro's privacy unreproved, was uncovered, and as the words "Do you know me, boy?" sounded in his ears, Marandhan recognized his father. The shaven head had strangely altered the aspect of that once so well-known face, and time had traced in three short years many new wrinkles upon the brow, but in all the sternness of proud independance the priest concealed the warrior—Nagasena Wahanse was Baddoola Modliar.

"Back," said the stern father, as his son would have embraced him; "back, and let me know if I am to embrace a Kandian chief's son or the renegade bastard of an English officer. Speak, boy."

"My father's will is mine," said Marandhan, meekly, awed by the strange incident and the absolute obedience to parents inculcated by his faith.

"Good," said Baddoola, as he embraced his son; "good, my boy, you were right to be grateful for benefits received, but you must never lose your nationality. Who can tell the day when we may yet be free? Gatro will forgive my son, will he not?"

"If he is obedient to his father's will I forgive him," said Gatro.

"I am," said Marandhan, kneeling.

"Then, think no more of England, boy, and take leave of Colonel Carroll and his family. You will receive my orders through Gatro. Speak not of my existence to a living mortal; nay, whisper not even my name to yourself. Be obedient and you may yet be happy; disobey me," and as he spoke, he scowled, as only the ferocious can scowl —"disobey me and you die. I would rather put my dead son into his grave than see him a traitor to his country and his creed, however exalted his station."

CHAPTER IX.

MARANDHAN'S HISTORY CONTINUED—VOYAGE TO BURMAH.

Proteus. "Yet writers say, as in the sweetest bud
The eating canker dwells, so eating love
Inhabits in the finest wits of all."
Valentine. "And writers say, as the most forward bud
Is eaten by the canker e'er it blows,
Ev'n so by love the young and tender wit
Is turn'd to folly."
Two Gentlemen of Verona, act i., sc. 1.

THE sudden apparition of his father, the imperative commands laid upon him, the absolute filial obedience required by his faith, all contributed to overpower Marandhan's resolution, and to force him to submit. The threat of death, if he disobeyed, he knew was by no means an idle one, for the priesthood were everywhere in the island, and at Colombo or Kandy he was equally under their control and in their power, whilst Budhism consigned him to the lowest depths of infamy and degradation if he died in disobedience to his parents. These considerations were too powerful to be shaken or overthrown by boyish resolution, however impetuous or impulsive, and as he returned to his European home that day, he reflected, with a boy's sorrow, upon all that he was to give up, and upon the sacrifice he was to make. Another reason, too, conduced to his arrival at this determination, however unwillingly it might have been made—Colonel Carroll had himself said, that, once arrived in England, he would probably see the family no more, and under these circumstances he saw little reason why he should risk so much to remain with them for a few months longer only. He speedily, therefore, communicated his resolution to the household, and the Colonel, instead of urging him to go, or endeavouring to alter Gatro's intentions, as Marandhan flattered himself he might have done, calmly acquiesced in the decision and commended him for obeying his pastor and his guardian. It was not so with Belinda, however. *She* was not guided by the cold rules of prudence, but by the warmer sentiments of the heart, and she grieved for her poor Marandhan, whom she tenderly loved and thought she ever should love, as if her young heart would break at the separation.

"Never mind, Marandhan," said she, putting her arm round his neck and her warm young cheek near his, "never mind now; we shall soon grow big. You will be a man and able to do as you like by and by, and then can you not come and live near us or with us as you have done? And I'm sure my papa will not object to it, for you know Gatro will have no power over you when you are a man. I asked him and he told me so. We will write to each other every month until then, and when you come to England I will sing to you, and play for you, and we shall ride about the country as we do here, and shall be very, very happy. Shall we not, Marandhan; why do you look so grave?"

"Alas, Belinda," said he, "this can never happen, I fear. When you grow up, you know, you will be a very handsome woman, and men will want to marry you; Englishmen, English gentlemen, Belinda, and do you think then that you will think of me?"

"How cruel of you to speak so, Marandhan," said she, wiping her eyes, "I shall always think of you. If I am grown up to be a woman, and if I am handsome and people want to marry me, what has all that to do with remembering you? I can't help growing up and getting tall; they say I am getting too tall already. I can't help being handsome if I am so; I can't help people wanting to marry me if they do, but I *can* help forgetting you, Marandhan—I *will* help it. I will write to you and I will think of you, and if you come to England and ask me, I will marry you, and perhaps we shall all come back to Kandy and live here again—in this very house, perhaps. Wouldn't that be delightful?"

"Very, very delightful," said Marandhan, catching her enthusiasm, "and I should love you better than any English gentleman, and do all I could to make you happy. I would lay down my life, Belinda, to make you happy."

By such conversations did the youthful couple try and prepare themselves for the separation which was impending, castle-building in the air deliciously, as they wandered hand-in-hand over the hill sides or by the margin of the lake, or as they lay sheltering themselves from the rising or the setting sun under some thick tree.

At length the day came that Marandhan was to leave his European home for ever—a chamber in the grim old temple, with its dim twilight and musty hangings had already been prepared for him, in the richest style permitted in such a building, but to the youth's eyes, very inferior to the lovely one he was to quit, so full of light and beauty. The richly decorated mat and ottoman in the one, were but poor substitutes, he thought, for the simple, neat little bed in the other. The elaborately carved ebony *almirah* for his clothes he did not consider a sufficient substitute for the plain oaken chest of drawers he had used in his

European home; and however attractive the piles of palm leaf pothas, with their board covers, and the string wrapped round them, might once have been to him, when he knew of no other literature, he esteemed them more lightly now, that he had commenced to peruse and to enjoy Shakespeare's Plays and Bacon's Essays. A small European library, however, he even now possessed, for he had spent some of his funds in purchases of books at auctions which had already taken place in Kandy—a heterogeneous collection truly, but sufficient to keep alive the knowledge of, and the appetite for, European literature—the Bible and Tristram Shandy; the Pilgrim's Progress and the Cook's Oracle; the Whole Duty of Man and a treatise on military tactics, rested side by side in this strange collection, and were all equally perused by their possessor, if not with much profit religiously or intellectually, at all events, to the improvement of his philological information.

From the brow of the hill, which afforded the most extensive view of the country beyond Kandy, did Marandhan watch the carriage which conveyed away all whom he then loved from him for ever, and as it rolled uneasily along the badly made road, soon to be exchanged for saddle horses, by means of which alone, the greater part of the journey could then be accomplished, a fair hand waved a handkerchief from the carriage window as its owner had promised, and told of the affection which the girl Belinda had for the boy Marandhan. A turn in the road, and they were gone; and the young Kandian felt as if, in this wide wide world, he were quite alone. He neither saw nor heard of them more. Colonel Carroll was in Kandy subsequently, but not when Marandhan was there, and two years afterwards the Colonel left the island altogether, but not before he had the father's title of Modliar conferred by the Governor upon the son. Whether Belinda ever wrote, or whether, as is more probable, she thought no more of her boyish lover, he never heard, but he did not, on that account, think the less of her, or the less frequently ponder on her appearance and character as on that of an angel whom he had seen afar off, as it were, in a dream, a bright, beautiful, ethereal, boyish dream.

Marandhan now entered upon a new existence, totally different from any that he had passed before. Gatro still instructed him, but as he was rapidly approaching his seventeenth year, and was regarded by the other inmates of the temple, rather as a man than as a boy, he began to assume an independence and a self-confidence which he had never exhibited before. At first, indeed, his life was a dull and monotonous one.

He visited the spots where Belinda and he had walked and conversed, he rowed in the boat all alone, thinking of the moonlight excursions he had shared with her, he shut himself up in his chamber and threw himself upon his mat to commune with her again in the recesses of his own heart, and then he would seize his pen to write to her and tell her how fondly he loved her, and how fondly he should ever love her. But no letters came in reply, or, if they did, he did not get them; and, when many months had passed away, and still no answer to his warm confessions reached him, he brooded more and wrote less, until at last he wrote not at all; but, indignant at this total desertion of him, he became still more gloomy, still more reserved; and, feeling no sympathy with the hearts or the beings around him, he resigned himself to solitary melancholy, and often meditated suicide, as all youths do or have done at some period of their lives.

From this state of torpor and listlessness he was aroused by the presence of his father at the temple. He saw him twice before his father spoke to him, and he knew it was not for him to speak first. At length Nagasena, as Baddoola was now called, entered his chamber one day when he was thus meditating over a European book, which he had been reading, and which was still open in his hand.

"Gloom seems to have settled early on your

young heart, Marandhan," said Nagasena, "and I am not grieved that it is so, for, in the subject condition of our country, there is enough to make any Kandian gloomy. A mission of political importance from the priesthood of Ceylon to that of Burmah takes me to Rangoon, possibly to Ava. Will you come with me? A vessel awaits me at Batticaloa; you will see the sea as you desired; you will see, too, another Budhistic country, still independent, a sample of what Ceylon ought to be, and yet one day may be."

"I shall be delighted to go, Nagasena Wahanse," said Marandhan to his father, earnestly, "nothing would give me more pleasure."

The life and hope and energy that, for a time, had almost forsaken the active youthful frame of Marandhan, now returned in a full tide. Something to rouse him from the self-nurtured torpor into which he had been thrown by his own brooding reflections was all that he required to make him the sprightly, active youth he had been; and now the prospect of crossing the sea moved him to bright anticipations of new and delightful sights and sensations. The current that for many months had been dammed up, broke forth impetuously on the impediment to its progress being removed, and swept the rubbish that had accumulated on its surface away at a single bound. His preparations for departure were soon completed. Some new dresses, some splendid presents, and a few European books constituted, with his rifle, his entire baggage, yet, so far as use was concerned, the latter might have been dispensed with, for Nagasena Wahanse was now too strict a Budhist, to permit of any destruction of animal life, under any pretences. War, however, he would willingly have engaged in. So strange are the inconsistencies in the conduct of the most consistent of men! Man was the only animal he would have allowed his son willingly to shoot.

With joy did Marandhan see the intervening hills gradually shutting the vale of Kandy from his eyes, with its massive old temple and picturesque lake. He had been too happy in that valley for three swiftly passed years, to relish his further life in it; and, for some reason, to him inexplicable, Gatro had uniformly opposed his visiting the estate which, by Colonel Carroll's earnest intercession, had been preserved for him, and the revenue of which was still being hoarded until, according to English law, he could claim possession. His father and he departed on horseback, palanquins being provided for the more inaccessible parts of the jungle where riding would be unpleasant, and as they crested the hills towards the rising sun, Marandhan thought again of the rides he had often taken with Belinda, of how they two had so often cantered over this very road, and of the joyous hilarity by which such rides were generally enlivened. He looked back upon the European bungalow in which he had spent so many happy hours, as if he never expected to see it again, nor did the thought give him much pain, for it was now tenanted by a new family who had no sympathy with the Kandian stranger. All was changed indeed, since that day when, in the opposite direction, the white handkerchief from the rolling carriage, had been waved to him fondly again and again, as long as a glimpse of the hill-top could be obtained from it where he was known to be posted. All was changed—and Marandhan not less than all, for he began to feel himself a man, and chided himself often for allowing his childish fancy for a child to take such a hold of his heart. Often did he ask himself why he should think of one that thought no more of him, why as he became a man, he should not feel and act like one, and pluck out boyish thoughts from his heart.

Of all the fallacies that beguile the youth, there is perhaps none so fatal to happiness as this—the impression that the man should destroy and eradicate the lingering thoughts of the boy, those sweet aërial fancies that have been as delicious perfumes to the soul, breezes of paradise laden with the scents of far-off flowers and fruits, different in truth from those of earth. Can any subsequent success in life give to the soul that full enjoyment and perfect content which it received from early triumphs and early joys? What boy thinks of the future when present success has been attained, or allows anticipations of evil, foreboding of the time to come, to jar the exhilarating soul-music which entrances the whole being when youthful ambition has been satisfied, or youthful desire fulfilled? and what recollections can give more happiness than those of such youthful triumphs?

His father noted and approved the change in Marandhan's temper as they advanced, and although entirely mistaken, both as to the cause of the previous gloom, and the present exhilaration, flattered himself that he saw through his son as through the clearest glass, when he was, in fact, but looking into the mirror in which he saw himself reflected.

The exhilaration was, in reality, not so much one of mind as of body. The exercise was grateful to the youth, and in a consciousness that he was now rapidly becoming a man he exulted, whilst a struggle was going on in his mind to overcome and destroy the feelings of boyhood, a struggle in which, with his characteristic energy, he persevered till quite successful.

Seeing, however, with the blindness of pre-occupied men, his own thoughts reflected in his son's bosom, his own thoughts which seemed ever fixed upon his country, a shrine at which he was willing still to sacrifice every domestic feeling, Baddoola painted in glowing colours to the youth, what Kandy had been when independent, and what it still might be if its sons were true. He told him of the scenes he had witnessed and taken a part in, when European ambassadors were kept waiting for hours by the native potentate, for an audience; when a Kandian noble spoke on terms of equality with the highest European officer, military or civil; when all the power was in the hands of the king, the nobility, and the priesthood. Marandhan's enthusiasm was easily kindled, and it was to kindle that enthusiasm that Baddoola spoke, far more as a warrior and a noble than as a priest. Nor did he omit Budhism, and its present degradation, compared with what it had been. He conjectured, and rightly too, that the youth was attached to his religion; and what it had been a point of pride for him to maintain in European society, its present degradation would but implant, he thought, the more firmly upon his generous mind.

As they rode side by side, or in the palanquins when they were able to converse, or when they stopped to take their meals, and to avoid the heat of the day, the fiery father plied his son with such topics, urging them with all the eloquence and persuasion of which he was master, upon a willing and easily-roused listener. Marandhan looked upon it as an appeal to his manhood, and felt all the braver at the idea, all the more disposed to side wholly with his preceptor, and to discard all other considerations from his mind. For three days was he plied thus; on the first at intervals and but occasionally, being himself requested to state his opinions freely and unreservedly; on the second and third more warmly, until, on the fourth, as they descended a hill, whence the first view of the sea had burst in all its majestic grandeur upon the young man, with Batticaloa, their destination, directly beneath them—the object of all this persuasion and cajolery became apparent.

"You see, then, Marandhan," continued his father, "you see then the position in which our country is placed, are you willing to perform your part for its restoration?"

"Undoubtedly," said Marandhan, as he felt

the blood of a man, and no longer that of a boy, tingling in his veins at such a question—"undoubtedly."

"Then heed me;" proceeded his father. "By force of arms, at present, we can do nothing. Success can only be obtained by a vast organization of every part of the country, which must be the work of time, and which I am labouring to advance. To extend such an organization, which shall distribute arms, swear in men, and act everywhere at once, the priesthood is the only available engine—the least interfered with too by our conquerors. Its secrets are safe, and its ramifications extend over every part of the island. If we succeed then, there will be a simultaneous rising at Trincomalee and Galle, at Batticaloa and Jaffnapatam, at Kandy and Colombo, and then let us see what European discipline can accomplish. The forts will be seized at once, and our country freed. Is it not a glorious prospect?"

"Truly it is," said Marandhan, catching something of the enthusiasm of his father, whilst he entertained an uneasy feeling as he thought of Colonel Carroll.

"Would you join in such an enterprize?" asked his father.

"Willingly," replied the youth, "but Colonel Carroll should be spared."

"Of course," was the reply, "but the perfect organization I want will be the work of time, and all the priesthood, without exception must join it first; ere that is attained Colonel Carroll will probably have left the island, for it is the policy of the English never to let men who know the country remain in it; they are immediately removed elsewhere when they have become really acquainted with us. Now to join this confederacy, to aid this grand design, you must become a priest.

"A priest!" said Marandhan, as he thought of Belinda, and the union they once dreamt of, "a priest!"

"Yes, a priest," said his father, earnestly, "but you are not yet of age for the purpose, and it would be better for you to secure our only remaining property first, and then you will have a large sum in ready money, and the produce of the estate to spend in the good cause."

"And have you intended all along to make me a priest?" asked Marandhan, who by no means relished the prospect of perpetual celibacy.

"Of course I have," was the reply, "else why have you not been betrothed like other youths?"

"Why, indeed," said Marandhan, "I had forgotten that."

"What say you then?" asked the father.

"I have no objection to become a priest," replied the young man, "that is—at the time you advise," for he reflected that long ere that, the question of his ultimate marriage with Belinda, which did not even then seem very probable, would be definitely settled.

"Then you shall take an oath to that effect in the great pagoda of Rangoon, and ratify it over the tooth of Budha in Kandy on our return," said his father. Marandhan winced a little inwardly at this intimation, but said nothing.

The town of Batticaloa offered little to excite the attention of the active young man, save the prospect of the sea which he gazed at as if he should never weary of regarding it—some ancient ruins of once-hallowed temples in the vicinity were little esteemed in comparison. A native bark of the largest size used by Orientals, was preparing to cross the Bay of Bengal on their arrival, but was not ready for sea for three days. The steady monsoon, blowing uniformly and freshly, carried them to Burmah without incident or accident, but not without the usual penalty of sea-sickness, the tribute Neptune exacts from those, who, for the first time, or but seldom, venture on his territory.

Arrived in the Gulf of Martaban, they coasted

along the island of Syriam, up one of the estuaries of the Irrawaddy. The new country, and the magnificent rivers, equally delighted Marandhan, and, for the first time in his life, he tasted something of the true enjoyment of the traveller. The glittering spires of Rangoon, and the pagodas of the neighbourhood, gaudy with gold and paint, that shone brightly in the full sunbeams, spoke to his heart of a flourishing Budhism in all the pride, pomp, and circumstance of political favour, and still retaining a firm hold over the minds of the people, not politically frowned upon and almost effete in influence, as in Ceylon. Nagasena was received with great state by the hierarchy of Rangoon. The Burmese first learned their religion from Ceylon, and they have ever since remained grateful for the blessing, looking upon the favoured island that guards the sacred tooth of Gotama, as blessed by Providence above all other lands, and as that where Budhism is maintained in its greatest orthodoxy, notwithstanding the claims of the Grand Llama of Thibet, and the efforts he has made to extend his influence to the south-east.

But whatever the mission with which his father was entrusted, and Marandhan was then, and still is, ignorant of its nature, it did not appear to prosper, and he found it necessary, after some months' residence in Rangoon, to go to Ava, whither the young man willingly accompanied him. They travelled as they had travelled in Ceylon, partly on the Pegu pony, so famous throughout the East for its speed and strength, and partly in richly-decorated palanquins, before which the people prostrated themselves as they passed. Sometimes by the banks of the Irrawaddy, where the river often spread out like a sea, and the picturesque hills and trees on the opposite side formed the appropriate background of the picture. Sometimes deep in forests and jungles that rivalled those of Ceylon in their luxuriant foliage and wild beauty. They travelled ever onwards to the north, and, ere they reached the capital of his golden-footed majesty, they had passed over five hundred miles—five hundred miles of the richest portion of the earth's surface, which, now scantily occupied by three or four millions of oppressed and ill-governed people, might support a population of thirty or forty millions under an improved system.

If the distant view of Rangoon, with its innumerable gilded spires and vast pagodas, had astonished Marandhan, accustomed to the poverty, artistic and metallic, of Ceylon, it may be easily conceived that he was still more surprised when the magnificent prospect of Ava first burst upon his view. From a gently sloping hill to the south-east of the city, in which a tributary of the Kaunee takes its rise, they first saw the city in the low ground beneath, the Irrawaddy, even here of considerable breadth, spreading far off to their left, and flowing away directly west, its waters only apparent here and there through the forest of minarets and domes and spires which crowded the view, especially in the northern quarter of the city. Far away in the distance, at the other side of the stream, and further to the north, could be discerned the gilded spires of the temples of Sagaing rising above the foliage which surrounded them, and the tops of which only, at that distance, could be faintly distinguished. The entire scene made an impression upon the mind of the young man which the placid life of his later years has recalled vividly to his memory, retouching the picture, as it were, with a delicacy and finish which idealism alone can give.

His life in Ava, which was but of a month's duration, was one continued scene of interest and wonder to him. The monarch himself, whom he saw three times; the head of the priesthood, whose power was little inferior; the splendid temples, made as gorgeous as gold, precious stones, silver, and paint could make them; the immense monasteries, where hundreds of devotees, in their yellow robes, were daily to be seen in prayer or reciting the sacred books, whilst other hundreds copied out these books, or the commentaries by religious sages of other years upon them; the images of Budha, radiant with elaborate ornament, and the great white elephant sacred to Gotama, all these were persons and objects to make an impression upon a young heart not easily effaceable, and which kept him, for the time being, in a constant ferment of gratified curiosity. Amidst these scenes Belinda was seldom thought of, and his father rightly concluded that the gorgeous religion of Ava would do more to reconcile Marandhan to the priesthood than any exhortations of his.

Before they were to leave the capital a farewell visit of a formal character was to be paid to the head of the priesthood in the principal temple of the Sairwa, or northern side of the city. It was to be a visit of state, and Baddoola spared no pains and no expense to make his own and his son's appearance as rich and imposing as possible. A large attendance of the inferior clergy surrounded the high-priest, as he sat in the great chair of state, sometimes occupied by the monarch, which was placed near the altar of Budha. Marandhan and his father approached to the centre of the temple, hand in hand, in the direction of the high-priest, and then his father, advancing a step before him, threw himself upon his face on the marble floor, at the same time speaking in Pali, the sacred language equally of Burmah and Ceylon, and studied generally by the priesthood alone. Gatro had taken pains to make Marandhan a proficient in this language, another sign, had any been wanting, that he had evidently long been intended for the priesthood—

'I, Nagasena, emissary from the priesthood of Ceylon, and the humble slave of your sacred majesty, come to the high-priest of Burmah, whose virtues are more lustrous than the sun, and whose words are wiser than the words of the sages, to take my leave. Will my lord permit his slave to approach?"

"Welcome, Nagasena Wahanse, honoured brother and friend, welcome. I joy to see you, and grieve at the cause," said the hierarch.

Nagasena approached and embraced the high-priest, whilst Marandhan remained standing where his father had left him.

"Will my lord permit his slave to ask him if Marandhan Modliar, son of Baddoola Modliar, of the holy island, may approach my lord's glorious presence, to receive a blessing of my lord's bounty, more precious than diamonds, more enduring than adamant?" asked Nagasena.

"He may approach," said the high-priest.

Marandhan then likewise threw himself upon the ground, and crying "holy, holy, holy!" advanced towards the altar.

"Young noble of the holy island," said the high-priest, "I bid you sorrowfully farewell. Neglect not your religion, and remember that the ever-blessed Gotama has declared that those who take refuge in him, in the word, and in the priesthood, shall be blessed as gods in the next birth."

Marandhan threw himself again upon the ground, and would have withdrawn, but was arrested by his father's voice.

"Will the sanctified allow his slave once more to speak?" he asked, addressing the high-priest. "The young man intends to enter the holy order of the priesthood on attaining age. Will the sanctified allow Marandhan Modliar, the son of Baddoola Modliar, of the holy island, to swear here upon the altar of our God that he will devote himself and his property to our holy religion?"

"He may swear," said the high priest, after a surprised pause.

Taken thus aback, Marandhan could not avoid the oath which he feared and disliked. An attendant priest placed some relics on the altar, and, taking the young man's hands in his own, held them over the relics, whilst he caused Marandhan to touch the altar with his forehead as he said, "I swear." A little sacred corn and water were then given him to eat and drink, and the oath was administered.

As they returned that day from the temple, the father and the son, they said not a word to each other of the unwonted transaction. Marandhan was annoyed and vexed, looking upon himself as duped; and his father was probably too much engrossed with other matters to mind him much. It was not that the thoughts of Belinda still occupied his mind—far from it; the novelties of the past month had effaced all tender recollections of her; nor was it that he had any particular objection to the life of a priest, save the general obligation to celibacy; but he regarded himself as unfairly dealt with in this sudden requirement of the oath, which he had originally been told should be taken in Rangoon; and he felt displeased with his father, with the high priest, and with himself. Baddoola, however, either disregarded his vexation, or did not notice it; nor was he generally so communicative or inquisitive as to enter freely into conversation with his son about matters that concerned either of them exclusively.

The journey back to Rangoon accomplished,

they looked out for a vessel to take them again to Ceylon: but it was several months before a large native ship was found for the purpose, which intended shortly to sail for Colombo. During these months he vigorously pursued his Budhistic studies, the treasures of large stores of Pali books being here open to him in the temples. He studied hard indeed, partly because his natural mental activity impelled him to it, partly because he had little else to do, and partly because he had made a promise to Gatro to make the best use of his time in that respect.

At length, however, the ship that was to take them to Colombo was ready. Again did the steady monsoon bear them back in safety to their beloved island, the unvarying breeze wafting them, as with the wings of a bird, swiftly to the West; nor was there any anxiety visible on the faces of any on board, save, for a time, when they were coasting along the southern shore of Ceylon, and when there seemed a chance of their having got so near the land as to be unable to tack off again. The danger was but temporary, however, and afforded the only incident of interest connected with the voyage, as a voyage. Yet to Marandhan that passage of twenty days' duration from Rangoon to Colombo was one of the most influential circumstances that had yet occurred in the history of his strange and chequered existence. It left its impress upon every day of his subsequent life, and has not ceased to influence it up to the present moment.

The ship was a European vessel, which had formerly been engaged in the trade just beginning to spring up between the Gulf of Persia and the Straits of Malacca. It had been sold, however, in Calcutta, and was bought by a native merchant, who manned it with an Asiatic crew and Arab officers. On the present occasion it was bound with a cargo of rice from Rangoon to Colombo, for, strange to say, Ceylon, which formerly supported five millions of inhabitants, according to the best authorities on the subject, does not now grow sufficient rice to feed its modern population of half a million. The present cargo was an experiment to try whether "the holy island" might not, as well and more cheaply, be supplied from Burmah as from India. The cabins in the after-part of the ship were left pretty much in the same condition, as regards arrangement, as they had been when occupied by Europeans. Two large stern cabins, with windows looking out upon the sea on either side of the rudder, were by far the finest in the vessel, and of these Marandhan and his father had one, whilst the other was occupied by a Burmese merchant and his family, who was about to settle in Colombo. Thatwhang, the merchant, was wealthy, and the rapacity of the new Governor of Rangoon, as well as the sufferer's inability of obtaining justice in Ava, induced him to forsake his native country, and rather place himself under the protection of English laws in Ceylon than expose himself and his family to the injustice and want of principle of native officials.

In frequent voyages backwards and forwards, Thatwhang had obtained an accurate knowledge of the Singhalese language, and had long been preparing for his emigration by obliging his family to learn it too. His departure from Rangoon was rather a flight than a voluntary removal, however, for, were his intentions known, the strong hand of tyranny would have prevented its accomplishment, or held his wife and family as hostages for the citizenship of Thatwhang—a measure which the merchant was aware it would be highly pleasing to the Governor to put into execution. To save himself, then, from injury, his property from enormous exactions, and his family from disgrace, Thatwhang was obliged to relinquish his home, and betake himself to a foreign country. As he had had for years mercantile dealings with Colombo, he felt the less difficulty in transferring his property thither; and as Ceylon was still a

Budhistic country, he did not fear the loss of their faith amongst his household.

In his person and mien Thatwhang was a favourable specimen of the half Chinese, half Malay race from which he had sprung. He was muscular and of the middle height. His brilliant black eye, ever moving and flashing restlessly, allied him to the Malay; whilst his comparatively fair skin and ample cheek-bones proclaimed connexion with the Chinese race. His courage, jealousy, determination, and rigid adherence to his faith were the characteristics of the one; his love of money, adroitness in getting it, and skill in keeping it when once obtained, the peculiar national features of the other.

The love of Thatwhang for Budhism induced something like friendship between him and Baddoola, whom, as the priest Nagasena, he honoured; whilst, instead of courting the friendship of Marandhan, he kept him as much as possible at a distance—a reserve which the offended young man returned with interest. At the same time Baddoola soon discovered the merchant's extreme love of money, and despised him for that, as much as he honoured him on account of his affection for Budhism. Surrounded as they were by Mohammedans and Hindoos, their mutual faith was a bond of union between the three, which Marandhan felt the more offended Thatwhang should break so unnecessarily and offensively. He lost, therefore, no opportunity, during the first few days of the voyage, of conciliating the good-will of the Arab captain, in which, with the aid of a judicious present of some excellent tobacco, he quite succeeded, nor of returning the distant gaze of Thatwhang, and showing him, in every possible way, that to him his friendship or enmity was alike indifferent. A week, however, had scarcely elapsed ere Marandhan's interest was excited by the family of the merchant, and he began to repent his rude behaviour, even although he conceived himself justified in it by the equally rude conduct of Thatwhang.

He was passing by the cabin which contained the merchant's family one morning later than usual,—his time and that of his father being spent principally on deck,—when he saw a fair form standing at the door giving orders to a Burmese servant. The face was uncovered, and its colour, almost European in its delicacy, at once attracted his attention and observation. Nor was he indifferent to a pair of lustrous Oriental eyes, whose long lashes added a charm to them that our northern beauties, in Marandhan's opinion, for the most part, want. True, the face was fat,—the cheeks were decidedly fleshy,—but the mouth was beautifully formed, and the figure, if it had not the grace of a nymph,—indeed there was no denying it was altogether fat,—was adorned by a strange costume that set off its somewhat large proportions to admiration.

The gaze of the young man, ardent and somewhat bold, was not unobserved by the lady, nor—to judge by the way in which she drew a thin veil over one side of her face to hide the portion of it which was turned away from Marandhan, and to form a groundwork for an exquisite profile—was it by any means unpleasant. He could not do more, however, than loiter for a moment, in vain efforts to open the door of his own cabin, as he gazed upon the stranger, and it was, at all events, some consolation to him to hear the other door shutting and the servant departing, as he succeeded.

"That's surely not a Burmese face," thought he, to himself, "it's too well proportioned for that; there are no large cheek bones in it; besides, she's so fair; heigh ho! what a pity she's so fat, I wish I had spoken to her."

Marandhan's interest, however, was excited, and, as he walked the deck that day with the Captain, endeavouring to carry on a conversation in the few words of Hindoostanee with which he was acquainted, he returned Thatwhang's supercilious stare, when they happened to meet, with as near an approach to a smile as possible,—with, at all events, the blandest expression of countenance he could assume. Thatwhang looked again, yes, there was no mistake. Marandhan, instead of elevating his eyebrows and drawing up one side of his upper lip, was benevolently extending the corners of his mouth and looking at him in the most friendly way.

"He has found out at last, I'm rich," thought Thatwhang, doubtless, to himself, as he continued to chat with Baddoola.

"That Burmese merchant has his family on board, has he not?" asked Marandhan of the Captain, floundering through the Hindoostanee, much in the same way as the griffin who first takes up his abode in the East, and observes to his servant, "there was a coal-hole,"* when he wishes to tell him to open the door.

"He has,"—replied the Captain, adding much more that was unintelligible to Marandhan.

"Indeed," said the latter, "and do they never walk on deck?"

"They do at night," was the first part of the answer, followed by a large appendix, that the young man in vain endeavoured to translate for his own edification.

* *Durwāza kolo*, Hindostanee for 'open the door.'

"Ah," he replied, "is it possible? Are the women handsome?" he asked again, imperfectly, after a pause.

"Don't know," said the Captain, and then he proceeded to mention "veils," and "muffling," and "fat," and "thin," in a way that quite baffled Marandhan's comprehension. At last he gave up the effort to understand, and listened merely to a whole torrent of words.

"Indeed," said he, when it was ended, "at night—"

The Captain looked at him and laughed, but Marandhan did not understand the joke, and remained unmoved.

That night, instead of sleeping, Marandhan remained awake, and listened attentively in order to discover whether any symptoms indicated that his fat friend in the next cabin was about taking exercise upon deck. "What a pity she's so fat," thought he again to himself, as he lay awake, "with so handsome a face." The heavy breathing of his father assured him that he, as usual, had gone to sleep,—there was evidently no disturbance in his mind, respecting handsome faces, fat or otherwise. At length, just as Marandhan himself was dropping off to sleep, despite his watchfulness, the shutting of the door of the next cabin, which he distinctly heard, convinced him that some one was stirring. He left his mat-couch hastily, therefore, and, dressing himself without loss of time, made his way upon deck. There they were, every one of them, quietly pacing the deck, but so softly and noiselessly that the slightest sleeper below could not have been disturbed. It is not the custom of Budhists to conceal their females thus, and it was, therefore, quite inexplicable to Marandhan why Thatwhang should act so,—hence another cause of curiosity, besides his interest in the handsome face. Yes, there was no mistake about it, Thatwhang, with his short muscular figure was there, and two dreamy-looking female figures in strange costumes beside him. The Hindoo sailors were lying lazily about in the fore part of the ship, and, save an Arab officer that was smoking near the steersman, and the steersman himself, the Burmese party and Marandhan, were the sole occupants of the quarter-deck. It was a bright starlight night, but there was no moon, nor would there be for hours, long ere which Marandhan concluded the ladies would have retired.

Marandhan, too, began to walk the quarter-deck, and, as he passed Thatwhang, who was by the side of the two ladies, he saluted him in a friendly way, with the usual greeting, "Peace be with you!"

Thatwhang grunted out an acknowledgment, that was not very intelligible and passed on. Marandhan did not heed that, however, but occupied himself in inspecting the female figures as they passed. They were both nearly of the same height, both dressed alike, both so closely muffled with veils that no glimpse of their features, in the moonless night, could be obtained. One, however, she who walked beside Thatwhang, was evidently stout—"the handsome fat woman," thought Marandhan. The other was much thinner, but nothing of her figure could be distinguished.

"The moon will not rise for some hours," observed Marandhan, as he passed Thatwhang again.

"Not for four hours," growled the Burmese.

"Bear of a Chino-Malay," exclaimed Marandhan to himself, as he passed on.

Arrived near the steersman, however, he stopped, and addressed some observations to the Arab officer, who courteously replied to him—Thatwhang approached again.

"We shall probably be within sight of Ceylon in four or five days more," said Marandhan to him.

"Very probably," said Thatwhang, as he wheeled round with his fair companions, to walk forward again.

"What did you say?" asked Marandhan, stepping after him, and walking by his side.

"I merely said, probably," said Thatwhang.

"O, indeed," continued Marandhan, "yes, the Captain told me to-day, he should not at all wonder if we sighted Dondera Head in four days, that is, if the wind holds, but of course all depends upon that. If there were any change or interruption, it would be a different matter altogether."

"Would it?" asked the imperturbable Burmese, increasing his speed.

"Of course," argued Marandhan, increasing his, likewise. "You see, if the wind changed, we might be driven to the north or south, or even east again, which would carry us far away from our course."

"Indeed," was Thatwhang's only reply.

"However," continued Marandhan, "it's fortunate there is not much danger of that. At this season of the year, they say, the monsoon is very steady and unchanging."

"Do they?" said Thatwhang, drily, and then turning round to his companions, they stood still and he addressed some words to them in Burmese.

"I trust," said Marandhan, boldly, "I shall not be the means of depriving the ladies of their walk. If so, I shall return to my cabin this moment."

"By no means," said a sweet musical voice that issued from "the handsome fat one," as Marandhan called her to himself—"by no means, we shall merely walk together on the other side, whilst you and my husband walk on this."

"Not on my account, Madam," said Marandhan, to whom the prospect of a private conference with Thatwhang was infinitely more disagreeable than returning to bed, "no, certainly not, it would be unpardonable in me to disturb your family arrangements. How fortunate we have been in getting so quiet and well-ordered a ship!"

"Very," began the handsome fat one," but ere she had time for another word, Thatwhang interposed, "We have already kept you long enough out of your bed, won't my honoured friend Nagasena be expecting you?"

"He sleeps by himself," said Marandhan, "and if you remain quiet for a moment, you will most probably hear him snoring, as only a priest can snore."

The ladies laughed, and Thatwhang instantly replied—"Your observation savours of irreverence, Sir; the priesthood should not be made an object of ridicule."

"By the canine-tooth of the ever-blessed Gotama," said Marandhan, sternly, "I meant no impiety. It's no sin, surely, to say that a priest snores when he *does* snore. I can hear Nagasena from this. Listen."

"There is irreverence in your words and manner, young man," said Thatwhang, gravely; "it is to me like eating sour mangoes to hear you talk."

"I am sorry to hear it," replied Marandhan; "but doubtless you will find the mangoes sweeter if you talk yourself. Peace be with you; adieu, and you madam, and you."

So, turning on his heel, he made his way into the cabin. "That's his wife," thought he to himself; "well, he need not be so jealous of her I'm sure—she's fat enough to prevent jealousy." Before many minutes had elapsed he was fast asleep, dreaming that a fat Burmese, with bright black eyes, was asking him if he would purchase his wife.

But although Marandhan professed to himself to be perfectly satisfied with what he had seen and heard of the Thatwhang family, he still, in reality, longed to be better acquainted with them. The wife's face was undoubtedly a handsome one, and if the thinner lady, and as he had already persuaded himself, the younger one, were daughter to the stouter, there was little doubt that she too must then be handsome. "But then I'm to be a priest," thought he, as he reflected over the matter next morning, "what can it matter to me whether she is handsome or not? Heigh ho! I wish it were not so, but it can't be helped now; however, I'll see them at all events." Accordingly, about the same time as he had previously observed the lady talking to the servant, having left Thatwhang in conversation on deck with his father, he went softly below, and, to his great joy, found the door of the cabin containing the interesting family open. A curtain appeared to divide it into two apartments, and as he passed, a youthful, graceful, and elastic figure appeared from within the curtain, and called "Quatchee;" now Quatchee was the name of the Burmese female servant that attended on the family, and the impression of the young lady, as she looked out, evidently was that the person advancing was Quatchee—hence her appearance.

"Your servant is not here," said Marandhan, gallantly; "shall I call her?"

Before giving any answer, the young lady spoke in Burmese, and was answered from behind the curtain by the same voice that Marandhan had heard the night before, during which interval he felt himself unable to detach his eyes from the beautiful form and face before him.

"I fear I trouble you much," she answered, at length, "but if your goodness prompts you to undertake the mission, I shall be obliged."

There was no excuse for staring longer, so Marandhan turned on his heel to seek Quatchee.

"As handsome as the other," thought he, as he walked forward, "and without the fat, too. I certainly never saw a woman's face that was perfect before, for Belinda was only a child after all."

"Quatchee will attend the light of the morning presently," said he, as he returned and found the young lady still standing near the door.

"Your Excellency—" she replied, in Singhalese, which, to the young Kandian was all the more attractive, because broken and imperfect, "your Excellency has taken too much trouble, and I am thankful."

At this moment the elder lady made her appearance, and also thanked him for his kindness. He was preparing a speech full of compliment and devotion, when the wrinkled old Quatchee brushed by him, and shut the door after her, leaving him staring at it as if he could see through it,—not distant more than a yard's length. It was not a blessing that he murmured upon Quatchee, as he entered his own cabin, and threw himself upon his couch.

"A priest, a priest," he muttered, "and so

much elegance, so much grace, so much beauty in the world that I might perhaps be possessed of. I'll *not* be a priest—my oath was extorted from me, and if it holds good I'll be a Christian or a Hindu or a Mohammedan. I'll *not* be a priest, and I'll go and tell my father so this instant—he can but have me excommunicated."

So saying, he rushed out of the cabin, and made his way, agitated and excited, rapidly upon deck. The cool breeze fanned his forehead as he emerged from the companion-ladder and saw his father looking out upon the sea at the ship's stern, with his back towards him. "Are you mad?" whispered reason to him, as he rapidly strode forwards and faced his father's countenance, so placid when composed—so terrible in anger.

"Well, Marandhan?" asked Baddoola, quietly, as his son thus rudely interrupted his reverie.

"I—I fear I disturb you," said the young man, his resolution oozing out of every pore, as he looked deep into the dark eye of the chief.

"No," said his father; "what is it?"

"There was a huge shark at that side of the vessel just now. I never saw so large a one before," replied Marandhan, blushing at the falsehood, and mortified at his own want of determination.

"Is that all?" said Baddoola, turning round, "where?"

They looked for the monster for some time in vain; no one had seen it.

"Nevertheless," muttered Marandhan to himself, as he walked off, "I will *not* be a priest."

Again and again, on many days, did he go past the cabin that contained so much hidden beauty within, but the envious door was not open, nor did the lovely form make its appearance. Fortune favoured him, however, before the conclusion of the voyage. A few days before they arrived at Colombo, Thatwhang was confined to his bed, and having had an unoccupied cabin at the side prepared for him, removed thither, giving up the stern cabin altogether to his wife and daughter. The second day that he was thus compelled to abstain from going on deck, Baddoola, for whom the merchant had the highest esteem, and Thatwhang himself, were closeted alone for some time—mysteriously as Marandhan conceived—and the result of the conference was, that, on that very night, after they had retired to rest as usual, Baddoola arose, —Marandhan diligently watching him, whilst he pretended to be asleep,—and escorted the two ladies to the deck.

In a few minutes he was joined by Marandhan,

who observed, as he came up with the party, "Then you are not ill?"

"No," said his father; "my respected friend, Thatwhang, merely asked me to walk with his family this evening, as he was prevented by illness."

Marandhan took his place by the side of the daughter, and walked for some time in silence, listening to a learned discourse of his father's upon merit and demerit, and their influence on future existence.

There was not room for the four to walk comfortably abreast, and by degrees the two parties became separated, the younger couple falling behind the elder.

"My name is Marandhan Modliar of Ceylon," said he. "May I beg to know the name of the fair star of the morning?"

"My name is Zeefa," said she, in the soft, musical tones that had already captivated the young man's attention, "and I have lived with my father, Thatwhang, nearly all my life in Rangoon."

"And the pride of Burmah, who walks with the priest, is your mother? Pardon the curiosity of a stranger;—when the heart is full, why try and stop the mouth?"

"Sardee is my mother," she answered, "but she is not of Burmah originally. Her mother was an infidel of Circassia, her father a Mussulman of Northern India—she forsook her religion and her home in youth for Thatwhang."

"What power can keep the dove's mate from her consort? Where love draws the distance is soon past," said Marandhan, with all that Oriental warmth and poetic licence which rose naturally to his lips.

"What can the eagle know of the feelings of the bulbul, or the priest of love?" she asked.

"I am not a priest," he replied, hastily.

"But you have sworn to be a priest, and intend to be one," she argued.

"Yes—no—yes," he stammered forth, whilst his frame was agitated with contending emotions. "Listen, Zeefa, and I will tell you all."

"Marandhan," said his father, turning round at the moment, "the lady would visit her husband; conduct her to Thatwhang."

"Would that her fat ladyship had postponed her visit," growled Marandhan to himself, as he handed her down the companion-ladder. When he returned his father was pacing the deck beside the fascinating Zeefa, and there was no opportunity on that night for making the disclosure he wished—

No opportunity on that night, nor on other similar nights, for, manœuvre as he would, Sardee and he invariably walked together for the future, both Baddoola and she determined apparently that there should be no mutual confidence between the young people. Nor did this circumstance add to Marandhan's amiability, as he walked the deck with "the handsome fat one," and every night as he went to bed he muttered "she grows fatter and uglier every day," and Sardee, doubtless, on her part, thought what a disagreeable young man that was, and how much his conversation belied his appearance. So it is, indeed, ever in life,—where there is no desire to please and to be pleased there is no pleasure—seen through green spectacles all the world is green.

Before they landed at Colombo, Thatwhang was up again, and able to enjoy his usual walks, the attendance of Marandhan and his father at night being dispensed with, and, except by an occasional glance, Marandhan had no opportunity of telling Zeefa how truly and how fondly he loved her, and how ready he was to give up, not himself only and his future life to her, but his father and the priesthood also. She received such glances without displeasure, nay, the young man flattered himself with pleasure rather; and, as he curled his black moustache and whiskers and beard, all growing luxuriantly, like the jungle of his native island under a tropical sun, he thought that perhaps after all it was not so wonderful that she should be pleased, and, further, that it would be a great pity to lose, under any circumstances, the aforesaid curling moustache, whiskers, and beard.* Nor were these looks so unintelligible to Zeefa as might at first be supposed. Where there is so little intercourse between the sexes as is usually the case in the East before marriage, the eye often takes the place of the tongue, and the Egyptian or the Chinese belle will easily translate a glance into a sentiment, and a few reciprocal glances into a dialogue. She puts more trust too in such telegraphic signals than her fairer sister of the West in the most violent protestations; so that ere the good ship,—the "Fazeel Careem,"—had borne her freight safe into the roadstead of Colombo, Zeefa felt convinced, on her side, that this young noble loved her, and was ready to sacrifice then, at all events, his chances in the priesthood for her hand.

"We must go to Kandy at once," said Baddoola, as they left the vessel, "that you may ratify there your oath respecting the priesthood." Marandhan said nothing, but thought much.

An agent of Thatwhang's had taken a house for him in the vicinity of Colombo, near a village

* The Budhist priests shave the head and face completely in Ceylon.

called Galkisse. So much Marandhan learned, and no more; nor could he ever find an opportunity of saying adieu to the fair Zeefa. On the road to Kandy then they went, no time being lost in useless delays in Colombo; horses and palanquins, and the usual retinue, forming their party as before. Marandhan's mind was made up; he determined that he would not go to Kandy to ratify his oath; on the contrary, that he would go back to Colombo, and, if possible, renew his acquaintance with Zeefa. He wished, however, to avoid an open rupture with his father, for he knew not to what lengths Baddoola's violent temper might impel him, did he openly declare that he would not go to Kandy. Having made presents to their escort of opium, on the second day of the journey, he resolved to put his scheme into execution that very night. They occupied the house of a wealthy native, who, at this period, was in Colombo with his family, and, accordingly, their own servants were the only ones about in such numbers as to give him any annoyance; but as there was no suspicion of his intention entertained, the probability is that he exaggerated the difficulty.

Stealing out, then, when his father and the attendants were asleep, he left the house behind him, and tramped vigorously back towards Colombo in the clear moonshine, taking nothing with him but the clothes he wore, and the stock of money he had obtained on landing in Colombo. For some distance he went on foot; but, meeting a Pegu pony in a shed by the road's side, he made a bridle of his halter, leaped upon his back, and rode furiously to the West. The pony had all the mettle of his race, and, with the exception of half an hour's halt to refresh both parties, bore him, ere the sun had risen more than an hour the next morning, to the Kalany River, in the vicinity of Colombo. Here he bribed a poor man to take the animal back during the ensuing night, and leave him in the vicinity of the shed, whilst he continued his route to the native town of Colombo, or the Pettah, as it is called, on foot.

He was wearied with the violent exertion and fatigue he had undergone, and, in a Mohammedan tavern, where his money made him welcome, he slept during the greater part of the day. In the evening he sallied forth to find a temporary home for himself in the neighbourhood of Galkisse, in which he succeeded without much difficulty or delay, for the Governor of Ceylon was building a veritable palace in the neighbourhood, on a hill jutting out into the sea, called by its European possessors Mount Lavinia, and houses of all kinds were fast springing up in consequence around.

He took care also to write to the Government Agent in Kandy relative to his property, of which he would soon be entitled to claim possession, and asking him to remit to Colombo the arrears of the annual allowance left him by Colonel Carroll, who, he found, had sailed some months ago for England.

Of his father he heard and saw nothing for some time,—his sudden disappearance, so secret and unforeseen, putting Baddoola completely at fault; and it was not until some time after the agency of that wide-spread secret police, the priesthood, had been set in motion by Gatro, that he was discovered.

Having found out Thatwhang's house, Marandhan, like a skilful general, proceeded to reconnoitre it leisurely, determined to have an interview with Zeefa before he formally mentioned the matter to Thatwhang himself. The house was situated in the middle of a garden, which was completely surrounded by a wall of no great height; and as the merchant now felt secure, he was proportionately less cautious in secluding his wife and daughter—permitting them to drive out as they listed in a close carriage, and to walk in the garden as much as they pleased, whilst he was at his mercantile office in the Fort.

For several days did Marandhan go to the

garden regularly, watching an opportunity when he might speak to Zeefa alone. Often did he see her and her mother walking together; but he muttered to himself that he had enough of the fat one, and wished for her society no more. At length their visits to the garden were discontinued altogether for a time; and, although the young man suspected the cause, yet he was not certain of it until he had bribed a Singhalese servant engaged in the house to inform him. He was quite correct in his anticipations. Sardee had been confined,—and a boy, to Thatwhang's great delight, had been added to the establishment. From the same servant he learned also that several of Sardee's children had died in infancy, and that the handsome Zeefa was the only one alive.

At length the wished-for opportunity occurred. Zeefa resumed her daily walk in the garden, and now, without her mother. Marandhan would never have tired, he thought, of contemplating her, and described with enthusiasm her appearance on that important day. She was just approaching womanhood—the fair rounded outlines of maturity gradually replacing the angularities of adolescence. A pair of wide trousers, covered with a short skirt, formed the lower portion of her dress, whilst the outline of the bust was distinctly shown by a tight-fitting boddice of richly ornamented muslin. Her arms were naked from the elbow, and disclosed those rounded, firm, delicately-muscular proportions, which are seldom seen in perfection in the North. Her skin was fair, for the tropics, not darker, indeed, than that of many Spanish brunettes; and her finely proportioned features such as a Grecian artist would have immortalized in his Venus. Her large black eyes floated deliciously in a watery light, and were shaded with long eye-lashes,—both in keeping with the masses of black clustering hair, which, although simply braided on the forehead, fell thickly on the shoulders in wavy masses, from beneath the veil which shaded, but did not hide, the head.

As she entered a walk at the extremity of the garden, concealed by thick bushes of cinnamon from the observation of the house, Marandhan stood before her, and, with a cry of surprise, which did not sound unjoyfully in his ears, she welcomed him.

"O, Marandhan," she cried chidingly, "why seek me again, to your own and to my evil? You have sworn to be a priest; Zeefa, therefore, and you should avoid, not seek, each other. Unless, indeed, your eyes have spoken falsely, and instead of loving me, you do but mock me."

"Far from it, Zeefa," he cried; "the oath

which I swore to become a priest was extorted unwillingly from me by Nagasena. I never wished to bury myself in a wihare. I am a noble of Ceylon, with an hereditary estate to order and control, and I never will be a priest."

"Your guilt will be fearful," said she. "I pity you."

"If Zeefa loves me," he continued, "I care nothing for guilt or obloquy;—the lion does not more joyfully undertake the contest with the leopard than I with the disesteem of others, if Zeefa only loves me."

"Alas, Marandhan!" said she, "would that we had never met. I saw and loved you some days e'er you had seen me. My eyes have too plainly told you that, and they do not lie; but Zeefa prefers death to shame."

Marandhan would have replied, with all the gallantry of which he was master, to this heroic speech; but before it had concluded, short as it was, a hoarse voice, which he compared to the sharpening of a saw, called out the young lady's name. It was Quatchee; Marandhan knew the voice but too well, and had scarcely time to take his beloved Zeefa into his arms and imprint one luscious kiss upon her lips, when they heard steps, as if a gigantic goose with shoes on (such was his simile) was coming down the walk. The young man remained concealed behind the cinnamon bushes, whilst Zeefa walked forward, glowing with love, and shame, and pleasure, to meet the importunate old monster.

Marandhan felt happier than he had been for a long time as he walked to his temporary home that day—happy in his love, happy in his own resolution, happy in the bright anticipation of much happiness to come. "Now for Thatwhang," thought he, as he crossed the threshold of his room.

The tall figure of a priest, whose countenance Marandhan knew but too well to be that of his father, rose as he entered.

CHAPTER X.

MARANDHAN'S HISTORY CONCLUDED.

> "Love bade me swear—love bids me to forswear;
> O sweet suggestive love, if thou hast sinned,
> Teach me, thy tempted subject, to excuse it."
>
> *Two Gentlemen of Verona*, act ii., sc. 6.

HIS father was in his apartment when Marandhan returned from the interview with Zeefa, in which she had declared her love, and inferentially expressed her willingness to become a Modliar's wife. Every one has observed, doubtless, how suddenly a dark cloud often obscures the brightest sunshine, and discharges itself in deluges of rain upon the earth. Everything that was bright, and glowing with light before, droops or looks gloomy at once. Happy faces are changed at once into anxious ones, and light joyous airs into those of hurry and anxiety. By such a simile was it that Marandhan expressed to me the change which passed over him when he saw his father rising at his entrance. He had been all happiness and joyful anticipation before, but this sudden apparition damped his gladness, and turned back his bright feelings upon his heart in gloom and the darkest shade.

" Marandhan," said his father, as the young man entered, "am I to welcome you as a son returning to his duty, or to curse you as a renegade from his religion and the cause of his country? Speak, and deceive me no more. The jackal is not more false and treacherous in his alliance with the lion, than you have been to me."

" Nagasena Wahansc," said Marandhan, "even the deer that has been baited will turn upon its pursuers, and I, anxious to love and obey you, am yet forced to speak the words of undutifulness and disobedience."

" Am I to understand, boy," asked his father, threateningly, "that you now dare to tell me you are resolved to oppose me, and to break the oath you solemnly swore on the altar of Budha, before the high priest of Ava? Has the degeneracy of Ceylon come to this, that a son of Baddoola should declare himself not only an apostate from his creed, but even an enemy to his country?"

" The dove is not truer to her mate than I will be both to my religion and my country," replied Marandhan.

"Then you will fulfil your oath?" said his father.

"No, Nagasena Wahanse, I will not fulfil an oath extorted from me by fraud and forced upon me by violence. I will live and die free, as a Kandian Modliar should."

The expression of his father's face became dark and threatening as Marandhan boldly uttered these words, and the young man feared that the interview would not terminate without some fatal issue, but he resolved, for his part, not to oppose his father by force, and if he attempted his destruction to offer no resistance.

"Extorted by fraud," muttered the furious priest; "forced upon you by violence. You lie, dog—in your throat you lie! Free, saidst thou! Free!—how canst thou live free with British lords for thy masters, whose slightest wish thou must obey. False, perjured, spiritless boy!"

"I am thy son," said Marandhan, "and will not revile thee. These British lords that thou hatest so have taught me so much good. I was told that I was to take the oath in Rangoon, not in Ava; I was taken unawares, suddenly, in the midst of a host of priests. It might have been death had I disobeyed. There were fraud and violence both in it. I intended to tell thee that I would not be a priest before the oath was actually required. Would you take the unwilling by stratagem, shave his crown, and put on the yellow robes? Would that make a man a priest? Where the mind is not hallowed, what holiness or sanctity can there be in the outward garb or appearance?"

Baddoola appeared to listen to his remonstrance more calmly than he had anticipated, and asked him fearfully and huskily, after a pause—

"Thou sayest that thou art true to thy creed and to thy country. How canst thou be true if thou art not willing to give up all for them?"

"I am willing to give up my property," began the young man,—but he was fiercely interrupted.

"*Thy* property, unmannered slave of the white faces!—thine, how thine?"

"Mine by the present law," said Marandhan, "but yours in every respect besides. If the giving up of that can soften your anger it is yours to enjoy, nor shall I touch a pice of the revenue. You can devote it to the restoration of Kandian independence if you will. Me you can command, and I will act as you please to promote the same object. What more can you desire? But a priest I will not be?"

"I care not for the priesthood," said his father, vehemently, "I care only for my country; but the priesthood alone can know our secrets, and to join us effectually you must join the priesthood. Why will you not be a priest?"

"Because I will not take a holy office upon me with an unsanctified heart," replied Marandhan, boldly; "because I will not mock our faith by professing to renounce the world when my soul clings to it."

"Is that all?" asked his father.

"That is all," was the reply.

"Then matters may be arranged. The priesthood can do all things. You love some one?"

"I do," said Marandhan.

"And you would have her?"

"I would."

"It shall be done, then, if she be not a European, for that might blast our enterprise."

"She is Zeefa, the daughter of Thatwhang, the Burmese," said Marandhan.

"Good. It can be done. Zeefa shall be taken to Plapla, in the forests of Rohona. She shall be yours for a year. Will you *then* become a priest, —when the year expires?" asked his father.

"I would die rather than suffer violence to be used towards her. Shame, shame! your project is infamous!" exclaimed Marandhan.

Baddoola scowled fiercely. The muscles of his face became distorted with violent rage. His eyes glared upon his son like those of a tiger, and his whole frame seemed agitated with sudden convulsions.

"Then, die, wretch!" he exclaimed, as he drew a dagger from his girdle, and rushed forwards; but before he had reached Marandhan, who stood motionless against the wall, the infuriated priest fell heavily, the dagger sheathing itself in his son's leg, and a torrent of blood issuing from his mouth. He had burst a bloodvessel in his fury, and now lay dying at his son's feet. Help came, but was of no avail. The fatal tide could not be staunched, and in a few minutes the form that had been the rallying point of Kandian conspiracy,—the life of the secret workers for Kandian independence,—was a helpless corpse.

It was some weeks before Marandhan could walk abroad, in consequence of his wound—weeks of gloom and sorrow, of sadness, misery, and almost of despair. Bodily pain and mental distress combined to prostrate him utterly, and it was not without the keenest anguish that he reflected that his father had died with a curse instead of a blessing for him on his lips. But reflection and a powerful mind came to his rescue. He knew that he had not been wrong in his convictions and determination, and that, however anxious to obey his father, compliance, in such a case, would have been criminality.

There is no healer of the crushed heart like time, however;—a sorry reflection truly, even under the best of circumstances, implying much that is ignoble everyway in our composition. Day after day brought its balm to heal Marandhan's wounded soul, and in a few months his warm hopes and earnest aspirations after happiness were rekindled, and illumined him internally and externally as before. He thought again, and thought much, too, of Zeefa, and now that his father was dead, and he wanted but a few days to be of age and claim his property, he saw no reason why he should not speedily conduct his beloved Circassian-Burmese to his jungle home.

He called boldly, therefore, upon Thatwhang, making as much display as possible, and resolved to act the superior rather than the inferior in his subsequent communications with him. Thatwhang did not know him at first, and dazzled by his badge of nobility, received him with great respect.

"You probably forget, Thatwhang Appoohamy," * he began, "the young man who accompanied you from Rangoon in the *Fazeel Careem*—I am he."

"I remember Marandhan Modliar well," replied Thatwhang; "the young man who was under the guardianship of my respected friend Naga-

* *Appoohamy* is equivalent to Mr., a common title of respect.

sena Wahanse, who died suddenly lately; the young man who had sworn in the great pagoda of Ava to be a priest."

"I was inveigled into that oath against my consent," replied Marandhan; "it was never my wish to become a priest, and to prove to you that I have no desire now to be one, I come to solicit your daughter Zeefa in marriage. I saw her during the voyage, and we loved each other. If she consents to the match, surely you will not refuse my offer."

"*She* consent," said Thatwhang, indignantly, "what has *she* to do with it? Ha! ha! good, very good! We are to ask our daughters, leave to marry them, are we, now adays! Marandhan Modliar, my daughter is not for you, she is engaged already. It is not likely that she should grow almost to womanhood, without being betrothed. Her husband is in Calcutta, and is the head there of a very respected house, my friend Meersham."

"Meersham," said Marandhan, "why I have heard the name ever since I could hear anything. Who does not know the house of Meersham and Thisthat?"

"Who, indeed?" asked Thatwhang.

"And how old may Meersham be?" asked Marandhan.

"Not more than fifty, I should say," replied Thatwhang, "but what has that to do with it? He is my friend—the head of an excellent house—a good Budhist and a rich man. What can any girl want more?"

"And do you fancy, Appoohamy, that Zeefa will like such a husband?" asked the young man, soothingly, and yet earnestly.

"Do I fancy—what a question—yes, of course I do. You might have asked me, am I sure of it with more reason—of course I am," replied the stolid Burmese, grinning so as to display a shining set of teeth that seemed to stretch from ear to ear, as the large mouth distended.

"Thatwhang," asked Marandhan, again, "will you be guided by reason and wisdom?"

"Will a child eat sugar, or a young man deceive a virgin?—Of course I will," was the reply.

"Then be guided by Zeefa's choice between us. I am a noble: my property is ample; my family traces back its pedigree to the time of Prackramabahu the great. If you can make your daughter happy, why not do so? Ask her, Appoohamy, and be guided by her choice."

So urged Marandhan. Thatwhang looked at him as if he doubted whether the young man could be serious, and then burst into a roar of laughter.

"Be guided by *her* choice," he echoed, "ha, ha! Reason and wisdom in truth. Did you ever see bread-fruit growing on a upas tree, or hear of wisdom issuing from a young maiden's lips? You joke with me, my friend, but let me assure you I like your joke; it's the best I have heard for a long time. Wisdom truly, ha, ha!"

"Laugh at me if you will, Appoohamy," said Marandhan, blandly, "yet surely it is not so strange to ask you to consult her whose happiness or misery is to result from your resolution. Be advised, I pray you,—ask her?"

"Ask her what?" said Thatwhang, peevishly.

"Whether she will have the Calcutta merchant, Meersham, or the Kandian noble, Marandhan," urged the youth.

"By the collar-bone of the ever-blessed Gotama, but it is too absurd," said Thatwhang, laughing again, as he rose to go into an inner room, probably with the intention of carrying out the joke, "but," said he, as he turned again and reseated himself, "what's the use of asking? She has never seen Meersham, and she has seen you. Any woman would prefer the man she has seen to the one she has not, if she have any sense at all. O no, it's no use, it's too absurd," he concluded, as he sank back upon his couch.

"And what is your objection to me?" asked Marandhan.

"My objection to you, young man," said Thatwhang, gravely, "why many objections. It is not only because the crow is black that the dove avoids it. You are not a merchant. You are irreverent. You swore to become a priest in the great pagoda of Ava, and you do not intend to keep your oath."

"I have told thee the oath was extorted from me—stolen unawares," urged Marandhan, warmly, "why then will you mention it again? If I am rich enough, what does it matter whether I am a merchant or not? and there is not a more fervent believer in Budhism than I am,—how then can I be irreverent? Bethink thee, Appoohamy, why give your daughter to one that may not value her as I should? Why make her miserable, perhaps for her whole life, from an idle whim of your own?"

"Rateel," shouted Thatwhang, calling a servant, as he walked away, "see if the Modliar's carriage is in waiting, and show him to it. Peace be with you, Modliar,—adieu."

"Zeefa shall be mine in spite of you and Meersham," muttered Marandhan, as he left the house.

He kept his word, too. Thatwhang had evidently no idea of the perfect understanding that subsisted between his daughter and the young Modliar, and his frequent absences at his office afforded the best possible opportunities for Marandhan to communicate with the loving maid, and to plan measures for their departure together. Nor was the vigilance of Quatchee, who acted as much in the capacity of duenna as of servant, equal to the ingenuity of the youthful couple. As there seemed no probability of Zeefa's marriage with Meersham being celebrated speedily, Marandhan did not spoil his measures, and frustrate his schemes, by being too impatient. In fact, until he took possession of his property,—that on which he now resides,—he had no home to which to take the fair Zeefa, and he therefore prudently resolved to defer her abduction for the few days still remaining; to go to Kandy, enter upon the possession of his estate, and the funds which had been so long accumulating; and then, having fitted out his new home in a way worthy of the reception of such a treasure, to bear off his bride to it in triumph.

This prudent course of conduct he successfully carried out. The British Court of Justice in Kandy put him formally in possession of his estate without delay. A large sum was paid over to him in ready money, the revenue of the property, with interest, from his twelfth to his twenty-first year, and he was received by the peasantry on his estate with unbounded enthusiasm. There was much to be done in repairing the house, much in the improvement of the gardens and grounds, but he could only wait on the present occasion to make the place habitable, and kept his further improvements for future leisure.

Returning to Colombo then, where he invested the money for which he had no immediate use, and where he had now a host of friends, willing to help him in anything he desired, he concocted measures with Zeefa for her abduction. Her mother and she were accustomed to drive through the neighbouring district daily in a palanquin carriage. She would not venture, however, to break her design to Sardee, whose reverence and fear for Thatwhang were too great to permit her to sanction, much less to aid, her flight. The ingenuity of Zeefa, however, was quite as great as that of young ladies generally is, and surely there have been few of them, whether Oriental or Occidental, who have found much difficulty in deceiving their mammas, particularly in the affairs of the heart,—affairs in which deception of every kind is too often looked upon as venial, if not as perfectly natural and unblamable.

At an appointed time, therefore, when everything was prepared, Zeefa drove out alone, the carriage having been previously packed by a servant, bribed to accompany her, with what clothes and ornaments she most valued or required. In order to lull suspicion, the servant who was to accompany her, at first remained behind, but subsequently came running after the vehicle, stating that by Sardee's orders *he* was to attend the young lady, and the ordinary *syce*, or groom was to return. Thus with a coachman ignorant of what was intended, and with a servant behind apprized of all, and ready to carry through the whole affair with Oriental duplicity, Zeefa drove off,— her eyes bathed in tears at the prospect of thus deserting her mother, whom she loved as a daughter ought,—but her heart fluttering with love and joyful anticipation at being the bride of the Kandian noble. By the new attendant's directions the carriage drove to the house of a friend of Marandhan, who was there eagerly awaiting her. Here it was intended the betrothal should take place; and the family, in the midst of which Zeefa now found herself, had everything prepared for the purpose.

One aged friend personated the father of the bride, another the father of Marandhan, and by these were set forms of words repeated, intimating that these youths did here lawfully and legitimately pledge themselves to matrimony at a future day when the stars should be propitious, and the devoes (Budhistic spirits) willing; that, in consideration of this betrothal, and as witnesses of it, presents were here exchanged; and that, at some future period, the betrothed parties should proclaim themselves husband and wife to their friends.

Taking Zeefa then by the hand, Marandhan led her to a couch at the upper end of the room, where, as they seated themselves before the assembled guests, he called upon them to witness how gladly he received her from her father to be the wife of his home, and the mother of his children. A dish of curry was next presented to them, from which each ate a portion—an action symbolical of the nominal equality between the two, and of the putting away of all pretensions of superiority on either side; in a word, of her being his *wife*, and not his *mistress*. They then drank from the same goblet, presented together some flowers upon the temporary altar of Budha prepared for the purpose, and were hailed by the few friends assembled on the occasion as legitimately espoused. True, the marriage rites were yet to be celebrated; but these as often succeed as precede their occupation of the same house;

and as the betrothal must precede the marriage at least a month, everything was done on this occasion that could have been done.

Whilst the comedy within was being performed, another was enacting without. Long ere the ceremony had reached its conclusion, the coachman was fast asleep upon his box, according to the invariable rule of all Asiatic and some European coachmen when detained for a time. The wardrobe of Zeefa was quietly taken out; and whilst Marandhan and his bride were preparing for their departure, the servant slammed the door and mounted behind, shouting out to the coachman to drive on quietly by a circuitous road home. The coachman seized his reins, fancying his young mistress was within, the horses started off, and in a minute the empty palanquin carriage was gone, the servant slipping from behind to assist and accompany Zeefa. Another carriage was speedily at the door, into which Marandhan led his bride, radiant with love and beauty; a female attendant was upon the box, and everything prepared for her comfort and entertainment. The carriage was soon exchanged, however, for saddle-horses, upon which they made their way to a house in the jungle, where they were to spend the night, and which, from its seclusion and the unfrequented character of its locality promised security and comfort. The next morning they renewed their journey, still shunning the high road, travelling away to the base of Adam's Peak, and so, by the forest paths, —sometimes by means of palanquins, sometimes on horseback,—to the neighbourhood of Ruminacaddee where the cultivators of his estate were awaiting their young lord and his bride, in anxious expectation of the presents which must accompany their nuptials.

In the mean time, Thatwhang spared no exertions to discover the fugitives, but in vain. They had had an entire day's start of him, and, as he fancied they would certainly be on the road to Kandy, his search proved fruitless. The lapse of a few months, however, restored his equanimity, and, after Zeefa had written several penitent and affectionate letters, in which she strongly urged how miserable she would have been with Meersham, who was fifty years of age, and how happy she was with Marandhan, who was only twenty-one, she received, at length, a short and business-like epistle from him, stating that he was in receipt of her letters of such and such dates, stating so and so, that it was his intention to visit her soon according to her invitation, and that her mother, whose letter was enclosed, had written more fully.

Since then, with the exception of occasional journeys to Colombo, and one trip on business to Madras, Marandhan has lived constantly on the property on which he now resides—books and agriculture his delights and employment—he and Zeefa leading a happy and an useful life, in the education of their children, (some of whom have already attained maturity,) and in the management of their property. Thatwhang died a few years afterwards, of grief, it was supposed, at the failure of a speculation in which he had embarked half his property; his wife, the mother of Zeefa, however, still lives, residing with Marandhan, and now in all the childish harmlessness of extreme old age. The son who was born to her shortly after her arrival in the island, died in infancy, like the rest of her children, as did two others subsequently, so that Zeefa remained the sole possessor of her affection and esteem.

APPENDIX TO VOL. II.

FOUR DIALOGUES BETWEEN A BUDHIST AND A CHRISTIAN.

PREFATORY REMARKS.

THE conversations which I had with my Budhist friend Marandhan, on the first principles of religious philosophy, were interesting and beneficial to both of us. It is not until one has actually encountered an opponent on some particular point long since laid down in his own mind as settled, that he discovers how much there is to say on the opposite side, or how ingenious the arguments by which his tenets may be assailed or those of his adversary upheld. To the majority of Christians the idea of entering into an elaborate discussion to prove that there is a God, and that Budhism is false, may appear to be an absurdity; not so, however, to the inquiring mind that finds itself thrown into a Budhistic stronghold, and often assailed, without a chance of honourable escape, save by victory. In such a situation, he who would not root error more firmly in the minds of those around him, is forced to reconsider the foundations of his belief, to examine the position which his adversary has taken up with critical minuteness, to seek diligently for the weak and assailable points in that position, and, when they have been found, to batter away at them perseveringly and unremittingly. An intelligent Budhist is by no means the easily vanquished opponent, in an intellectual combat, that many would be disposed to believe; and it is not until he has opened his batteries upon the ramparts of Christianity, and been foiled, that he will permit himself to reconsider the entire question. For the inquiring mind, ready and willing to extend its researches beyond the limits of its own experience, I cannot help flattering myself that the following Dialogues will possess some interest, however poor the logical ability displayed by either combatant, or however limited the range of his reading and the scope of his reflections.

It has been argued that such conversations, on the highest and holiest of subjects, are out of place in a light and popular work like the present. I cannot discover the incongruity. In life itself, the serious and the playful, the grave and the merry, are so intermingled and combined that it is not always easy to separate them, or to prevent the association of ideas combining them together. Who has not felt again and again that a ludicrous incident will often accompany the profoundest and most serious convictions in the mind, and that too, in spite of every effort to the contrary and in diametrical opposition to the wishes of the individual? Life is made up of such incongruities, and a work therefore which professes, however feebly, to portray any phase of life, must contain, if it be faithful, examples of the good and of the bad, of the grave and of the gay, of the serious and of the jocose.

I must not be supposed to maintain that the most sacred and the most trivial matters should be constantly brought together, or that any amalgamation of them is desirable, or even tolerable. I maintain no such proposition. I merely argue that, as life is a collection of important and unimportant events, so far as our finite judgments can weigh them;—of thoughts holy and unholy passing through the mind and leaving their impress more or less vividly stamped upon it behind them;—of recollections, some invested with all the halo of sanctity and revered as sublime, whilst others are indissolubly associated with the ludicrous or the fantastic—as life is so strange a mixture, so odd a compound, so incomprehensible an enigma,—there can be nothing wrong in adding as an appendix to a collection of light sketches, professing to describe life, a few dialogues of a more serious and solemn character than the rest of the work—dialogues which the thoughtless will not trouble themselves to peruse, but which the more reflecting may possibly find worthy of their attention.

DIALOGUE I.

Persons.—MARANDHAN *and* KNIGHTON.

K. I was sorry to find, from our last conversation,* that you had little faith in modern science, to me one of the grandest facts, if not the grandest, of this nineteenth century in which we live. It forms, as I before urged, the great distinguishing feature between the civilization of the West and that of the East, and of course, in my opinion, the principal point of superiority in the former.

M. You mistake me. I do not pretend to condemn the accumulation of scientific facts respecting nature, or the investigations of modern students of nature. In so far as practical benefit is derived from these facts and investigations, every one must admit their utility and importance; but when you urged the mental advantage of these scientific inquiries, the influence they exercise on the human mind, as one point of superiority in the Western over the Eastern world, it was then, and then only, I ventured to differ from you, and subsequent reflection has but strengthened my impressions.

K. You astonish me. You admit the advantage of

* See vol. i. chapter v.

such speculations and investigations when practical benefit can be derived from them, or, I suppose, when man's labour is diminished, its effect increased, or some convenience supplied to him which he must otherwise do without. You admit these as benefits flowing from modern science, and you deny the far more ennobling, the far loftier results upon the human mind itself—the elevation of ideas, the expansion of thought, the unfolding of the world within, which must necessarily arise from a knowledge of the grand truths of physical science as cultivated at the present day.

M. I do so because I regard physical science, as at present cultivated, as essentially irreligious. I may not be supposed to know enough of that science to be competent to pronounce an opinion upon it at all, isolated as I am from all that is cultivated and polite,—but, if an attentive study of the best treatises, procurable by me, on astronomy, geology, and chemistry, if an earnest desire to arrive at truth, if an attempt long continued to understand nature by a study of the works of nature, can entitle me to give an opinion, I *am* competent to do so. Nothing that is irreligious can in my opinion be beneficial, whether it be merely a tendency or a dogmatic assertion, and hence my conviction. Religion teaches man that he is the great being of this world, for whom it was constructed, and whose origin and destiny are immutably bound up with those of the globe he inhabits; modern European science says "not so—man is but a link in a vast chain—the world has its destiny and origin totally apart from his, he is a mere cypher of a day compared with the eternity of the universe around him"—in fine, that he was made for the world, not the world for him.

K. I acknowledge the value of the religious sentiment in man as fully, and will maintain that opinion with as much tenacity, as you can do, but I see no opposition between it, when true and hallowed, and modern science. Your argument, in fact, amounts to this, that, starting with the idea that the peculiar religious system in which you believe is true, you will not admit anything that appears to you to militate against it in the slightest degree! You will excuse me asking is that a philosophic conviction? Would it not be more so to ask first, calmly and dispasionately, What is truth? and then say, every thing or any system that contradicts this truth must be falsehood,—and surely if one system does so, that is no reason why every system should.

M. There are certain points in which all religions agree, and these points go to form what you have designated, and happily so in my opinion, the religious sentiment. Having ascertained those points, and established those convictions in my mind, am I, then, inconsistent in denying the utility of a kind of knowledge which tends insidiously to upset those convictions, or to uproot those truths formerly ascertained? No. If physical science gives me no information respecting my destiny, but rather tends to throw a doubt on the truths of religion which does, assuredly I will not glory in it, or boast of it, but use it cautiously, as men do the lightning which they laboriously collect in jars, and which is waiting but the most trivial accident to cause their destruction. Shall I not cautiously deal out little by little, in the way and order I esteem best, the leading truths of this science to my children, and shall I not arrest, if I can, their indiscriminate promulgation amongst my fellow-countrymen, rather than promote it?

K. All truth must be harmonious. There can be no contradiction between one truth and another, although the one may belong to a science and the other to religion.

M. Unquestionably. But, seen dimly and partially by the rush-light glare of some presumptuous physical philosopher, may not one truth be made so to appear as to contradict another, and a more valuable one. May not the physical truth be so described as to convey a hint that the religious is a mockery,—just as Gibbon, in his history, loses no opportunity of leading the mind of his reader to condemn, despise, and reject Christianity? Is it not a fact, that, in proportion as intellectual eminence is claimed by any class of men, the religious sentiment in them appears to be obscured or eradicated, and that, relying on their physical science, which appeals to the senses, they become disposed to deny all that cannot be submitted to the same mathematical test? Was it not such cultivation that partly led to the irreligious tendencies of the French revolution?

K. I do not at all agree with you, but am not sure that I thoroughly understand you. You infer a seeming contradiction, if not a real one, between natural science and religious truth.

M. I do. Natural science is disjointed and partial, incomplete and unconnected, and appears to contradict some of the most universally received principles of religious faith in its present form. When the whole has been carefully elaborated, every part diligently investigated, and a grand harmonious *kosmos* of material science constructed, I doubt not that it will be found to form a beautiful portion of the great temple of religion, but we are far from that point yet, and hence its evils.

K. I begin now to understand and comprehend your ideas on the subject, shadowy and obscure to me before. You argue against natural science from its imperfections, and you believe that incorrect impressions respecting parts of it militate against religion and the religious sentiment generally. In other words, you argue from the abuse, not from the use, of that philosophy. In the same way the noblest convictions of humanity, nay, religion itself, might be condemned. Would you regard a spade, then, as a useless, dangerous weapon, because it had been used, on some occasions, to injure or destroy an adversary? or would you take a watch away from the man who could not explain its mechanism, but was thoroughly acquainted with its use?

M. Had I seen a spade frequently so applied, and seldom used for its legitimate purpose, I should be fully entitled to consider it a dangerous weapon; and did I find the owner of the watch falling into the most egregious errors, or injuring himself and his neighbours, by trusting it when it went wrong, or had stopped from want of winding, I should say he would be better without it.

K. I must then return to the simple dogmatic assertion, which discussion alone can enable us to judge of as true or false, that there is no contradiction between religion and physical science,—no opposition,—no clashing of principles or deductions,—no undermining of the one by the tenets of the other—that is, I mean between true religion and the sober philosophy of matter, thus excluding on the one side all religious systems but one, on the other all the wild vagaries which diseased imaginations have founded upon their jaundiced views of physical science.

M. I understand you. There may be opposition or contradiction, you would infer, between Budhism and natural philosophy, as cultivated in these our days, but none if Christianity be substituted. You want to put my religious faith upon its trial, and I am willing that it should be, for, from friendly and candid discussion such as ours, uninfluenced by passion or interest, nothing but good can result, and I should have but a poor opinion of Budhism if I feared its investigation. At the same time, without wishing to shift the assault from the Eastern to the Western faith, allow me to ask if such an opposition or contradiction, real or seeming, has not been felt in

Europe, why those elaborate works, which I have seen so frequently advertised, intended to demonstrate the harmony between geology and the Bible, why those astronomical discourses of Chalmers and others, to prove that astronomy and Christianity do *not* tell different tales or inculcate contradictory dogmas, why those defences of the Mosaic account of the creation, why those vindications of the Pentateuch, why those apologies for the Bible, why those analogies of religion, natural and revealed, with which the prolific press of England yearly teems?

K. The noblest instruments are abused in unskilful or malicious hands. Individual writers, many of them of great intellectual power, have wrested the truths of natural science into arguments against Christianity, just as Gibbon did history; and, in reply to such sophistical but often able productions, those that you have alluded to were rendered necessary, and notwithstanding the unhappy titles of many of them, such as the 'Apology for the Bible,' for instance—as if the Bible needed an *apology*—they will be found, for the most part, not only to prove conclusively a harmony, but an identity, between the teaching of the material world and of the spiritual, as interpreted by Christianity. The individual idiosyncracies or blindnesses of writers making a wrong use of their learning will not of course lead the judicious to any injurious conclusion with reference to the utility of that learning itself.

M. I acknowledge myself answered upon that single point, yet surely you will allow that the very number of these defences proves the extent to which modern science has been used as an instrument of attack.

K. I may safely do so, I conceive, without damaging the strength of my position. Intellectual pride or vanity, the affectation of novelty and superiority, a thousand circumstances, may induce a clever writer to devote his pen to attacking commonly received opinions; and, as the world takes everything unknown, or imperfectly known, for extraordinary, they could not find a weapon better suited to their purpose than the science so recently developed with such marvellous rapidity. Hence, in my opinion, the sooner this science becomes more generally known, the sooner will it be rendered useless as an assailant upon religious truth.

M. If so many, well skilled in its details, are ready and willing to use it so, is it not highly probable, that in increasing, in an arithmetical ratio, the number of its students, you are but increasing, in a geometrical, the number of the enemies of your faith?

K. This does not appear to me at all to follow, inasmuch as the novelty of the study and of the truths taught by it is hereby removed. Not to pursue this point further, however, at present, perhaps you will allow me to ask you a question or two about Budhism, respecting which my ideas are confused and unsatisfactory. I am the more emboldened to do so by your frank avowal that you have no objection to discuss its dogmas, and their relationship to modern science. Do you believe in the existence of a Deity or not?

M. In the Christian idea of a God we do *not* believe—that is, we have no faith in, or knowledge of, a self-existent first cause — immaterial, omnipotent, and eternal—from whom all things proceeded. We believe matter to be eternal as spirit, both subject to general laws by which they are ever changing, never at rest till perfect bliss and happiness be attained, which can only be attained by spirit of course, never by matter. Change we look upon as an evil inherent in matter, a part of its constitution. Its cessation, immobility, unchangeableness, fixity, we regard as the *summum bonum*, which we designate *nirwana.* This the spirit can only attain by shaking off change and its causes. Matter and spirit we regard, with Plato and Pythagoras, as equally eternal and equally indestructible, as existing *from* all eternity *to* all eternity, and hence the necessity for a God, in your sense of the word, is done away. We believe, however, in several spiritual essences of less or greater power, inhabiting various regions, some styled the gods, others the angels, others the devils, of Budhism, by European writers. Further, we believe that the all-powerful, the omniscient Budha, our man-god, after leaving us his instructions and his commands, has departed to the world of spirits, having attained, by his perfections, the highest and noblest condition of spiritual existence; a state which he has himself spoken of as one of "exalted felicity," the incomprehensible *nirwana*—incomprehensible to us, while thus wrapped and folded in the bandages of earth, ever tied down by grovelling bodies intended to be subdued and conquered, and used by the spirit, and for its benefit—a state which all, after repeated transmigrations, more or less numerous according to the excellence or other of the spirit, may attain; in which there will be no more sorrow, no more evil, no more desire, no more longing, no more clinging to objects; in which the spirit will be in its normal and most perfect condition, free from all the defilement and pollution of earth and imperfection.

K. What an extraordinary system! containing much that I esteem good, and very much that you will pardon me for believing to be pernicious. In the first place, with regard to the existence of a Deity such as we believe in, you acknowledge matter and spirit subject to general laws, by which, you said, they were ever changing, till the haven of perfect peace was finally attained, and yet you do not believe in the lawgiver! Now, tell me, Marandhan, can you conceive of laws without a lawgiver?

M. In the ordinary sense of the word *laws* I cannot;

but, hold! I use the word here because I cannot get a better. I do not mean laws impressed externally, but principles inherent in matter and spirit, and of these I can as easily conceive as I can of matter and spirit being equally eternal, which even some of your most distinguished Christian writers have admitted, as Milton, for instance. Have you got his 'Paradise Lost' at hand? I will show you in that where it is implied; and in one of his prose controversial works I have seen it openly, broadly, stated and advocated.

K. I am aware of it: we need not refer to the passages at present, as they would little assist our argument. Do you, who have read and thought so much, mean to tell me that you can look around upon creation, upon the wonders of the heavens and the earth, upon the adaptation of being to being, of contrivance to contrivance, upon the evidences of design in the human frame and elsewhere, and then deny the existence of a great Architect and Designer—a great Supreme First Cause?

M. I thought that argument from design had been abandoned by recent writers on the subject. However, permit me to say, allowing me the same liberty of speech which you claim for yourself, that if I saw any evidence of unity of design in the various objects around us, I might try and get over the many other difficulties in the way of such a belief as you advocate; but as long as I see one animal the prey of another, as long as I see pain and grief, and death, and madness in the world, I cannot believe in such a designer. What would you say of the mechanician who, in inventing a machine, so placed one part that it must evidently and inevitably interfere with and counteract another, destroying the very product which the other laboriously fabricated? Again, I cannot conceive of a spiritual essence calling matter into existence, an object so totally dissimilar, so contrary to itself: as well might I conceive of light producing darkness or heat cold—you will surely allow me to doubt here, when even Christian philosophers, with a predisposition to believe the dogma, have been staggered and overthrown by it. Again, you say design implies a designer; there is evidence of design in the world, hence there must have been a designer of the world. I cannot tell you the logical mood and figure of this syllogism, but such I believe to be its logical form. But, alas for the conclusion, it proves too much; for, if we admit the designer, then is not his own existence another evidence of design; are not his power, his majesty, his prescience, his justice, &c., also proofs of similar design, and where was the designer here?

K. Your first objection is the existence of evil in the world. I am sure, however, that you have but to reflect a moment on the subject to perceive that the free will of man and the imperfection of matter necessarily imply the possibility of such evil, and once admit the possibility of the smallest amount and the objection is overthrown. Could there have been free will without a freedom of choice between good and evil?

M. Infinite wisdom might surely have reconciled what to us may appear irreconcilable. You admit a Deity of infinite power and of infinite goodness, and yet you see around you death, sorrow, disease, pain, want, suffering of every kind, in the highest and in the lowest animals.

K. Pardon me, but you wander from the argument. You have omitted the consideration of infinite justice, which is as necessary to be remembered as power and goodness.

Your second objection was that you could not conceive of matter created by spirit—you meant, I presume, you could not understand it, for you can surely form a conception of it, if you can form a conception of spirit and matter separately. Now it is not to be wondered at that we should not understand all that infinite power can accomplish. However, I do not mean to insist upon this point. Our Bible says, that "in the beginning God created the heavens and the earth." The Hebrew word "*bara*," here translated "created," has by some been supposed to imply nothing more than reforming, and, as the point may be regarded as doubtful on that account, although the evidence preponderates amazingly in favour of the idea of creation, it would be useless to discuss it now.

Your third objection, which has the appearance of carrying much more weight with it, does not appear to me better founded than the first. Were we to take up a watch, and to examine its construction and movements, we should say at once here is design, there must have been a designer, further than that from the watch we could not go. Afterwards meeting the man, and hearing that *he* was the designer, from an examination of his frame and powers, from an investigation of the dependance of one part of his body upon another, of the adaptation of powers to necessities, we might again conclude, here must have been a designer also; he is not eternal, he did not make himself, chance could not have adapted ends to wants so beautifully, there must have been a designer here too. So far our argument would be perfectly legitimate; but, were we to presume to go a step beyond that, and to say that designer must have had another designer, we go beyond the reach and ultimate power of our abilities; we know too little of the Great Architect to presume to examine him as we should a man. We may not say here are powers adapted to produce certain results, harmoniously joined together, design in fact, where is the designer? A being infinitely above our comprehension and capacities, whose power, knowledge, and wisdom are without bounds, whose very nature is beyoud our understanding, is not to be subjected to reasoning adapted only to the business of man. Unless we could measure his powers and capabilities by some definable standard, unless we could inspect, examine, judge, weigh and understand infinite power, infinite wisdom, infinite knowledge, infinite goodness, we should have no right to argue as you indicated; just as the ephemeris, whose life is limited to a day, would certainly be wrong in arguing about an indefinite period of time; or the insect inhabiting a drop of water during its brief existence, which drop it never leaves, about the ocean.

Nor, again, would your own creed solve the difficulty. Matter, with certain principles or innate laws; spirit, with certain powers existing from all eternity, would more certainly lead us back to a designer than a contemplation of the attributes of the Deity, according to your view.

M. Precisely, and hence, to my mind, the fallacy of the whole argument from design; and you will not be angry with me, I am sure, when I say that your argument appears to me to savour more of sophistry than of truth—ingenious, not convincing, I should be tempted to designate it at present. But it requires consideration.

K. It appears to me strange, extremely strange, that an argument which has been regarded as so conclusive by thousands of the most able minds of all countries should be lost upon you, who seem so open to the truth, so willing to consider the matter apart from prejudice or passion. I fear this result is to be attributed to my method of stating it, not to the argument itself.

M. From the way in which Christian writers generally bring forward their tenets, one would suppose there were no other form of religion in existence but Christianity alone. You, yourself, in speaking of the numbers who have been believers in the Christian Deity, convinced by that argument,—or early training and that argument combined,—seem to ignore the fact that, according to the computation of the learned German, Professor Neumann, there are three hundred and sixty millions of Budhists in the world, and there have probably been nearly as many for the last thousand years. Your writers even speak of the universal consent of mankind as one proof of the existence of such a God, when here is nearly a half of the human race proclaiming their disbelief in it for ages. The press, however, is yours, and until it becomes more universally used in the East, literature will be all your own.

K. I did not say that the numbers believing in the Christian Deity were any proof of his existence. My observation was, that there must be much in an argument which had convinced thousands of the most enlightened of mankind—men of great logical acuteness and of cultivated minds—even contrary to their own wishes.

M. Is it not a fact, however, that you and most Christian thinkers regard Christian enlightenment, and Christian cultivation, and Christian philosophy, as the only kinds worthy of the name, oblivious of the early civilization of China and of India, of Greece and of Rome, which were independent of Christian influences altogether? We, too, have had our thinkers and our writers, our moral and mental philosophers, and our logical disputants; nor was a tenet argued in the metaphysics of Greece, nor probably is there a tenet, apart from purely Christian ones, argued in the metaphysics of modern Christendom, which was not a subject of discussion a thousand years ago in India and Ceylon. Modern treatises on this subject that have had all the charm of novelty in the West, would be looked upon as piracies upon the ancients amongst the *literati* of the East.

K. There is, doubtless, much truth in your observation, and until we know more of the early literature of the East, that of the West will be constantly liable to the same objection. To return to Budhism, however, and to leave the first point we have discussed for future thought, does not Gotama Budha, the founder of your faith, speak of four great continents upon the earth, communicating with each other here and there?

M. He does.

K. Does he not also speak of a great mountain, called Maha Meru, in the centre of the earth, around and above the summit of which are the abodes of gods and inferior spirits?

M. He does, but—

K. Pardon me. Does he not also speak of a material fire within the earth, the abode of the damned and the wicked?

M. He does.

K. Now, Marandhan, let me beg you to consider this matter impartially, without prejudice or pride. If these assertions were made by one professing himself omniscient, do they not prove to us, who know the elements of geography and geology, that he was not so.

M. I am astonished you should make such an objection to our faith, Mr. Knighton. The blessed Gotama found such ideas of geography prevalent amongst his hearers when he taught them the practice of virtue. His object was to teach them far higher things than physical science, and hence his acceptance of the geographical ideas then prevalent. He alluded to these localities as widely-spread objects of belief merely. Had he primarily introduced them, there might have been weight in your objection. Does not your own Bible do likewise? Is the account there given of the creation that given by geology? Did not Joshua command the sun to stand still upon Gibeon, and the moon in the valley of Ajalon? Had it been otherwise, would what was written have been comprehensible at all in those ages? I think not, and the very weakest objection to Christianity has always appeared to me to be that which presumptuous men have founded upon such expressions. The discrimination I willingly grant in reference to Christianity, I confidently ask in reference to Budhism.

K. And thus you bring me back to the point from which we started, whether natural science and religion are not, as now taught, hostile to each other. Not that I allow for a moment that any analogy exists between the instances you have brought forward from the Bible, and those which I have adduced from your creed. The locality of heaven and hell, the points of belief respecting gods and angels, are surely too important to be taken, in any faith, from the common belief of the parties to whom it is addressed. Did Christianity inform us that there was a vast mountain in the centre of the earth, which is spherical, which mountain was the abode of spirits who are immaterial, and that the centre of the world was occupied by a material fire in which spiritual natures were eternally or temporarily punished for sin, I for one should throw it overboard, and say I will have none of it. My reason has been given me to judge of truth and falsehood, and what contradicts that reason cannot be truth to me.

M. A strange conclusion, truly, seeing that you admit a contradiction already, the mystery of the Trinity. Suppose it were intended to mean a material mountain, which I do not believe, would it not be more tolerable or possible to believe in Maha Meru, all modern science notwithstanding, than to believe that three are one and one is three?

K. There is a difference between what is above, and what is contrary to our reason. The dogma of the Trinity is a mystery, as you call it, incomprehensible by our finite minds, but, being the nature of the all-powerful, not contradictory to our reason. Could man, with his bounded narrow intellect understand the infinite? it would be strange indeed if he could, far stranger than, that there should be points respecting it which are above his comprehension.

M. I cannot see how the Budhistic tenet would be contradictory to his reason, and the Christian only above it,—did you reverse the proposition I might be more ready to assent to it. But it is of the very nature of religion that it should contain much that is incomprehensible or unaccountable to our reason,—which must in fact be matters of faith,—and, therefore I do not lay much stress upon the objection at all. As to the great central fire of the world, I see nothing whatever absurd in the idea, even with all the lights of modern science. It is not so long ago since a scientific man proposed to visit the world in the centre of the earth, and invited Davy and Humboldt to accompany him to the north for that purpose, believing that the entrance would be found where the aurora borealis was most brilliant, for he maintained that that light was itself an emanation from the region within.

K. He must have been mad.

M. Perhaps he was. Is it, however, so improbable, that the centre of the earth is a vast mass of fire ?

K. By no means,—but is it not absurd to suppose a material fire injuring a spirit, injuring anything else in fact than a material substance ?

M. Unquestionably, yet in all religions, in yours and mine at all events, this material fire is taken as a type of the punishment reserved for the wicked. Do not nine-tenths of the hundred and fifty millions of mankind that profess Christianity, nominally or really, associate hell and material flames always in their minds, and would they not be startled did you tell them you did not believe in any such lake of fire ?

K. True, very true. You have thought much and read much on the subject of religion, Marandhan, and I would willingly sacrifice much to see you embrace as heartily what I believe to be truth, as you have embraced what I consider error,—but with reference to Christianity you forget the resurrection of the body.

M. I am willing to accept the truth unreservedly wherever I find it, and as I ride home through the forest to-night by the light of that glorious moon, and those twinkling stars I shall weigh well all that we have talked of, and believe me, I shall spare no pains to extract the truth and reject the error.

K. Then allow me, ere you depart, to press these two points upon your consideration during your ride to-night. The argument from design in favour of the existence of the Deity, and the direct contradiction which modern science gives to much that Budhism teaches as truth.

M. I will do so—honestly, candidly, unreservedly as I ought. And you, are you above taking a hint from an unfortunate, unenlightened Budhist?

K. How can you ask such a question?

M. Well then, remember this. The accounts your English books give you of Budhism, are, for the most part, compiled by missionaries, or, at all events, from information supplied by them,—they being naturally the best informed of your countrymen on the subject of foreign faiths. Such an account, therefore, as a Protestant, would give of Roman Catholicism, or a Roman Catholic of Protestantism, may be expected from a missionary, of Budhism—that is, it *may* be a fair and candid one, but will most probably be quite the reverse.

So saying, my Budhist friend mounted his horse, and rode leisurely away into the dark shadows of the trees.

DIALOGUE II.

Seated as before in my verandah, a little table between us, to hold the few books to which we referred, both reclining in easy chairs, and yet both eager and interested, the blue hills in front of us, the primeval forests and brawling water-courses around, amid which the jungle cock and the teal, the bustards and the herons, were composing themselves, with loud cries, for the night,—we spent two evenings a fortnight after in discussions of a similar kind to those of our former conversation. I do not pretend to convey word for word anything like all that was said, but whilst endeavouring to give as much as possible of the peculiar manner and style of each, merely to note accurately the subjects we touched upon, the arguments used, and the order in which we passed from one to the other.

M. The argument from design, in favour of the existence of such a Deity as Christianity recognizes, becomes more forcible as I reflect upon it the more, yet it is after all but an argument drawn from analogy, the most fruitful of all sources of fallacies, the line of reasoning of all others, perhaps the most uncertain, and the most likely to lead us astray. But this contradiction I cannot get over — Christianity recognizes a being of infinite goodness and infinite power, and yet evil, crime, misery, despair, death exist in the world, and have existed in all history. A being of infinite power might certainly have brought such beings as ourselves into existence, if we can conceive of spirit creating matter at all, but infinite goodness would certainly not have called miserable wretches into being to linger through a life of vicious degradation and constant unhappiness here, and to endure endless torment hereafter.

K. Alas, Marandhan, your objection is to the imperfection of man's judgment, not to the inconsistency, if we can reverently suppose such a thing possible, of God's government! Of the limitation of man's faculties neither you nor I can entertain a doubt. We are both equally convinced that his reason is bounded, erring, and imperfect. Can we then expect that he should fathom the heights and depths of Divine wisdom, or understand all the objects of Divine actions? to suppose that we can do so, is to point out the bounds of the infinite, to understand the incomprehensible, to weigh the imponderable. To me it would be more extraordinary that we should understand every portion of the Divine economy, than that there should be much a mystery to us, much that the poor, imperfect, confined mind of man cannot comprehend.

M. I fear I cannot be convinced by such arguments as those—I am to consult my reason up to a certain point, that is as long as it leads me to your conclusions, but the moment it diverges from those conclusions, and would find out another way, I am to abandon it as dangerous and unsafe.

K. Not so. I appeal to that very reason itself in every case. I do not ask you ever to forsake it. I ask it, is it likely we should understand all that infinite power contrives and executes, and it answers, no, it is by no means probable. I ask it, if a design does not imply a designer, laws a lawgiver, and it answers, yes, certainly. Thus, its conclusions in both instances are those which I allow, and to which I adhere.

M. And thus you ignore and evade my objection, that goodness and power combined could not have constituted such a world as we inhabit; that the existence of evil supposes either the existence of some independent antagonistic principle, as the Parsees believe, or the action of inherent principles and innate laws in spirit and matter, independently of all external influence, as we Budhists maintain. To say that benevolence was not the rule of creation, destroys at once the Christian hypothesis of a Deity, and the love which we are desired to have for him becomes an impossibility—terror taking it place: to say that the free-will of man implies a certainty of error is to deny infinite power, for surely what man can conceive of as possible, infinite power could effect, and man can conceive as possible the construction of a world on purely benevolent principles, in which happiness should be unalloyed, misery totally unknown.

K. And free-will?

M. And free-will either excluded altogether, for where is the necessity of a principle in which millions do not believe, and hundreds of millions do not enjoy? or else so subordinated to right and the production of good, as to exclude evil altogether.

K. The idea of free-will appears to me inconsistent with such concomitant circumstances, and of no being responsible like man, can I conceive, without his being endowed with such a principle—justice brought into consideration in addition, resolves all the anomalies of life and existence, inasmuch as justice requires that punishment should follow crime as shadow its substance. On a principle of pure and unalloyed benevolence we do not assert the worlds were framed, but that they were so framed as to exhibit to all intellectual existence, the glory of God—of this great machinery we form an insignificant fragment, our convictions and impressions of no injury to any but ourselves if false, as long as they are unimpressed on others, but if true, redounding to our own benefit and the glory of our Creator.

M. You speak enigmas I cannot understand, and which I fear require Christian training to be comprehensible at all. A being of infinite power can surely want praise, or belief, or glory, from atoms such as we, as little as we from the animalculæ that pervade water, and should we not rather despise than commend the man who sought such.

K. There is no analogy whatever between the two cases. Intelligent obedience and praise, or such glory as I speak of, can only come from intelligent minds, and to me the proudest aspect of man's troubled life is the relation in which he stands to the Deity—his capability of raising his soul in respectful adoration to the Giver of all good, the Fountain of every blessing—the communion which, by infinite condescension on the one side, and the highest exaltation on the other, he is permitted to hold with Omnipotence—and the favour with which his virtues are benignantly regarded by the condescension of the Architect of the Universe. These things which are not of the earth, earthy, are proud features of his life and existence upon the world, this view the highest aspect in which he can be regarded, this consummation the noblest end of his exertions. Who can overestimate the sublimity of the thought that we are thus linked to all that is great and grand in nature, that there is an intimate relationship between God and man, that our existence here is but the portal to an eternal existence with the Almighty hereafter, an existence to be enjoyed in all the plenary freedom of spiritual power and spiritual volition. These my dear Modliar, are grave thoughts, such as rouse the man's soul, who is not sunk in idle vicious sottishness, who is not all material; thoughts that make him walk abroad, a happier and a prouder mortal, with a glow of love and hope in his heart which nothing temporal can give or take away. Would that you could realize them! but your cold metaphysical creed gives you no such ideas—you worship an abstraction that looks upon you with no love, that is indifferent to your success or failure, you seek merely the cessation of existence as the greatest of earthly or heavenly blessings!

M. Is all this argument or declamation?

K. Declamation in part, certainly, but the earnest declamation of an earnest soul becomes an argument.

M. It does. You would argue then that Christianity is a more satisfactory creed than Budhism, because it holds out, not cessation from transmigration as its summum bonum, but perfect happiness of some new and spiritual character.

K. More satisfactory certainly to the enquiring, hoping mind on that account. As to transmigration, I can scarcely speak of such a belief seriously, or suppose an intelligent mind like yours believing in it.

M. If Christianity then be more satisfactory because it promises bliss hereafter to only a few of its votaries—for "strait is the gate and narrow is the way that leadeth unto life, and few there be that find it,"—what shall we say of Mahommedanism, which promises, not an ideal abstract heaven, but such an one as realizes material bliss, not to a few, but to all its votaries. If I should seek a satisfactory creed merely and not truth, should I not embrace it in preference?

K. I do not argue that because more hopeful and satisfactory, therefore it is true, but merely that as being so, it is, in so far as that point goes, more worthy of the convictions of an earnest soul.

M. Possibly it is, yet let me remind you, that our nirwana is spoken of by Gotama himself as a state of "exalted felicity," that many Budhists believe it is an absorption into the first principle of all things, and that we all regard it as a complete release from every form of suffering and anxiety; of the positive enjoyment, I cannot speak so certainly, nor have my researches in the New Testament taught me much of the actual form or character of that blessedness promised to the saved.

K. The blessedness you speak of is represented as of the most exalted character, its particular attributes and constitution being concealed as incomprehensible by us at present, "Eye hath not seen, nor ear heard, neither have entered into the heart of man the things which God hath prepared for them that love him,"—this, surely, is sufficient to picture forth to us something of an inconceivably perfect character; nor is it wonderful, indeed, that spiritual bliss should be ineffable in what is so closely connected with materiality as ordinary language.

M. You cannot conceive of transmigration being seriously believed in by an intelligent enquiring mind—such was the observation you made a few moments ago. So far can early training prejudice us against truth we are not used to! Transmigration has been the belief of the vast majority of mankind from the remotest times to the present. The comparatively small minority of Christians and Mohammedans being the only civilized rejecters of the doctrine; China, the Eastern Peninsula, India, Thibet, Tartàry and Mongolia, Persia and Egypt have all been, at various times, upholders of this faith, and, from the East, Pythagoras and Plato received it, and introduced it into Greece, and yet you can scarcely suppose that any intelligent mind seriously holds it!

K. Your rebuke is just. My remark showed great want of thought, and was the result of early prejudice. What such a man as Pythagoras believed in, and even Plato appeared to favour, as a legitimate speculation, cannot be either absurd or ridiculous, however strange to me, and those professing my faith.

M. If a coincidence between the doctrine of Budhism and that of Grecian philosophy pleads in favour of the former, I can point out many such, for, although incapable of reading the Greek classics in the original, I have diligently studied all the translations I could procure—the eternity of matter and spirit, the doctrine of the metempsychosis, with the prohibition to destroy animal life its necessary consequence, the prohibition of all intoxicating drinks, the command to eat only at particular times, and the general denial of all luxury, were common to the systems of Pythagoras and Gotama, whilst their moral codes were not only similar but identical—the whole, in my opinion, learned by the former from the disciples of the Budhist prophet, who were very widely dispersed abroad over the East by zeal and persecution, shortly after his death. Between the system of Plato, and that of the founder of our faith too, you will find the most marked and extraordinary coincidences, particularly in two classes of doctrines, first, those relating to the origin of the earth, its primeval condition, its history, and its destination; secondly, in those relating to the origin, history, and destination of the human soul.

K. The primeval condition of the world! I should like to hear the Budhistic doctrine on that head.

M. It is, that the primeval beings which appeared on the earth were infinitely superior to the race of men as seen at present. In the Sutrapitaka, section Dighaniko, Gotama describes them as "subsisting on the element of felicity," as "able to move easily through the air," as "delightfully situated" and "existing in unity and concord," whilst in the Janawanso, one of our standard works, the description, although more ample, is substantially the same. If you have a translation of Plato's Dialogues I think I can show you similar descriptions in them.

K. I have an attempt at translation, but, so poor a one, that, after reading a few pages, I closed the book and never opened it since.

M. If the sense of the author is only faithfully transcribed, I care little for the style—here is the passage to which I allude, in the Statesman; describing the early condition of mankind, Socrates says, "God was then the common prince and father of all; just as man now tends inferior animals, so he then governed man himself; cruelty and hatred were then unknown; war and sedition were unheard of. God himself guarded man; he was his supporter and shepherd. There were then no magistrates, no civil polity. In those happy days, man sprung from the bosom of the earth, which spontaneously yielded him, untilled, corn and fruit. He had no need of raiment, for changes of temperature were unknown, whilst the perennial verdure formed his downy bed." And a little further on, he adds, "Everything there was beautiful, harmonious and transparent; fruits of an exquisite flavour grew spontaneously; the earth was watered by rivers of nectar. They there breathed the light as we do the air, and the water of that earth was purer than our air." Allowing for the more florid style of the East, the descriptions of Gotama and of Plato are almost identical.

K. Both, we Christians should say, giving an account of what tradition bore dimly down in the lapse of ages respecting the garden of Eden.

M. Precisely what a missionary at Kandy said, in conversing on the same subject! Every part of the belief of other people and of other creeds that can be tortured into a resemblance to the tenets of Judaism or Christianity is a dim tradition of the truth obscured by the lapse of ages—every dogma in which we contradict such tenets, a device or invention of man.

K. We certainly think so. Perhaps it would be wiser to keep the impression to ourselves. But you asserted likewise that Plato agreed with Gotama in his account of the history of the human soul—that history in Budhistic belief is summed up in one word metempsychosis, and you must have read Plato's Dialogues to more advantage than I, if you have found that tenet, in all its latitude, advocated by Plato, as it certainly was by Pythagoras, if his disciples Ocellus Lucanus, Demophilus, Timæus the Locrian, and Jamblichus speak the truth.

M. It is but natural that I should have regarded this subject with more than usual interest, as an article of my religious belief, whilst your attention has been probably absorbed by other matters. In the Phædo, and, as you have the Greek before you, at chapter forty, Cebes says

"This probably will need no little persuasion and proof, that the soul of a man who dies, exists and possesses activity and intelligence."

"You say truly," said Socrates, "but what shall we do? Are you willing that we should converse on these points, whether such is probably the case or not."

"Indeed," replied Cebes, "I should gladly hear your opinion on these matters."

"I do not think," said Socrates, "that any one who should now hear us, even though he were a comic poet, would say that I am talking idly, or discoursing on subjects that do not concern me.* If you please then, we will examine into it. Let us consider it in this point of view, whether the souls of men who are dead exist in Hades or not. This is an ancient saying, which we now call to mind, that souls departing hence, exist there, and return hither again, and are produced from the dead. And if this is so, that the living are produced again from the dead, can there be any other consequence than that our souls were there originally; for surely they could not be produced again if they did not exist; and this would be a sufficient proof that these things are so, if it should in reality be evident that the living are produced from no other source than the dead." He then proceeds with his favourite argument that contraries produce contraries, summing up with this explicit statement at the end of chapter forty-five: "For, Cebes," continued Socrates, "as it seems to me, such undoubtedly is the case, and we have not admitted these things under a delusion, but it is in reality true that there is a reviving again, that the living are produced from the dead, that the souls of the dead exist, and that the condition of the good is better, and of the evil worse."

* It must be remembered that this dialogue immediately preceded the execution of Socrates—hence the above remark.

K. I have not much fault to find with these translations. The plain sense of these passages undoubtedly is, that Socrates left it to be inferred that transmigration in a more or less limited manner, was to be believed in.

M. The doctrine is stated without reservation, and most explicitly, in the Timæus, in the introduction to which, speaking of its concluding chapters, the translator says, "from which it appears that Plato entertained the Pythagorean doctrine of the transmigration of souls." I suppose by "entertained" he meant believed. Turn to tbe seventy-second chapter, "And now the discussion which we announced at the beginning, concerning the universe, as far at least as concerns the generation of man, is very nearly completed, for as to the rest of the animals, how they were generated, we will only briefly describe, except where necessity bids us enlarge: for a person may think that he is thus more in measure as concerns such an enquiry," whatever that may mean—but the rest is plain; "On this subject then let us speak as follows:—Of the men that were born, such as are timid, and have passed through life unjustly, are, we suppose, changed into women in this second generation. At that time then, and for that reason, the gods devised the love of copulation." We need not enter into the anatomical details, pass on to chapter seventy-three, "Next succeeded the tribe of birds having feathers instead of hair, which were fashioned from men without vice indeed, but light-minded and curious about things on high, yet conceiving in their folly that the strongest proofs of these things are received through the sight, that is, the senses. Again, the race of wild animals, with feet, was generated from men, who made no use of philosophy, nor ever enquired into any thing that concerned the nature of the universe, and this, because they no longer employed the circulations in the head, but followed the guidance of those parts of the soul that reside about the breast. Owing to these pursuits, therefore, they fixed their forelegs and head earthwards, as suited their nature—having also, long and variously shaped heads, where the circulations of each were compressed by inactivity:—and hence their race became quadruped and multiped, the Deity giving a greater number of feet to those more than usually unwise, that they might be the more drawn towards the earth. But as regards the most unwise of these, which extend all their body along the ground, as if they had no longer any need for feet, the gods formed them without feet to creep on the earth. The fourth class is that living in the water, which was produced from such men as were to the last degree unthinking and ignorant, and whom those transformers of our nature did not think deserving of a pure medium of respiration, because they possessed a soul rendered impure by extreme transgression—but drove them from the attenuated and pure atmosphere into the turbid and dense-breathing medium of water:—and hence arose the tribe of fishes and oysters, and all other aquatic animals, which have received the most remote habitations, as a punishment for their extreme ignorance. After this manner then, both formerly and now, animals migrate into each other; experiencing their changes through either the loss or acquisition of intellect and folly."

K. I might take a few objections to some parts of these translations—the difference may possibly arise, however, from differences in the Bipont text which I use, and that of Stallbaum used by the translator. But that is beside the question. You have brought forward quite sufficient to prove that Plato held or favoured the doctrine of the transmigration of souls; sufficient to prove to me how very hasty, foolish and inconsiderate I was in regarding that doctrine as an absurdity beneath the serious belief of enlightened men. What Pythagoras,

Plato, and Socrates, and more than half the world besides, for ages, have regarded as true cannot be ridiculous unless seen from an erroneous or a prejudiced point of view. But you have forgiven my indiscretion. Will you allow me then to direct your attention to the very Dialogue from which you last quoted, the Timæus, chapter nine? "With reference to what exists," says Timæus, "it must necessarily have arisen from some cause. To discover then the Creator and Father of this universe, as well as his work, is difficult;"—a little further on, in the tenth chapter, he proceeds, "Let us declare then on what account the framing Artificer settled the formation of the universe. He was good, and in the good, envy is never engendered about anything whatever. Hence being free from this evil, he desired that all things should, as much as possible, resemble himself." Throughout the whole Dialogue indeed, it is assumed, as almost an axiomatic truth, that design implying a designer, and effects a cause, there is and has been a great Artificer and Beginner of all things, by whom were all things, and without whom was not anything made, that is made, in whom we live, and move, and have our being.

M. In the twenty-seventh chapter you will find that he comes nearer our creed than the passages you have read would lead us to believe, but I am willing to confess, from looking at the whole Dialogue, that his idea of the Creator is more consonant with the Christian belief, in consequence of the personality attributed, than to ours: yet strange to say, I never so regarded it before, so much depends upon the point of view from which we regard what we see, hear, or read. You have read the Timæus and the Phædo, without seeing the metempsychosis, and I without seeing the personal, active, forming, regulating, and renovating God. You will find throughout both, however, that the eternity of matter is assumed. Yet

I must not allow you to draw me away from the subject we commenced with, the transmigration of souls. I should like much to know your objections to the dogma.

K. It is not easy to improvise objections to a dogma which one has not dispassionately considered. But one fundamental objection to it is, I think, apparent. The souls of the vicious, it supposes, transmigrate into low and grovelling animals, those of the virtuous into superior men and women, or gods. Now vice, so far from invariably stupifying the vicious, often sharpens the more their intellect. It depends upon the kind of vice to which the individual has been addicted. Some descriptions there undoubtedly are, which tend to degrade and debase the intellectual faculties, and such souls one would willingly consign to the swine and the sloth, could he look upon transmigration as a fact, but these are rather the exceptions than the rule.

M. Quite true. But you must remember that the dispositions of the inferior animals are almost as various as their external forms. The intellectual acuteness which vice frequently gives, we see exemplified in the activity and slyness of some beasts and birds of prey, which often exhibit an amount of quickness of perception, patience, perseverance, and ingenuity in catching and destroying their enemies or procuring their food, which man cannot equal, or indeed approach, save in the savage state.

K. There is so evident a distinction between the instinct by which inferior animals are guided, and the reason which directs man, that any community of soul between them, appears to me impossible.

M. Have you ever seen any definition of reason which did not include much that is common to man and other animals? In the sagacity of the elephant, the sympathy of dogs with their suffering companions, the imitative powers of the monkey, the well-ordered commonwealth and powers of transmission of thought of beavers, bees, and ants, do we not discover powers and capabilities equal to those displayed by the lowest order of mankind? Is there any so cogent reason why the naked, brutal savage, that wanders ignorant and depraved through the bush of Southern Africa or Australia, his speech a species of kluck-kluck, more resembling the cackling of geese than the articulate utterance of man, his utmost reach of intellect how to trap the wild buffalo or kangaroo, and his intellectual cultivation confined to the perception of want of food, or some other appetite, with the means of supply—is there, I say, any so cogent reason why *he* should be possessed of a soul, and the chimpanzee, that wanders in troops, and similarly provides itself with food, and exhibits superior strength and sagacity, should not?

K. In the process of degradation we can scarcely wonder that, during centuries of neglect and increasing barbarism, man should have become so fallen; the only wonder, indeed, is, that he still always retains a power over nature, and other animals, which stamps him its lord and theirs. In no case do we find man so sunk that he has become the slave of inferior animals—in every case he has subdued some of the highest of them, as if to prove, even in deep degradation, his superiority. His religious rites, found in some form or other, however rude, amongst every people, would alone be sufficient to stamp him supreme in this lower creation—telling, as it does, of his aspirations, forming a connecting-link to unite him to things higher and better and nobler than himself, a convincing proof that however near debasement and deep defilement may approximate him to the irrational, he has a soul which binds him to the spiritual and the God-like. The very fact that, as improvement spreads, this lowest savage state of man must disappear, proves the capability of the most degraded to be raised, and their capacity of taking, under proper influences, the position which man ought to take in the world. If there were any truth in the supposition that man is but a higher species of monkey, why are no traces of the intermediate links of the chain discoverable? why no animal half-monkey, half-man? why no races which we should find a difficulty in classifying under one or the other head? All nature leads us by analogy to the supposition that, if that dogma were true, something of the kind would be discoverable. The mineral world, in its crystallization and chemical affinities, leads us by nice and almost imperceptible degrees into the vegetable, there the chain is unbroken from the simplest cryptogamia up to the most complicated sensitive plant or sun-flower, and still by nice and almost imperceptible degrees are we led along from the vegetable to the animal kingdom, as in the sponges and animalculæ —nay, there are even beings which appear to be vegetables at one period of their existence, and animals at another.* All the lower world is then one vast chain of which the links are traceable and discernable, step by step. We arrive at the highest of irrational animals, and there we meet an abrupt end. There is no transition species to man, none that, for a moment, can be mistaken for such. He stands at the head, unquestionably, unmistakeably so elevated, removed far from all beneath, as an animal peculiar in his origin, his history, his destination. And what causes this peculiarity, if not the immortal soul within him? which he certainly possesses, and they, I should conclude, as certainly want?

M. You are right in saying the lowest savage state of man must disappear as civilization and improvement spread. But how will it so disappear? Not by the

* "Infimæ formæ (algarum) inter vitam animalem et vegetabilem fluctuant, quædam sub diversis evolutionis stadiis utriusque regni cives."—*Endlicher Gen. Plant,* p. 1.

taking of the degraded savage and placing him amongst more elevated men, but by his extermination. As the civilized advances the uncivilized retreats, retreats into the ocean at length if his steps can track out no other course. "You must go," cries enlightenment, "God and man are equally tired of your degeneracy. Delay not, I advise you, or the consequences will be serious. I will pay you for your land if you want payment, but if you do not, or will not accept payment, then I will take it, I must have it—such is my mission, yours is to go and be damned. Go then—" "Whither," asks helpless savagery, wringing its pitiful hands ungracefully to heaven, "—in God's name whither?" "Anywhere," is the reply, "simply anywhere or nowhere. You say it is perhaps death to go—possibly it may, but it is certain death, I assure you, to remain." There is a short struggle, and savagery retreats, whilst civilization takes its place, with a self-satisfied consciousness of performing its mission on earth.

K. Too often the case, yet not always. Attempts have constantly been made, and are still making to raise the fallen brother to something of a level with the more refined.

M. But the fallen brother will not be raised and dies—savage freedom pulling him energetically at one end, and enlightenment, with great violence, at the other, until he is torn asunder in the struggle, and so ends another chapter of human history.

But any intermediate link between man and the lower animals is wanting, you argue, to prove that he differs from them in degree only, not in constitution or essence. He is unmistakeably at the head of the animal creation, you say, a being of a totally different order and character from the inferior animals by which he is surrounded; so far your argument appears plausible, and I can only meet it by referring to instances of extraordinary sagacity in various animals, which go to confound all fine-drawn distinctions between instinct and reason,—instances which you have but to turn to any book on natural history to discover. But when you proceed to argue that man is evidently of a different character from the other animals because we find no links in the great chain of creation, connecting him with those beneath him, although throughout all the kingdoms of nature we find such gradual advances prevail,—no great leaps from bad to good, or good to bad, but a sliding, so to speak, by nice and imperceptible degrees from the one to the other—when you use such an argument as this, you rather strengthen my position than invalidate it. In the first place I assert that there is such a chain, and that the orang-otang, the chimpanzee, and the monkey, are the links required—their skeleton approximating to that of the lowest type of mankind, just as the skeletons of the vast antediluvian saurians lead us from the lowest of the amphibious reptiles by slow and almost imperceptible degrees to the mammalia of the present day. In the second place, were there no such links, or were such links lost, my position would not be invalidated, for, on the same principle I might argue that the elephant was an animal *sui generis*, like man, evidently put at the head of the quadrupedal mammalia, inasmuch as there is no animal that ever I heard of half-elephant and half-ox, or half-elephant and half-hippopotamus, to connect him with those of the more ordinary types. Mules and hybrids are the exceptions not the rule, and to expect them in the case of man and the other animals is not to be moderate and philosophical.

K. It really amuses me to find you rummaging sciences of every description to support a dogma which I thought so utterly indefensible and improbable, at the same time that I regard your ingenuity as quite thrown away, as sophistical and not philosophically logical. With respect to the elephant, and your argument on that head, geology upsets it—the required links do not now live, it is true, but have formerly lived. In so wide and vast a field as modern science, however, there is scarcely a tenet, however absurd, to support which some seeming analogy or contrast, some point of resemblance or of contradistinction, may not be brought forward.

M. Thus you arrive again with admirable self-complacency at the absurdity of what is in me an honest conviction; but if an absurdity, one shared in by more than half the world.

K. Pardon me. In this discussion you have greatly the better of me; setting out in the study of modern science and literature, with this metempsychosis as a settled dogma, true and irrefutable, in your mind, you have doubtless found much to favour your belief, to which you willingly opened your eyes, whilst you involuntarily closed them to what might militate against it. Remember the importance of the point of view from which we regard anything—its subjective aspect—a reflection which you yourself made but a short time ago. I, on the other hand, have never studied the matter *pro* or *con*. Writers in Europe have long ceased to argue respecting it, and I could not, at this moment, even name a book in which I should probably find a calm discussion of the question by the light of modern science. Our warfare, on this particular point therefore, is at a disadvantage to me. You come mailed *cap-à-pié*, in tried armour which you have doubtless proved before, whilst I have been foolish enough to provoke a contest, trusting to the sticks and stones I may find in my path. Let not then the indiscretion of the champion damage the cause he is endeavouring to uphold. You, in your own house, are surrounded by the most eminent literature of your religion, whilst the temple libraries afford you access to any controversial work you may desire to consult. I, on the other hand, am banished from all such intellectual banquets as a good library affords, and am obliged to be content with the few good books I have brought with me into the jungle, and the many bad ones the popular lending library of Kandy affords.

M. But surely, Sir, the cultivation bestowed upon you by a European education, renders you more than a match upon such subjects for a benighted Budhist, who is obliged to extract his religion from the writings of men ignorant of modern science, and who has no such controversial works, as you have referred to, to consult, for there are none such in existence. The combat is undoubtedly unequal, but the inequality lies all upon the other side. Am I to suppose, then, that you regard your arguments against the transmigration of souls as answered, or will you favour me with weightier objections?

K. By no means. You believe that some of the inferior animals can transmit their thoughts to each other, either by language, or something which answers the same purpose?

M. I do. I have seen a hive of bees thrown into the greatest possible commotion in the course of a few minutes by the removal of their queen. The moment the loss was discovered emissaries went in every direction, evidently with the intention of informing all the others of the circumstance, and, in a few moments, all was confusion, commotion, disorder, where all had been order, quiet, and regularity, so shortly before; so that I think facts bear me out in supposing man not to be the only being endued with language in the world.

K. There is a great distinction between man and the inferior animals which we have not yet noticed, and which, in my opinion, is quite sufficient to lead us to the conclusion that man is endued with some high principle or motive power which they are altogether without. The distinction is between the perpetual progress and advance of the one, and the eternal immobility of the other. Man is ever contriving new implements for his own use, ever adding to his knowledge and its sources, making use of those additions in a practical way too; man is ever investigating, ever active, mentally as well as physically; there is, with him, no standing still in the race of life; ever pressing from the old into the new, from the past into the future, he alters, improves, invents, perpetually. The inferior animals, on the other hand, remain ever the same; the beaver of to-day makes its dam precisely as the beaver of five thousand years ago; the nest of the swallow was as well built a thousand years ago as it is now; the cells of the bee, the dwellings of the ant, the sagacity of the elephant, the affection of the dog, all remain the same. Progress is man's law; theirs is immobility. Is the man of to-day the same as the man of the time of Sesostris was? or is it probable that the man of five thousand years hence, if such there be, will at all resemble the man of to-day? Here then is a fact which implies one to be the possessor of a great principle unknown to and unfelt by the other, which makes the one the fitting heir of everlasting life, the other the heir only of that material frame from which it sprung, and to which it must all return.

M. There is much poetry in the idea, whatever may be said of its philosophy. Were that progress you notice universal amongst mankind, there would be much truth in the observation too. That the inferior animals remain for ages the same in habits, dispositions, mental powers and capacities, I am willing to admit, that is, so far as man's limited experience goes, and of course he can go no further; but that man is universally a progressive animal I deny. You argue not from man, but from the European, whose proud boast it is, and always must be, that he has taken the lead in the race of civilization in these latter years. But allow me for a moment to draw your attention to other men. Do the Bushmen of Southern Africa, the Black-fellows of Australia, the Indians of America, the Esquimaux of the Arctic Regions, or the Veddahs of Ceylon exhibit this progress? Nay, to leave the more degraded races, is it not a perpetual reproach, flung by Europe at China and India, that they are the same now they were in the earliest ages? Do we not constantly read of "a certain immobility," which is said to be the curse of Asiatic life?

K. No. I will not be driven from this position by specious examples. I speak of the race as a race, not of the European, the American, the Asiatic, the African, or the Australian, but of man collectively as a great race of animals on this globe. You will not surely tell me that you regard man as standing still, or retrograding? You cannot surely deny that there is evident progress in his career? The very intercommunion between the most distant nations, unknown to each other before; the very grandeur and vastness of the attempts made to promote the acquaintance of people with people; the emigration, the colonization, the interchange of thought with the rapidity of lightning; the diffusion of useful minerals, vegetables, and animals over the world; the increase of knowledge—these, and a thousand other ingredients of nineteenth-century illumination, all tend to mark and prove the onward progress of mankind; a progress to which there is nothing whatever analogous in the inferior animal creation, which is indeed wholly excluded from it altogether. If it be not the living soul of man urging him on to mighty deeds, and higher destinies, what is it that thus impels him forward? Why do not the inferior animals, if they possess similar souls, share in the general improvement, or exhibit, at the very least, a tendency to tread the same steps, to march in the same way?

M. You have put this argument in a very forcible way,

and in the strongest possible light, yet there is something partially unsatisfactory to me in it, notwithstanding its weight in an abstract point of view. Were the progress you notice universal and uniform, not spasmodic and intermittent, I should acknowledge at once that some great distinction there evidently was between man and other animals, however I might endeavour to account for it; but a progress so irregular and partial, so influenced by times and places, does not appear to me to be the result of the operation of a principle common to all men, otherwise we should find this progress as marked in the life of the savage as of the civilized European. It seems to me rather to be the result of language and of printing than of the soul.

K. Hence one reason why I asked you about the language of inferior animals. As you acknowledge they have some means of communicating their thoughts to one another, it appears to me that you have excluded yourself thereby from appealing to this at all as the source of the progress of mankind, for if man has made so good a use of an implement common to him and the inferior animals, why should they alone have possessed, without improving, it?

M. Quite true. I see fully the force of your argument, and its aim. Objecting partially to the premises, however, I am not likely to arrive at the same conclusion, and so I fear our discussion must terminate, as discussions too often do, by each being only the more fully persuaded of the truth of his own tenets. You assume man has been making, since his fall, a gradual advance, which the lower creation has not. I allow that the inferior animals remain as they were, but, at the same time, I deny that man has been making that even, consistent progress which you claim for him. My impression is that, in order to enable us to arrive at the conclusion you wish, it would be necessary to believe that the progress of man had been uniform, uninterrupted, and universal, whereas, without all doubt, it has been, on the contrary, spasmodic and intermittent, partial and irregular; and, so I conclude by observing that I see no valid reason in nature, in mental or material philosophy, why the doctrine of the transmigration of souls should not be considered consistent with the harmony of the universe,—true in itself and useful in its results.

K. I have not succeeded then in bringing my arguments before you in a sufficiently forcible way, and must leave the subject to your calm consideration and unbiassed reflection. If Budhism be true as a whole, it must be true in its parts; if false in its parts, it cannot be true as a whole. I trust one of these days to see you, like myself, a Christian; and then, I doubt not you will see, with me, the falsehood of transmigration as a dogma, its failure as a moral tenet, and its total inadequacy to act as a stimulant to virtue or a dissuasive from vice. Adieu, my dear friend, I await the conclusion of your deliberations within yourself, respecting the existence of a great Supreme First Cause, with the most lively anxiety, and, till you have settled that point, do not hope for much otherwise.

And so our conversation ended.

DIALOGUE III.

K. I have reflected much, Modliar, on the objection you brought forward, during our last conference, to the doctrine of the Christian Deity—that the imperfection and evil in the world implies either no Deity at all, or one uninterested in humanity, or one of limited goodness or power. The more I consider the subject the more I feel assured that the result stated by no means necessarily follows. Let us look at the *à priori* argument from causation for a moment first. You admit causation generally?

M. Yes. I admit that certain effects proceed from certain determinate and pre-acting causes.

K. Well then, the world, and the universe, of which it forms an insignificant portion, is a great effect which implies a pre-acting, and, of course, a pre-existing, cause. The more this world is examined, too, the more we dive into the powers and principles by which it is regulated, the more the idea of simplicity in its arrangements is developed;—the further we advance in a knowledge of the constituent elements of things, and of the laws by which these elements are separated and combined, the nearer are we led to unity and uniformity as the end of our researches. Classes of phenomena are found constantly to belong to, and to be deduced from, a single elementary principle, and the whole tendency, equally of all philosophy and of all science, is to bring us back to some one fundamental principle or law which explains numerous classes of truths and diverse methods of operation. Does not all this lead us to some one great Being, the ultimate cause and end of all things? does it not imply the existence of a great Architect and Ruler, the ultimate principle, the remote agent, to whom we approximate the further our researches are carried?

M. The argument is a powerful one, and no one can see its force more fully than I do; since our first conversation on the subject I find my mind has been gradually undergoing a revolution, which leads me by imperceptible degrees to this Supreme Architect, this great Primary Cause. A thousand obscurities that have long darkened my mind previously, disappear as the conviction grows upon me, and I seem like a man awakening out of a long trance, and only just beginning to see objects around him as they really exist. But still great and apparently insurmountable difficulties stand in the way; and, whilst on the one side all is light and sunshine, on the other the darkness increases, and the mind begins to despair of ever piercing it, urging the inquirer to cast the whole speculation aside and rest content with the dogmatizing of others. A Being, infinite and eternal, self-existent and uncaused, having all power and all knowledge, from whom and by whom are all things, is a great and a sublime conception, and that there is such a being is an impression daily forcing itself, as I have said, more strenuously on my mind. But when you come to add to this idea that of infinite goodness, the intellect dissents, and cries "hold,"—infinite goodness, say you, O whence then evil of every kind—pain, sorrow, distress, death and calamity; whence the sufferings of the good, the misery, too often long-continued, of the virtuous? These are facts which I cannot reconcile with the ideas you have so powerfully enforced, and the result of our conferences tends to be to make me a heretic to the orthodox Budhism of Ceylon, and a member of the sect called the Aïshvarika of Nepaul, a sect who acknowledge an Adi-Budha supreme, infinite and immaterial, the sole cause of all things, who, having once exerted his almighty power in creation, now leaves the universe to its fate.

K. I by no means fear such a result: I have too much confidence in your head and heart to fear it. You delighted me with the former part of your observations, and I shall not allow myself to be depressed in spirits by the latter. Suppose matter existing, whether, by the supreme fiat of a creator, first called into being, or as existing from all eternity, it matters not—suppose it existing. Connected with this idea of matter are there not necessarily imperfections adhering? is not the idea of space, which cannot be separated from it, in itself an imperfection; for does not the perfect exist everywhere, and not in one place more than in another? there can be no idea of space in connection with what is perfect, universal, all-embracing, which must be everywhere. To us there is space, to all animals, because we are not perfect, but imperfect, manifestly in many ways; but to the perfect, the self-existing and eternal, in all places at once, everywhere acting, there is no space, no distance of object from object, of being from being. The idea of space then which necessarily adheres to matter, and without which we cannot conceive of matter existing, without which we know matter does not exist, is in itself an imperfection.

M. So it evidently appears. I have never regarded it in that light before.

K. Might we not similarly go over other necessary attributes of matter, such as time, divisibility, and others, and show that they too are imperfections?

M. Imperfections in so far as they do not adhere to the perfect.

K. More than that—inasmuch as they could not adhere to the perfect; could not, by any means, be attributes, properties, or concomitants of anything which was not essentially imperfect.

M. Then, allowing this?

K. Then, allowing this, evil, with its necessary consequences, is a certain and incontrovertible deduction. Imperfection implies the want of that which would constitute perfection; implies more too, the liability to evil of every kind, the possibility—nay, the extreme probability—of falling into this evil and being drowned in it. Once admit, then, the existence of matter, whether, as I suppose, called into existence by the fiat of an Almighty Creator, or, as you believe, existing, like the Creator, from all eternity; once allow this existence, and whether united with spirit or not, imperfection necessarily adheres to it, is indeed so to speak of its very essence. There can be, in fact, but one perfect. All others must be imperfect; divide spirit, and it becomes imperfect, because it becomes possessed of properties at once, which render it so; and thus, of no such material world, of no such universe as this we inhabit, of no such being as man, can we conceive, without supposing it and him liable to error, to evil, to pain, sorrow, distress, misery, and death. So much for his material frame. Now for his spiritual.

Consciousness implies will. If he is to use this will as he pleases, he must be at liberty to use it in a bad, as well as in a good, way. Did he use it always in a good way, as he had the option of doing at first in this his probationary state, doubtless much of the imperfection of his body would be neutralized; indeed, we can conceive of its being so far neutralized as to be of little or no inconvenience, the very condition which is conceived of as paradisaical. But he has not always so used it. Christianity and Budhism equally tell us that he has used it ill for thousands of years; that, of his own free will, he chose error instead of truth, vice for virtue, and consequent misery for happiness; and, as a general rule, the more he retraces his steps and embraces virtue instead of vice, and truth instead of error, the more nearly does he return to that happy condition which he has forsaken. Deprive him of free will, and consciousness becomes extinct, for consciousness implies a self-directive power which is the very essence of free will—he is no longer then an accountable or an intellectual being, no longer a man.

M. You argue with a force and vigour to-day, which I find it difficult to combat. There is a logical terseness in your expressions, and a strength in your arguments which perplex me. I am not prepared to deny the position you have taken up, either with regard to man's physical or intellectual nature. Both require a reflection and consideration which I shall not fail to give them, and, believe me, my object is not to exhibit myself as an intellectual gladiator, but merely to discover truth. Do not forget, however, that hitherto we have been solely engaged in considering what you look upon, as the weak points of Budhism, and that if there are some difficulties in our faith, there are also some in yours. I must still, however, adhere to my former observation, that, what man can conceive possible, Almighty Power could execute, and therefore, I see no reason why a universe, spiritual if you will, might not have been constructed, in which perfect virtue and happiness amongst all creatures should have been the rule without exception.

K. In other words, you think man's finite capacity, "cabined, cribbed, confined," as it is in the present state of his existence, can tell the infinite wisdom of the Almighty how things might have been constructed so as to be better than they are.

M. No. If we merely abstract the idea of infinite goodness from the Christian conception of the Deity, we arrive at what appears to me to be the truth. The Aïshvarika of Nepaul, as I have already stated, have, in my opinion, realized that truth, and the tendency of our controversy is still to throw me into their ranks.

K. But you have not yet given that consideration to the remarks which I have just made on the material frame of the universe, and on man's physical and spiritual nature, which you have promised.

M. I have not, and until then, I suspend my judgment, I should like to know, however, as you have already said so much that is novel this evening, whether you see any fresh reasons for considering matter as a product of time, and as a creation, and not eternal and uncreated.

K. I have thought much on all these subjects, and

read much, and, with respect to the origin of matter, or whether it ever had an origin, it appears to me that we must necessarily consider it as in a constant state of progress—indeed, geology proves this.

M. Must, then, the ultimate appeal be to that popular physical science, the study of which I have always regarded as irreligious in its tendency?

K. Do you not believe then, that, in the changes and revolutions of the earth's history, as an earth, there is a progress, a tendency to development and evolution of some kind? Do you not believe that, as century by century, and cycle by cycle has elapsed, finding the earth now in one state, now in another, there has been a gradual unfolding of its powers, a gradual onward tendency in its history?

M. I must be cautious of the admissions I make to one who so often turns them against myself. Speaking as a student of science I should say, yes; as a religious man, no. Geology tells me of some such progress, of an early age when lower animals existed without man, of a time when the earth was unfit for man, and that since then there has been an improvement, an onward progress, fitting it to be the abode of man. But Budhism, on the other hand, tells me that the earth goes through stated periods of changes and revolutions eternally, changes and revolutions stretching through immense cycles of time and ever recurring.

K. Admitting that there is a Deity then, a truth which you are now disposed to allow with me, although we may differ about his attributes, admitting that he has shaped and fashioned the universe, is not such an idea of progress towards some consummation ultimately to be attained, a necessary consequence!

M. It certainly appears so, or the whole creation would be aimless and objectless.

K. Precisely so. Well, had the matter of the universe been existing from all eternity, it must ere this have reached that goal, that consummation, that ultimate limit and object of its existence, that point, whatever it is, to be obtained.

M. Why so?

K. If the matter were so acting and so progressing from all eternity, surely in eternity the end must have been attained, the object of its existence fulfilled, to suppose otherwise would be to suppose that arrival at that consummation, required a longer period of time than eternity to complete, an evident absurdity. Therefore, if, as geology teaches us, and as, indeed, the world itself teaches us in the history of mankind, there be a gradual progress onward, a gradual development, a progressive approach towards some point not yet attained, then the universe must not have existed from all eternity, must, in other words, have been created in the beginning, otherwise we are led into the palpable absurdity of concluding that a longer time than eternity was required to reach that end.

M. Nothing can be plainer. Taking that material science as our guide, which I regard so suspiciously as the enemy of religion, we are evidently led to that conviction, and the conviction as evidently harmonizes with Christianity. As I have already intimated, however, Budhism evades this difficulty.

K. Or rather, as it appears to me, to avoid one absurdity falls into another.

M. I do not quite see that. Could you bring forward as conclusive an argument against the metempsychosis as you have this evening on some other points, I must confess the edifice of Budhism, in my mind, would be completely shaken.

K. The metempsychosis is a purely unfounded hypothesis, which artfully evades many difficulties, and was evidently originally propounded to alarm the vulgar. It was so regarded, at all events, by the very Greek philosophers who pretended to embrace it, "As we cure diseases of the body," said Timæus the Locrian, an eminent Pythagorean, "by unpleasant medicines, if they will not yield to the more agreeable, so do we correct the evil propensities of the soul by false terrors if they will not yield to true. On this account it is that we threaten the cowardly with becoming women hereafter, dedicated to disgrace; murderers with becoming wild beasts; the libidinous with being changed into the forms of goats and swine; to the heedless and the rash, we threaten aerial bodies, doomed to eternal wanderings; and lastly, to the slothful and luxurious, the careless and the obstinate we consign the stupid minds and awkward forms of the aquatic fowl."* And an ingenious method of getting rid of much difficulty in psychological speculation, it undoubtedly is, but this, at all events, is to be said against it, that it is wholly unsupported in science and nature—that not one scientific fact, not one established principle of physical or spiritual philosophy can be adduced in its favour.

M. Pythagoras may have regarded it in the light you have stated, but Socrates and Plato evidently did not, if the slightest dependence is to be placed upon the translation of the works of the latter. And as to its not being supported by any scientific fact, a religious dogma, in my mind, needs no such support. Indeed, were such a principle as that to be universally carried out, where should we rest? Scientific facts would be the test of religious truth, and thus the revolution which appears to me to be but too rapidly advancing as it is, in which

* Timæus, Περι ψυχας, κοσμω, και φυσιος. Opuscula Mythologica Galæ. Amstelodami, 1688.

science, or rather physical philosophy in some form, whether scientific or otherwise, usurps the place of religion, would be consummated at once.

K. You are right. Religious dogmas must not be judged of in that way, yet surely there is no irreligion in the pleasure which one derives from a contemplation of the harmony between scientific and religious truth.

M. Once admit the principle that a religious dogma can be rendered more certain by scientific facts adduced in favour of it, and where shall we end? Shall we not look for such support in every case, and in relation to every article of religious belief? Here is the very irreligious tendency of modern science, of which I feel so convinced. In every religion there must be much taught which man can neither explain nor comprehend, it is of the very essence of spiritual truth that it should be so, and, if such be the case, how dangerous a rule to admit that the most overwhelming testimony from physical or psychological philosophy can add, in the faintest degree, to the reasons why we should firmly hold one tenet or doubt another.

K. I see plainly the force of your objection, but I think you state it too absolutely. What man can help being influenced by any great amount of testimony from science in favour of a dogma which his religion teaches him to be true? Does it not produce a conviction in his mind of such a character as to make him more earnestly embrace the whole system and fling his doubts to the winds?

M. Its action would to me appear to be extremely insidious. He finds one dogma so supported, and he, therefore, believes it more firmly; then will he not similarly look for such support in reference to other dogmas? Is it not natural that he should say to himself —"My religion certainly teaches me so and so, I wish science taught me the same, or even hinted at it," and, if he cannot discover this hint, will he not be likely to say to his own heart with a sigh,—"it would be infinitely more satisfactory to me if science taught so too, but I must try and believe it notwithstanding." What must be the product of such thoughts but a pernicious scepticism that saps the very foundation of religious belief?

K. You state the case very absolutely, and I cannot go quite so far as you do in the conclusion you arrive at. Fortunately, between Christianity and established scientific facts, as now understood, there is so intimate a union that the difficulty does not present itself in the way in which you state. There are dogmas, certainly, which science can neither render more or less credible,—with which it has, in fact, nothing whatever to do,—and, for these, no sensible man would look for any intimation from science of the existence or non-existence of such truths. Take, for instance, the nature of the Almighty. It is evident that science may give us certain proofs of the existence of some such Being. By an induction of the most certain kind we are led to that belief, his attributes too are shadowed forth in his works, not obscurely either or darkly, but with precision enough to satisfy the acute observer fully; further than this, however, it is not possible that science could go. The nature of that wonderful Being, and any particulars of that nature, must evidently come from Himself alone, man cannot see Him, and finds it difficult to grasp the overwhelming attributes which nature tells us He is endowed with, and here, where science stops, religion begins. Truths, which the unassisted intellect of man could never arrive at, are there proclaimed, which, as being far above all science, need no confirmation from it, and cannot, therefore, be controverted by anything that science teaches.

M. To a mind constituted like yours, ready to bow to authority when the intellect or the heart would speak a word which authority would condemn, such a conclusion may appear obvious; but I much doubt if the habit of judging the truths of religion,—and grand fundamental truths there are, such as those of morality, common to all religions,—by the rush-light of modern science, with all its disjointed facts and crude speculations, does not, in most men, beget a scepticism which tends to overturn the edifice of religion altogether in their minds. To me, therefore, there seems no alternative between absolute submission to authority, a belief in all that that authority teaches, unreservedly and sincerely, a faith in the authority itself which regards its voice as divine, and a universal scepticism that doubts all, believes firmly in nothing but in sensuous impressions, and ultimately lands its possessor in the haven of infidelity. You will allow that, in going through the world I have kept my eyes open, and the more narrow my sphere of observation, the more likely am I to have thoroughly investigated that sphere. As one who is indifferent to both of the great sects of Christianity, too, my observation will at all events be allowed to be impartial. Even here in Ceylon, I have seen how rancorous is the hatred between Protestants and Roman Catholics, and my reading often proves to me, that in Europe it has been for centuries still more so. Well, with respect to these two great bodies of Christians, I have observed this—and I am sure you will not be offended at my mentioning it.

K. Certainly not, any observation of yours on the subject I should be glad to hear.

M. Well, this:—Protestants *talk* most of their religion, Roman Catholics *believe* most. The former seem more enlightened on the subject, the latter put their trust in Christianity more firmly and more unhesitatingly.

Many of the former seem to be sceptics, and none of the latter. Of this, too, I feel certain that, generally speaking, the latter will make more sacrifices for their religion than the former. Of their respective morality I say nothing; but, of this I feel persuaded, that the trust in authority of the latter leads them into a safer and more fearless reliance upon their religion, than the private judgment, as influenced by modern science, of the former.

K. And of their respective morality—I should like to hear your opinion?

M. My impression is, that the one is not a whit worse than the other. Take as a proof of the truth of my observation, the recent efforts made to obtain a missionary for the planters, whose duty it should be to go from one estate to another to keep alive religious feeling in the jungle, and to afford the benefit of Sunday services in central situations. You were ready to subscribe regularly and liberally, I know, and one who rides so far as you often do to engage in religious service of course would; but, considering the number of planters in this province, how small a proportion was willing to aid the original proposers of the scheme in carrying it out! I saw the list in the newspaper, not one-twentieth part of the entire planting population, and yet all had been applied to! Now, had they been Roman Catholics instead of Protestants, do you think that result would have followed?

K. Probably not. The unhappy disunion amongst us was the cause, however, of the failure of the scheme.

M. Another result of private judgment.

K. Perhaps so. We are wandering, however, from Budhism, and although I have already stated the most important considerations I intended to bring forward this evening, yet there is another point I should like to bring before you for your calm consideration. It is this—the inadequacy of the motives it presents on the one side for a moral and religious life, and of the dissuasives it holds out from a bad one on the other. This is an objection which almost every European writer on the subject notices. To tell a man if he is vicious in this life he will become an inferior animal in the next, is surely no sufficient inducement to make him give up present gratification when he can obtain it; to tell him, if virtuous and self-denying, he will be born again as a happy, virtuous man, or ultimately as a god, does not appear to me likely to make him yield a single opportunity of enriching himself at the expense of others, or of obtaining any pleasure or advantage forbidden by his moral code.

M. All religious motives to virtue and dissuasives from vice are future. Future reward or future punishment is held up in every religion as a stimulant in the one case, as a terror in the other. Now, of the exact degree of this punishment, it is not possible we should have so distinct an idea as to render it always present and influential with us. It can only be exhibited under the form of material punishment of some kind. In this respect Budhism is certainly not a whit behind Christianity, for, whilst it threatens degradation in the scale of animal life for the minor offences, it holds forth the doctrine of a great central fire for the thoroughly depraved—a fire which is the abode of infernal spirits; and you have yourself seen on the walls of our temples, representations of the torturing of the vicious by those evil spirits in another world. Again, Budhism holds out a progressive advance to *nirwana*, as the reward of virtue and self-denial.

K. And this *nirwana* itself is an abstraction that no one can understand—a kind of annihilation in fact! Now, do you for a moment regard that as so glorious a thing that men will strain energetically after it, and sacrifice much to obtain it? Do you suppose that any man will give up a present gratification, or persevere in virtuous resolution contrary to instinct or desire of any kind, merely to reach annihilation hereafter?

M. It does not appear probable, when put in that light, certainly. Yet though *nirwana* is often spoken of as the cessation of everything that implies existence, yet this is not the impression universally prevalent amongst Budhists on the subject. They regard it as a thing to be desired; and if any definite ideas are entertained by any on the subject, they are probably summed up in that of absorption into the universal spirit. Where, as amongst the Nepalese Budhists, a great supreme being is recognized, *nirwana* is invariably regarded as an ultimate union with him, absorption into his essence.

K. Can that which the most intelligent of Budhists finds so much difficulty in explaining be an object of desire to the vulgar, such an object of desire as that they should deny themselves, and pursue virtue to attain to it?

M. Probably not. But to be a rich, powerful, happy and prosperous king hereafter, is surely something that they can understand and appreciate. If already rich, powerful and prosperous, then to be a spiritual existence, a god upon Maha Meru, is a thing that can be understood. *Nirwana* is ever far in the distance, only those who believe themselves approaching perfection ever hoping to attain it in the next birth. I must confess that the object of my Budhistic life, however you may smile at the idea, was to become a deity on Maha Meru hereafter; and that I have never once believed myself so far advanced on the road to perfection as to entitle me to the blessings of *nirwana*.

K. Surely nothing more conclusive against *nirwana*, as an object of desire, could possibly be adduced.

M. Perhaps not. Yet our system of secondary rewards

and secondary punishments prevents much of the evil that might thence be anticipated. You will find, I think, on examining into the matter, that the whole system is so nicely put together, that any apparent defect in one part is compensated for by some substitute in another.

K. I have already frequently had to confess this fact, and have found it one of the principal obstacles to attacking it effectually. On this point of *nirwana*, however, the defect is so self-evident, that it cannot escape the eye of the most cursory observer.

M. Yet in truth speculative opinions respecting the exact character of the blessedness reserved for the consistently virtuous and religious have little influence on the mass of mankind. The morality of a creed, or its success or failure as a moral system, can only be judged of impartially by the lives of its professors, so that after all it resolves itself into a question of testimony.

K. I am astonished you should make such an admission. The testimony on this point is so overwhelming against you, that your observation has completely taken me by surprise, yet I look upon it as an extremely just one.

M. Do you mean the testimony against the morality of Budhists generally ?—if so, I must confess it runs counter to that which I have seen. This, however, I must premise, that the evidence of Christian missionaries on the subject cannot be received. They must look upon all heathen creeds with a jaundiced eye. It is impossible that they can judge, either the religious system or the lives, of opponents of Christianity impartially. Did I want to know the characteristics of your faith, or the probable influence of its dogmas, should I go to a Mohammedan priest to learn either the one or the other ? Should I not, on the contrary, regard his testimony on the subject with extreme suspicion ?

K. You wrong an earnest, able, honest and praiseworthy body of men, who, I am convinced, would scorn to give false evidence as much as you or I. But putting this testimony aside, there is that of Robert Knox, who, two hundred years ago, was so long a prisoner in Kandy, the testimony of Mr. Hodgson from Nepal, and of every one, I believe, who has written about China, all proclaiming vice and immorality the rule, virtue the exception.

M. Against which evidence I must bring forward that of MM. Klaproth, Abel Remusat and Bournouff, who have all borne testimony to the civilizing influence of Budhism. "The three religions the most widely spread in the world," said the first of these three great Frenchmen, "are Christianity, Budhism and Mohammedanism. The two former have contributed to civilize and to improve human nature; but it cannot be said that the third has had altogether the same effect." And again, "the fierce nomades of Central Asia have been transformed by it," that is, by Budhism, "into virtuous men; and its influence has been even felt as far as Siberia." *

K. From such general observations nothing I fear can be concluded particularly, respecting the moral influence of Budhism as a system of religion. I am willing to acknowledge indeed, that, in so far as I am acquainted with them, of all the religions of the world, Budhism appears to come next to Christianity in its civilizing and humanizing influences. But, if it be a boast to the former, that it has transformed the nomadic races of Central Asia from wild savages into semi-civilized and comparatively virtuous men, what shall we say of the latter, which has turned the wild races of Northern Europe, the Goths and the Vandals of Roman history, and of proverbial barbarity, into the most polished races of mankind? Again, Budhism is professed by the great majority of the common people of China, indeed by the vast mass of the population; and,

* Nouveau Journal Asiatique, tom. v. p. 306.

if the accounts of all travellers be true, there is not a population under heaven in which unbridled licentiousness, lying, cheating, knavery, venality, and oppression, reign more undisputedly and universally.

M. I am not very extensively read in the theological literature of England; but, from what little I know of it, and from what I see noticed of it in literary journals and reviews, it does appear that the clergy of Europe have no very exalted idea of the morality of their people generally, nay, were I as well read as you are in such works, I doubt not I could bring down a host of extracts from the time of Chaucer to that of Byron, to prove that the very vices you have named have flourished luxuriantly in England itself. The very last number of Blackwood's Magazine, which I saw on the table of the Kandy library, plainly asserted that this was the very age of shams and humbugs;—that the shopkeepers of England delighted in false weights and measures, and told falsehoods respecting the goods they wanted to sell, proclaiming that good which they knew was bad, and that cheap which they knew was dear;—that they thought nothing of declaring goods to be the stock of a bankrupt, of which it was necessary to dispose at once, when the assertion was a lie;—that simony was a prevalent sin, both amongst clergy and laity, and was so common as to be lightly thought of, or even excused;—that men did not believe what they read in the newspapers, for that much of the reports in them were false, that they all required confirmation, and that the statement of a circumstance in an advertisement did not render it, on that account, the more likely to be believed; nay, he even went so far as to say, if I remember aright, that it rendered it the more likely to be disbelieved, but that, of course, must have been only a rhetorical flourish;—that men who sold milk put water into it to increase the quantity, and then sold the whole as pure;—that others who sold sugar, tea, and similar articles, likewise adulterated them, and then asserted them to be good and unadulterated;—that opinions were often advocated, not because the writers believed in them, but because the advocacy suited the interests of party in political, polemical, or social controversy;—that situations, which should be given to merit, were often yielded for money, nay, that advertisements offering and asking for such, were often seen in the newspapers;—that great numbers of women, many thousands he said, made a trade of prostitution, and others, of both sexes, of thieving. Now, I am quite willing to allow that much of this was merely stated to render the article piquant, that individual cases must have been taken as general examples, and that the writer was more anxious about putting together a lively, interesting diatribe, than a full and fair exposition of the general state of the country, for, were it literally true, the frame-work of society must evidently be unhinged, and revolution impending; but, nevertheless, he would not have ventured to write so in so respectable a journal if there were not some truth in his assertions. What then am I to conclude? that the morality of England is much superior to that of China? that there are not vice, injustice, crime, in abundance in both? that, in fact, as little regard is not paid to the moral precepts of Christianity in one case, as to those of Budhism in the other?

K. All the evils you have enumerated are to be found in the large towns of England, but not universally. There are men who sell pure articles, and who tell the truth, or what they conscientiously believe to be such, of their wares. Of the relative proportions of the two classes I have no means of forming a judgment, but, in so far as I have seen, in no other part of the world is there so much virtuous happiness, both in town and country, no other in which domestic joys are so earnestly sought, and so highly esteemed—there is doubtless much too to condemn, in large bodies of mankind cooped up in comparatively small spaces, there always will be such, but, at the same time, all must not be blamed because some are worthy of censure,—the worst of such articles as that you refer to is that they give a false view of things, they bring the evil prominently forward, ignoring the good, and giving no data by which the relative preponderance of one or the other might be estimated.

M. Quite true,—then how foolish to form one's estimate of a people from such superficial judges ! and what European writer can have so intimate an acquaintance with the country, or even the private town life of China generally, as to warrant his passing a verdict on the whole ?

K. You are right, Modliar. So difficult is it to get proper testimony on either side that I fear any argument founded on that which is procurable, will not carry much weight. Let us look at the two creeds irrespectively of such effects. Christianity, with the simplicity of truth, which is essentially one and undivided, plainly declares that those who obey shall be happy, and those who wilfully disobey unhappy in a future state of existence; it tells us that this is a state of probation, as indeed all nature tells us too, and that our lot in another world will be irrevocably determined by our conduct in this. It holds out a simple promise and a simple threat as the persuasive and the dissuasive, at the same time inviting us to the good by the most affecting motive, by the most powerful principle, in our nature—love and gratitude, it says, urge us to the one, and eternal happiness, of a perfect order, is the reward—reject all this and the end is the death of soul and body, eternal exclusion from God, from the good, from the great, from the sublime, from all that is lovely in the universe. What system can be at once so simple and so clear, so definite and so grand ? On the other hand, Budhism, with the complication of art, informs us that ere the final haven be attained, there are many phases of existence to be passed through, that fail now, and you may succeed again; that unless your wickedness is of the most diabolical kind, the punishment in the next birth is merely the assumption of some animal form, from which you may again emerge into manhood, that thus the day of repentance and of reformation may be indefinitely protracted, and lives of sensuality and selfishness permitted if not excused. To this selfishness—pure, absolute, uncompounded selfishness indeed—the whole system urges on its professor; it says not a word to his gratitude, even Gotama himself has done nothing for him, was solely employed, during his existence on earth, in completing his own salvation, without reference to that of others. Gods and devoes are contemplating his struggle without interest or encouragement to him. He is alone in the universe, no sympathy, no helping hand held out to him, from the spiritual world. Not a word is said to his love. He is commanded to love indeed, to love a cold abstraction—justice, honesty, integrity, virtue—to love the good and hate the bad, but no word of sweet consolation is uttered to him, telling him that his God loves him, or has ever proved that love in time or in eternity. The whole system is a vast metaphysical abstraction, more like the coinage of an acute and virtuous philosopher's brain, than an emanation from above. Ponder the contrast, my dear Marandhan, and then ask yourself which bears upon it the greatest semblance of truth, the system that appeals to the head and the heart combined, or that which professes to be addressed to the head alone.

M. What you have enunciated last is indeed the entire contrast. The one appeals to the head and the heart, the other to the head alone. But what guide can possibly be more likely to lead us to error than the heart, nay, what guide has led men into such diabolical extremes as the perversions of the heart have done?—perversions which its too great cultivation naturally leads to. Our system leads to selfishness you say. O Mr. Knighton, ignore not the evils of Christianity when you descant so eloquently on those of Budhism. What is the vast system of monachism, whether in the West or East, but a system of pure unmitigated selfishness? Was it Budhism or Christianity that fostered this in Northern Africa and Southern Europe, to so alarming an extent, in the middle ages? Why did men retire to the deserts and caves, and lead lives of voluntary seclusion from their fellows but from the purest selfishness? Are not monasteries and nunneries, in so far as religion is practised in them, existing monuments of selfishness? Not indeed where benevolence issues open-handed from them to succour the distressed, or relieve suffering, but where the devotees apply themselves solely to their religious duties, and leave all the rest of mankind to their fate. Is selfishness then a product of Budhism alone, nurtured and flourishing luxuriantly in the congenial soil of the East only, or is it not rather, the natural instinct of humanity, which will exhibit itself irrespective of all creeds? Nor can you tell me that what the majority of Christians still approve of is an abuse of Christianity, otherwise I may say the same of all the testimony you can adduce relative to Budhistic conduct. But, sir, I have a far graver charge to bring forward against your boasted system—a charge which tends to set it in a more odious light than any other system under heaven. No other religion that I have ever heard of has legalized and systematized persecution. No other has ever established such a fearful enormity as the Inquisition, and, not only established it, but permitted it to flourish for centuries. Were ever torments more diabolical invented by North American Indians to put an end to their captives, than were administered in the dungeons of the Inquisition to its unfortunate victims, in order to make them confess crime of which, perhaps, they were often innocent? Is this the religion of love and sympathy, of philanthropy and benevolence?

K. Alas, there is too much truth in your statements, although little in your deductions. The monachism and asceticism of which you first spoke are not, in my opinion, natural offsprings of our religion, but extraneous institutions endeavoured to be grafted on it. The Inquisition was a fearful institution, although doubtless its evils have been much exaggerated by party spirit,—but even Roman Catholics of the present day, will tell you that it was an abuse. These abuses of Christianity are fruitful themes, but were we similarly to argue from the abuses of other matters, we should discard the holiest and best principles of our nature, the most fruitful sources of good. Benevolence itself has often done much mischief when unregulated by wisdom and when impulsive merely. A desire to convert others to truth, in itself an amiable principle, has led to persecution in its abuse. The good is Christianity's in these and similar cases, the evil human nature's. And as a proof that these evils appertain to human nature generally, allow me to ask if there has not been persecution in the East as well as in the West? Have not Budhists, Hindoos, and Mohammedans persecuted too? Why then attack one system for an abuse common to all? In the New Testament you will find no such measures as those adopted in later times, either advocated or tolerated. By *its* tenets and precepts, by *its* rules and ordinances, Christianity should be judged, not by the lives or conduct of those who, whilst they professed reverence for its principles, violated them in the most outrageous manner.

M. I do not think persecution has ever been systematized and made an institution, as it was in the Inquisition, by any other faith but Christianity. Budhists have persecuted, but only in times of strong religious and political excitement, and contrary to the express command of Gotama himself.

K. Which fact goes to prove the very principle I advocated, that a religious system must not be judged of by the abuses of its professors, but by the spirit of its tenets and precepts. Consider the matter thus calmly and without bias, Modliar, and I shall yet have the happiness of hailing you as one who has cast off the trammels of error and emerged into the fulness of liberty. Consider the points we have discussed this evening, the attributes of the Almighty, the inadequacy of the motives which would persuade a Budhist to virtue, and dissuade him from vice, the want of heart—of all generous feeling flowing from the heart—in the system, and the selfishness engendered by it, naturally and inevitably, and then ask yourself on which side does truth lie—on the side illustrated by the simple grandeur of Christianity, or on that obscured by the complicated mechanism of Budhism.

DIALOGUE IV.

M. You have not lately turned our conversations into the channel in which you formerly delighted to lead them.

K. Alas, Marandhan, I feel too keenly my own unworthiness to assume the character of the champion of the purest and most sublime of all faiths to tempt the discussion further.

M. Every one is open to the same reproof, and to the same condemnation on reflection: "Use every man after his desert, and who shall 'scape whipping."

K. True, very true; a most satisfactory plaster for the chapped conscience. I may continue the speech by saying, 'the less I deserve, the more merit is in your bounty."

M. If it be any consolation to you to know that you have opened my eyes to a great fundamental truth, to the most sublime of all conceptions, and have made that truth—that sublime conception—an article of faith with me, you have that consolation, and I trust it may give you something of the satisfaction in the hearing, which it gives me in the believing.

K. You refer to the belief in the Deity.

M. I do.

K. It is a great comfort to me to think that I should have been the means of setting you on the right road thus far. I have thought much on the subject of our colloquies lately, and I believe myself able to prove from the Almighty power of the Deity—from that one attribute alone—that all his other perfections may be deduced.

M. I shall be delighted to hear you; I am not much further advanced than I was when we last conversed on the subject. I can see clearly, and without a doubt at present, that the universe around leads me back to a great primeval cause—that all the laws by which nature works, and which may be looked upon as the agents of the conservation of the universe, are but the impress of a great Architect and Ruler, who originally formed, and now sustains, the myriads of worlds in existence around us; but that this Architect and Ruler is a being of infinite goodness I cannot discover. Doubtless one would like to believe so—it would be more comfortable to fancy so than to fancy otherwise, but that is no sufficient ground for embracing such a tenet. It would rather appear to me that, in the construction of the universe, some great idea is being worked out infinitely above man's conception, or ability to conceive, in which great scheme this world bears a most subordinate part, and we, an utterly insignificant one; that our existence is a consequence of the existence of the globe which we inhabit, not the object for which that globe was created, as your religion would have me believe; that in fine, man is left to himself in the things of the world and that, whatever becomes of his soul, the Deity does not regard, as of any moment, his actions or convictions here. This is truly a cheerless unsatisfactory belief, or rather it appears so on a cursory inspection of it, for when we go deeper into it, it is by no means so dreary as fatalism, in which so much of the world, and so many even of your own creed, put their faith.

K. You shall not rest there if I can prevent it. Whatever consolation metaphysical abstractions can deduce from such a creed, there is nothing that can engage the heart or the affections in it. Were such the truth, man would be indeed a miserable being, totally excluded from all communion with his Maker, and some of the noblest qualities of his soul would be thus deadened and disused. From what you have already stated, I infer that you acknowledge the almighty power of the Deity.

M. Certainly, in so far as we can conceive of what is beyond our ability. Almighty, humanly speaking, the universe proves its great Architect to be.

K. I mean by it, capable of performing all things of which we can conceive, not contradictory or absurd.

M. In that sense the sublimity of the universe proves the Deity to be almighty.

K. In order to be so it is necessary that the Deity should be everywhere, as he cannot act where he is not, and, being almighty, it follows therefore he must be omnipresent.

M. Decidedly. Indeed, the very conception itself presupposes a principle pervading all nature, able to do all things, and everywhere present.

K. The being everywhere present must be conscious of everything, and therefore omniscient.

M. Unquestionably. Almighty power then implies omnipresence and omniscience.

K. Much more. The Being knowing all things, and able to do all things, must be infinitely happy.

M. I do not see that quite so plainly as the other points.

K. In what does happiness consist, but in the ability to attain to what will make happy, and is desired. A being that knows everything, must know in what the highest possible degree of happiness consists, and having all power, achieves it at once.

M. Yes, so far as that can lead us to the consideration of infinite happiness I can go with you.

K. But remember that to such a Being there can be no lapse of time—time and space are annihilated, and therefore happy once is ever happy, and to have the highest possible degree of happiness is to be infinitely happy.

M. I see that clearly now. You must pardon my snail's progress.

K. A Being of almighty power, infinitely happy, will surround himself with happy beings.

M. With none other were he infinitely good; but others exist.

K. You jump a little at conclusions. Is it not of the very nature of happiness to desire the happiness of others? Does not the prospect of misery damp the happiness of the happiest? Would not the infinitely happy, almighty Being therefore, surround himself with happy beings?

M. It appears indisputable.

K. You grant that. Well, omniscience must have seen all possible worlds, before this one, for instance, was called into existence, and almighty power would construct the best only, when infinite intelligence had discovered what it was. The infinitely happy Being, desiring happy inhabitants of this world, would sanction only that system which admitted of the greatest number of happy inhabitants to result from it.

M. All which goes to prove, that this is, in fact, as Dr. Pangloss maintained, the best of all possible worlds.

K. Do not condemn my conclusions before I arrive at them, and before I have fully stated them. Does it not appear that when in the Divine mind, all possible worlds were being contemplated, infinite happiness desiring happy beings, and almighty power ready to execute the work about to be allotted to it, in the best possible way—does it not appear, under such circumstances, I ask, that the idea determined to be realized would be that embracing the greatest possible amount of good, with the least possible amount of evil?

M. Certainly, I agree with you fully. But why the least possible amount of evil? Why any amount of evil at all? Why not all good? Infinite happiness, desiring happy beings only, would not surely bring into existence those whose lives must be only misery—long-continued, perpetual misery indeed.

K. You agree with me so far however. The beings to be so produced could not be perfect. In order to form the idea of perfection, infinite power, knowledge and wisdom would be required, and indeed, as I formerly argued, there can or could be, but one perfect. These beings then could not be perfect?

M. In the absolute sense of perfection, such as you have just stated, of course not. All could not of course be almighty, omnipresent, and omniscient. But how vast is the gulf between that idea, or that of happy spirits on the one side, and the knowledge which our own senses give us of the deep degradation and debasement into which man can fall, does fall, and has ever fallen, on the other. Do you mean to assert that these fine-spun syllogisms, however beautiful uninterrupted and attenuated, can span that vast and all but boundless chasm?

K. You are too eager. Let us review the position at which we have arrived. Almighty power, which you grant existing in the great Architect of the universe, implies omnipresence and omniscience; implies also infinite happiness;—the infinitely happy Being would surround himself with happy intelligences, and would call into existence only that system which would produce the greatest possible amount of happiness, with the least possible amount of misery. But matter is imperfect. Spirit, separated from the great and pervading Spirit of the universe, has in it the elements of imperfection. There can be no active intelligence without volition—this volition must be free and uncontrolled, to make it serviceable for any good purpose. Without such free will, the being so constituted might be a well-regulated machine, wound up, like a clock, to go so long in such and such a way, but could not experience intelligent happiness or exercise its mind as it listed, and therefore the existence of such a being would be one of constant restraint, uneasiness, unhappiness, in fact, of more—of absolute torture. Now the universe is composed of matter, which is, in its nature, imperfect; man is a compound of this imperfect matter, and of a spirit which, as being separated from the great pervading Spirit, is therefore, in so far, imperfect likewise. He is a compound of two imperfections—an imperfect body and an imperfect soul. Free will gives him the option of using both, not to secure his own happiness, but to ensure his own misery, if he so wills. He deliberately chooses, actuated by a thousand conflicting ideas—he deliberately chooses, not the path of happiness, but the path of misery; he perseveres in this way. For years he perseveres, nay, for centuries. He sinks deeper and deeper into the abyss, until so far gone that no efforts of his own can retrieve him—a thousand motives prevent his accepting the assistance offered—and so we find him in the lowest depths of degradation and debasement. .

M. Nothing can be more interesting than your speculations on this difficult subject, nothing more ingenious than your arguments. To me, however, they are not perfectly satisfactory, however much the declaration may astonish you. Infinite power, infinite wisdom, infinite happiness, are all attributes of the Deity, which you have clearly deduced from nature and from man. But when you add infinite goodness, my mind revolts from the idea, conscious as I am of what goes on around me, and of what worse exists elsewhere in the world. Infinite wisdom doubtless foresaw what the result of the creation of this world would be, to go no further at present, although, if the other worlds are all filled with such beings as man, the argument is made a thousand times stronger. Infinite knowledge and foresight would, doubtless, have foreseen such a world as ours, in contemplating all possible worlds. Infinite power might call such a world into existence, but infinite goodness would assuredly refrain. When, in contemplation, the misery of which millions would be the victims, the disease, crime, sorrow, punishment, despair, and death, which would pervade it, arose before the Divine Mind,—would infinite goodness sanction such a scheme ? nay rather, would not infinite goodness thrust it away, as altogether an unfeasable project, a thing to be zealously avoided and prevented, not encouraged ? We are inevitably led, it appears to me, to what I stated at first, a belief that this world is but the working out of a portion of some vast problem, of which we know nothing; that its excellences and its defects are equally subserving some vast purpose of which we are profoundly ignorant; that man is but a moving atom in the scheme of the world, insignificant and uncared for, just as the world is but comparatively an atom in the working out of some other vast scheme.

K. Your views contradict themselves, or rather one part contradicts the other. A Being of infinite wisdom made the world, yet the world is not made as well as it might be! such is the drift of your observation. I, on the other hand, maintain, that there was no possibility of its being better. Again, to judge of man's existence by the small part of it passed on earth, is to judge of the butterfly, in the state of the caterpillar. We know the miseries, the trials, the sorrows, the distresses, the deaths of this life, but we know nothing of the glories of another. It is the belief of many Christians that all will ultimately reach that better life, and that all the expressions which imply the contrary in our Bible are to be regarded as figurative or hyperbolical. Again, you allow that the Almighty is perfect, the only perfect being, yet you would deny one of his perfections—infinite goodness. You perceive that to escape one difficulty you fall into many.

M. There is much in what you have said about judging of man's existence from this life only, which strikes me very forcibly. The foundations of Budhism are so thoroughly shaken in my mind, that I have little difficulty in giving up the doctrine of transmigration, and looking to something nobler in another world than our unsatisfactory nirwana, and were the universalism you hint at, a tenet of Christianity, as Christianity is generally preached, there would be little difficulty in its making its way amongst Budhists. But you are aware that any one would be regarded as heterodox by the majority of Christians, who held such a doctrine. Nor, indeed, in our previous conversations have you hinted at such a dogma, or, perhaps, my obtuse faculties prevented my observing it.

K. It is a tenet which was extensively spread throughout England at the time of the Revolution, and which is making rapid progress, I understand, in America, at the present day. I have never upheld the dogma myself, nor, indeed, have I given it much consideration, but it is right that you should know such a doctrine is held by many. They argue that the sacred volume abounds in hyperbolical expressions, that "for ever" is constantly put in it for a long and indefinite period. Abraham and his seed, for instance, were again and again promised the holy land "for ever," unconditionally. And what can be more explicit, they ask, than the declaration that "as in Adam all die, even so in Christ shall all be made alive," where the salvation is made as universal as the fall. But this is a particular tenet of a peculiar sect, and it will be better for us to keep more closely to the grand object which we are considering to-day—the Divine Nature. My belief is, that from an attentive study of the works of nature, every attribute of the Almighty may be discovered, and, from these attributes, the transition is simple to the grand truths of Christianity.

M. The attribute of goodness is that alone which has presented any difficulty to me—once impressed with the conviction that a great primary cause was required to produce the grand effects of the universe, I felt little difficulty in arriving at the ideas of Almighty power, infinite knowledge, and perpetual happiness. Infinite goodness, however, has always seemed to me inconsistent with the state of things which I see around me in the world, and my impression now is, that it is only by taking such a view of the future life as you suggest, that we can arrive at that idea at all. It makes much plain that was before obscure, and gives an overwhelming conception of the benevolence and love of the Deity.

K. The difficulties are wonderfully lessened by such a

conviction, however dangerous many may esteem it. But in considering so transcendant an idea as the Divine existence and nature, there will always be difficulties to our finite and imperfect minds.

M. There are undoubtedly difficulties, turn where we will, and direct our attention to whatsoever side we please. The human mind itself, with its wonderful collection of sensations, perceptions, feelings, emotions, and intellectual struggles, is an enigma to us, in many respects. How much more the Divine Nature, in all its majesty and grandeur!

K. It is a source of great pleasure to me to think that I have, in any way, been the instrument of leading you to this magnificent conception, and, I doubt not, you have but to persevere from that fundamental conviction to arrive at the ultimate truths of Christianity. The Bible, remember, is the only ancient book which gives us anything like a consistent account of the origin of the world, and the early history of our race. As a whole, you will rest in the conviction that Christianity is the only religious scheme which will satisfy the requirements of an ardent, honest soul, and the questions of acute intellectual inquiry.

M. Believe me, I shall investigate the system with a full and entire desire to arrive at the truth. and a determination, when I have found it, to embrace it earnestly and unreservedly.